Asia and Europe in the New Global System

Asia and Europe in the New Global System

Intercultural Cooperation and Competition Scenarios

Edited by

Sung-Jo Park
Freie Universität Berlin

and

Sierk Horn
Freie Universität Berlin

First published 2003 by
PALGRAVE MACMILLAN
Houndmills, Basingstoke, Hampshire RG21 6XS and
175 Fifth Avenue, New York, N.Y. 10010
Companies and representatives throughout the world

PALGRAVE MACMILLAN is the global academic Imprint of the Palgrave
Macmillan division of St. Martin's Press, LLC and of Palgrave Macmillan Ltd.
Macmillan® is a registered trademark in the United States, United Kingdom
and other countries. Palgrave is a registered trademark in the European
Union and other countries.

ISBN 1–4039–0496–0

This book is printed on paper suitable for recycling and made from fully
managed and sustained forest sources.

A catalogue record for this book is available from the British Library.

Library of Congress Cataloging-in-Publication Data
Euro-Asia–Management Studies Association. Conference (18th: 2001: Free
University Berlin)
    Asia and Europe in the new global system: intercultural cooperation and
    competition scenarios/edited by Sung-Jo Park and Sierk Horn.
      p. cm.
    "Selected papers presented at the 18th Annual Conferences of the Euro–
    Asian Management Studies Association (EAMSA) in November 2001" – Pref.
    Includes bibliographical references and index.
    ISBN 1-4039-0496-0
      1. Asia – Foreign economic relations – Europe – Congresses. 2. Europe –
Foreign economic relations – Asia – Congresses. 3. Industrial management –
Asia – Congresses. 4 Industrial management – Europe – Congresses.
5. Intercultural communication – Asia – Congresses. 6. Intercultural
communication – Europe – Congresses. 7. International trade – Congresses.
8. Competition, International – Congresses. I. Park, Sung-Jo. II. Horn, Sierk.
III. Title.
HF1583.Z4 E8518 2001
337.504—dc21   2002192657

10 9 8 7 6 5 4 3 2 1
12 11 10 09 08 07 06 05 04 03

Printed and bound in Great Britain by
Antony Rowe Ltd, Chippenham and Eastbourne

Contents

List of Figures

List of Tables

Foreword

This volume collects selected papers presented at the 18th Annual Conference of the Euro–Asian Management Studies Association (EAMSA) in November 2001. The main theme of this conference was 'Asia and Europe in the New Global System: Intercultural Cooperation and Competition Scenarios'. EAMSA was founded in November 1984 and its first conference was organized by the East Asian Institute of the Free University of Berlin and the Science Centre of Berlin. Thirty participants came from all over Europe and Asia for that occasion, the first in a series of annual conferences each attracting participating audiences of around 70 people. A popular feature has been the publication of selected papers from these events, either as a special issue of an international journal or as a monograph.

When we look back over the past 18 years, we can see how our principal concerns have developed. During the first four to five years our discussions were centred on internationalization, the globalization of Japanese business and the transferability of Japanese management. Themes then shifted to a comparison of European and Japanese management, and competition and cooperation between them. In the 1990s, discussions predominantly focused on Asian business, on newly-industrializing economies (NIEs) and on ASEAN, the growth of the Asian economy, and business operations of Japanese and European companies in East Asia. Our most recent area of attention, as shown in the conference theme from which these papers are derived, has been the analysis of various issues of business and management emerging in both European and Asian companies, in response to the new environments of globalization.

Our current theme is simultaneously one of our most challenging and most important and calls for further investigation into competition and cooperation, not only between European and Asian companies but also among East Asian companies such as Chinese, Japanese, Korean, Taiwanese and ASEAN businesses with the participation of China in the World Trade Organization (WTO) at the end of 2001 and the adoption of the Euro as a common currency over much of Europe in January 2002.

I firmly believe that this publication, under the editorship of Sung-Jo Park and Sierk Horn of the Freie Universität Berlin, will mark a significant contribution to the above area of study. On behalf of EAMSA,

I would like to thank Daimler-Chrysler AG, Schering AG, Palgrave Macmillan, OAK-TFH, WZB, the Embassy of Japan, Kobe Graduate School of Adult Education and the Commerz Bank for their financial support for the 18th annual conference of EAMSA. Last but not least, I am grateful to Katrin Quandt and Barbara Fense for enabling the conference to be realized.

YOSHIAKI TAKAHASHI
Chairman of Euro–Asian Management Studies Association
Professor of Chuo University

Notes on the Contributors

Tetsuo Abo is Professor Emeritus at the Faculty of Economics of Teikyo University. His fields of study are multinational enterprises, and international economic relationships in the Japanese, American and European economies. He has been Guest Professor at the University of Rennes in 2001, Visiting Professor at the University of California, Berkeley, in 1994 and Guest Professor at the Free University of Berlin in 1984 and 1997. His recent main publications in English are *Hybrid Factory: The Japanese Production System in the United States* (New York, Oxford University Press, 1994); 'Electronics Assembly Industry', in H. Itagaki (ed.), *The Japanese Production System: Hybrid Factories in East Asia* (Macmillan, 1997); 'Changes in Japanese Automobile and Electronics Transplants in the USA', in H. Hasegawa and G. D. Hook (eds), *Japanese Business Management* (London: Routledge, 1998); 'Hybridization of the Japanese Production System in North America, Newly Industrializing Economies, South-East Asia, and Europe: Contrasted Configurations', in R. Boyer, E. Charron, U. Jürgens and S. Tolliday (eds), *Between Imitation and Innovation: The Transfer and Hybridization of Productive Models in the International Automobile Industry* (New York: Oxford University Press, 1998); and 'Spontaneous Integration in Japan and East Asia: Development, Crisis, and Beyond', in G. L. Clark, M. P. Feldman and M. S. Gertler (eds), *The Oxford Handbook of Economic Geography* (New York: Oxford University Press, 2000).

Sayeeda Bano is a Senior Lecturer in Economics at the University of Waikato, Hamilton, New Zealand. She received her BA (Hons) and MA in Economics from Patna University and her MPhil from Jawaharlal Nehru University in New Delhi, India. After being awarded a Canadian Commonwealth Scholarship she completed an MA at the University of Alberta, Edmonton. She then received a PhD from Simon Fraser University in Canada. She has lectured at the University of Dar-Es-Salaam and the Centre for Foreign Relations in Tanzania and was an economist at the New Zealand Institute of Economic Research (NZIER) prior to taking up her appointment at Waikato in 1987. She was a visiting Professor at the University of Ottawa during 1991/92. She was a visiting scholar at Jawaharlal Nehru University in 1999. Her main teaching areas are international trade, international finance, international economy, and the Asian-Pacific economies. Her professional research interests are: inter-industry and intra-industry international trade; international trade in services; balance of payments; the role of the World Trade Organization and the Asia-Pacific Economic Cooperation group in fostering world trade and development; intra-industry international trade between New Zealand, Australia, the Organization for Economic Co-operation and Development (OECD) and Asian nations; economic reforms in India and New Zealand; the development of regionalism and economic integration; links between Special Drawing Rights (SDRs) and development finance; and the role and status of women in Islam. Her publications include *The Extent and Determinants of Intra-Industry International Trade: The Canadian Experience* (Gower, 1991); book reviews; articles in international journals; six book chapters; seven monographs and working papers; 28 articles in edited volumes and numerous international conference papers and seminar papers.

Dieter Beschorner is Deputy Head of the Department of Business Planning at the University of Ulm in Germany. He studied Electronic Engineering and Industrial Engineering and Economics, gaining a PhD in 1976 from the Technical University of Munich. He lectured on Economics at the Universities of Bamberg, Speyer, Vienna and Freiberg (Sachsen) from 1979 to 1992. Since 1992 at the University of Ulm, Faculty of Mathematics and Economics. Deputy Dean and Member of the Commission for Restructuring Faculty of Economics at the Technical University Bergakademie Freiberg/Sachsen (1991/92). Memberships in the Euro–Asian Management Studies Association and the Vereinigung für ökologische Wirtschaftsforschung. Research activities in the fields of Economics and Ecology, International Management, Controlling and Ecological Management Systems and Auditing.

Nobuyuki Chikudate is Associate Professor of Organization Theory in Department of Management Studies, Graduate School of Social Sciences, Hiroshima University. He received his doctorate from University at Buffalo, State University of New York, and completed post-doctoral trainings at the Johns Hopkins University. His specialities include organizational culture, business ethics, comparative management and intercultural communication. His major articles have appeared in the *Journal of Applied Behavioral Science*, the *Journal of Business Ethics*, *Journal of Management Studies*, and the *Management International Review*.

Zahiruddin Ghazali is Lecturer at the School of Finance and Banking, University of Utara, Malaysia. He teaches corporate finance and capital markets. His research areas cover capital markets, corporate capital structure and real estate. He is the author of 'Do shareholders benefit from acquisition?', in *Bankers Journal*, March 2000. Chapter 12 was written with the help of his colleagues at the University of Utara.

Hasegawa Harukiyo is Senior Lecturer in the School of East Asian Studies and the Director of the Centre for Japanese Studies, University of Sheffield. His research interests are in Asian business and management. His publications include *An International Comparison of Business and Management* (Tokyo: Chuo Keizaisha, 1993) (in Japanese, co-author); *Steel Industry in Japan: A Comparison with Britain* (London: Routledge, 1996); *Japanese Business and Management: Restructuring for Low Growth and Globalization* (London: Routledge, 1998) (co-editor); *The Political Economy of Japanese Globalization* (London: Rouledge, 2001) (co-editor). He is also general editor of a new international journal, *Asian Business and Management* (Palgrave Macmillan, 2002).

Martin Hemmert gained his qualification for full lecturership in business administration from the University of Essen in June 2001 where he lectures on business administration. From 1998 to 2001 he was DFG Research Fellow at the Institute of Production and Information Management, University of Essen, Germany, and from 1993 to 1998 he was Research Associate at the German Institute for Japanese Studies in Tokyo. In 1993 he recieved his doctoral degree in business administration from the University of Cologne, where he also completed his studies of Business Administration (MBA 1989). From 1990 to 1993 he was Research Fellow of the Institute of Business Research at Hitotsubashi University, Tokyo.

Tadamasa Imaguchi is Professor of the Faculty of Business and Commerce at Keio University, Japan. His fields of research focus on management and organization. From April 1985 to March 1997 he worked at the Department of Business Administration of Kyoto Sangyo University, Japan and from August 1991 to August 1992 he was a visiting scholar of the Faculty of Commerce and Business Administration at University of British Columbia, Canada.

Ulrich Jürgens studied economics and political science at the Freie Universität Berlin from 1965 to 1969. He was Assistant Professor of Political Science at the same university between 1969 and 1977. In 1977 he became a research fellow at the Social Science Research Centre, Berlin

(WZB) and in 1989 he became Adjunct Professor at the Institute for Political Science of the Freie Universität Berlin. From 1989 to 1999 he was deputy director of the research unit Regulation of Work at the WZB and since January 2000 he has been the head of this research unit. At the WZB he conducts international comparative research in the fields of industrial politics, work organization, and organizational development with a focus on the automotive industry.

Akira Kuroda is Professor at the Toyohashi Sozo College in the Aichi prefecture in Japan. He is also Visiting Professor at the Teikyo University of Science and Technology in Japan. His subjects are financial management, small industry, foreign investment and technology transfer. From 1984 to 1988 he worked for the Department of Industrial Promotion, Thailand. Between 1965 and 1967 he worked for the Small Medium Enterprises Agency in Japan. From 1963 to 1993 he worked for the Shoko Chukin Bank. He studied at the University of Tokyo from 1957 to 1963, and was with the University of London from 1993 to 1997.

Xinjian Li became a doctoral student in the Department of Business and Commerce of Keio University, Japan, in April 1998. From April 1997 to March 1998 he was Visiting Researcher at the Department of Business Administration at Keio University. From September 1996 to April 1997 he served as Associate Professor at the College of Business Administration of China University of Mining and Technology, and from August 1990 to August 1996 he was a lecturer at the same institution. His current research topics centre around international joint ventures, business administration in China, corporate strategy and business organization.

Hendrik Meyer-Ohle majored in Japanese studies and business administration at the Philipps University, Marburg, where he also received his PhD with a dissertation on dynamics in Japanese retailing. From 1995 till 1999 he worked for the German Institute for Japanese Studies in Tokyo. Since January 2000 he has been Assistant Professor in the Department of Japanese Studies at the National University of Singapore. He has published on the distribution and service sector in Japan as well as on international marketing strategies of Japanese companies in Asia.

Mohamad Hanapi Mohamad is Associate Professor at the School of Management, University of Utara, Malaysia. He teaches international business, corporate strategy, corporate finance, international marketing, and multinational firm and business management. His research areas cover corporate performance, international business, industrial organization and corporate finance. He is also editor and reviewer of the *Asian Academy of Management and Malaysian Management Review*. He is adviser to the MARA Professional College, Institute of Technology, Darulnaim, and to the National Accreditation Board.

Romdej Phisalaphong is a PhD student at the Tinbergen Institute, Erasmus University Rotterdam, the Netherlands. The title of his doctoral dissertation is 'The Impact of European Economic Integration on Inward Foreign Direct Investment from Japan'. From 1997 to 1999 he studied at the Graduate School of Economics, The Universty of Tokyo, Japan, where he gained a Master's degree in economics. From 1997 to 1998 he took part in the special programme, 'Globalization and Regionalism', at Sophia University. From 1993 to 1997 he studied at the University of Tokyo, where he gained a Bachelor of Economics degree at the Faculty of Economics. From 1992 to the present he has received a Royal Thai Government Scholarship.

Fred Robins holds a BA and MA in economics and an MSc and PhD in marketing. He teaches and researches at The Graduate School of Management, University of Adelaide. He is also a member of The University of South Australia's Marketing Science Centre. Prior to his academic career he had public sector experience in Europe and Asia and, later, private sector experience in public relations and as a marketing manager. He has lived and worked in a range of European and East Asian countries and has been a frequent visitor to the major cities of the Asian region for many years. He is a regular contributor to MBA programmes in Australia and overseas. He researches the activities of international business in the Association of South East Asian Nations markets and publishes articles on Asian business in international academic journals. He has also written on the contrast between Asian and Australian trade and industry policies and, more recently, produced an MBA course in e-marketing. This year he has presented papers on 'Contemporary Business Development in East Asia' at the Tenth World Business Congress in Zagreb and 'Online Security and Privacy' at the International Conference on Global Business in Bratislava. He has also written a chapter for a new book on Asian post-crisis management, co-edited by Frank-Jurgen Richter, and published by Palgrave Macmillan.

Kenji Suzuki has been Assistant Professor at the European Institute of Japanese Studies, Stockholm School of Economics, since 1999. He received his doctoral degree in political economy from the University of Warwick, UK in 1999. From 1995 to 1996 he studied at the London School of Economics (MSc). In 1992 he graduated from University of Tokyo. His main publications are 'Policy Network of Competition Policy: Comparative Political Economy of Britain and Japan' (originally a PhD thesis, which will be published by Routledge in 2002) and 'Companies' Use of Web Information in English: An Analysis for International Investors', *Journal of Asian Business*, 16 (4) (Winter 2000).

Thoraya Younes is a PhD student at the University of Ulm, Germany. She received the Master of Business Administration (in English) from Yarmouk University, Irbid, Jordan in 2000. From 1987 to 1991 she studied at Yarmouk University, Irbid, Jordan, where she received a Bachelor of Business Administration. From 1993 to 2000 she worked for the Jordanian Government of Education, teaching commercial transactions, economics, office management and public relations in high schools. From 1991 to 1993 she also worked in the Department of Statistics of the Jordanian Ministry of Planning.

List of Abbreviations

A-A	application-adaptation
AEEU	Amalgamated Engineering and Electrical Union
APEC	Asia-Pacific Economic Cooperation
ASEAN	Association of Southeast Asian Nations
BoJ	Bank of Japan
BU	business unit
CAR	cumulative abnormal returns
CEO	Chief Executive Officer
CGF	Corporate Governance Forum of Japan
CRM	customer relationship management
DVD	digital video disk
ECIT	European Confederation of Independent Trade Unions
ECOM	Electronic Commerce Promotion Council of Japan
EMF	European Metalworkers' Federation
ESOP	employee share option plans
ETUC	European Trade Union Confederation
EVA	economic value added
EWC	European Works Council
FDI	foreign direct investment
FICs	Forum Island Countries
GATS	General Agreement of Trade and Services
GATT	General Agreements on Trade and Tariffs
GMM	generalized method of moments
HQ	headquarters
HRM	human resource management
ILO	International Labour Organization
IMF	International Monetary Fund
ISCT	integrative social contracts theory
IT	information technology
JETRO	Japan External Trade Organization
JMNESG	Japanese Multinational Enterprise Study Group
JV	joint venture
KLSE	Kuala Lumpur Stock Exchange
MD	Managing Director
ME	Middle East
METI	Ministry of Economy Trade and Industry

MNCs	multinational corporations
MoF	Ministry of Finance
NGOs	non-governmental organizations
NICs	newly industrialized countries
NIEs	newly industrializing economies
NSOs	National Sales Organizations
NYSE	New York Stock Exchange
OECD	Organisation for Economic Co-operation and Development
PC	personal computer
PFL	Pacific Forum Line
R&D	research and development
ROE	return on equity
SCANS	Securities Clearing Automated Network Services
SEA	Southeast Asia
SIMM	Single Index Market Model
TSE	Tokyo Stock Exchange
UNCED	United Nations Conference on Environment and Development
UNICE	Federation of European Employers
VER	voluntary export restraint
VTRs	video tape recorders
WTO	World Trade Organization

Introduction: Interculturality as a New Global Competitiveness Factor

This book is an anthology of the contributions presented at the annual conference of the Euro–Asian Management Studies Association (EAMSA) at the beginning of November 2001 in Berlin. The studies embrace not only topics such as foreign trade (inter-regional, intra-regional), foreign direct investment, technology transfer, and the comparison of management systems, but also intercultural communication and marketing, corporate governance, e-business and, last but not least, the economic development of countries in East Asia, with particular reference to China.

Since their foundation in 1984, EAMSA meetings have followed the tradition of choosing a specific conference subject oriented towards the most current and timely issues. At the beginning of the 1980s, experts concerned with economic and technology cooperation between Asia and Europe came together. They focused on the analysis of the superiority of the Japanese management system and the comparative advantage of its economy *vis-à-vis* the West, as well as on the question of how corporate strategies in the West should cope with the so-called Japanese challenge. For this reason, EAMSA was first called the 'Euro–Japanese Management Studies Association'.

Some years later, experts and EAMSA members were forced to realize that the analytic scope could not remain confined to Japan alone. Since NIEs ASEAN member countries and China had, in the meantime, begun to show excellent economic performance, the entire region of East and Southeast Asia had to be taken into consideration. The volume of intra-regional trade and foreign direct investment increased enormously, while trends towards an intra-regional division of labour began to emerge.

These regional economies gradually posed a real challenge for the Western-dominated world economy, even though they were still far from cementing an EC or North America Free Trade Agreement integration. Thus, handling the economies in the region *in toto* led to re-naming the Association the 'Euro–Asian Management Studies Association'.

The headline of the 2001 Annual Conference was 'Asia and Europe in the New Global System – Intercultural Cooperation and Competition Scenarios'. The Organizing Committee identified the implications and consequences of *intercultural management, communication* and *marketing* as the most significant issue among the current relevant topics.

The end of the Cold War in 1989 was perceived as a new challenge for tackling *inter-systemic* problems. The integration of the former socialist economic systems into a capitalistic world economy – that is, the challenge of *transformation* – deserved the highest priority.

Transformation difficulties were scarcely addressed when massive globalization had to be faced. Uncertainty overwhelmed individual countries in their effort to seek the best solutions of how to continue with liberalization, de-regulation, privatization, innovation, and so on.

The events of 11 September 2001, however, signalled an entirely new dimension for re-thinking notions and strategies inherent in the ongoing globalization, especially problems of intercultural confrontation and cooperation. The issue of *interculturality* suddenly became the focal point of academic and political debates. Was this the antithesis of Francis Fukuyama's thesis, 'absoluteness of Western liberalism'? Some people already saw Samuel Huntington's *Clash of Civilizations* confirmed. Others concluded that the building of a new peaceful world order required the *coexistence of cultures* as a precondition. In short, the current escalation of global conflict reminds us of the necessity and urgency of sincere debate on new perceptions of the cultural dimensions of globalization.

The most imminent question is how *culture*, in the context of Euro–Asian cooperation and competition, should be perceived. In the past, Japan, Korea, China and Taiwan were believed to lack the ability to develop capitalism, as has been argued by philosophers and social scientists such as Gottfried Herder, Karl Marx, Friedrich Engels and Max Weber, among others. However, these countries are the only areas that have successfully learned from Western capitalism and have been able to compete with Western capitalist economies. Thus, experts began to take a great interest in exploring the reasons for the region's economic success. Confucianism was now widely perceived as the key dimension for this regional miracle, and debates on the *monocausal* or *functional* correlation between Confucianism and economic performance have not ceased.

Ironically, Confucianism – which is believed to positively determine the high economic performance in East Asia – has lately been considered a significant breeding-ground for the development of the *crony capitalism* which probably contributed to the recent financial and economic crisis in the region. A balanced answer to the question of the extent to which Confucianism affects economic development, positively or negatively, still calls for intense research.

Back to the concept of *culture* in a broader sense: not only reglions, ideologies, morals and ethics, but also norms, values and attitudes in daily life are gaining increasing importance in the process of globalization. The common question of how individual countries are being affected by globalization implies the formation of a *standardized and uniform* global economy and society. However, in doing so, differences between economic and management systems, as well as societies, will tend to be ignored. Reality indicates that efforts by individual countries to maintain and develop their cultural identity should be taken into consideration when working out successful strategies for 'global players'. In other words, integrating local culture and mentality into global strategies seems to be the key to success. 'Think global, act local' comes to mind again. In this sense, the studies included in this book follow the above-mentioned framework.

Corporate governance: shareholder value versus stakeholder value

This topic has, in fact, provoked serious debates among experts. Chapters 2 and 4 focus particularly on the comparison or, in other words, on the inter-play of Western (European) and East Asian (Japanese) management principles and styles. Chapter 3 is evidence of the extent to which personal and information networks have significant repercussions on the decision-making process in the banking sector of Japan.

Intercultural management, communication and marketing

In this field, Chapters 1 and 14 deal with the applicability of Japanese management concepts and ethic principles compared with those of the West. The authors depict its limitations, which stem from socio-cultural and other local constraints.

Human resources development and industrial relations

With regard to global education and share option possibilities, Chapters 11 and 12 provide an in-depth analysis of the case of Malaysia. Chapter 2 indicates the difficulty of using the Japanese concept of human resources development and worker participation in the UK.

E-business

E-business has recently gained increasing importance. Chapters 15 and 16 are largely based on empirical evidence which shows the variety of emerging structures, their specific patterns in e-business, and the scope of online marketing.

Technology transfer and technology dependence

Chapters 5 and 13 present a profound empirical study on the practice of technology transfer and the reality of technology dependence. The former contribution is based on quantative data analysis, as well as on the author's personal experience in the Asian region. The author sheds light on the practical impediments in the transfer of know-how and technology which can be attributed to corporate strategies and cultural variables. Chapter 5 is a large-scale quantitative analysis on the corporate technology access strategies of German and Japanese companies.

Trade, investment and the Chinese market

Chapter 8 contains an in-depth comparative analysis of Japanese firms and the degree to which the formation of the single European market determines corporate decisions as regards future investment strategies. Chapter 10 shows the impact of the Single European Market on the Middle East Region (Jordan), especially in the field of environmental problems. Chapter 9 provides a special study on the cooperation between Japanese and Chinese firms. The authors present an extremely fruitful differentation of cooperation practices. Last but not least, Chapter 6 discusses new trends in the trade services of selected Asian nations, South Pacific Forum Island economies, and OECD countries.

***

In summarizing all of the contributions, it can be emphasized once again that the 'intercultural communication, management and marketing' factor (*interculturality*) is believed to play a crucial role in enhancing global competitiveness. This means that the expertise necessary for efficient Euro–Asian transaction and cooperation must be based on profound intercultural insights, experiences and strategies.

*Freie Universität Berlin*SUNG-JO PARK
SIERK HORN

1
Japanese Hybrid Factories in Germany: Survival in a Different Environment

Tetsuo Abo

1   Introduction

It is commonly assumed that managerial conditions in Germany are not favourable to Japanese manufacturing firms. It is notable, however, that some Japanese transplants not only manage to survive but even achieve solid results through the partial application of Japanese management and production techniques, and the adaptation to (or adoption of) particular location-specific management advantages in Germany.

This chapter will address the following points:

1 How do Japanese transplants in Germany manage to cope with rigid social regulations and customs, such as the *Tarif* system based on AZUBI (to be described later), which are implemented through negotiations with labour unions and work councils (*Betriebsrat*)?
2 How do Japanese-style flexible production systems and 'mechatronics' (mechanical and electronics) technologies manage to coexist with German-style rigid work organization and mechanical engineering technology?
3 What are the advantages to Japanese manufacturers of having their production bases in Germany in terms of markets and logistics? What are the advantages of being in Germany in terms of supplying functionally advanced and high quality products to the German market, or in terms of parts procurement from suppliers and OEM (Original Equipment Manufacturer) contracts with local manufacturers in eastern European countries?

4 What is the significance of recent changes in German society, such as the revision of the AZUBI system; the arrival of part-timers as a new addition to the workforce, with the cooperation of manpower agencies; and the emerging frontier in former East Germany?

The Japanese Multinational Enterprise Study Group (JMNESG), of which I am a member, carried out large-scale field research in Europe in 1997 and 1998 as part of its comparative hybrid factory investigation project in major regions such as North America and East Asia. The group conducted plant visits in Germany during the research on continental Europe in 1998.

2 Outline of the surveyed companies

The present study surveyed the plants of eleven Japanese (see Table 1.1) and three German companies. Since it was difficult to obtain sufficient data from German plants to permit a detailed comparison with their Japanese counterparts, it was not possible to include such analyses in the application-adaptation evaluation. Instead, I will refer to the characteristics of individual plants and companies as necessary. Table 1.1 shows the overall characteristics of Japanese plants located in Germany.

Of these eleven Japanese plants, five manufacture electronics components, three manufacture automotive parts, and three are electronics assembly plants. The majority of these plants are therefore parts-related; there are no Japanese auto-assembly plants in Germany. This distribution of plants by industry type itself reveals much about the characteristics of Japanese plants in Germany.

First, while the cost of labour in Germany is high, there is also a sophisticated level of skills and technology in the areas of precision manufacturing and assembly that are suitable for the production of higher value-added and advanced functional materials. Second, the domestic market for automobiles and other types of manufacture provides steady demand from customers with sophisticated expectations. Numerous parts manufacturers cater to this demand and are also in a position to supply the products to the greater European market, and especially to the EU. In the auto-related industries, typical examples include APa, which is a manufacturer of springs, and APb, a joint venture between the Japanese company APJ and a German company APG, which produces oil seals, and APc, which manufactures air bags. These companies predominantly supply German auto manufacturers, and Japanese manufacturers to a much lesser extent. Electronics component

Table 1.1 Japanese transplants in Germany as of September 1998

Company	APa	APb	APc	EPa	EPb	EPc	EPd	EPe	EAa	EAb	EAc
Industry	Auto parts	Auto parts	Auto parts	Electro parts	Electro parts	Electro parts	Electro parts	Electro parts	Electro assembly	Electro assembly	Electro assembly
Start of operation	1971	1976	1996	1988	1984						
Mode of entry	New/ wholly-owned	Joint venture	New/ wholly-owned	New/ wholly-owned	New/ wholly-owned	New/ wholly-owned	New/ wholly-owned	Joint venture/ wholly-owned	New/ wholly-owned	New/ wholly-owned	Joint venture/ wholly-owned
Capital			DM24 million		DM15 million	DM295 million			DM26.29 million	DM69 million	DM8 million
Ownership	100%	40%	100%	100%	100%	100%	100%	100%	100%	100%	100%
Number of employees	174	62	240	225	192	650	450	280	661	430 (part 100)	153
Japanese	10	1	6	2	7	19	11	5	13	4	5
% Japanese	5.7%	1.6%	2.5%	0.9%	3.6%	2.9%	2.4%	1.8%	2.0%	0.9%	3.3%
Products	Ball bearing: 48.7 million	Auto pump seal	Air bag, and related: 200 million	Magnet head VCR: 11.4 million	IC (memory, asic)	16 DRAM	DRAM (wafer), module	tuner, switch	Large high grade copier: 60 k	PC: 1 million	HDD spindle motor, R&D
Volume/ capacity	Fabrication unit: 2.1 million	Electronics mechanical:		Cylinder VCR	DRAM, etc., 8,240 kp	wafer: 120 k	DM185 million	RF Modulator	toner filling: 1,120 k	(notebook type)	mass production: 170 k
[1998]	Auto tensioner	total 500 million		Switch, etc: 246 million	IGBT module, EN-FAX	assembly: 2.4 million		power supply etc.: DM163 million	ink filling: 3,980 k	(desk-top type)	tester
Export ratio	32%	15–20%	5%	a little	14% (1997)				83%		
Destination	France 18%, UK 14%	Brazil, Australia, UK, France	USA		USA			Continental Europe	UK 18%, France 16%	All Europe	USA, Japan, UK, France, Thailand

HDD = hard disk drive
IGBT = insulated gate bipolar transistor
PC = personal computer
R&D = research and development
RF = radio frequency
VCR = video cassette recorder

manufacturers exhibit basically the same tendencies. However, since German electronics product assemblers are not as competitive and do not provide the same degree of demand as the German auto manufacturers, component manufacturers tend to focus on the overall European market, which also relies on Japanese electronics manufacturers. Managing these semiconductor and other manufacturing plants is not an easy task.

Third, in the field of product assembly, it is difficult for simple volume production plants to exist in Germany for longer than they have done in Japan. The only types of plant that have survived are those producing EAa's large advanced photocopiers, EAb's notebook personal computers (PCs) with their concentration on miniature, precision technology, or the small motors developed and designed by EAc. Small wonder that even Japanese manufacturers hesitate to get involved in local auto assembly, which includes world-class high- and medium-quality automobile manufacturers.

Some companies established plants in Europe at a surprisingly early date. Companies such as APa, APb and EAa began operations in the mid-1970s as part of the overall move towards local overseas production on the part of the Japanese manufacturing industry, and parallelling the first group of Japanese companies to explore such activities in Asia. Likewise, in 1980, EPc became the first Japanese company in its field to begin operations in Europe at around the same time that it ventured into the USA, where trade friction had become a major issue. These early ventures are notable in comparison with the numerous cases of Japanese direct investment in the UK, which was to become the powerhouse of the European electronics industry, beginning in the mid-1980s.

The reason behind these early ventures into Germany was probably the companies' appraisal of the importance of Germany to the rest of Europe, in terms of supply and demand. Particularly from the supply aspect, companies such as APb, EAa, and later EAc took note of the high levels of skills and technology in Germany's machinery industry. For this reason, they had the desire to develop advanced functions and new products through joint ventures or other forms of cooperative effort with local industry rather than simply introduce Japanese technology. In this regard, most of the Japanese who were dispatched to these plants were unanimous in their high praise for the manner in which mechanical engineering know-how had been adapted to the work place, as well as for the high level of traditional trade skills. This does not mean, however, that it led directly to an aggressive expansion of local production operations. The following characteristics explain this.

Japanese manufacturing plants in Germany were limited to small or medium-scale operations. As Table 1.1 shows, the largest plant employed about 600 workers, with the majority well below that number. This compares unfavourably with France, Holland, and some countries in southern Europe, where several plants employed more than 1,000 workers, not to mention the plants in England, most of which employed more than 1,000 workers while six had more than 2,000 workers. In other words, it seems that Japanese companies ventured into Germany with great expectations at an early date, and when things failed to work out as anticipated, further progress was stifled. Many of the local Japanese managers admitted as much and, with the wisdom of hindsight, suggested that they might have been better off not coming in the first place. Needless to say, the major reason for this opinion was the various costs associated with labour. As will be discussed later, the high level of wages and salaries was not the only problem; other labour-related difficulties included regulations such as working hours and restrictions relating to the labour unions and the system for employee representation. Moreover, another aspect of this problem was that the advanced mechanical technology and worker skills typical of the German industrial environment could not easily adapt to electronics-related or IT-related technology, or to the Japanese system of multi-skilled workers and flexible work organization. A number of companies such as EAa and EAc started out as partners in a joint venture, but ultimately opted to go it alone for this very reason.

In comparison with the historical developments described above, recent Japanese foreign direct investment (FDI) has dealt more positively with the new situation in Germany. Table 1.1 shows APb as one example, but there are other new, large-scale plants that are not subjects of the present study. These include the EPe plant for the manufacture and development of cathode-ray tubes (established 1995 with 1,300 employees at Esslingen), a Komatsu plant for the manufacture of large hydraulic shovels (1996; 650 employees; Dusseldorf), and a giant Siemens-Matsushita joint venture producing electronics components (1999; 10,000 employees; Munich; see Toyokeizai 2000).

Behind these recent developments lies an aggressive strategy for internationalization on the part of German industry as it confronts new aspects of EU integration, and a trend, particularly among increasingly globally competitive Japanese parts manufacturers, to select Germany as the location for their production centres. One reason for a growing preference for continental Europe over the UK on the part of Japanese corporations is the delay in bringing sterling into the European monetary union, which distances the UK from the rest of Europe. Even in Germany, traditional labour practices and customs are crumbling under the impact of trends and events such as Japanization, the integration of East and West Germany, the advent of major global- or European-scale competition, and market capitalism. This is particularly evident among the new type of companies and plants that foreign companies and former West German companies are establishing in former East Germany. Representative among these is the General Motors (GM) plant that we visited in Eisenach, as well as the APc plant. Another development likely to have important consequences for future investment, although it was not very notable among the plants that we visited for the present study, is the widening range of jobs for which companies employ part-time workers. In other words, the rigid social and system frameworks within which management had to operate in the past are becoming more flexible, and in many respects this works to the advantage of local production by Japanese companies.

3   Hybrid evaluation

3.1   Analytical framework: application-adaptation (hybrid) model

The application-adaptation (A-A) model, which was developed by the JMNESG, seeks to determine the extent to which the Japanese-style production system, summarized in terms of 23 elements and six groups (see Table 1.2–3), has been successfully introduced and applied at foreign subsidiaries of Japanese enterprises (Abo 1994, chs 1 and 2; Itagaki 1997, ch. 1). The A-A model emphasizes those aspects of the production system that are vital to achieving high product quality and efficient production over a wide range of operations. The focus is on employees' strong sense of identity with the company, and on the flexibility that derives from *genbashugi* (work site-orientation) operations. The model was completed around the latter half of the 1980s, just before the beginning of the bubble economy in Japan. Although there have been some changes in the Japanese system since the crash of the bubble, nevertheless we continue to believe that the model is appropriate and useful as a prototype with which other models at home and abroad can be contrasted. The focal point of the A-A model is the human factor, which underlies and reinforces the Japanese systems. Not only is this closely related to the historical and cultural background of Japanese society, but it is also largely based on in-house education and training. Therefore, our hypothesis is that when Japanese firms 'apply' their technological advantages to foreign countries, they will face problems in 'adapting' to the local managerial environment. This is a 'dilemma model' in the sense that it exposes the difficulties inherent in the A-A aspects of the system. However, various types of application and adaptation generate different 'hybrid patterns' of Japanese elements and local elements at the subsidiary plants, largely depending on socio-cultural backgrounds, which are greatly influenced by the historical and geographical contexts of each respective society. We use a five-point scale ('hybrid ratio') to determine where to position the overseas plants of Japanese firms relative to the Japanese and the local models. A score of 5 indicates the highest possible degree of application (and consequently, the lowest level of adaptation: e.g., a Japanese plant operating in Japan). Conversely, a score of 1 represents the highest degree of adaptation (and would reflect conditions at a non-Japanese plant operating in its domestic environment).

3.2   Overall industry average

The overall industry analysis of application and adaptation, according to Table 1.2, produces a high average score for application. Although no Japanese auto-assembly plants are represented in this group, the average application score of 3.2 is close to that of plants in the UK (3.3) and higher than plants in other countries such as France (3.0) and Italy (2.8). The problem, however, concerns the composition of elements revealed in the hybrid evaluation.

3.3   Six-group, 23-item evaluation

The six-group evaluation, shown in Table 1.3, shows a conspicuously high application score for group III, procurement (3.5, +0.5)[1] as well as for group VI, parent–subsidiary relations (3.4, +0.5). This is not only high for other countries in Europe, but also relative to major countries or areas in other parts of the world. On the other hand, the score for group I, work organization and administration, which represents the human-method core of the Japanese production system, is not particularly high (3.1, +0.1), while group V, labour relations, receives the lowest score (3.0, −0.3). Group II, production control, receives the second highest score, following the UK. However, as in most other cases, regional discrepancies in this group are minimal. A detailed discussion of these points, as well as each of the 23 items in the groups, coupled with Figures 1.1 and 1.2, follows.

First, as mentioned earlier, the high degree of application for parts procurement is largely related to the fact that many of the larger Japanese companies in Germany are parts manufacturers. The companies

Table 1.2 Hybrid evaluations of 23 items in Europe

		UK	Germany	France/Benelux	Italy/Spain/Portugal	Hungary
1	Job classification	4.4	3.1	3.5	2.9	3.3
2	Job rotation	3.3	2.8	2.8	3.0	2.5
3	Training	3.5	3.2	3.0	3.1	3.0
4	Wage	2.8	2.7	2.9	2.6	3.0
5	Promotion	3.4	3.2	2.8	3.2	3.0
6	Supervisor	3.4	3.4	3.0	2.9	2.8
7	Equipment	3.9	3.9	3.2	2.6	4.8
8	Maintenance	3.0	2.7	2.7	3.1	2.5
9	Quality control	3.6	3.5	3.0	3.1	2.5
10	Operation management	3.6	3.4	3.2	3.2	3.0
11	Local content	1.9	3.6	2.8	2.0	2.0
12	Suppliers	2.7	3.8	2.8	2.1	2.8
13	Methods	2.9	3.0	2.6	3.0	2.3
14	Small group	2.7	2.6	2.7	2.3	2.0
15	Information	3.6	2.8	3.2	2.7	2.3
16	Unity	3.7	3.0	2.8	2.6	2.5
17	Employment policy	3.3	3.1	3.1	3.4	2.5
18	Employment security	3.4	3.0	3.6	3.2	2.5
19	Union	4.2	3.2	3.9	3.1	4.3
20	Grievance	3.0	2.8	3.3	3.0	3.3
21	JPN ratio	2.4	3.0	2.6	2.4	2.3
22	Power delegation	3.0	3.6	2.9	2.7	4.0
23	Local manager	3.0	3.5	2.9	2.8	3.5

Table 1.3 Hybrid evaluations of six groups in Europe

		UK	Germany	France/Benelux	Italy/Spain/Portugal	Hungary
GI	Work organization/administration	3.4	3.1	3.0	2.9	2.9
GII	Production control	3.5	3.4	3.0	3.0	3.2
GIII	Parts procurement	2.5	3.5	2.7	2.4	2.3
GIV	Team sense	3.3	2.8	2.9	2.5	2.3
GV	Labour relations	3.5	3.0	3.5	3.2	3.1
GVI	Parent/subsidiary	2.8	3.4	2.8	2.6	3.3

themselves have little choice but to procure many of their own parts
and materials from Japan or other Asian sources, for two reasons: first of
all, the parts makers have to meet stringent quality and function standards from product assemblers competing on the German, European or

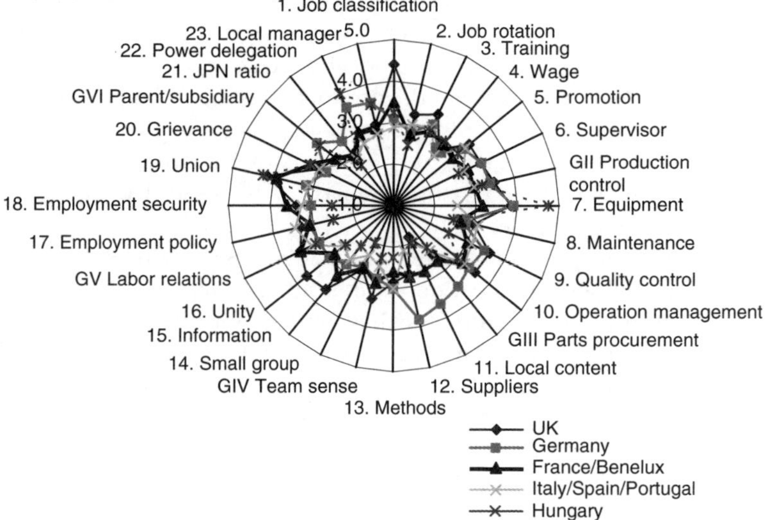

Figure 1.1 Hybrid evaluation of 23 items in Europe

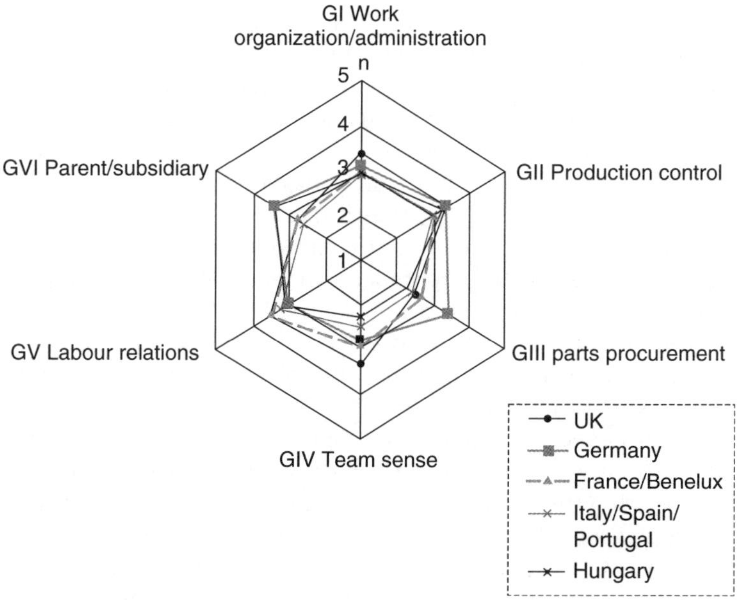

Figure 1.2 Hybrids of six groups in Europe

global markets. Second, these assemblers expect the parts makers, particularly when they are Japanese or other foreign companies, to help them meet 'Euro-one' and other EU local content regulations. In other words, the parts makers cushion the product assemblers from local content requirements by providing the logistics to raise quality and lower costs through the procurement of high quality and functionally advanced parts and materials from Japan, or low-priced components from other sources in Asia.

Second, next to parts procurement, parent–subsidiary relations have the second highest application rating among Japanese plants in Germany, and in all of Europe for that matter, coupled with Hungary. Indeed, the only case of a higher application rating for this item anywhere in the world was a 3.6 point evaluation recorded for Japanese plants in the USA ten years ago. Even there, an interim survey carried out in 1993 revealed a marked shift towards adaptation (Abo 1998b) while yet another survey completed in 2000 confirmed this trend. It is likely that in 1998, the plants in Germany represented the highest degree of application of parent–subsidiary relations among all overseas Japanese plants anywhere in the world. Notable among the items in this group is item 21, ratio of Japanese expatriates, with an application score of 3.0 (+0.4). Judging from the manufacture of products that involve a high degree of technical difficulty, or the large number of small and medium-sized operations (which facilitate a high ratio of Japanese expatriates) problems would arise in the overall plant management without a comparatively large number of Japanese employees.

This is certainly not because of any lack of supervisory or management skills on the part of German managers. In fact, we were greatly impressed by the enthusiastic, skilled managers in a number of plants who have made a sincere effort to introduce and apply the various methods practised at the parent plants in Japan. At EAa, a group of five German engineers who visited the parent plant in Japan to prepare for the introduction of a new process of manufacturing ink cartridges demonstrated their craftsmanship and system engineering skills and techniques in various ways. For example, they formed 'novice teams' with other inexperienced Japanese employees and succeeded in starting up the process without any help. They also designed 'computer inspection method' systems for problem identification during parts inspection in the copier assembly process, and they also invented devices for waste disposal within the plant. At EPb, highly motivated German managers who had made numerous training trips to Japan guided the creation of a score sheet to record workers' multiskill competencies, along with a detailed job chart. At EPa, German engineers improved Japanese equipment used in the assembly of tact switches, thereby achieving a higher operating rate than the parent plant in Japan. The Japanese parent company of EAc formed a 50 per cent joint-venture subsidiary with a German company that had expertise in the manufacture of spindle motors for personal computers. However, since the German partner lacked managerial skills, EAc turned it into a 100 per cent owned subsidiary and strengthened management by increasing the number of Japanese expatriate employees (3.3 per cent plus two trainees). In the case of an EAb plant for the assembly of personal computers, the quality control formation rate reached 30 per cent despite the complete absence of a bonus system. In addition, enthusiastic, self-initiated *kaizen* activities include a system for collecting suggestions from employees.

As these many interesting cases show, German workers who demonstrate leadership on the shop floor and voluntarily utilize their technical expertise and competent job skills also contribute to a fairly high level of *kaizen* activities as well as creative job performance. However, for a number of reasons, it is a little problematic to entrust the overall management of the plant to these employees. First, extreme cases such as EAc demonstrate that German workers have a slightly narrow perspective when it comes to plant operation. It is unfair to expect them to broaden their views of plant management, or to expect them to coordinate those operations with those of other plants outside Germany, not to mention those in Japan. Second, and somewhat related to differences in management styles, while Germans tend towards a perfectionism that will only be satisfied with expert, comprehensive solutions, Japanese managers, despite their interest in system development or process changes, will act in moderation, always giving due consideration to cost factors. In this respect, ultimately there is no choice but to leave such decisions up to Japanese managers. Finally, in most cases, the German domestic market is of greatest importance to German plants. Consequently, as long as it is a profit centre, it will be necessary to have Japanese managers in charge who, as the representatives of Japanese headquarters, are concerned with market strategies such as sales and purchases.

Third, the reason that certain human-related item-groups such as work organization and administration, or labour relations, do not exhibit such a high degree of application is that there are such pronounced differences between Germany and Japan in terms of the various customs and systems governing jobs or labour. When a Japanese company attempts to introduce the methods employed at its parent plant, it often encounters a spate of restrictions on its implementation. This German system framework is not as diametrically opposed to Japan's as was the case in the USA. Although there is a strong emphasis on specialization in Germany with regard to job methods, as mentioned above, this is quite limited and not nearly as exhaustive as the detailed job descriptions in the USA. Likewise, neither is the wage system so tightly linked to job classifications. The German system also utilizes a type of team approach, and in some aspects it also supports the long-term employment that cultivates teams.

In the background, however, there is strong evidence of horizontal divisions in the organizations which are rooted in a traditional social hierarchy. Such rules and practices take precedence over the organization system that is imposed from within a particular corporation and which centres on the functions of the labour union. These characteristics do not coexist well with the vertical structures of the Japanese production system. This refers in particular to the employee representative council (*Betriebsrat*) that exists in the organization completely separate from the labour union. In fact, the council is closely related to the labour union, and its position and functions are rather delicately defined. An understanding of this point requires a brief explanation of its relationship to wage classes, known as '*Tarif* wages'.

The *Tarif* is the German version of a European qualifications system for specifying the relationship between traditional jobs and the wage classes (or salaries) earned by workers doing those jobs (cf. Jürgens 1998b; Nihon Rodo Kenkyu Kikou 1998; Sudwestmetall 1995). It is based on an agreement between management and the labour union that conforms to the business organization law, and according to which ten agreement areas throughout the country determine wage levels (in the case of white-collar workers, 'salaries') across as few as 8 or as many as 12 (in most cases 10) wage classes (*Lohngruppe*). The qualifying conditions for each class are determined by agreement between the labour unions and the employer associations in each area, and simply expressed in a standard document. In the case of Sudwestmetall (November 1995, owned by EAc), there are 10 wage classes: class 1 refers to simple jobs that require no prior knowledge or training; those up to class 4 reflect respectively more experience and some specific knowledge; classes 5 or 6 require two months' or more training; class 7 and above require the completion of special training or the equivalent level of skill. This special training and education is a particular system for the training of tradesmen (*Facharbeiter*) through a combination of vocational school (AZUBI: Auszubildende) training and in-house apprenticeship. Originally, *Facharbeiter* training was a fusion of the traditional in-house worker training system and a special German-style, external training system. Today, however, it has become standard training for about two-thirds of all male labourers and is no longer considered a particularly special qualification. The wage levels that correspond to these wage classes in 1995 were approximately DM2,501 for class 1, DM2,934 for class 7, and DM3,894 for class 10 (monthly). Moreover, maintenance workers are those selected from the class 7 to 10 group who also fulfil other conditions such as a ten-year experience at the plant. Line leaders (*Linie Leiter*) seem to be selected from the 9 or 10 wage class.

Otherwise, the highest qualification for a plant worker is that of *Meister* (a standard classification since the Second World War, and distinguished from a similar term for 'craftsmen' in the handicrafts industry) which requires about 2 years of special training and education after the *Tarif*, culminating in a diploma (*Diplom*) on graduation. The salaries for a *Meister* would be about DM5,500–6,500 a month (in case of plant EAC). The *Meister* qualification used to be a prerequisite for becoming a foreman in the traditional job-rank sense. Recently, however, it has not been unusual to become foreman without this qualification, and indeed, at the Japanese transplants, it is common for a foreman not to have this qualification. Even in German companies, apparently, if there were plans to develop flexible plant or organization management operations to cope with changes in the internal or external environment, the present qualification system leaves little room for compromise and is thus difficult to utilize.

On considering how Japanese companies have dealt with this system for qualifications, we see that among the eleven plants surveyed, four have not established a labour union, although all except one plant located in former East Germany have an employee representative council. Also, while it is required that any work place with five or more employees has an employee representative council, were it not for the request from the employees there would not be any need for this council. The determination of wages and salaries in the majority of cases clearly conforms to *Tarif* wages and, in fact, each of the eleven plants, including the one that does not have an employee representative council, determines wages and salaries in accordance with this system. In any case, the discrepancy between this situation and the Japanese system is nowhere near as great as that between the American job-centred and Japanese person-centred wage systems.

In other words, the focus of attention shifts to dealing with job functions per se. In the case of standard jobs, wage classes are determined with reference to an example contained in the labour agreement. However, in the absence of such an example, a committee made up of representatives from the company and the employee representative council decides on the wage class. As described above, this *Tarif* wage system is basically a job wage, and management does not have the right to shift an employee to a different job unilaterally without regard to the type of job that matches his particular job qualifications. However, in comparison with US-type job wages, there is a greater degree of tolerance and flexibility. That is to say, first, a specific wage class specified through *Tarif* wages may be applicable to a number of different job types. Therefore, since job shifts within a particular wage class have no effect on wages, it is possible to transfer workers between different jobs within their respective wage classes. Second, since each wage class only specifies a certain minimum wage rate, it is possible to encourage workers to accept job rotation by offering them incentives such as performance bonuses based on worker assessments. However, it is probably impossible to exceed the level specified as the minimum for the next highest wage class. Third, even though these wage class practices may reflect certain social regulation frameworks and thus take precedence over the organization imposed by a corporation, they are ultimately determined by the wage class committee and thus do, in fact, reflect internal company conditions. But again, this depends largely on the position of the employee representative council. In cases where the labour union exerts considerable influence over the council, these things do not always work out as planned.

Under such conditions, many of the Japanese transplants choose not to press the matter. Instead, they tend to leave work organization and its operation in the hands of their German managers. This may account for the unusually sketchy responses from many Japanese managers when asked to provide detailed answers on matters concerning work organization. But in other cases (e.g., both EPb and EAb plants of the same company Y, and the EPa plant) companies have actively utilized performance bonuses based on the introduction of the straightforward worker assessments mentioned above. There are other cases such as APa, where, in order to train and develop mechanical maintenance technicians, the company succeeded in negotiating with the employee representative council for a pay increase equivalent to an entire wage class. In short, to a certain degree it is possible to conduct blue-collar worker assessments in Germany and to stretch the limitations of the wage-class system in order to develop broader, more diverse job skills, and thereby pursue a more flexible process management. Indeed, it is fairly standard among German firms that an average 13–16 per cent of the contractual wages are subject to some kind of worker assessment. However, this does require the readiness to spend time and trouble observing conventions and practices such as, in particular, patient negotiation with the labour union or the employee representative council. In the majority of cases, these Japanese firms did not resolve to undertake the type of cost-intensive, all-out mass production manufacturing operations that would warrant such a commitment of effort. As mentioned previously, they have assumed the form of operations that allows them to utilize German technology and production skills in order to manufacture functionally advanced components and higher value-added products, mainly for the German market, and on a scale that is appropriate for this demand. Consequently, they basically allow plant management to pursue a 'Japanese style' that is understood and accepted by German managers.

Fourth, at the level of the 23-item analysis, group I, items 5 (promotion) and 6 (first-line supervisors) for the Japanese plants in Germany receive about as high a score as Japanese plants in Britain (Table 1.2, Figure 1.1). In fact, due to the somewhat flexible internal promotion system to the first-line supervisor (*Linie Leiter*) and foreman classes, the process ensures the development of plant managers who are broadly skilled in operational as well as managerial aspects. In contrast, however, all items in group V (labour relations) receive a lower score. This is partly on account of the presence of Germany's strongest labour union, IG Metall, which represents workers in the metal-working industries, such as electrical machinery or automobile manufacturing. In spite of the fact that the union has become fairly flexible, the employee representative councils require extra, painstaking negotiations for any attempt to modify existing regulations or practices. It must be said that the strength of these systematic constraints in Germany greatly restricts the ability to develop the type of accommodative labour relations seen in Japan.

Fifth, the high average item scores for group II (production control) reflect the high scores for items 7 (production equipment), 9 (quality control), and 10 (process control). In fact, with the exception of item 8 (maintenance), these item scores for Japanese plants in Germany are the highest in continental Europe. Japanese production equipment is indispensable because, as mentioned above, it is difficult to bring in Japanese elements through human-related items and, moreover, because of the need to supply functionally advanced, high-quality products to the German market. In the case of quality and process control, German managers implement Japanese production methods competently and effectively, although not exactly in the Japanese style. However, the reason that maintenance receives a lower score is that, as mentioned earlier, the process of skills training has only been partly introduced and implemented on an in-house basis; fundamentally, it conforms to systems and institutions external to the company. For example, it is not easy for these companies to carry out training for firm-specific, multiple job skills, and it is especially problematic to find methods of rewarding this training.

3.4   Four-perspective evaluation

Let us now reconsider the results of the six-group, 23-item hybrid analysis by using the 'four-perspective evaluation' which looks at the substantive content of technology transfer. According to this evaluation, 'method' refers to the transfer of intangible elements such as the technique and know-how that are necessary to build the organization and carry out personnel administration. This requires transplanting a considerable number of Japanese skills and technologies to the local soil. 'Result', on the other hand, concerns the transfer of the visible elements of 'ready-made' hardware such as machines, parts, and even Japanese personnel. After repatriation, it is possible that these elements will have left no trace whatsoever on local soil.

As expected, Table 1.4 and Figure 1.3 confirm the overall high application scores obtained from the hybrid analysis. Moreover, there is a conspicuously high application score for 'material result', as measured along the horizontal axis of this figure.

The results are not surprising, in the light of the high application scores for all group III procurement items (and, in the case of the auto and electronics parts manufacturers, particularly local content and suppliers) as well as equipment. There are two ways to consider this. On the one hand, it shows that it is not easy for Japanese transplants in Germany to transfer and successfully implement the Japanese system and technology in their all-important parts manufacturing plants. Therefore, to compensate, they must bring in 'ready-made' Japanese parts, materials and equipment. On the other hand, this reflects the particular importance that set makers attach to the

Table 1.4   Four-perspective evaluations of hybrids in Europe

	UK	Germany	France/ Benelux	Italy/Spain/ Portugal	Hungary
Method: human	3.4	3.0	3.0	2.9	2.7
Result: human	2.7	3.3	2.8	2.6	2.9
Method: material	3.2	3.1	2.8	3.1	2.4
Result: material	2.8	3.8	2.9	2.2	3.2

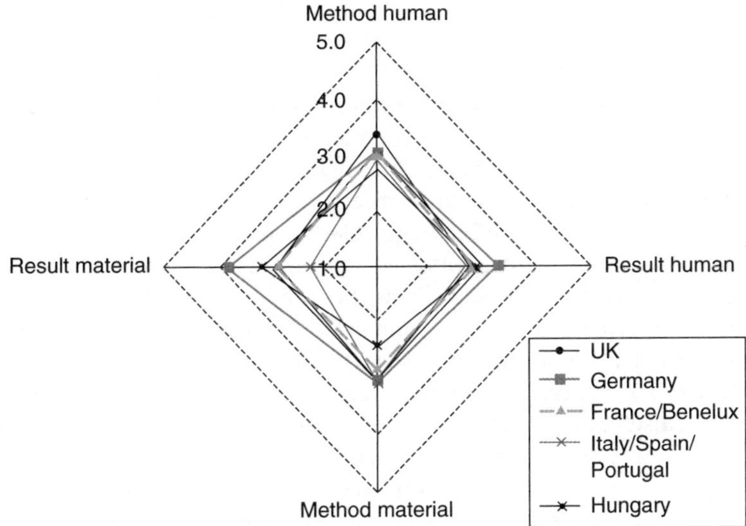

Figure 1.3 Four perspectives of hybrids in Europe

production and supply of functionally advanced, high quality products in Germany.

This is also evident in the high application scores for 'human result' in Japanese transplants in Europe. That is to say, not only is there a high ratio of Japanese expatriates, but the position of local managers (item 23) is also quite low. In other words, there is little commitment to developing the authority of German managers, and compared with their counterparts in the UK, far less than we would expect (see Table 1.2, Figure 1.2). As mentioned earlier, we encountered quite a few Germans at the rank of shop floor manager, but their presence seemed far less noticeable above that level. Outwardly, a certain degree of localization does seem to be taking place, as shown by three companies at which Germans are positioned at levels from plant manager to president, and two companies where Germans occupy other upper management posts, such as vice-president. However, there is a strong sense that these are only nominal appointments and, moreover, at all of the other companies, Japanese personnel dominate the positions of authority almost exclusively.

In the case of medium-scale parts manufacturing plants, such a wide variety of know-how on the part of local managers is not considered necessary for the creation and development of opportunities in the local market. Rather, priority is given to effective local application of products and technologies already held by the parent plant.

In contrast, the material-method aspect group is among the highest application scoring groups in Europe, despite the existence of some striking differences between the German and Japanese systems, such as education and training (which, as pointed out above, partly accounted for the low application in maintenance). One reason for this high over-all score is that, as exemplified by the electrical product assembly plants, although these companies followed the outward form of the German system and practices, in substance they applied Japanese production control. In other words, the companies followed German-style *gen-bashugi*, such as having specialists carry out the maintenance or quality control job functions. In practice, however, these specialists took it upon themselves to acquire Japanese methods such as 'creating quality in the process', and as a result of their interaction and communication with quality and process engineers, were able to achieve a wide range of *kaizen* effects. This is a case of what we have called 'revised application'.

4   Performance evaluation

How does the business performance of these plants compare with their hybrid evaluations? When the field research was conducted in the autumn of 1998, with the exception of some of the semiconductor plants, most plants were operating in the black. The scale of their profits, however, was not particularly large. Many of these operations had also succeeded in erasing their cumulative losses. Overall, despite the high cost of labour, and although their performances were not particularly impressive, these Japanese transplants did manage to survive in Europe and, more significantly, in those countries whose markets were especially important.

On the other hand, not many of these transplants are entirely satisfied with their situations, particularly those that had set their sights on the German market in the 1970s, that were impressed with the country's high levels of skills and technology, and that took the lead in local investment strategies there. We heard of several who reconsidered their strategies in the light of later circumstances, or believed that England might have perhaps offered a more suitable environment after all. While this is no doubt their honest opinion, other companies feel differently. Although few in number, companies such as APa represent a new wave of investment that took place in the early 1990s. The value of locating a plant in Germany may gradually change as the integration of the European economy progresses. However, the significance of establishing a production centre in a country that will remain, at the very least, the focal point of the auto manufacturing industry, will probably only increase. With respect to these and other points mentioned above, we will now proceed with an overall hybrid evaluation of these Japanese transplants in Germany.

5 Overall evaluation

Overall, the most distinguishing characteristic of these hybrid evaluations is a strong, result-oriented, high application pattern. High application scores for material results were particularly conspicuous through the bringing in of parts as well as production equipment. A high ratio of Japanese expatriates also contributes to a fairly high application score for human results. The application of methods, on the other hand, is more limited.

Behind this type of application pattern there is a willingness to accommodate some of the strongest system frameworks in Europe, such as social systems that regulate the management of industrial enterprises in Germany (the labour union, the employee representative council, and *Tarif* wages, as well as other customs and practices). Even where such systems do not exist, the companies follow wage systems that are similar to *Tarif* wages. This is perhaps the reason why the general commitment of Japanese expatriates to local operations seems fairly weak and, as will be discussed below, why production is left largely in the hands of German managers and German technical specialists. Many of the Japanese personnel seemed unable to provide an adequate response to our questions concerning work organization or the nature of small group activities, a situation we rarely encountered in other regions.

With the rather limited application of human method elements, and faced with a market that demands high-quality functionally advanced products, it is almost inevitable that Japanese transplants will turn to 'bringing in' ready-made elements from Japan. This is the easiest, most effective way for them to clear the various social and cultural hurdles that stand in their way.

Since it is almost inconceivable to run large-scale, mass-production plants in such an environment, companies generally adopt a form of mixed-model production (small-lot production of a variety of products) of high-quality, functionally advanced parts intended mainly for the auto industry. With the growing expansion of the EU, and the lowering of economic trade barriers with eastern European countries such as

Hungary, Poland and the Czech Republic (with which Germany has strong historical relations), this type of strategy is becoming increasingly necessary. In fact, German enterprises themselves are already establishing manufacturing plants for compact, inexpensive automobiles in Western European countries such as Spain, Portugal and Belgium, in Eastern European countries such as Hungary, Poland and the Czech Republic, in former East Germany, and close to the border with France. Among the Japanese transplants in Germany that are the subject of the current study, EAb has sub-contracted the production of certain low-end components for its notebook PCs to EMS (Electronics Manufacturing Service) in Hungary (Headquarters hearings, February, 2001), and EPe has established a subsidiary plant in Slovakia (twin operation) employing approximately three times more workers than its plant in Germany.

Because it is related, I would like to mention briefly the somewhat special situation that exists in the former East German region. APc is the only Japanese transplant in the region to be included in the present research. Although Japan lags behind, some small and medium Japanese transplants have recently begun to appear here. German investment from former West German companies arrived first, followed by that of US multinational enterprises. The 'German' investor, in this case, is the well-known GM plant at Eisenach, which was established with the helpful mediation of Opel, GM's German subsidiary. This plant is seen as representing the introduction of a very 'Japanese-style' operation, based on what GM learned in America about the Toyota system (such as NUMMI, New United Motor Manufacturing Inc., which is a joint venture plant between GM and Toyota in the USA: see Jürgens 1998a). We were given a simple tour of this plant during the research trip in 1998. It was the author's personal impression that it was a very 'lean' plant indeed. However, this may have been the result of witnessing the huge surrounding 'logistic district' right next to the plant, where almost all parts, components, and sub-assembly plants necessary to produce a simple car model were together in one place. It comes as no surprise that they were able to deliver 'just in time'.

The specific characteristics of plant management at the Japanese transplants in Germany were previously referred to as 'German-style *genbashugi*'. This creates the image of a hybrid system that combines German traditional precision machinery technology (mechanical technology) and the worker skills necessary to support it on the shop floor with the flexible work organization system resulting from Japanese-style mechatronics technology and the principles of mixed-model production. This is a form of *genbashugi*, since those in charge are mainly

German-style expert technicians under the guidance of managers and engineers, while Japanese-style manufacturing technology blends with German-style methods and system frameworks, and the technicians perform *kaizen* and small-group activities enthusiastically at the shop floor level. A notable difference between this system and the way it operates in Japan is, however, that it generally fails to extend to the regular shop floor workers. Consequently, we are treating this model as an interesting case of 'revised application'. Since it makes fairly heavy demands on time and effort, it is sometimes viewed as 'excessive application' from the perspective of the basic necessities of the Japanese-style production system. In any case, it is probably best to say that its effectiveness is restricted to special cases such as the one described above.

Changes are also beginning to emerge in German society itself, as a certain easing of regulations in this strongly rule-driven society gradually unfolds. Basically, in the face of a declining rate of unionization and a rising unemployment rate, unions (and especially employee representative councils) are becoming more accommodating in their dealings with management. There is broad progress in areas such as the implementation of worker assessments and more flexible application of the *Tarif* wage system that uses these assessments. There are also negotiations that could lead to a longer working week (from 35 to 37.5 hours per week in order to prevent a wage cut at EAa), to the introduction of overtime, and to more liberal rules governing the employment of part-time workers. There are two categories of part-timers, one of which is the 'fixed period' part-timer. Although their period of employment is limited, certain conditions, such as eligibility for social insurance, are the same as those for permanent employees. Another part-timer category contains those who are employed via temporary staff agencies and who do not pay social security if they earn DM600 or less per week. Originally to be found mainly in the service industry, this type of part-time employment has rapidly spread to the manufacturing industry. Although not many of the Japanese transplants that are the focus of this study employ personnel from this category, there are several examples of an increase in 'fixed-period workers' which reflects a softening of the rigid employment conditions that existed before. All of these developments have served to relax the rigid German-style systems referred to above. They can be considered the German version of trends sweeping across the whole of Europe, as these countries seek to reinforce market-oriented capitalism and increase their competitiveness in the face of globalization and rapid European integration. From the German perspective, these changes represent efforts to prevent German manufacturing enterprises from leaving the country, and there is no question that they produce an easier, more tractable local environment for Japanese enterprises.

From the above, we see that while the significance of having a manufacturing centre in Germany is not a simple matter, there are clearly certain merits. Maintaining a manufacturing presence in Germany, which is the industrial and economic (if not the financial) heartland of Europe and particularly of the EU, and which represents a very important market comprising consumers with sophisticated and exacting demands, is a matter of strategy. Above all, this strategy is related to establishing a foothold in general business activities, including sales and research and development (R&D), in this country and this region. In this way, the relationships that are established with other companies or the transaction channels with its customers can later contribute to the development of an undertaking on a much larger scale throughout the whole of Europe.

The strategic position of Germany in particular as a conduit to eastern Europe is expected to become increasingly important in the future. Due to their geographical and cultural proximity to the countries in that region, the role of the plants in Germany will be to support a system for volume production at plants located in eastern European countries. Support of this kind could range from logistical concerns such as the supply of application designs or functional components, to leadership and guidance in plant management. This is similar to the role played in recent years by plants in Korea, Taiwan and Singapore, as they occupy a position intermediary to the parent plants in Japan and their volume production subsidiary plants in Southeast Asia, China and India, and provide necessary support to these plants.

However, although the rigid system framework of German managerial culture is bound to impose a number of limitations, it is not entirely a handicap for the bringing-in of the Japanese-style production system. This is because, in a limited participation style of work and shop floor environment, it creates considerable potential for manufacturing high-quality functionally advanced parts or precision machinery and tools, although the *genbashugi* of training and work place management that revolves around the traditional German tradesman system is not as accommodating as in Japan.

I should emphasize that the foregoing observations are all in the context of an economic region that is in the process of moving towards the economic integration that we know as the EU. It is precisely because it exists within the protective barriers that surround such a vast market that it is possible to carry out local production in a country with wages as high as they are in Germany. According to 'Euro One', a set of import regulations that represents a somewhat extreme form of this protective barrier, the parts manufacturing industry in the region is able to undertake local production with the help of fairly relaxed local content regulations. The assembly industry, which then purchases 'local products' from the parts industry, even at comparatively high prices, is able to compete effectively with Asian imports, on which 40 per cent import duties are levied.

It is also important to point out that the drop in the exchange rate of an internationally strong currency such as the German mark against the British pound or the American dollar is not insignificant for Germany, or indeed for the whole of the EU. The balance of trade and balance of payments clearly demonstrate that the current exchange rate against the pound and the dollar undervalues the German mark. This is not merely because of overvaluation of the pound and the dollar based on the Internet bubble and the related stock-market speculation boom, but also because the process of paving the way for the Euro effectively depresses the exchange rates of some of the participating currencies. The adoption of the Euro will, in effect, probably boost the relatively weak participating currencies, while depressing the rates of the stronger ones. In this way, the exchange rate for the Euro will settle near an average of the rates for all participating currencies prior to monetary union. In other words, it is possible that the Euro will be undervalued as a result of the inherent difficulties of nations participating in the monetary union to make the necessary adjustments. In any case, as far as Germany is concerned, it is inevitable that the value of the Euro will be less than that of the German mark. This means that it will eventually be easier for enterprises located in Germany to export their products, either to other countries in Europe or abroad.

The final point to stress is the stability of enterprises with production centres in Germany or in other locations in the EU. Europe is presently conducting a large experiment in regional economic integration that is bound to include a certain measure of trial and error. Although it may not achieve the sudden economic growth that we see in Asia or the USA, its policies on monetary union, interest rates and the environment demonstrate that it gives the highest priority to stability and safety. This German example of European commitment to stability compares favourably with trends and events in other parts of the world: America faces the possibility of economic turmoil through the destruction of pax Americana, which began in the 1970s, and a collapse of the 'Internet bubble' that grew in the 1990s; Japan has yet to recover from its loss of confidence following the collapse of its bubble economy in the 1980s; Asia is now just beginning to recover from its financial crisis in the 1990s and could be seriously affected by the dramatic collapse of the American bubble. Germany will gain even greater confidence in the future and this will probably further increase the value of having an enterprise located in that country. However, in the midst of this commitment to stability, a number of representative German corporations have recently been in difficulties. It was perhaps on account of having been burned by US-style market-oriented capitalism that companies such as BMW, Daimler-Benz and the Deutsche Bank pursued large-scale international mergers and acquisitions (M&As), and are now either facing failure or serious problems. Evaluating these developments properly could be an interesting project.

Note

1   + and – refer here to the mean deviation in European countries or regions.

References

Abo, T. (ed.) (1994), *Hybrid Factory: The Japanese Production System in the United States* (New York: Oxford University Press).

Abo, T. (1998a), 'Hybridization of the Japanese Production System in North America, Newly Industrializing Economies, South-East Asia, and Europe: Contrasted Configurations', in R. Boyer, E. Charron, U. Jürgens and S. Tolliday (eds), *Between Imitation and Innovation: The Transfer and Hybridization of Productive Models in the International Automobile Industry* (New York: Oxford University Press).

Abo, T. (1998b), 'Changes in Japanese Automobile and Electronics Transplants in the USA', in H. Hasegawa and G. D. Hook (eds), *Japanese Business Management* (London: Routledge).

Abo, T. (2001), 'Competition and Cooperation between the Japanese and British Management Models in the UK: International Transfer Problems of Intangible Management Systems', in P. Banerjee and F.-J. Richter (eds), *Intangibles in Competition and Cooperation: Euro-Asian Perspectives* (New York: Palgrave).

Itagaki, H. (ed.) (1997), *The Japanese Production System: Hybrid Factories in East Asia* (Basingstoke and London: Macmillan).

Jürgens, U. (1998a), 'Implanting Change: The Role of "Indigenous Transplants" in Transforming the German productive Model', in R. Boyer, E. Charron, U. Jürgens and S. Tolliday (eds), *Between Imitation and Innovation: The Transfer and Hybridization of Productive Models in the International Automobile Industry* (New York: Oxford University Press).

Jürgens, U. (1998b), 'Transformation and Mutual Interaction of the Japanese, American and German Production Regimes in the 1990s', Paper presented at the Conference 'Germany and Japan in the 21st Century: Strengths Turning into Weaknesses?' at the Max-Planck-Institut für Gesellshafts-forschung and Japanisch-Deutsches Zentrum Berlin, Berlin, 22–24 January.

Kazama, N. (1997), *Doitsu-teki Seisan Moderu to Furekishibirit* (*German-style Production Model and Flexibility*) (Chuo Keizaisha, 1997).

Nihon Rodo Kenkyu Kikou (1998), *Doitsu Kigyo no Chingin to Jinzai Ikusei* (*The Japan Institute of Labour, Wage and Training Systems of German Companies*).

Schlunze, R. D. (2001), 'Locational Adjustment of Japanese Production System in Europe', in *2001 AJBS Conference Best Paper Proceedings*, 14th Annual Conference, 11–13 June, Seinajoki.

Sudwestmetall (1995), Tarife Metall- und Elektroindustrie Sudwurttemberg-Hohenzollern, Gultig, AB, 1 November.

Toyokeizai Data Bank (2000), *Kaigai Shinshutsu-kigyo Soran* (*Directory of Overseas Japanese Firms, 2000*) (Toyokeizai Shinpo-sha: Tokyo).

2
Two Faces of Corporate Governance in Britain: Symbiotic Diffusion of Human Resource Management/Japanization and European Works Council

Hasegawa Harukiyo

1   Introduction

The topic of corporate governance has already received much discussion in the USA, Japan/Asia and Europe, but so far the scope of its implications have not been broadly explored. This chapter suggests an enlargement of the debate by presenting a new perspective which should go some way to providing a more comprehensive understanding of issues relating to enterprise governance in a capitalist economy.

The underlying issue of corporate governance is essentially an issue of democracy within capitalism. More specifically, it concerns the nature of governance and its manifestation in legislation, institutions and practices both within and without corporations: about who governs whom and in what style, such that it becomes an issue of social relations and methods of management, and about how business organization is to be managed for the optimum achievement of its objectives. As democracy is generally understood to be a 'virtue', reforms in legislation, institutions and practices towards that end tend to be considered positively, at least insofar as they contribute to corporate competitiveness, efficiency and profitability. Governance is thus form, process and function in managing social relations and it manifests in particular forms depending upon the level at which it operates.

The most popular area of corporate governance has been the relationship between shareholders and board members/Chief Executive Officer (CEO). In this study, however, we limit our discussion to reviewing why the issue of corporate governance emerged in the USA with an association with principles of democracy. Our particular focus is on the

governance of employees and industrial relations in British corporations. Human resource management (HRM) and the European Works
Council (EWC) are examined and discussed as effective means of governance, thus enlarging the scope of corporate governance; and we
consider these to be integral parts of its mechanism. If effectiveness is
not achieved in these, the longer term future and social acceptance of
corporations will be compromised, even if the governance of the
board/CEO has been successful. How governance is created in these two
areas by means of particular managerial methods will be explored as a
manifestation of conflicting forces of capital and labour. To shed light
upon HRM and EWC in Britain will help us enlarge the scope of corporate governance and understand corporate governance as an important
issue of democracy within corporations.

2   Human resource management and European Works Councils as managerial methods of corporate governance

Since the 1980s, the way large US corporations have managed their
affairs has received attention in discussions of corporate governance. The
backdrop to this was the process of changes in US capitalism during the
1970s, in particular the increasing influence of institutional investors
(such as pension funds) upon corporate boards and CEOs and their
accountability to shareholders. Peter Drucker commented as early as the
mid-1970s on this new phenomenon, calling it 'pension-fund capitalism'
(Drucker 1993, 74). This phenomenon is of great significance for
academics, as it has far-reaching implications for American democracy
itself, as well as for major issues of corporate culture, such as 'ownership',
'control' and 'governance' (Yoshimori 1996; Sako and Sato 1997; Scott
1997; Takahashi 1999; Uetake and Nakata 1999; Shibuya 1999).

Shibuya (1999) addresses the issue of relevance between 'control
mechanisms of finance capital' and 'democracy within large corporations', as extant in 1970s US capitalism, in his investigation of the 1974
US Senate committee discussions on governance operation. He suggests
that elucidating the reasons why the Senate debated the control mechanisms of finance capital would help establish a perspective of analysis on
the relations between corporate governance and institutional investors.

The current corporate governance discussion thus dates back to the
above hearings on corporate disclosure and ownership. This discussion
was in essence about the basic values of US democracy and the nature
of its capitalism. More specifically, it showed that US capitalism had
developed to the extent that more than one-seventh of the nation's

population had become either direct or indirect shareholders, hence legitimizing the protection of large US corporations (Okamoto 1974). However, the discussion then spread and developed into a debate on how to modify corporations to deal with global competition, so that in practice the discourse on corporate governance became an effective ideology of corporate reforms oriented towards enhancing 'shareholder values' (Keizai Kikakucho 1998; *Harvard Business Review* 2000; Keidanren 2000). These discussions have been supported by neo-classical principles (market orientation), while in the process an organizational approach (social democratic) has also emerged as an alternative to the neo-classical approach. It is the social democratic approach which asserts the legitimacy of stakeholder capitalism on the basis of the accountability (democracy) demanded by the various stakeholders, such as shareholders, employees, suppliers, trade unions, communities, and so on (Drucker 1993; Kelly, Kelly and Gamble 1997; Scott 1997; Wheeler and Sillanpaa 1997; Korten 1999; Rengo 1999).[1] To advance the discussion, governance is here defined as form, process and function aimed at creating order in the relationship between two parties. Thus, issues of who governs whom and to what end can be identified as issues of governance. In a capitalist economy it is manifested in relationships such as those between shareholders and board/CEO; management and employees; management and trade unions; and management and community. Throughout the dynamics of such relationships, the authority of capital functions at both political and economic levels; and governance, the political face of capital, is used to achieve economic objectives (i.e., efficiency and profitability).

This logic of individual capital is not always compatible with the interests of labour in enterprise and public welfare in general, so that issues of corporate governance become conspicuous when perceived incompatibility increases. Owners of capital will assert their rights and authority to further their governance, while labour (employees) interests may also assert their inclination towards more socially oriented governance.

Governance thus functions to regulate those relations between capital and labour that manifest as relations between different categories of people in an enterprise. Those who exercise governance in large corporations exercise power via the authority of capital in order to achieve corporate objectives. Dynamics at each level of corporate governance manifest in forms of organization, management methods and legislation (see Table 2.1).

Corporate governance can thus be postulated as a more holistic function of individual capital, and it works throughout the enterprise;

Table 2.1 Typical corporate governance: types, actors, objective, methods and relations

Types of governance	Actors	Objective of governance	Methods of governance	Relationship
Governance of board and CEO	Shareholders governing board and CEO	Profitability, accountability	Legislation/ external/ internal monitoring	Shareholders versus board and CEO
Governance of employees	Management governing employees	Efficiency	Management methods (HRM)	Management versus employees
Governance of industrial relations	Management governing trade unions	Assimilation/ compliance	Legislation/ industrial relations management (EWC)	Management versus labour unions
Governance of community relations	Management governing community	Symbiosis	Company as member of the community (corporate citizenship)	Management versus community

however, different methods are adopted at each level. Corporate governance in this broader sense came into existence with the emergence of modern business enterprises, with the beginning of the capitalist economy. Even today it exists in any company, regardless of variations in styles of ownership. When Berle and Means wrote *The Modern Corporation and Private Property* (1932), their major finding and discussion point was the 'divorce of ownership from control', providing the foundation for today's narrow definition of corporate governance: a company must govern itself in a way that will satisfy shareholders. This leads to the current major corporate discussions over the relationship between shareholders and board members, the central concerns being efficiency, profitability and competitiveness. If a company wishes to grow, a 'divorce of ownership and control' may be necessary, but also generates problems of governance.

In the USA in the mid-1980s, this issue appeared as a corporate governance movement from institutional shareholders such as TIAA-CREF and CalPERS (Deloitte Touche Tohmatsu 2000). Large institutional shareholders in the US asserted 'efficiency', 'accountability' and 'higher profitability' in the name of 'corporate governance'. Thus, corporate governance has become a metaphor for corporate reforms of board organization towards higher profitability, leading to institutional and legislative reforms in favour of shareholders and against directors and CEOs.

Contrary to this narrow definition, broader perspectives of corporate governance include relationships between management and employees, management and trade unions, and management and community. This chapter will focus on the first two of these, as manifest in HRM and the EWC. These areas are worthy of attention in that they also relate to the phenomenon of globalization, an important set of conditions for the corporate governance movement in the area of top management.

More specifically, our hypothesis is that the diffusion of Japanization and HRM in the UK (in the 1980s and 1990s) and the introduction of EWC in the late 1990s brought about new forms of governance between capital and labour, with stronger managerial strategy and realistic labour compromise. This created a new phase of enhanced corporate governance in British companies.

HRM is certainly a product of managerial strategy to accommodate employees within a more effective corporate governance system. EWC is an ambivalent compromise between capital and labour, as manifest in its formation and in fierce face-offs between management and labour concerning plant relocations. If HRM is taken as a method developed in the USA and EWC as a style rooted in continental Europe, then contemporary British corporate governance has two faces, one looking to American HRM (Americanization) and the other to European EWC (Europeanization).

3 Human resource management and Japanization as employee governance

The governance of employees via HRM is of vital importance in management's quest to increase organizational 'efficiency' and profitability. It has been argued that during the 1980s Britain shifted from personnel management to HRM (Berridge 1992) and in this process Japanization played a catalytic role in the local diffusion of HRM.

During the twentieth century, accompanying the decline of British capitalism, the USA became a management paradigm provider to the rest of the world. It was the source of 'scientific management' (Taylor 1911/1967) in the 1920s and 1930s, which spread around the world though with varying degrees of influence. Britain and Japan were themselves affected, but here scientific management merged with existing concepts and practices.

The human model adopted by scientific management was to regard employees as motivated by an economic incentive: the 'economic man' model (Watanabe 2000a). The style of management was collective in the sense that a wage was paid for a job regardless of differences in worker morale and enthusiasm. Unions were able to control job allocation and even promotion. Industrial relations in this context were collective and conflict-laden, being in a state of adversarial pluralism.

However, in Britain technological conditions, in particular production scale, were much smaller than in the USA, so that the deployment of scientific management was limited in various ways. Indeed, in many companies there was no strong need for it, as traditional personnel management was still effective and trade unions controlled jobs and promotion. As it was, industrial relations were quite conflict-prone, as demonstrated by the frequent strikes and disputes prior to the 1980s. To deal with this, Labour governments in the 1970s attempted to resolve the prevailing adversarial relations by nationalizing large corporations and promoting industrial democracy through the participation of employees/unions in decision-making at both board and plant levels (Hasegawa 1996). Unfortunately, these measures were less successful than had been hoped and were promptly rejected with the election of the Thatcher government in 1979, which set out an opposite strategy of privatization (Hasegawa 1996).

Britain is in fact a classic case of a large capital exporter, a situation which tended towards overlooking domestic capital investment. This in time led to the need for industrial regeneration as well as employment creation. This character of British capitalism pulled in overseas capital from the USA, Europe and, more recently, Asia. Japanese capital's foreign direct investment was a typical example of Asian FDI and was accompanied by principles of Japanese management and practice, thus creating hybridity in management approaches at affected plants in Britain (Hasegawa 1998).

In the 1980s Japanese influence upon British management, usually known as Japanization, impacted upon British academics (Ishida, Yasui and Kato 1998). Large-scale Japanese FDI became a conduit for Japanization, channelling it through three principal routes; greenfield investment, as in Nissan and Toyota; acquisition, as in DAKS Simpson; and technological tie-ups, as in Rover and Honda. Japanization was arguably a strong catalyst for the diffusion of HRM in Britain, as vital elements of HRM were already incorporated within Japanese management (Hasegawa 2001).

The forces for a paradigm shift from personnel management to HRM are also found in the USA from the latter half of the 1970s to the 1980s

(Okada 2000; Tanaka 2000), when the competitiveness of US manufacturing industries declined under growing competition from Japan and Germany. In addition, developments in production technology, changes in labour markets and union organization, and also the perception of workers may be taken as factors promoting this shift. These factors impelled companies to adopt a new approach to employee management, shifting from inflexible job-centred management (the Fordist approach) to HRM. The objectives were flexibility, high quality and low-cost management, suitable for competition in a global era of trade relations.

Changes, therefore, have looked towards flexibility in production systems, an internal labour market and the accommodation of industrial relations within management itself, and required a shift from traditional, collective and restrictive industrial relations to a more harmonious, cooperative and accommodating environment. Theoretically this is a shift from the prior 'engineering' approach towards one based more on human relations, psychology and sociology, the prevailing assumption seeing the worker as a social, autonomous and self-actualizing human being.

In Japan, so-called Japanese management was an effective method of governing employees during the high economic growth period lasting from 1960 until the mid-1970s. Since then, the influence of new technology has contributed to a more sophisticated 'multi-mass production' system better suited to the low-cost, high-quality, flexible and versatile markets emerging under conditions of global competition. Japanese management, as developed in the high-growth period, had already subsumed elements of HRM based upon human relations and organizational behaviour theories, as well as other theoretical approaches seeking to harness employee motivation to corporate objectives. The continuing influence of US management styles upon Japan from the 1960s made Japanese management an amalgam of Japanese conditions with US HRM input. It is therefore no surprise to find that Japanization had synergetic effects in Britain with the general diffusion of HRM there. Table 2.2 shows a comparison of personnel management typical in Britain, HRM in Britain and Japanese management, showing similarities as well as differences in respective areas.

Looking at the comparisons in this table, similarities between HRM and Japanese management are clear. The difference between personnel-type governance on the one hand and HRM and Japanese management on the other lies in a basic outlook on employment relations. Personnel management is founded upon 'divide-and-rule' according to job, tending

Table 2.2 Personnel management, HRM and Japanese management

	Personnel management in the UK	HRM in the UK	Japanese management
Employment principle	Employee as a resource for company: detailed job-centred relations	Employee with values of commitment: flexible job relations	Employee as member of organization
Human model	Economic individual model	Social, autonomous, self-motivated individual model	Social, autonomous, self-actualizing individual model
Method of governance	Class division: blue versus white-collar; supervisory versus middle; middle versus senior; senior versus directors	As little status distinction as possible, as typically shown at Rover: all employees are 'associates'	No status distinction: majority of board members are former employees who were promoted
Management theories	Analytical and engineering approach but limited use of human relations, psychological/sociological approaches	Full use of human relations, psychological/sociological approaches	Full application of human relations, psychological/ sociological approaches but modified to Japanese perception and values
Education and training	Limited use of in-enterprise education and training	Extensive use of both external/in-enterprise education and training	Extensive use of in-enterprise education and training
Industrial relations	Adversarial/pluralist	Consultation and if possible assimilation: unitarist	Consultation and if possible assimilation: unitarist

thus to rigidity, while governance in the HRM or Japanese management mode is based more upon the 'organic inclusion' of employees, creating internal flexibility within the enterprise. This type of governance, however, requires a certain change in industrial relations, from pluralist to unitarist. This shift will tend to imply either no unions or a 'consultation' type of industrial relations, as distinct from strong unions or a 'negotiation' type of industrial relations.

The shift from personnel management to HRM in Britain took place in the 1980s for a combination of reasons (Berridge 1992, 64):

- internationalism
- Japanization
- excellence theories
- technology
- economic pressure
- entrepreneurialism

In the USA the emergence and development of HRM from the late 1970s was also due to a combination of factors (Claydon 1997, 752):

- decline of manufacturing competitiveness in the late 1970s
- change in macro-economic conditions (low economic growth, globalization, increased competition)
- change in labour market (decline in blue-collar workers, increase in female labour)
- decline of union power (membership decline, negotiating power, concession bargaining)
- perception change (from collective to individualization)
- managerial strategy and ideological change

In Japan, the so-called Japanese management also underwent modification, though retaining its key concepts. The human model adopted by scientific management was to regard employees as motivated by an economic incentive – the 'economic man' model (Watanabe 2000a). The style of management was collective in the sense that a wage was paid for a job regardless of differences in worker morale and enthusiasm. Unions were able to control job allocation and even promotion. Industrial relations in this context were collective and conflict-laden – a state of adversarial pluralism. Since Japan had already introduced some core concepts of HRM, current debate there, rather than portraying a shift towards HRM, revolves around managerial reforms to deal with globalization (Kumazawa 1997; Kinoshita 1999; Watanabe 2000b; Nikkeiren 2001). The focus of present reforms is an individualization suited to more flexible production systems, employment and industrial relations, the ultimate target being improved efficiency, flexibility and competitiveness.

Japanization for Britain was no wholesale importation of Japanese management systems; excluded from the package were basics such as the employment system (lifetime employment and seniority promotion) and industrial relations (enterprise unions). What was taken on board were methods and techniques of production management that were effective in enhancing quality while reducing cost, when implemented under conditions of HRM as developing in Britain at that time.

The most effective symbiosis of HRM and Japanization was in changing corporate culture and introducing single-status systems, single union/negotiation practice, education and training programmes, and most importantly a shift from 'job-oriented' to a more 'organization-oriented' approach to employment. This last point is really a core issue for HRM, which aims at high commitment and 'trust' from employees; this has naturally affected a crucial aspect of existing British industrial relations, causing shift from a pluralist to 'cooperative' unitarist approach.

Japanization can thus be taken as a metaphor for the realignment of British management towards HRM. It has received a degree of acceptance from trade unions as it allows some 'liberation' from rigid Fordist governance of employees. This 'liberation' is, however, at best limited, since it was after all introduced and implemented by enhanced managerial initiative and prerogative rather than through the democratic participation of employees (Hasegawa 2001).

As Japanization effectively functioned as a locomotive pushing British management along the HRM track, it can be discussed in terms of convergence theory. HRM has now become a 'universal' preference of management in large global corporations. Japanization should therefore be seen not simply as a phenomenon on its own, but as a process contained within the general dynamic of HRM diffusion in the UK.

While HRM spread in Britain in the 1980s and 1990s as a new method of employee governance (Beardwell and Holden 1994/1997), the UK government signed the Social Chapter at the Amsterdam summit on 17 June 1997; the actual implementation of EWC was set for December 1999. This implied another stage of corporate governance, namely the governance of trade unions by means of Europeanization.

4   The European Works Council as governance of trade unions

This section examines EWC as a new phase of industrial relations and an important method of corporate governance in the area of industrial relations. We identify two ambivalent but integrated forces (capital and labour) interacting, while reviewing the general background and its implications for the UK, and two cases of sudden plant closure, where the exercise of managerial prerogatives has demonstrated how the power of capital can override that of labour.

The philosophical source of EWC dates back to 1970, when the EU Commission proposed a 'European Company Law' stipulating the 'participation' of employees (AEEU 1998). Its spirit thus lies in belief in industrial democracy and various proposals towards this end have been put forward, including successive versions of the European Company Statute, the fifth Company Law Directive and the Vredeling directive (which proposed employee 'information' and 'consultation' in European companies: AEEU 1998). None, however, reached legislation due to strong opposition from employers, governments and problems arising from the diversity of national systems of employee representation (AEEU 1998). In the end, EWC emerged out of a compromise born of European experiences in industrial democracy and labour and civic rights.

Historically, the 1989 Social Charter included a European-level instrument of information, consultation and participation in European-scale enterprises. However, the UK government opposed its adoption as a Directive and discussions were stalemated (AEEU 1998) until the government opted out of the social policy element of the Maastricht Treaty in 1993. This allowed other member states to adopt the EWC directive, circumventing Britain's veto by submitting proposals under the terms of the Maastricht Social Protocol (AEEU 1998). In September 1994 Council Directive 94/5 EC, on the establishment of EWC, was established. This made all EU member states liable to incorporate the Directive into national legislation by 22 September 1996, with the exception of the UK. It was only on 17 June 1997 that the (now-Labour) government signed the Social Chapter at the Amsterdam summit, committing Britain to implementing the EWC Directive by December 1999. Prior to this, 53 UK companies and 165 non-UK companies had concluded 'voluntary' agreements with UK trade unions (AEEU 1998).

The scope of the Directive is extensive, covering 2,000 enterprises or groups, and 10–15,000 subsidiaries. EWC representatives total 40,000 officers and shop stewards, holding over 5,000 meetings per year; 15 million workers are covered by the Directive (AEEU 1998).

The objective of EWC succeeds the original philosophy of industrial democracy as defined in Article 1, 'to improve the right to information and to consultation of employees in Community-scale undertakings and Community-scale groups of undertakings'. The meaning of consultation is defined in Article 2 as 'the exchange of views and the establishment of dialogue between employee representatives and central management of any more appropriate level of management'. As regards the content of information and consultation, Annex 2 (Subsidiary requirements) states that the EWC has the 'right to meet central management annually to be informed and consulted about the enterprise's progress and prospects concerning':

- the enterprise's structure and economic and financial situation
- the probable development of the business and production and sales
- investment
- substantial changes concerning organization, new working methods or production processes, transfers of production, mergers, cut-backs or closures of undertakings, establishments or important parts thereof, or collective redundancies (EWC Directive, Annex, Article 2)

The crucial issue for workers is the meaning of 'exchange of views' and 'dialogue'; it must be asked to what extent the right of workers can be protected by 'exchange of views' and 'dialogue', when corporate decisions have to be made quickly under increasing global competition? Can employee representatives prevent managerial decisions to relocate their plant? In the same Annex (at the end of Article 3) it states that 'the meeting shall not affect the *prerogatives* [emphasis added] of the central management'. In practice this prerogative may function in various ways, quite often against the civic welfare of workers.

The spirit of the EWC is to pursue simultaneously two objectives, Economic Europe and Social Europe, by means of 'information disclosure' and 'consultation', the idea being that industrial democracy contributes to Economic Europe. In reality it is very difficult to maintain a balance between such ambivalent forces. In the following cases we see that managerial prerogative tends to override the civic/social logic and companies who are driven into global competition will regularly ignore even the spirit of 'consultation' and 'dialogue'.

4.1 Global corporate strategy and EWC

It was Hoover's withdrawal in 1993 that alerted the EC to the vulnerability of labour to boardroom decisions of globalized companies, and the consequent need for protective measures (JETRO 1994). Question marks remain, however, over the effectiveness of the EWC, as shown by the 1997 Vilvoorde case which highlighted both the ineffectiveness of legislation and the persistent problem of maintaining a balance between capital and labour (Economic Europe and Social Europe).

Is balance possible, indeed, or just some kind of Utopia? Is all effort of labour to compromise nothing more than assimilation into the logic of global capital?

4.1.1   *The closure of the Vilvoorde plant*

On 28 February 1997, the French company Renault announced, without consulting the EWC, its intention to close its plant in Vilvoorde, Belgium, in July 1997, and to transfer production to Spain. Some 3,100 jobs at Renault and 1,000 more at supplier and sub-contracting level were threatened (European Foundation for the Improvement of Living and Working Conditions, or eironline 1997). In the current Directive, companies are asked to 'inform' and 'consult' when such a corporate decision is discussed. Penalties and conditions laid down in the Directive – as well as national legislation – are not, however, sufficiently strong to deter companies from ignoring, if they choose, their legal obligations. In fact, the legislation – which was a result of time-consuming compromise between capital (employers), labour (trade unions) and the EU Commission – itself has inclusions which companies can use to their own advantage if labour interests are not strong enough at both political and work place level.

The aim of Social Europe, to assist poorer regions financially, has been circumvented ironically by both global capital and local government. Renault's case shows how a company, weakly placed in global automobile competition and in need of rationalization, can effectively play off national interest and its own individual global corporate interest.

Renault's relocation to Spain was planned with the benefit of subsidies from the EU (7 million ECU from EU regional development funds), Spanish government and local regional government (4 million ECU); but the relocation would create 500 new jobs, a fraction of those lost in Belgium (eironline 1997). This demonstrated how global capital can profit from 'aid shopping' from both the EU and local government for global rationalization.

Renault's destination, Valladolid, is in Castile-Leon, one of the EU's poorest regions, attracting subsidies of up to 40 per cent of total investment, which in the Renault case was valued at ECU 76 million (Reuters, 6 March: for the Renault case and the future of Social Europe, see eironline, March 1997).

The issue here is to what extent the Commission can intervene in commercial decisions of global capital and how far legislation can be tightened to promote Social Europe without undermining Economic Europe. Legislative measures relevant to this issue are the EWC Directive

(94/45/EC), the Collective Redundancies Directive (75/129/EEC) as amended (92/56/EEC) and the Organization for Economic Co-operation and Development (OECD) Code of Conduct for Multinationals (eironline 1997). None of these is legally binding, however, as there is no penalty which exceeds the profits likely to accrue from ignoring the spirit of the legislation. To be resolved is the matter of how much the EU and OECD want to regulate the decision-making of global capital.

What about the labour movement and its strategies? Do they really mean to confront global capital? European and international trade union organizations were unanimous in their condemnation of Renault's closure of their Belgian plant without prior consultation. The European Trade Union Confederation (ETUC) is demanding the introduction of new measures and stricter penalties, plus the introduction of strict rules to avoid corporate misuse of Community financial subsidies (eironline 1997). The European Metalworkers' Federation (EMF) stressed the importance of holding broad-based discussions at European level on the future of the industry (eironline 1997). The main issues raised by them for comprehensive discussion are:

- problems of overcapacity
- the promotion of cooperation between European manufacturers to explore new markets, cut costs and share production sites
- the adoption of an integrated transport policy
- the development of environmentally friendly vehicles
- a constructive partnership between the assembly sector and its suppliers
- the reorganization and reduction of working time (eironline 1997, 7)

The World Labour Confederation condemns companies who abuse procedures adopted at international level and the disrespect of relevant national laws. The European Confederation of Independent Trade Unions (ECIT) stresses the need for reforms in the EWC Directive (eironline 1997).

The strike movement organized by Renault's European Group Committee and supported by EMF suggested the birth of a Europe-wide workers' solidarity. French and Belgian unions collaborated and support came from Spanish representatives. They agreed to oppose the closure of the plant, explored legal avenues, and organized a one-hour strike on 7 March. Management finally addressed the EWC at a meeting on 11 March, but merely reiterated the rationale behind the closure. Alternative options suggested by employee representatives were rejected by management (eironline 1997).

In the above case we can see the difficulty and inherent ambivalence of striking the right balance of interest between capital and labour. The dilemma has already been built into the Directive, and companies are naturally ready to maximize their advantage; all the more so if, like Renault, the company is struggling globally. Unions can at best only delay the implementation of corporate decisions; capital prefers relocation to more advantageous environments in terms of wage, social cost, infrastructure, markets, quality of labour and productivity. This freedom of movement is indeed exactly what the EU, as a manifestation of regionalism, intends.

4.1.2   *The closure of the Kilo plant*

Fujitsu Siemens, the German–Japanese joint venture, decided in December 1999 to close down a profitable computer plant located in Kilo, Finland, by the end of March 2000, at the cost of 450 jobs (eironline 2000). This was a similar case to Renault, again suggesting that the EWC directive is not effective enough to resist such sudden relocation decisions. The strategy of management was to concentrate production at the Augsburg and Sommerdan plants in Germany. As the Kilo plant was just an assembly plant it was easier to deal with in terms of relocation of satellite plants to more advantageous locations (eironline 2000).

When employees asked for information and consultation, it was refused on the grounds that, as the company headquarters was located in Germany, Finnish legislation did not apply (eironline 2000). Legal enquiries were carried out by the Metalworkers' Union to find out whether the company was in compliance with the conventions and regulations of the International Labour Organization (ILO), the EWC Directive and with OECD guidelines for multinational companies. The preliminary fact-finding report of the Ministry of Labour stated that no laws, agreements or Directives had been violated (eironline 2000).

A country such as Finland, where many companies are subsidiaries of global capital with headquarters elsewhere in Europe, is vulnerable to this kind of problem. It has been alleged that Siemens did not dare to rationalize its German units for fear that the powerful IG Metal metalworkers' union would mobilize against it (eironline 2000). Companies may thus be motivated to relocate their plants to where tax benefits are greatest, markets are nearer, labour and other costs are lower, and trade unions are more compliant. Globalization in Europe, within EU regionalism, has created flexibility within Europe and has meant more freedom for global companies in selecting their locations. Yet, in areas where global capital wants to evacuate, this globalization within EU regionalism contradicts the principle of Social Europe, which aims to enhance employee welfare overall.

There are two ways to challenge this dichotomy. One is to strengthen legislation and prevent global capital relocating their plants; the other is to leave things as they are, and leave either local government or EU to compensate laid-off employees. The former measure would strike at the heart of globalization within Europe, and thus the economic concept of the EU itself. The latter, which aims to deal with the matter indirectly, will solve problems temporarily but might lead to areas of widespread economic social depression and dependency.

The next section suggests a middle course of action, which would activate an interesting process of political economy to address the problem.

4.2   The political economy of EWC

The recent Nissan case shows an interesting case of the political economy of global capital and its relation to local government and EU regionalism. On 25 January 2001, Nissan (currently owned by Renault) announced that they would continue production of the Micra at Sunderland (UK) instead of relocating it to France (*Observer*, 14 February 2001). Although production of the new Micra is to begin in 2003, Nissan had been considering shifting production because of the high sterling rates, high costs and lower profitability in the UK. Nissan Sunderland is a major plant; it is claimed to be the most efficient in Europe and, following Rover's decline, the largest. It manufactures 320,000 units per year and has a capacity of 500,000 units. Its departure would directly have made 1,300 people unemployed, and affected another 11,000 in component suppliers in north-east England. Its loss would have been a severe blow; but Nissan are now to invest £235 million, increase employees from the current 4,500 to 5,000, and raise production capacity from 320,000 to 500,000 (*Observer*, 14 February 2001; AEEU 2001).

Was there any consultation on this matter? The final decision seemed to have little to do with any 'dialogue' and 'consultation' at EWC, although French unions were said to have helped by declaring that their factories were already overworked (*Observer*, 14 February 2001).

Nonetheless, industrial relations did not seem to be an issue in the decision as to whether to move operations to Flims in France or stay in Britain. Unions in both France and the UK seem to depend upon political lobbying and decisions. The crucial factor was national and regional level political dynamics, in particular between the UK government and the EU Commission over funding to private companies (FT.com site, 17 January 2001).

Nissan/Renault decided to remain in Sunderland for three reasons: (1) efforts were to be made to reduce operation costs by 30 per cent, (2) the UK government would offer £40 million subsidy, (3) attitudes to the Euro were taking a positive turn. A local plus point for Renault was the 'excellent' industrial relations at Nissan: just one hour's production had been lost to industrial action in its 16-year existence, and it had a reputation as a strike-free plant.

The UK government aid package for Nissan was approved by the European Commission on Wednesday, 17 January 2001. Mario Monti, EU Competition Commissioner, said:

> Our initial doubts led us to open a formal investigation procedure in September 2000, as we have also done in cases of support measures to car manufacturers in other member states. The Commission is now satisfied that the proposed aid to Nissan is in line with the Community rules for state aid and the specific rulebook for aid to the motor vehicle industry in particular.
>
> (FT.com site, 17 January 2001)

Thus, direct conflict was resolved by the political economy of global capital and local government, and EU endorsement. Does this mean that political economy will establish itself as a means for achieving compromise between global capital and local employees? How does this kind of political economy relate to corporate governance?

5   Human resource management and European Works Councils as dialectics of corporate governance

HRM was introduced by managerial initiative as a new method for the governance of employees; EWC emerged similarly, with input from trade unions and in the interests of industrial relations. How should such a shift in governance be interpreted in terms of the dialectical development of the relationship between capital and labour?

Such a structural shift in governance implies enhancing the control of capital by enhancing the accommodation of labour. From a management point of view, HRM and EWC are reasonable methods of governance, compatible with globalization and regionalism. Internal and external flexibility in labour deployment and freedom of relocation have become available through new forms of governance. Unless labour develops a progressively democratic strategy leading to a dialectical development of social and regional governance, the balance will tend to tilt towards capital.

There are two ways in which this aim may be approached. One is by reform of the international legislation of the EU, OECD and ILO to embrace global capital in social principles of local and regional community; the other is to reinvent democracy in enterprise and create a new democratic mode within business organizations. Capital has already reformulated its governance system to its advantage in the areas of top management, employee management and industrial relations. The countervailing power of labour and society, namely the exercise of social authority, is not equivalent to that of global capital and the governance of capital seems to have dominated in the process of globalization.

The dialectics of corporate governance operates at each level of governance. HRM as a form of advanced employee governance may contribute to 'efficiency' and 'profitability'. EWC is understood as an advanced form of governance by both management and unions; for management it is a means towards competitiveness, while for labour it is a measure for employee participation and social welfare. For the latter to be realized, however, the authority of labour (society) needs to be translated into forces of democracy both within and without enterprises. Dialectical development in corporate governance may incur partial liberation of labour and society within capitalism, but this is not possible if employees and trade unions remain quiescent or easily accept the governance offered by management, which exercises power with the overriding authority of capital. Social acceptability only comes with compliance with the social power deriving from social authority.

In the capitalist system, management adopts strategies to further the governance of employees and industrial relations and steers the ship in a choppy sea of global competition. It is natural therefore that managers constantly innovate styles and methods of governance to meet external changes. The US economy as an engine of world capitalism has continuously invented methods of governance in areas of employee management. Europe, on the other hand, has invented methods of governance in the area of trade unions and industrial relations, for it is in their mature capitalism that relations between capital and labour are comparatively sophisticated and social power most powerful.

Methods of governance tend to be emulated by capital in other countries simply because they are a means to an end. Americanization, Japanization and Europeanization are metaphors to describe how methods of governance are emulated by capital in other countries.

Intellectual reflections of Japanization in Britain also endorse the ambivalent nature of the relationship between capital and labour. Wickens (1987, 1995, 1999), describes and interprets Japanization as an ideal of employee governance for management; but Garrahan and Stewart (1992) critically depict Japanization as nothing more than a sophistication of exploitation and control. In between there are Oliver and Wilkinson (1992) and Bratton (1992), who take more neutral and realistic positions, aiming to strike a balance of relations between capital and labour.

As regards interpretations of EWC, various perspectives were expressed at its establishment in 1994. These can be classified into three positions; capital, labour and neutral or 'realistic'. The EU commission reflects the last of these, commenting on EWC: 'good industrial relations as the foundation for industrial competitiveness and economic development'; 'an important trial for the development of Euro Social Policy'; 'balanced content for both industry and labour' (JETRO 1995). This view implies that good industrial relations are vital for an economically viable Europe.

The ETUC hailed EWC as: 'a big step forward for European social policy and democracy' that 'will increase corporate efficiency upon new industrial relations' (JETRO 1995).

The UK government (Conservative) demurred: 'an increase in unnecessary costs, decline of industrial competitiveness, negative impacts upon FDI'; 'EWC will undermine the existing voluntary consultation arrangements'; 'inflexible, bureaucratic system which will delay the decision making of the companies'; 'compared with the US, Europe is creating a burden upon employers' (JETRO 1995).

The Federation of European Employers (UNICE) declared they would 'oppose the implementation of the Subsidiary Requirement as it will have negative impacts on industrial competitiveness'. They claimed that 'for the past five years [they had] demanded "revision" of The Subsidiary Requirements' as it would 'create rigid and bureaucratic industrial relations consultation mechanism' and 'cause negative effects on competitiveness, unnecessary costs, delay in decision-making, negative effects upon investment and result in bad employment prospects' (JETRO 1995). Similarly, the Belgium Employers' Federation felt that they were 'not able to support the "Subsidiary Requirements" as they were "bureaucratic and rigid"' (JETRO 1995).

Toyota is interesting in that it reflects a 'Japaneseness' in attitude towards EWC. On the surface both management and union (EMF) welcome EWC as an ideal means towards good industrial relations and competitiveness   (http://www/ecu-notes.org/esrjune96/dev4.html). Toyota signed an agreement with the EMF to establish a European Works Council on 3 June 1996. The Toyota European Forum (Toyota's version of EWC) consists of management and employee representatives from their major European plants. They meet annually and management provides information on manufacturing, distribution, sales and after-sales activities. The Forum also facilitates the exchange of views on pan-European issues and understanding to strengthen Toyota's position in Europe.

Tatsuo Takahashi, the Toyota Motor Europe Marketing and Engineering Managing Director, stated that 'In establishing the Toyota European Forum we wish to promote productivity and harmonious relationships to support the achievement of strong and effective Toyota European operations. Toyota believes that management and employees must enhance sound relations through mutual understanding and trust' (http://www/ecu-notes.org/esrjune96/dev4.html). Charlie McKenzie, the EMF Project Manager, commented 'We recognise that employees' job security and development depend on the Toyota European companies continuing to grow and be successful and that the objective is to achieve not only short-term success but long-term prosperity' (http://www/ecu-notes.org/esrjune96/dev4.html).

These statements suggest that labour organizations such as the ETUC and EMF welcome the formation and function of EWC. Yet employers and management generally have shown reluctant acceptance or even opposition to it, so Toyota is unlike other European employers in showing confidence that creating good governance in industrial relations will lead to enhanced competitiveness. It is possible that Toyota, as a relative newcomer in Europe, may have benefited in its company–employee relations from its new greenfield location, a situation lending itself to good governance.

In practice, capital readily takes advantage of EWC, as a method of improving industrial relations, until the opportunity or need is perceived for a different strategy. Then a different set of priorities comes into play, legitimizing selective exploitation of EU legislation and/or subsidies, or even unilateral dismissal of the EWC ethos.

While the European Commission is trying to strike a balance of capital and labour relations for the sake of pan-European economic development, the relative emphasis seems to be on economy and company rather than society: Competitive Europe is considered a prerequisite for Social Europe. ETUC seems to be in the same boat, provided that management is reasonably accepting of the industrial relations model stipulated in EWC. A major compromise has already been made by labour when it agreed to shift the structure of existing industrial relations from horizontal (industry-based) to vertical (enterprise-based), which is the most convenient structure for management in its dealings with labour. This vertical structure of industrial relations matches HRM in both concept and practice, thus facilitating the governance of top management.

In general, the balance has shifted greatly towards capital, and in particular management, even though EWC has been welcomed by British trade unions as a tool for alleviating local weaknesses. How far the union movement can go beyond national interests remains to be seen. If transnational or cosmopolitan solidarity develops, as well as local union and social movements, then it might be possible to envisage the development of a balance of power between capital and civil society, such that the dialectical development of a Social Europe compatible with Economic Europe may be realized.

At the close of the 1990s, the performance of EWCs since 1994 was subjected to extensive academic scrutiny, compiled by Waddington (1999) in the *European Review of Labour and Research (Transfer)*. Contributors' views were summarized by him as follows:

1 There is variation in the establishment and development of EWCs based in companies with different countries of origin. Country of origin is a likely source of persistent diversity in the operation of EWCs (Marginson 1999).
2 Sectoral differentiation (manufacturing versus finance) is also associated with variation in the operation and procedure of EWCs (Lecher 1999).
3 EWCs are used for management to draw greater compliance from employees if they are not adequately supported by unions (Veersma 1999).
4 Diffusion of acquisitions and mergers help to promote the influence of the 'Anglo-Saxon' style of management. Thus, there is need for training of representatives to meet different style of management (Edwards 1999).
5 Each national tradition in industrial relations influences the transposition processes of EWCs (Blanke 1999).
6 Need for enhanced inclusion of 'Europeanization', 'transnationality', 'supernationality', 'solidarity', 'multi-lingualism', 'multi-culturalism', EWC as a learning organization (Waddington 1999).
7 Need for tighter definitions regarding 'adequate information', 'consultation' (Waddington 1999, 250–1).

Three major issues appear here, and all are relevant to what has been discussed so far in terms of corporate governance: (1) variance of EWC in actual operation, (2) management taking positive initiatives in its operation for the governance of industrial relations, (3) need for EWC reforms to reflect the rights and benefits of labour and society.

The objectives of EWCs to provide 'information' and hold 'consultation' but not to go beyond 'managerial prerogatives' embodies a clear advantage for capital and implicitly imposes an extra burden on the pursuit of labour interests. The above survey clearly shows that if labour wants a greater say in affairs, then EWC clauses need to be rewritten; whether, however, capital or employers will agree to such revision is another matter.

6   Conclusion

The main theme of this article has been to investigate two areas and methods of corporate governance in Britain and to argue that there are two contributory aspects to this governance operating in the majority of large companies in Britain: Americanization (HRM) and Europeanization (EWC). We have endeavoured to examine corporate governance in its relevance to democracy in business management, seeing it as form, process and function of controlling relations between different categories of people in an enterprise.

The current corporate governance discussion emerged in the USA in the mid-1980s. From there it spread to Britain and Japan almost simultaneously, but picked up momentum in the 1990s, developing a focus on the relations between shareholders and board members/CEO. Debate mainly centred around reforms in legislation, organization and company rules, in order to enhance corporate performance in the stock market, and hence took a direction of minimal relevance to the fundamental issue of governance.

We have concentrated here, however, on governance relevant to democracy and examined HRM and EWC from this perspective. We looked at how the force of capital manifests and reacts with that of labour and society in the process of HRM and EWC, thus diverging from the popular functional approach that looks to method and reform to energise companies.

HRM suggests a paradigm shift from personnel management, which aimed at employee governance by controlling the 'visible realities' of employees. On the other hand, HRM seeks to accommodate employees at deeper levels using psychological and sociological insight, thereby in theory incorporating workers more holistically into the corporate ethos. In this sense, unless a countervailing force of democracy constrains that of capital, there is a danger of degrading working conditions and working life.

EWC, which realigned industrial relations from British horizontal (industrial-based) to vertical (enterprise-based), serves to develop HRM, while HRM creates favourable conditions for the further development and smooth functioning of EWC.

In general, it would appear that corporate governance has been reinforced by HRM and EWC in Britain in recent years. To what extent management will succeed in its efforts and to what extent labour will reassert its right to fair capital-induced governance remains to be seen. For labour, it depends on whether the movement can reorganize itself as part of democratic movement and invent concepts and methods compatible with the changing conditions of capitalist society. If this is achieved, labour may be able itself to initiate dialectical development in current relations between capital and labour which may lead to a new democratic corporate governance. For the time being, however, EWC and HRM are likely to continue to exert symbiotic effects that enhance capital-oriented corporate governance in Britain.

Acknowledgement

This is a revised paper in A. Kudo (ed.) (2002) *ISS Research Series* No. 3 (Tokyo: The Institute of Social Science, Tokyo University).

Note

1   In this connection, a noteworthy movement is the campaign by British academic and senior administrative staff for ethical investment of their pension fund. Their pension fund, the Universities Superannuation Scheme (USS), adopted a socially responsible investment policy focusing upon human rights and environment. USS has taken action against BP, Glaxo and Premier Oil as their major shareholder to monitor their behaviour (*Ethics for USS Newsletter*, 2001, No. 5).

References

AEEU (1998), *European Works Councils* (London: AEEU).

AEEU (2001), *Union Review*, 56 (February), 3, 8.

Beardwell, I. and Holden, L. (1994/97) *Human Resource Management: A Contemporary Perspective* (London: Pitman).

Berle, A. A. and Means, G. C. (1964), *The Modern Corporation and Private Property*, rev. edn (New York: Harcourt, Brace & World).

Berridge, J. (1992), 'Human Resource Management in Britain', *Employee Relations*, 14 (5), 62–92.

Bratton, J. (1992), *Japanization at Work* (London: Macmillan).

Claydon, T. (1994/97), 'Human Resource Management and the USA', in I. Beardwell and L. Holden (eds), *Human Resource Management: A Contemporary Perspective* (London: Pitman).

Deloitte Touche Tohmatsu (2000), 'Corporate Governance: taking responsibility for shareholder value' (1–3), *http://www.deloitte.com/publications/cgovernc.html* (20 March 2001).

Drucker, P. F. (1993), *Post Capitalist Society* (Oxford: Butterworth Heinemann).

Eironline (1997), 'The Renault case and the future of Social Europe', *eironline*, 1–11.

Eironline (2000), 'Closure of Fujitsu Siemens plant – a repeat of Renault Vilvoorde?', *eironline*, 1–4.

Ethics for USS Newsletter (2001), No. 5 (Oxford: Ethics for USS).

Garrahan, P. and Stewart, P. (1992), *The Nissan Enigma* (London: Mansell).

Hasegawa, H. (1996), *The Steel Industry in Japan: A Comparison with Britain* (London: Routledge).

Hook, G. D. and Hasegawa, H. (eds) (1998), *Japanese Business Management: Restructuring for Low Growth and Globalization* (London: Routledge).

Hasegawa, H. (2001), 'Globalisation and Japanization: implications for human resource management in Britian', *Japan Forum*, 13 (2), 159–76.

Ishida, K., Yasui, T. and Kato, M. (1998), *Kigyo Rodo no Nichiei Hikaku (A comparison of labour in business between Japan and Britain)* (Tokyo: Otsuki Shoten).

JETRO (1994), 'Oshu Roshi Kyogikai ni tsuite (On European Works Council)', *Euro Trend*, 17 (October), 2–24.

JETRO (1995), 'Oshu Roshi Kyogikai ni tsuite (About European Works Council)', *Saikin no Oshu Josei* (Recent European Situation) (Tokyo: JETRO, 1995).

Keidanren (2000), *Wagakuni Koporeito Gabanansu ni kansuru Ronten Seiri* (Summing up of discussion points concerning corporate governance of the listed companies in Japan) (Tokyo: Keidanren).

Keizai Kikakucho (1998), *Nippon no Koporeito Gabanansu* (Japanese Corporate Governance) (Tokyo: Keizai Kikakucho).

Kelly, G., Kelly, D. and Gamble, A. (1997), *Stake Holder Capitalism* (London: Macmillan).

Kinoshita, T. (1999), *Nihonjin no Chingin (Wage of the Japanese)* (Tokyo: Heibonsha).

Korten, D. C. (1999), *The Post-corporate World* (West Harford: Kumarian Press, Inc.).

Kumazawa, M. (1997), *Noryokushugi to Kigyo Shakai (Corporate society and ability orientation)* (Tokyo: Iwanami Shoten).

Nikkeiren (2001), *Creating a Society Rich in Choices: Nikkeiren Position Paper 2001* (Tokyo: Nikkeiren).

Okada, H. (2000), 'Keiei Senryaku no Tenkai to Jinteki Shigenkanri (Evolution of corporate strategy and human resource management)', in H. Shima (ed.), *Jinteki Shigen Kanrion (Theories of Human Resource Management)* (Kyoto: Mineruba Shobo).

Okamoto, S. (1974), *Kigyo Kakumei-ron (A theory of corporate revolution)* (Tokyo: Shogakuan).

Oliver, N. and Wilkinson, B. (1992), *The Japanization of British Industry* (Oxford: Basil Blackwell).

Rengo (1999), 'Rodo Kumiai kara mita Koporeito Gabanansu (Corporate governance as seen from labour unions)', in *Rengo Soken Report*, No. 129, 11–17.

Sako, M. and Sato, H. (1997), *Japanese Labour and Management in Transition* (London: Routledge).

Scott, J. (1997), *Corporate Business and Capitalist Classes* (Oxford: Oxford University Press).

Shibuya, H. (1999), 'Amerika no Kikan Toshika to Koporeito Gabanansu: Kenky Shikaku Settei no Kokoromi (Institutional Investors in the US and corporate governance: an attempt to set a theme of study)', *Shoken Keizai Kenkyu*, 22, 15–28.

Takahashi, Y. (1999), 'Saikin Nippon no Koporeit Gabanansu o meguru Kakushu Houfoku/Teigenn (Various reports and suggestions on recent corporate governance in Japan)', *Shogaku Ronsan*, 40 (3–4), 255–79.

Tanaka, K. (2000), 'Hyuman Risos Manajimento no Tenkai to Roshi Kankei (Evolution of human resource management and industrial relations)', in Y. Maruyama and K. Kawagishi, *Konichi no Kigyo to Keiei (Contemporary enterprise and management)* (Tokyo: Yachiyo Shuppan).

Taylor, F. W. (1911/67), *The Principles of Scientific Management* (New York: W. W. Norton).

Uetake, T. and Nakta, M. (1999), *Gendai Kigyo no Shoyu, Shihai, Kanri (Ownership, control, management of modern corporations)* (Kyoto: Mineruba Shobo).

Waddington, J. (1999), 'Editorial', *Transfer: European Review of Labour and Research*, 4 (3), 250–1.

Watanabe, T. (1998), 'The rise of flexible and individual ability-oriented management', in H. Hasegawa and G. Hook (eds), *Japanese Business Management: Restructuring for Low Growth and Globalization* (London: Routledge).

Watanabe, T. (2000a), *Jintenki Shigen no Soshiki to Kanri (Organization and management of human resources)* (Tokyo: Chuo Keizaisha).

Watanabe, T. (2000b), *Kyaria Jinji Seido no Donyu to Kanri (Introduction and management of career based personnel management)* (Tokyo: Chuo Keizaisha).

Wheeler, D. and Sillanpaa, M. (1997), *The Stakeholder Corporation* (London: Pitman).

Wickens, P. (1987), *The Road to Nissan* (London: Macmillan).

Wickens, P. (1995), *The Ascendant Organisation* (London: Macmillan).

Wickens, P. (1999), *Energise Your Enterprise* (London: Macmillan).

Yoshimori, M. (1996), *Nihon no Keiei, Oobei no Keiei (Japanese management and Euro-US management)* (Tokyo: Housou Daigaku Kyouiku Shinkoukai).

3
The Effect of *Amakudari* on Bank Performance in the Post-Bubble Period

Kenji Suzuki

One of the curiosities of the Japanese banking sector for Westerners is the close connection between banks and the financial authority, the Ministry of Finance (MoF). One of its main sources is *amakudari*, the practice whereby retired government officials 'descend from their heaven' to be employed in the private sector. It has a long history in the banking sector, as well as in many other industrial sectors of Japan. This chapter looks at whether, and (if so) to what extent, the effect of the *amakudari* connection altered after the collapse of the bubble economy due to increased criticism of bank–MoF collusion and the relevant institutional changes. Using model analyses of 82 listed regional banks, we found that the employment of *amakudari* executives reduced the likelihood of banks taking risks and that the traditional pattern of *amakudari* appointments to originally risky banks was gradually on the decline. These results may well support the idea that the effect of employing *amakudari* executives is undergoing change, so that it is now less likely to be used as a means of collusion between banks and the government.

1 Introduction

In the past, the *amakudari* connection was considered a useful means of supervising the development of the Japanese banking sector by the financial authority. Nevertheless, this method of supervision has been questioned since the collapse of the bubble economy in the early 1990s. Seven listed regional and second-tier regional banks failed in the 1990s, and all of them had employed *amakudari* executives during the bubble period (see Table 3.1). According to Hartcher, the practice of *amakudari*

Table 3.1   Listed regional and second-tier regional banks that failed in the 1990s and the number of *amakudari* executives employed in 1990

Name	Month and year of failure	Number of *amakudari* executives in 1990
Hyogo Bank	August 1995	2
Taiheiyo Bank	March 1996	0 (1 in 1987)
Hanwa Bank	November 1996	1
Tokuyo City Bank	November 1997	3
Tokyo Sowa Bank	June 1999	1
Fukutoku Bank (Namihaya Bank from 1998)	August 1999	1
Niigata Chuo Bank	October 1999	1

'provided ministry policy makers with no notable insights into how bank lending was contributing to the accumulation of a large speculative bubble in land and stock prices' (1998, 121).

It may be unjust to shift all the responsibility on *amakudari* executives, since many banks without *amakudari* also contributed to the bubble economy and suffered from its collapse. It is misleading to stress the incompetence of *amakudari* executives. The fact that they had no previous work experience in the banking sector does not necessarily mean they had 'no notable insights'. The recruitment of top executives from outside is not uncommon in the USA or elsewhere; it is merely a prejudice that government officials are incompetent in the private sector.

Given the fact that all failed banks employed *amakudari* executives, however, many observers suspect that the employment of *amakudari* has a negative effect on bank performance. Several studies have addressed this issue. Horiuchi and Shimizu (2001) conducted an empirical analysis, for instance, and found that banks with *amakudari* executives tended to take more risks than others. Van Rixtel and Hassink (1998) also drew a similar conclusion, emphasizing in particular the positive correlation between the employment of *amakudari* and the development of lending to risky industries, such as the construction, real estate and financial sectors.

Nevertheless, both studies focused largely on the period before the collapse of the bubble economy. The data set of Horiuchi and Shimizu only considers the period up to 1991. Van Rixtel and Hassink dealt with several data sets, but none of them covered the period after 1993. Considering the rise in criticism of the collusion between banks and the MoF, and the relevant institutional changes for the supervision of banks in the post-bubble period, it follows that the *amakudari* connection has had less effect, so that the gap between the performance of banks with *amakudari* executives and those without has lessened.

However, the validity of this hypothesis should be tested with empirical analysis, which the present study aims to do. Our analysis focuses on regional and second-tier regional banks. There are other types of bank in Japan (city banks, long-term credit banks, trust banks), but the *amakudari* practice occurs most commonly in regional and second-tier regional banks. Second-tier regional banks were originally mutual loan and savings banks, but were turned into ordinary commercial banks around 1990. It is therefore not necessary to differentiate between regional and second-tier regional banks. The phrase 'regional banks' is used here as a comprehensive term without differentiating between 'regional banks' and 'second-tier regional banks'. Due to the availability of relevant data, this study focuses only on the regional banks listed on the Japanese stock exchange.

The rest of the chapter is composed of four parts. The next section looks at the recent performance of regional banks and their *amakudari* practice as a whole. Section 3 discusses various models and examines the effect of *amakudari* executives on bank performance, showing the relevant results of the estimation. The discussion begins with the Horiuchi–Shimizu model, which we modified with other sets of explanatory variables. This leads to concluding remarks in the final section.

2 The performance and *amakudari* employment of Japanese regional banks in the post-bubble period

Some 82 regional banks were listed on the Japanese stock exchange and survived (i.e., did not go bankrupt or merge with/transfer to another bank) in the market up to the 1990s. Table 3.2 indicates the total assets, loans and deposits of those banks drawn from Kaisha Shikiho (Toyokeizai Shimposha). When the bubble economy collapsed in 1992, assets declined by 2.4 per cent. However, loans continued to grow until 1998. The growth rate of loans exceeded that of assets until 1997. Deposits showed a larger growth than assets and loans, except for 1992, 1995 and 1997. In 1999, assets and loans indicated a negative growth, reflecting the prolonged economic slump which particularly hit the main direction of loans from regional banks (i.e., small and medium-sized firms). However, even in that year there was a positive growth rate of deposits. The stable growth of deposits at the end of the 1990s corresponds to the growing propensity for saving among the Japanese, many of whom were encouraged to save money to provide for their retirement under a precarious pension system.

Table 3.2   Total assets, loans and deposits of 82 regional banks, 1992–99

	Assets		Loans		Deposits	
	billion yen	growth (%)	billion yen	growth (%)	billion yen	growth (%)
1992	224,657	−2.4	151,727	3.0	194,039	0.6
1993	227,492	1.3	153,828	1.4	196,947	1.5
1994	229,843	1.0	156,173	1.5	201,526	2.3
1995	233,824	1.7	161,717	3.6	203,375	0.9
1996	234,209	0.2	162,188	0.3	204,412	0.5
1997	233,476	−0.3	163,838	1.0	202,399	−1.0
1998	237,028	1.5	165,395	1.0	206,633	2.1
1999	233,051	−1.7	160,485	−3.0	209,045	1.2
1992–99 average		0.2		1.1		1.0

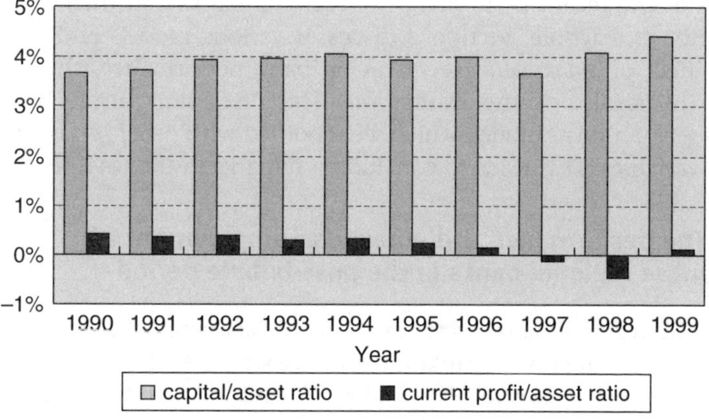

Figure 3.1   Average capital/asset ratio and average current profit/asset ratio, 1990–99 (82 regional banks)

Figure 3.1 shows the average capital/asset ratio and the average profit/asset ratio. The average capital/asset ratio stagnated for several years after the collapse of the bubble economy. It went into serious decline in 1997 due to the economic slump, but later turned up quickly, probably due to the rise in concern about risk management in regional banks. The average current profit/asset ratio was generally on the downturn throughout the post-bubble period. It was negative even in 1997 and in 1998.

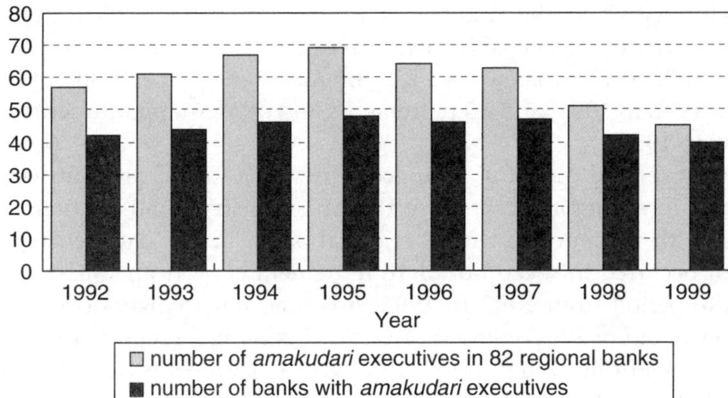

Figure 3.2 The number of *amakudari* executives in total and the number of banks with at least one *amakudari* executive, 1992–99 (82 banks)

Figure 3.2 indicates the total number of *amakudari* executives and the number of banks employing at least one *amakudari* executive. The source of the data is Kigyo Keiretsu Soran (Toyokeizai Shimposha). Both the number of *amakudari* executives and the number of banks employing them increased steadily from 1992 to 1995, but then declined. The most plausible reason for this change is that the MoF came under severe social criticism in 1995. Evidence of serious bribery scandals involving ministry officials and major banks emerged. In the same year, the ministry was also blamed for its failure to handle serious loan problems regarding housing loan companies effectively, as well as for bungling a criminal affair concerning Daiwa Securities in the United States. As a result, the number of *amakudari* executives was reduced from 57 in 1992 to 45 in 1999. It should be noted, however, that the number of banks employing *amakudari* did not decrease that much. Forty-two banks employed *amakudari* in 1992, dropping slightly to 40 in 1999. What did decrease, however, was the average number of *amakudari* executives per bank, as shown below. This amounted to 1.36 in 1992 and 1.13 in 1999.

	Year							
	1992	1993	1994	1995	1996	1997	1998	1999
Average number of *amakudari* executives per bank	1.36	1.39	1.46	1.44	1.39	1.34	1.21	1.13

With regard to the number of retirements (from banks) and new appointments, 52 *amakudari* executives retired and 36 were appointed from 1992 to 1999. There were 22 retirements and 30 new appointments from 1992 to 1995, and 30 retirements and six new appointments from 1996 to 1999.

Traditionally, the MoF arranged a new *amakudari* appointment to replace a retiring incumbent, so that the ministry could maintain control. With reference to the 82 regional banks in our data set, replacement occurred in seven out of 18 retirement cases from 1987 to 1991. In the period from 1992 to 1995, however, replacements occurred in only five out of 22 retirement cases. Furthermore, no replacements were made at all from 1996 to 1999, although 29 incumbents had retired during that period.

3   The effect of the *amakudari* practice on bank performance

3.1   Methodology and data

Horiuchi and Shimizu were among the first scholars to theorize and analyze the effect of the *amakudari* practice on the performance of regional banks. They formulated the relationship between taxpayers, banks and financial authority as one between principal, agent and supervisor. They viewed the *amakudari* connection as a sign of collusion between agent (banks) and supervisor (MoF) to their own benefit at the cost of the principal (taxpayers). It was assumed that, in contrast to other banks, the MoF allows banks with *amakudari* executives to expand risk exposure in return for the employment of (hence paying good salaries to) *amakudari* executives. It is difficult for taxpayers to detect this collusion if the regulating process is not transparent, as was the case in Japan (at least before the *amakudari* practice came under severe public criticism).

Based on this theory, they utilized the following dynamic panel data model in order to examine the hypothesis that banks with *amakudari* executives tend to take more risks:

$$EQT_i(t) = b_0 + b_1 EQT_i(t-1) + b_2 GAS_i(t-1)$$
$$+ b_3 PRO_i(t-1) + b_4 AM_i(t-1) + u_i(t) \quad \text{for } i = 1, ..., n \quad (3.1)$$

where $EQT_i(t)$ is the current capital/asset ratio of bank i at year t; $AM_i(t)$ is a dummy variable set equal to one if bank i employs *amakudari* executives at year t (taking zero if otherwise); $GAS_i(t)$ is the annual growth rate of total assets at the time; and $PRO_i(t)$ is current profit per total assets. The panel data consists of 123 regional banks from 1977 to 1991. This panel data model is 'dynamic' in the sense that the set of explanatory variables includes the capital/asset ratio of the previous year (i.e., $EQT_i(t-1)$). The dynamic panel data model is useful to integrate the previous state of the dependent variable, so that it clarifies the contribution of the other explanatory variables to the marginal change of the dependent variable at its given level.

The statistical method utilized for this model was the generalized method of moments (GMM), which is widely recognized as useful for the analysis of dynamic panel data models. While GMM has several different estimators, Horiuchi and Shimizu applied the one presented by Arellano and Bond, which does not require the assumption of strict exogeneity of explanatory variables, and is hence the most appropriate to their model.[1]

The model estimates that $EQT_i(t-1)$ and $GAS_i(t-1)$ are positive at the 1 per cent level; $PRO_i(t-1)$ is negative at the 1 per cent level; and $AM_i(t-1)$ is negative at the 10 per cent level. The negative contribution of $AM_i(t-1)$ to $EQT_i(t)$, which implies that banks tend to have a low capital/asset ratio if they employed *amakudari* executives in the previous year, is consistent with their hypothesis.

Nevertheless, several questions can be raised about the selection of explanatory variables for this model. First, it is difficult to understand why the authors used the employment of *amakudari* executives in the previous year, $AM_i(t-1)$, as an explanatory variable, but not the current year, $AM_i(t)$. It would be more natural to assume that the current employment of *amakudari* executives has an impact on the current capital/asset ratio.

Second, the significance of the asset growth in the previous year, $GAS_i(t-1)$, to the capital/asset ratio in the current year, $EQT_i(t)$, is not evident. Banks may be encouraged to increase their capital when their assets grow, but they are not necessarily encouraged to increase their capital/asset ratio as well.

Third, the contribution of the profit/asset ratio in the previous year, $PRO_i(t-1)$, to the capital/asset ratio in the current year, $EQT_i(t)$, is not clear either. It could be that profitable banks tend to reserve more capital, and thus have a higher capital/asset ratio. Yet annual bank profits are rarely stable, reflecting a volatile economic situation. Although a bank may have made large profits in the previous year and plan to increase capital in the current year, it could easily change this plan if profits in the current year are minimal. On top of that, it is difficult to understand why the contribution of $PRO_i(t-1)$ was negative. For the relationship between profit and capital, it would be better to assume the positive correlation between current profit, $PRO_i(t)$, and the current capital/asset ratio, $EQT_i(t)$, since more profit allows banks to reserve more capital.

In short, even if the above model indicated statistically significant relationships between the above explanatory variables and the dependent variable $EQT_i(t)$, their causality remains unclear and underexplained.

With respect to this, we modified the above model as follows. First, $AM_i(t-1)$ and $PRO_i(t-1)$ are replaced with $AM_i(t)$ and $PRO_i(t)$ respectively. Second, $GAS_i(t-1)$ has been removed. Instead, the loan/asset ratio, $LON_i(t)$, and the deposit/asset ratio, $DEP_i(t)$, are included as the risk indicators. When the loan/asset ratio rises, a sound bank may increase the capital/asset ratio to prepare for a growing risk. Likewise, the fall of the deposit/asset ratio may encourage banks to increase their capital ratio, partly because it indicates the reduction of the funds available to them, and partly because it may signal the fall of their social credit.

Hence a positive correlation is expected between $EQT_i(t)$ and $LON_i(t)$, and a negative correlation between $EQT_i(t)$ and $DEP_i(t)$. To summarize, our model is described as:

$$EQT_i(t) = b_0 + b_1 EQT_i(t-1) + b_2 LON_i(t) + b_3 DEP_i(t)$$
$$+ b_4 PRO_i(t) + b_5 AM_i(t) + u_i(t) \quad \text{for } i = 1, ..., n \quad (3.2)$$

Our expectation of this model is that b_1, b_2 and b_4 are positive, and that b_3 is negative. It will be negative for b_5 if the *amakudari* connection still functions as a means of collusion between the financial authority and the banks.

The observation period is from 1992 to 1999, since this study focuses on the period after the collapse of the bubble economy, and since the most recent data available at the time of writing is from 1999. However, the data set includes data from 1990 to 1991, as the Arellano–Bond GMM estimation requires data from at least two years prior to the observation period. The summary statistics of the data from 1990 to 1999 are presented in the Appendix.

3.2 Results

Table 3.3 shows the result of the GMM estimation with the models (3.1) and (3.2) using data of the 1990s in the left and centre columns respectively. Since two explanatory variables, the loan/asset ratio, $LON_i(t)$, and the *amakudari* connection, $AM_i(t)$, turn out to be statistically insignificant in the model (3.2), the variable $LON_i(t)$ is removed according to the backward variable selection (*F*-threshold is 2.0). The insignificance of $LON_i(t)$ is understandable, given that the amount of loan on the whole is not an adequate indicator of risk. There are safe loans as well as risky loans, and the reaction of banks should vary from one loan to another.

Table 3.3 The effect of *amakudari* on the capital/asset ratio of Japanese regional banks: the results of GMM estimation, dependent variable: $EQT_i(t)$, 1992–99 (82 banks)

Independent variables	Estimates		
	(3.1)	(3.2)	(3.3)
$EQT_i(t-1)$	0.457 (4.311)***	0.227 (2.545)***	0.274 (3.091)***
$GAS_i(t-1)$	0.012 (1.737)*		
$PRO_i(t-1)$	−0.338 (3.894)***		
$AM_i(t-1)$	−0.007 (1.952)*		
$LON_i(t-1)$		0.016 (0.577)	
$DEP_i(t-1)$		−0.051 (1.930)*	0.060 (2.999)***
$PRO_i(t-1)$		0.546 (9.408)***	0.645 (10.658)***
$AM_i(t)$		−0.003 (1.064)	−0.003 (1.929)*
Sargan test	31.063	27.753	33.265
Arellano–Bond m2 test	−1.109	0.435	0.395
No. of observations	656	656	656

Note: *t*-statistics shown in parentheses.
* $p<0.1$.
*** $p<0.01$.

The model without $LON_i(t)$, which we call model (3.3), produces the estimates shown in the left column.

The Sargan test statistics and the Arellano–Bond m2 test statistics show that all models are neither overidentified nor serially correlated, and can thus be considered as statistically robust.

The estimates with the model (3.1) are largely consistent with the results of the Horiuchi–Shimizu model despite the differences in the coverage of the data (Horiuchi and Shimizu included non-listed banks as well as listed banks) and the period. The coefficients of $EQT_i(t-1)$ and $GAS_i(t-1)$ are similarly positive and those of $PRO_i(t-1)$ and $AM_i(t-1)$ are similarly negative, although they and their *t*-statistics are not identical. This may suggest that the negative effect of the *amakudari* practice, argued by Horiuchi and Shimizu for the period between 1979 and 1991, still existed after 1992.

Negative effects of the *amakudari* practice are also confirmed by model (3.3), where the coefficient of $AM_i(t)$ is negative and statistically significant at the 10 per cent level. The other variables are also significant, and the previous capital/asset ratio, $EQT_i(t-1)$, and the current profit/asset ratio, $PRO_i(t)$, make a positive contribution, and the deposit/asset ratio, $DEP_i(t)$, makes a negative contribution, as already expected.

On this point, it should be remembered that our data set does not include the banks which failed during the 1990s. Since all of them employed one or more *amakudari* executives until the 1980s, the negative correlation between $EQT_i(t)$ and $AM_i(t)$ would be even clearer if they were included. Conversely, we reject the argument that the estimation of Horiuchi and Shimizu was biased towards some exceptionally bad banks. We obtained similar results from the data even without the banks that failed.

3.3   Further analyses

In estimating the effect of the *amakudari* practice, neither the Horiuchi–Shimizu model nor the Van Rixtel–Hassink model take more than the presence of the employment of *amakudari* executives into consideration. Nevertheless, the pattern of *amakudari* employment is far from identical. Appointment is made either to the presidential position or other less significant positions. The number of *amakudari* executives also varies from one bank to another. It is reasonable to hypothesize that these differences show different effects on bank performance. In order to verify this hypothesis, model (3.3) is modified in two ways. First of all, the dummy variable of the employment of *amakudari* executives, $AM_i(t)$, has been replaced by two dummy variables, $AMP_i(t)$ and $AMNP_i(t)$. $AMP_i(t)$ and $AMNP_i(t)$ denote the employment of *amakudari* executives in the presidential position and in other positions, respectively. When a bank employs two or more *amakudari* executives, $AMP_i(t)$ equals one (and $AMNP_i(t)$ equals zero) if one of them takes the presidential position. Second, $AM_i(t)$, has been replaced by $AMN_i(t)$, the variable which represents the number of *amakudari* executives. The results are shown in Tables 3.4 and 3.5.

From the results in Table 3.4, it follows that the employment of *amakudari* executives in the presidential position causes more negative effects than other cases. According to Table 3.5, moreover, the number of *amakudari* executives seems to be a significant variable, whose explanatory power is more robust than the dummy variable of *amakudari* employment. It is worth noting that the number of *amakudari* variables has greater significance than the dummy variable for *amakudari* employment in model (3.3). Given this result, it can be said that, as shown in Figure 3.2, the *amakudari* practice has generally had less effect since the number of *amakudari* executives decreased in 1996.

However, this does not mean that the effect of *amakudari* in each separate case has lessened. It is not surprising, of course, that the rise of public concern about *amakudari* and the restructuring of the supervision of banks in the late 1990s has led to a diminishing effect. The new agency for financial supervision, the Financial Supervisory Agency, was organizationally

Table 3.4 The effect of the *amakudari* employment in presidential and non-presidential positions on the capital/asset ratio of Japanese regional banks: the results of GMM estimation, dependent variable: $EQT_i(t)$, 1992–99 (82 banks)

Independent variables	Estimates
$EQT_i(t-1)$	0.270 (3.059)***
$DEP_i(t)$	−0.060 (3.018)***
$PRO_i(t)$	0.673 (10.418)***
$AMP_i(t)$	−0.005 (1.750)*
$AMNP_i(t)$	−0.003 (1.487)
Sargan test	32.631
Arellano–Bond m2 test	0.391
No. of observations	656

Note: *t*-statistics shown in parentheses.
* $p < 0.1$.
*** $p < 0.01$.

Table 3.5 The effect of the number of *amakudari* executives on the capital/asset ratio of Japanese regional banks: the results of GMM estimation, dependent variable: $EQT_i(t)$, 1992–99 (82 banks)

Independent variables	Estimates
$EQT_i(t-1)$	0.308 (3.182)***
$DEP_i(t)$	−0.089 (3.142)***
$PRO_i(t)$	0.616 (8.765)***
$AMP_i(t)$	−0.003 (2.475)*
Sargan test	23.071
Arellano–Bond m2 test	−0.369
No. of observations	656

Note: *t*-statistics shown in parentheses.
* $p < 0.1$
*** $p < 0.01$.

independent of the MoF, and hence the influence of *amakudari* executives on the supervising operation may well have diminished. To see the change over time, a further model was formulated by distinguishing between the effect of *amakudari* in the earlier period (1992–95) and the later period (1996–99). Therefore, model (3.3) is modified as follows:

$$EQT_i(t) = b_0 + b_1 EQT_i(t-1) + b_3 DEP_i(t) + b_4 PRO_i(t)$$
$$+ AM92\text{–}5_i(t) + AM96\text{–}9_i(t) + u_i(t) \quad \text{for } i = 1, \ldots, n \qquad (3.4)$$

Table 3.6   The effect of *amakudari* on the capital/asset ratio of Japanese regional banks (time-related dummy variables): the results of GMM estimation, dependent variable: $EQT_i(t)$, 1992–99 (82 banks)

Independent variables	Estimates	
$EQT_i(t-1)$	0.244 (5.734)***	0.253 (2.688)***
$DEP_i(t)$	−0.074 (3.438)***	−0.087 (2.905)***
$PRO_i(t)$	0.596 (8.960)***	0.564 (7.778)***
$AM92{-}5_i(t)$	−0.003 (−1.616)	
$AM96{-}9_i(t)$	−0.004 (2.211)**	
$AMNP92{-}5_i(t)$		−0.003 (1.964)**
$AMNP96{-}9_i(t)$		−0.004 (2.787)***
Sargan test	31.084	19.287
Arellano–Bond m2 test	0.098	−0.267
No. of observations	656	656

Note: *t*-statistics shown in parentheses.
** $p < 0.05$.
*** $p < 0.01$.

$AM92{-}5_i(t)$ and $AM96{-}9_i(t)$ are time-related dummy variables for the employment of *amakudari* executives from 1992 to 1995 and from 1996 to 1999 respectively. The effect of the number of *amakudari* executives is also examined by using time-related variables, $AMN92{-}5_i(t)$ and $AMN96{-}9_i(t)$. The results are shown in Table 3.6. $AM92{-}5_i(t)$ is marginally insignificant at the 10 per cent level, but $AM96{-}9_i(t)$ is negative at the 5 per cent level. $AMN92{-}5_i(t)$ and $AM96{-}9_i(t)$ are negative at the 5 per cent and 1 per cent levels respectively.

The results imply that the negative effect of *amakudari*, both in terms of employment and number, is greater and more significant in the second period than in the first period. In other words, the difference between *amakudari* banks and non-*amakudari* banks became even more salient in the later period. This may sound strange; given the changes stated above, it might be more natural to expect the negative effect of *amakudari* to decline as time goes on.

One possible interpretation of the results is that the appointment of *amakudari* became more selective in the later period, so that *amakudari* executives were only appointed to very unhealthy banks. Another interpretation is that non-*amakudari* banks were quicker to react to social criticism and the new type of supervision than *amakudari* banks. The results may reflect both.

Finally, let us examine the effect of *amakudari* on the Bank of Japan (BoJ). Following the Horiuchi–Shimizu model, the above models only

Table 3.7 The effect of the employment and the number of BoJ *amakudari* executives on the capital/asset ratio of Japanese regional banks: the results of GMM estimation, dependent variable: $EQT_i(t)$, 1992–99 (82 banks)

Independent variables	Estimates	
$EQT_i(t-1)$	0.289 (5.010)***	0.295 (4.993)***
$DEP_i(t)$	−0.050 (3.309)***	−0.048 (3.081)***
$PRO_i(t)$	0.675 (11.604)***	0.653 (11.709)***
$AMB_i(t)$	−0.000 (0.387)	
$AMBN_i(t)$		0.000 (0.140)
Sargan test	32.834	32.364
Arellano–Bond m2 test	0.714	0.744
No. of observations	656	656

Note: *t*-statistics shown in parentheses.
*** $p < 0.01$.

take account of *amakudari* from the MoF. Indeed, Horiuchi and Shimizu rejected the effect of *amakudari* from BoJ. According to them, BoJ *amakudari* do not affect bank performance because BoJ does not have the authority to supervise the management of banks directly, even though it plays the role of providing special loans for banks in trouble.

For unknown reasons, however, they did not utilize the GMM estimation in their study to examine this hypothesis. Meanwhile, Van Rixtel and Hassink treated *amakudari* from the MoF and BoJ equally, without any specific discussion. Therefore, it is meaningful to estimate the effect of BoJ *amakudari* in our study. Then $AM_i(t)$ in model (3.3) has again been replaced by $AMB_i(t)$ and $AMNB_i(t)$, which represent the employment and number of *amakudari* executives from BoJ respectively.

The result is that neither $AMB_i(t)$ nor $AMNB_i(t)$ is statistically significant, as shown in Table 3.7. Even if they are significant, their coefficients are almost equal to zero, so that the influence of BoJ *amakudari* is not observed at all. Therefore, we may conclude that the argument of Horiuchi and Shimizu is acceptable.

4 Conclusion

This chapter examined whether and to what degree the *amakudari* connection affected bank performance in the post-bubble period. The general overview indicates that the capital/asset ratio, which is regarded as an indicator of prudent bank behaviour, had grown by the end of the 1990s. In other words, banks appear to have performed more prudently. With the dynamic panel data analysis of 82 regional banks, we also found that the employment of *amakudari* executives still had a negative impact on bank performance. The impact was even greater when *amakudari* employees took up a presidential position. The number of *amakudari* executives is also significant.

Since the number of *amakudari* executives declined after 1996, the overall effect of the *amakudari* practice was reduced. However, the effect of *amakudari* employment on bank performance has become more negative and more significant in recent years. This is presumably because the appointment of *amakudari* became more selective, and concentrated more on unhealthy banks, and because banks without *amakudari* executives were more responsive to changes in the external environment.

It should be remembered, however, that the scope of our data is rather limited. Over 30 regional banks were not included in our data set. Data were not available either because they had failed and/or merged with another bank, or because they were not listed on the stock exchange throughout the period. It should also be noted that this study covers only a very short period. It is reasonable to expect that the effect of *amakudari* employment will be less significant in the future, due to the disengagement of the MoF from financial supervision. Nonetheless, it is still too early to make a judgement on the effect of the new supervisory scheme of the Financial Supervision Agency.

Appendix

Table A3.1   Summary statistics of the data set: continuous variables

Variable	Mean	Standard deviation	Maximum	Minimum
EQT	0.040	0.009	0.001	0.070
GAS	0.014	0.064	−0.152	1.506
PRO	0.002	0.005	−0.050	0.009
LON	0.685	0.063	0.449	0.850
DEP	0.876	0.035	0.717	1.036
AMN	0.737	0.814	0	4
AMN92–5	0.465	0.759	0	4
AMN96–9	0.272	0.583	0	4
AMBN	0.584	0.666	0	3

Table A3.2 Summary statistics of the data set: dummy variables

Variable	Mean	Standard deviation	Cases 0	Cases 1
AM	0.543	0.498	375	445
AMP	0.129	0.336	714	106
AMNP	0.413	0.493	481	339
AM92–5	0.329	0.470	550	270
AM96–9	0.213	0.410	645	175
AMB	0.489	0.500	419	401

Notes

This study is part of the project entitled 'Comparative Analysis of Policy-making Process for the Restructuring of the Financial System after Bubble – cases of Japan and Nordic Countries'. The author fully acknowledges the financial support of The Matsushita International Foundation for the project.

1   See Arellano and Bond (1991) for the explanation of their GMM estimation. Horiuchi and Shimizu also give a concise explanation.

References

Arellano, M. and Bond, S. (1991), 'Some Tests of Specification for Panel Data: Monte Carlo Evidence and an Application to Employment Equations', *Review of Economic Studies*, 58, 277–97.

Hartcher, P. (1998), *The Ministry: The Inside Story of Japan's Ministry of Finance* (London: HarperCollins Business).

Horiuchi, A. and Shimizu, K. (2001), 'Did *amakudari* undermine the effectiveness of regulator monitoring in Japan?', *Journal of Banking and Finance*, 25(3), 573–96.

Rixtel, A. A. R. J. Van and Hassink, W. H. J. (1998), 'Monitoring the monitors: *amakudari* and the ex-post monitoring of private banks', Discussion Paper No. 1785, January, London, Centre for Economic Policy Research.

Toyokeizai Shimposha, *Kigyo Keiretsu Soran*, various issues (Tokyo: Toyokeizai Shimposha).

Toyokeizai Shimposha, *Kaisha Shikiho*, various issues (Tokyo: Toyokeizai Shimposha).

4
The Transformation of Corporate Governance Systems in Japan and Germany: The End of Rhenian Capitalism?

Ulrich Jürgens

> Capitalism, we can now see, has two faces, two personalities. The neo-American model is based on individual success and short-term financial gain; the Rhine model, of German pedigree but with strong Japanese connections, emphasises collective success, consensus and long-term concerns. In the last decade or so it is the Rhine model…that has shown itself to be the more efficient of the two, as well as the more equitable.
>
> Michel Albert (1993), 18

1 Introduction

Corporate governance and policy reforms have been major topics for academic debate at the beginning of the new decade. There are many signs of changes in the traditional corporate governance systems in both countries; some are dramatic. This chapter focuses on two questions: first, how deeply have the changes already transformed the traditional systems in those countries? Second, what are the broader implications of these changes for the social systems of production, the 'styles of capitalism' in both countries?

2 Unravelling the traditional systems

The changes of corporate governance are part of a more general transformation process of last century's production regimes. They seem to indicate a universal process of levelling national specificities, of standardization. Thus it is not by accident that they follow on the heels of the lean-production movement which has introduced standard principles of production organization worldwide. That move was oriented at learning from Japan. The success of the 'Japanese model' had the adverse effect of reducing transformative, innovative forces in Japan. The lean-production movement was very much about socio-technical issues, about production and work organization, about workshop control and best-practice management. The main addressees were managers.

The corporate-governance movement raises the issue of who controls management itself. Clearly, this transformation is oriented at Anglo-Saxon models. This sudden and radical shift from the productionist themes of the lean-production debate to a shareholder value orientation and the New Economy debate took many observers by surprise (cf. Albert's projection of a long drawn battle between the two kinds of capitalism).[1] Suddenly Rhenian capitalism appeared to be an obsolete model.

In the debate about this secular shift two lines of reasoning can be distinguished: on the one hand there is the argument that the demise of Rhenian capitalism can be explained as a final phase in catching up the USA. In this phase protective mechanisms such as cross-shareholdings and lifetime employment (etc.) have become constraints to further development. National capitalisms can now meet the challenge of the pure liberal market model. The argument therefore is that a crisis of the stakeholder system marks the beginning of a development towards a more market-based 'shareholder' system. 'The Japanese economy has outgrown its former efficient set-up' (Schulz 2001).

The 'classic' Japanese corporate governance system, according to Kester (1991) consisted of implicit contracting founded on trust; extensive reciprocal shareholdings and trade agreements with few stakeholders; managerial incentives for overall corporate growth, and selective intervention and coordination by banks and by the state. On the background of governmental backing and central bank guarantees industrial groups (*Keiretsu*), with main banks (city banks) at their center, developed as stakeholder systems. The stakeholder model allowed companies and markets to develop at lower costs because it builds on a set of personal relationships and guarantees that do not require an established set of public rules, trusted enforcement mechanisms, and readily available sophisticated information (technologies) to raise and allocate huge amounts of investment capital. Enclosed and bound within networks of interlinked stakeholder arrangements, this system also proved more stable and secure against strong business swings and cycles. The market system, in contrast, builds on personal freedom and flexible independent decisions within a set of stable rules, allowing efficiencies beyond the stakeholder set-up when competing interests and trends need to be integrated in a diversifying economy.

On the other hand there is the argument that we have entered a new phase in the development of capitalism in which the capital markets and institutional investors play a dominant role in forcing companies to meet their expectations regarding corporate governance. The reassertion of shareholder power has a levelling effect on the variety of capitalism in general. In view of the lead the Anglo-Saxon system has, in terms of the new requirements, the demise of Rhenian capitalism can also be regarded as a convergence in the direction of the Anglo-Saxon system of capitalism.

While both lines of reasoning emphasize different driving forces and change dynamics, the unravelling of Germany's and Japan's post-war models in both arguments seems inevitable. These post-war models shared three basic similarities (cf. Jürgens and Rupp 2001; Jackson, forthcoming):

1   The central role of banks in a complex system of cross-shareholdings reflecting financial commitment of capital–corporate ownership concentrated among banks and inter-corporate networks rather than fragmented among individuals and institutional investors as in the USA. Japanese *Keiretsu* groups link corporations and banks within patterns of horizontal cross-shareholding, while pyramidal conglomerate holding companies (*Konzerne*) and dense bank-industry networks are important in Germany. These features restrict the role of the stock markets as markets for corporate control and create incentives for owners to influence management through 'voice' rather than exit. In the absence of markets, banks have played the central governance role (relational financing).

2   Industrial citizenship: labour has a voice in corporate governance. While the German system with its various co-determination laws can be characterized in terms of enterprise constitutionalism, the Japanese model can be characterized in terms of enterprise communities (Dore 2000).

3   A production-oriented, company-centred management system: in case of opposition from both capital and labour management in this system a balance has to be found between long-term returns to capital and labour. Management tends to be internally promoted and compensation schemes tend not to have strong shareholder-oriented incentives such as stock options but rather more egalitarian pay scales.

Indeed, in both countries changes towards an American style of corporate governance can be observed.

Government reforms of corporate law: in Japan, a key measure was lifting the ban on holding companies thereby facilitating centralized strategic management of multiple businesses. It is expected that the holding company will spread gradually with the effect that strategic management is centralized in smaller corporate boards thereby creating more arm's-length relations between businesses (cf. Jackson, forthcoming). Up to the current stage, however, there has been no great move towards adopting holding company structures.

In Germany, the key reform was the law on control and transparency of 1998, which limited multiple supervisory board memberships (and improving disclosure), and ownership stakes exceeding 5 per cent. Multiple voting rights and voting rights restrictions were eliminated, banks were barred from using proxy votes, and if their direct shareholding exceeded 5 per cent banks had to solicit more instructions from shareholders, and the supervisory board was given greater duties of financial oversight. Restrictions on share buy-backs and stock options, as in Japan, were removed.

The adoption of corporate governance codes on a voluntary basis: corporate governance principles were issued by the Corporate Governance Forum of Japan (CGF), a private study group of academics and business leaders. Supervisory boards and outside directors are widespread in Japan now. For instance, Hoya appointed half of its board of directors from outside the company in June 2001; Sony contracted outside directors and moved to a CEO system. A 2001 survey found that 35.7 per cent of corporations listed on the Tokyo Stock Exchange (TSE) had introduced CEO systems. The CGF remained cautious about a number of Anglo–American practices such as hostile take-overs and corporate lay-offs, and they have not called for reductions of cross-shareholdings.

In Germany a take-over code was introduced in 1995 on a voluntary basis. Provisions were liberal and provided little protection from hostile take-overs. Only 540 of 933 domestic listed companies and 79 of DAX100 companies participated. Under pressure from labour unions and leading companies Germany is now moving towards a national law allowing management to pursue a wider variety of take-over defences (as in the USA).

Adoption of international accounting rules: both countries had their specific accounting rules heavily criticized by international investors. While few Japanese companies obtained listings in the New York Stock Exchange (NYSE) in the 1990s, the major German corporations were either listed on the NYSE (out of the DAX30, 16 are listed on the NYSE; all others use international standards). Present reforms in Japan require corporations to increase transparency by reporting financial assets at market value beginning in March 2001, and cross-shareholdings beginning in March 2002.

Decrease of block ownership and cross-shareholding ('committed capital'): traditional patterns of stable and committed capital are weakening in both countries. The proportion of stable shares (owned by banks, insurance firms, corporations and the state) over the 1990s decreased from 64.7 per cent to 52.4 per cent in Japan and from 60.2 per cent to 52.8 per cent in Germany. However, the shareholder structure in both countries has not converged on the US pattern where nearly all shares are held by finance-oriented investors.

In Japan, changes in the shareholding structure have involved a partial unravelling of ties between horizontal *Keiretsu* groups. Between 1987 and 1999, the proportion of shares in listed companies owned by stable shareholders declined from 48 per cent to 38 per cent and cross-shareholding from 21 per cent to 11 per cent. In Germany, aggregate bank ownership has remained stable and insurance companies have increased their stakes; inter-corporate ownership has shown the greatest decline. (However this may be a statistical effect due to privatization of state enterprises and other factors; cf. Jackson, forthcoming.)

Banks losing their central role for financing of large corporations: while large corporations in both countries reduced their dependency on bank credits – not so much through issuing equity but through bonds, commercial papers and retained earnings – small companies have become more dependent on bank credits (cf. Deutsche Bank 1999; Jürgens and Rupp 2001).

While German banks have made moves into investment banking, Japanese banks are still closely linked to the corporate sector because of a lack of consumer credit. Thus they not only failed as efficient monitors during the bubble years in the late 1980s, they also failed during the financial crisis of the 1990s, when most small- and medium-sized enterprises depended heavily on bank credits.

Influx of foreign investors: the proportion of foreign ownership increased rapidly. Foreign shareholders accounted for 13 per cent of turnover of Japanese stocks in 1991 and this figure increased to nearly 28 per cent in 1999. Overseas investors are stepping up purchases of Japanese companies. Here, the trend of Japanese companies unloading less-profitable businesses to focus more on core operations and the slumping stock prices are working together as supporting factors. From January to May 2001, for example, overseas funds acquired 28 Japanese companies, compared with one in all of 1998, 13 in 1999 and 25 in 2000. Companies such as Ripplewood Holdings have already bought a whole portfolio of former icons of 'Japan Inc.'.

In Germany domestic institutional investors expanded dramatically after market liberalization. The percentage of foreign ownership has remained stable (Jackson, forthcoming, 23f).

Adoption of shareholder value targets: the most efficient and international competitive companies have adopted EVA (economic value added) or similar concepts (Kao, Advantest, Hoya, Sony). However, only 1.9 per cent of the corporations in a Nikkei survey of TSE corporations named EVA as the most important benchmark, while 38.2 per cent still named pre-tax profits and 18.7 per cent sales.

Stock options are spreading fast. Mitsubishi and Fujitsu added stock option provisions to their corporate charters. Overall a total of 63 companies either have secured shareholder approval or are planning to submit resolutions about stock option plans in June 2000/2001. Similarly, in Germany almost all DAX companies have introduced stock option schemes or gained approval to do so.

Concerning *shareholder value* as the lead target for corporate management, re-thinking in Japan seems to occur amazingly fast. While management in the traditional Japanese companies was clearly aimed at market growth and the interests of company employees, recently profitability and capital efficiency have become the main criteria for corporate success. According to a survey of directors of 1,307 major leading Japanese companies listed on Tokyo's stock exchange (1st section), carried out by the Research Institute for Advancement of Living Standards (RIALS), the think tank of Rengo, the Japanese Trade Union Confederation in about 50 per cent of companies the top directors now think that the primary role of management is to enhance capital efficiency and to maximize the profit of shareholders. Only 10.7 per cent disagree with these views. In 60.3 per cent of the companies the top directors expect that within the next five years return on equity (ROE) will become the primary target of their company instead of market share or growth in sales (Fliaster and Marr 2000, 250).

To summarize, there is no doubt that traditional systems have been changing in Japan as well as in Germany. While the speed of these changes is stunning there has been no large-scale transformation towards the US-shareholder-oriented model in either one of these countries. But it seems too early to speak of 'hybrid' models of traditional regime elements and a more 'marketized' approach. For the moment, the process should be regarded as open.

3   Conclusions

At the current stage of development it is hardly possible to grasp the broader socio-economic impact of these changes. Changes in corporate governance cannot be related in a cause–effect sense to the changes in supply relations, employee relations and industrial relations we can currently observe in Japan as well as in Germany. Several other reasons have to be taken into account in this regard.

In the debate about effects of shareholder value-oriented changes in corporate governance two possible negative consequences are emphasized in particular: the first is the result of the 'marketization' of social, financial, employment and supply relations. In view of the often cited strength of the 'relation-thickness' of the German and Japanese systems one may expect a high degree of conflict in the future. The second is the result of an increase in 'short-termism' which threatens to undermine the innovative potential and human resource base of the economy.

It has to be emphasized, however, that it is not appropriate to deduce such consequences from general principles or the 'logic' of the new approach. While it is true that traditional relationships are weakening or obsolete in many areas due to new financing practices, supplier relations and so on, it is also true that new practices are developing new social arrangements. Thus, a weakening of social relations due to their 'marketization' has fostered the development of new forms of networking and enhanced communication and cooperation across company borders.

Note

1   After the collapse of communism, Albert assumed the next battle to be between the systems of capitalism: 'This time the combat will pit neo-American capitalism against Rhine capitalism. ... The battle may ultimately come down to a confrontation between whole value-systems, and on its outcome will be decided the answers to such issues as the individual's place within the company, the function of the market place in society, and the role of law and authority in international economic affairs' (1993, 19).

References

Albert, M. (1993), *Capitalism Against Capitalism* (London: Whorr).

Deutsche Bank (1999), *On Corporate Financing in Germany and France: A Comparative Analysis*, October.

Dore, R. (2000), *Stock Market Capitalism – Welfare Capitalism: Japan and Germany Versus the Anglo-Saxons* (Oxford: Oxford University Press).

Fliaster, A. and Marr, R. (2000), 'Change of the Insider-Oriented Corporate Governance in Japan and Germany: Between Americanisation and Tradition', *Journal of Change Management*, 1 (3), 242–56.

Jackson, G. (forthcoming), 'Corporate Governance in Germany and Japan: Liberalisation Pressures and Responses during the 1990s', in W. Streeck and K. Yamamura (eds), *The Future of Nationally Embedded Capitalism in a Global Economy*.

Jürgens, U. and Rupp, J. (2001), *The German System of Corporate Governance – Characteristics and Changes*, Report for the EU-TSER Project 'Corporate Governance, Innovation, and Economic Performance in the EU', coordinated by W. Lazonick and M. O'Sullivan (http//:www.insead.fr/projects/cgep).

Kester, C. W. (1991), *Japanese Take-Overs – the Global Contest for Corporate Control* (Boston, MA: Harvard Business School Press).

Schulz, M. (2001), *The Reform of (Corporate) Governance in Japan. Why so Slow? Will it Succeed?*, Fujitsu Research Institute, Discussion Paper 01 – No. XX.

5

The International Organization of Technology Acquisition Activities: A Comparative Study of Japanese and German High-Tech Business Units

Martin Hemmert

Due to intensifying international competition, access to knowledge of cutting-edge technology in different countries and locations, and efficient management of internal technology transfer, have both become critical success factors for high-tech firms. This raises the question of whether and to what extent significant differences between firms located in different countries can be observed in international technology acquisition management.

A detailed study of 16 leading German and Japanese business units in the semiconductor and pharmaceutical industries reveals that technology acquisition in both industries is far more internationalized in German business units than in those of Japan. Most German business units, particularly in the pharmaceutical industry, have established a full-scale horizontal division of labour between vertically integrated R&D sites in their home country and those abroad. In contrast, the R&D activities of the Japanese business units surveyed are concentrated in their home country. Foreign R&D activities are limited to specific tasks and functions. Thus, in the case of Japanese business units, there is far less technology transfer from foreign sites to the home country than in the case of German business units. Accordingly, assessment of technology acquisition performance by the German R&D managers surveyed is significantly higher than that of their Japanese colleagues.

1 Introduction

As part of the ongoing integration of the world economy, internationalization of business firm activities will generally increase in the long term. However, the extent of this internationalization differs widely depending on the functional field taken into consideration. In contrast to other fields such as sales, production, and procurement, where the process of internationalization has progressed rapidly in many firms, business activities in the field of R&D, even in large firms, centred predominantly in the home countries until the 1970s. Multinational firms in R&D-intensive industries first began to set up international R&D locations on a significant scale in the 1980s, a trend that prevailed throughout the 1990s (OECD 1999). Qualitative research (Patel 1996) indicates, however, that R&D activities of most business firms are still centred in their home countries. Substantial internationalization has only taken place in a limited number of large firms.

In sum, empirical data indicate that, as far as internationalization is concerned, R&D is a latecomer to the functional areas covered by business firms. Therefore, assuming that the long-term tendency of business firms to internationalize will prevail in the future, most of this process still lies ahead for the vast majority of firms.

This raises the question of the organizational patterns to be installed when R&D activities are internationalized. Does internationalization impact significantly on the competitive performance of firms? Are some international R&D organizational structures superior to others in terms of competitive performance? How important are inter-industrial and intercultural differences to the analysis of this issue?

This chapter intends to contribute to the clarification of these questions. First, a review is given of previous research on the international organization of R&D activities. It is shown that whereas a significant amount of research has been conducted over the last decade, no conspicuous conclusion has evolved with regard to the impact of R&D internationalization on the competitive performance of firms. Thereafter, the results of an empirical study on the international organization of R&D in German and Japanese high-tech business units are discussed. They reveal that certain organizational patterns can be identified as clearly superior to others. The chapter concludes with some implications for business research and business practice in the field of the international organization of R&D.

2   Empirical research on the international organization of technology acquisition: an overview

As a first approach to analysing the internationalization of technological acquisition activities in business firms, statistical data from leading industrial countries are reviewed. At the end of the 1990s, German manufacturing firms spent about 20 per cent of their total R&D expenditures in foreign countries (Bundesministerium für Bildung und Forschung, or BMBF 2000, 51). Corresponding figures for US and Japanese firms were 12 per cent and 3 per cent, respectively (National Science Foundation 2000; Tsûshô Sangyôshô 2000), and strongly suggest significant country-specific differences in this field. The data also indicate industry-specific differences. The internationalization of R&D appears to be most advanced in the pharmaceutical industry and much less so in other fields, such as electronics. Finally, statistics revealed an increase in the relative importance of international R&D throughout the 1990s.

Due to the aggregate nature of statistical data, however, the information gleaned on internationalization of R&D is not very specific. Therefore, a review of empirical research on this topic is indispensable if a more precise picture of business firm activities in this field is to emerge.

Brockhoff and Schmaul (1996, 38) surveyed the performance of international R&D networks of German firms in various industries in relation to their degree of autonomy or centralization. They conclude that the average performance evaluation of R&D networks with a greater degree of centralization than of autonomy in foreign R&D units is substantially higher than that of more decentralized networks.

Other contributions are primarily founded on a qualitative, case-based approach. Reger (1997, 284–6) compares the international R&D networks of European and Japanese multinational firms in high-tech industries. He concludes that while European firms tend to establish vertically integrated R&D units, the R&D networks of Japanese firms are mostly based on small specialized units abroad. Similarly, Gassmann and von Zedtwitz (1998) analyse the division of labour in international R&D units of US, European and Japanese multinationals. They observe a general tendency towards vertical integration and horizontal specialization in R&D units in the home countries and abroad. Gerybadze, Meyer-Krahmer and Reger (1997, 25–8), who also refer to multinational firms from the three corners of the global economic triad, reach similar conclusions. Bartlett and Goshal (1998, 131–54) present case studies of multinational firms with innovations mainly generated in their home countries, and of different firms with highly internationalized R&D networks. They refrain, however, from a normative conclusion concerning the issue of whether one of the two organizational approaches bears more favourable results than the other.

Altogether, qualitative research on the organization of international R&D networks reveals that (1) the internationalization of the R&D

activities in business firms is generally increasing, (2) this internationalization concentrates mainly on large high-tech firms, and (3) there are considerable country-specific differences in this field concerning the degree of internationalization. European firms, in particular, appear to be more internationalized than Japanese firms, thus by and large confirming the above-mentioned statistical findings. Empirical studies have not, however, reached a definitive conclusion on the crucial issue of whether internationalization has a systematic impact on competitive performance in the field of R&D. This issue will subsequently be addressed by analysing the results of an empirical survey on the technology acquisition of multinational firms from Germany and Japan.

3 International organization of R&D and technology acquisition performance: evidence from Germany and Japan

3.1 Research methodology

The empirical survey on which the subsequent analysis is based was conducted during the second half of 1999. Since a substantial part of the R&D activities in high-tech industries is concentrated in a few large firms, research was focused on a detailed analysis of these leading firms rather than a large-scale survey. In order to assess the impact of different institutional environments and different technologies and markets, firms from different countries and industries were covered. This was attained by a survey of firms from two large industrialized countries (Germany and Japan) and two high-tech industries (pharmaceuticals and semiconductors).

Firms (as measured by their R&D and sales volumes in the respective industries) were contacted in their respective country and industry, with the result that a total of 26 high-tech strategic business units were requested to participate in the survey. In order to reduce business unit reservations about the disclosure of strategically relevant information to competitors, the whole survey was conducted anonymously. Eventually, 16 business units participated in the survey. The study therefore covers a large section of the leading business units in the respective countries and industries.

As seen in Table 5.1, the size and structure of the firms and business units from the respective countries and industries are similar in most respects. With the exception of the Japanese pharmaceutical firms, whose sales are highly concentrated on the pharmaceutical business,

Table 5.1 Structural indicators of firms and business units by country and industry, 1998

Indicator	Semiconductors, Japan $n=5$	Semiconductors, Germany $n=4$	Pharmaceuticals, Japan $n=4$	Pharmaceuticals, Germany $n=3$
A Average annual firm sales (US$ millions)	42,337	44,776	3,406	20,057
B Average annual sales of business units for pharmaceuticals/semiconductors (US$ millions, including firm-internal sales)	5,457	2,778	2,663	4,342
C Average share of business unit sales for pharmaceuticals/semiconductors of firm sales ($B/A \times 100$)	12.9	6.2	78.2	21.6
D Average annual R&D expenditures of business units for pharmaceuticals/ semiconductors (US$ millions)	680	403	336	734
E Average R&D intensity of business units for pharmaceuticals/semiconductors ($D/B \times 100$)	12.5	14.5	12.6	16.9

Note: Currency conversion from local currencies into US$ based on average foreign exchange rates released by the Federal Reserve Board.

Sources: Author's calculations based on data from annual reports, information directly obtained from firms and Semiconductor World (1999).

the sales volume of the business units (pharmaceuticals and semicon-ductors) accounts on average for only a minor fraction of the total sales of the firms. As might be expected from a general observation of these industries in both countries, the average size of the respective high-tech business units in German firms is larger in the pharmaceutical industry, while the average size of those in Japanese firms is larger in the semi-conductor industry. However, the average size in all countries and industries ranges between US$2.5 and 5.5 billion of annual sales, indi-cating a large structural similarity in the business units. The average R&D intensity is well above 10 per cent in all countries and industries, which confirms the classification of the business units as 'high-tech'.[1]

In order to gain maximum acceptance by participants, the content was discussed with business unit managers prior to the survey. Pre-tests were conducted with R&D managers from four business units – one in each country and industry – which were not part of the main survey.

The main study was based on three principal sources of information:

- quantitative data on international R&D of the strategic business units surveyed
- assessments of the internationalization and performance of tech-nology acquisition activities given in questionnaire form by R&D managers of business units
- additional information on internationalization and performance of technology acquisition provided by interviews with R&D depart-ment heads of the business units surveyed

Various quantitative data on the internationalization of R&D were col-lected from the individual pharmaceutical or semiconductor business unit in each participating firm. A questionnaire survey was then carried out with numerous R&D managers of each business unit surveyed. This approach was chosen to gain a precise picture of the international flow of technological knowledge in the business units. The questionnaire survey and subsequent interviews therefore focused on the function of technol-ogy acquisition, a key function of R&D.[2] A total of 235 questionnaires was sent out to the business units. Of this number, 165 usable responses were returned to the author. Thus the total response rate was 70.2 per cent.

Based on a preliminary analysis of questionnaire responses, addi-tional interviews subsequently took place with business unit managers concerning the internationalization of their technology acquisition activities. As in the questionnaire survey, the assessments of several respondents from each business unit were sought to gain a detailed pic-ture of the overall situation in the high-tech business units. Between

September and December 1999, 44 R&D managers from 15 business units[3] were interviewed altogether.

The questionnaire survey and the interviews were conducted exclusively in the native languages of the respondents (German and Japanese). All respondents were home-country based (i.e., located in Germany or Japan).

3.2   Findings

3.2.1   *Internationalization of R&D and technology acquisition*

In the first, quantitative part of the survey, data on international R&D sites by region and by vertical R&D function was supplied by the business units (Figure 5.1). Not surprisingly, all business units surveyed maintained activities covering all vertical R&D functions at their home country sites. There is also a clear concentration of host country R&D sites in North America and Europe. Concerning the coverage of the various R&D functions at host country sites in different regions, however, significant differences between industries and home country locations of the business units are observable.

In general, the host country R&D sites in the pharmaceutical industry cover more functions than those of the semiconductor industry, and the business unit sites of German firms cover more functions than the sites of Japanese firms. The German pharmaceutical business units cover all vertical R&D functions with their R&D units in North American and European host countries as well as at home. In contrast, the international R&D sites of Japanese business units in North America and Europe only partially cover research and pre-clinical development functions. There is a concentration of overseas R&D on product development in both German and Japanese semiconductor business units, whereas research and process development functions are covered by international R&D sites only in a minority of cases.

The data also suggest that the R&D functions closest to the final product (product development in the semiconductor industry, clinical development in the pharmaceutical industry) are the most internationalized due to a need to develop and design products separately for markets in different countries.

The data on the quantitative distribution of R&D in different regions, which was also collected in this part of the survey, reveals an even clearer picture (Figure 5.2). The R&D expenditures of the German business units in the pharmaceutical industry are almost evenly distributed between the home country, the rest of Europe and North America.

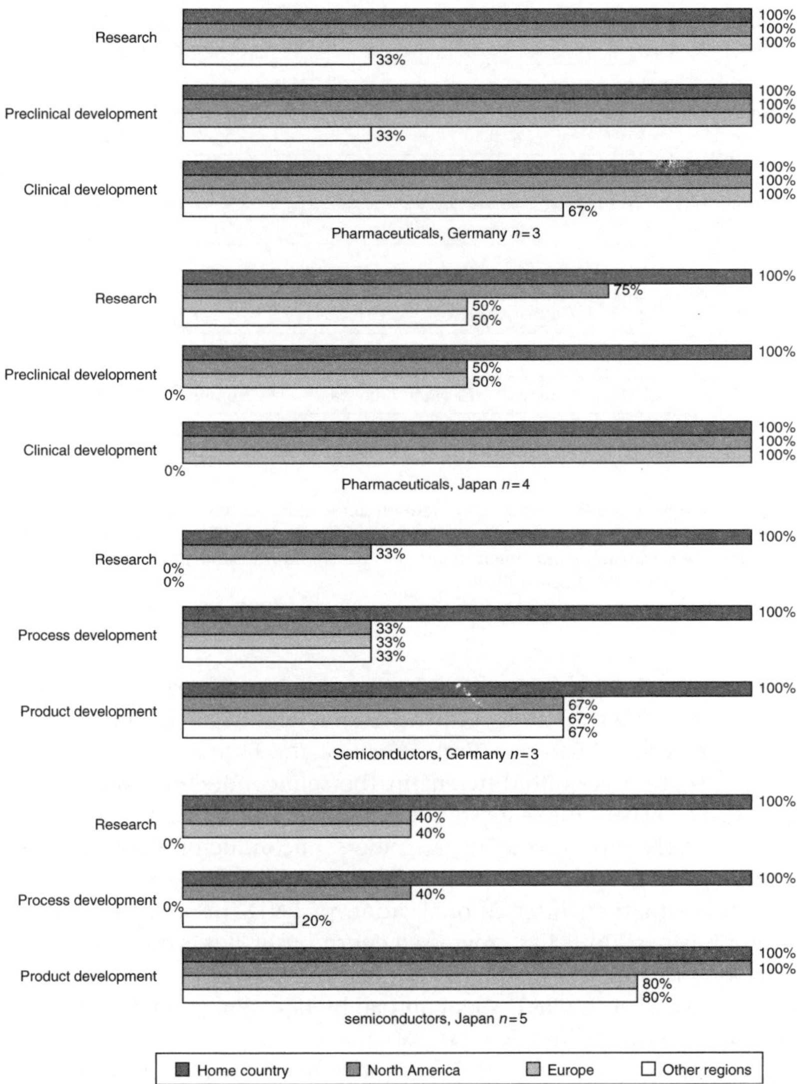

Figure 5.1 International distribution of the R&D sites of the business units surveyed

Note: *n* = number of business units. The percentages indicate the proportion of business units in each home country and industry which cover the respective R&D functions with their R&D sites in each region. One German semiconductor business unit which had its headquarters abroad was excluded from this part of the analysis.

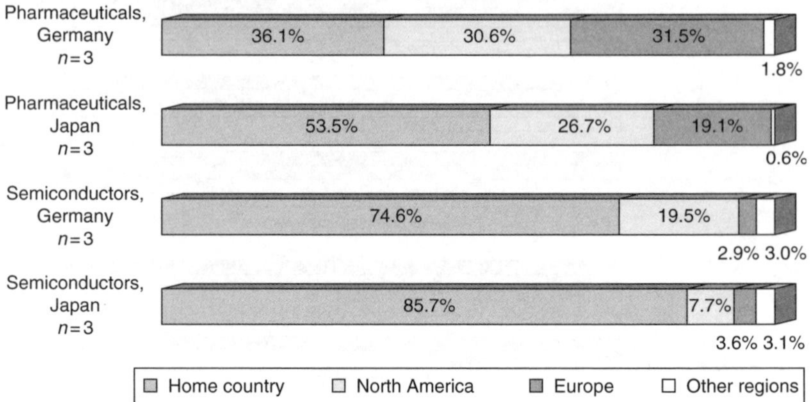

Figure 5.2 International distribution of R&D business unit expenditures by region

Note: *n* = number of business units. One German semiconductor business unit which had its headquarters abroad was excluded from this part of the analysis. Three business units from Japan (two in semiconductors, one in pharmaceuticals) did not supply data on the regional distribution of their R&D expenditures.

In contrast, the pharmaceutical business units in Japan spend more than half of their total R&D in their home country, with most of the remainder divided between North America and Europe.

The situation is quite different in the semiconductor industry. The bulk of R&D spending is located in the home countries. This tendency is particularly pronounced in Japanese semiconductor business units, which spend the overwhelming part of their R&D at home. Compared with this situation, internationalization of R&D in German semiconductor business units has progressed enormously. But even here, almost three-quarters of the total R&D expenditures are spent in the home country. Most of the R&D spent abroad by Japanese and German semiconductor business units goes to North America.

The results of the questionnaire give a more precise picture of the internationalization of R&D in the business units. As mentioned above, each questionnaire was answered by an R&D manager representing one technological field in the firms that were surveyed. Therefore, each case in the subsequent statistical analysis represents one technological field within an individual business unit, and not an entire firm or business unit.

The internationalization of technology acquisition was measured by the indication of whether technology was acquired (1) exclusively from domestic sources, (2) from domestic and foreign sources, or (3) exclusively from foreign sources. A list of five internal and nine external technological sources was provided to measure the degree of internationalization in each case. The distribution of responses (Figure 5.3) shows that while external technological sources have both foreign and domestic locations in most cases, internal technological sources, with the exception of subsidiaries and group firms, have exclusively domestic locations in the majority of cases. This result suggests that even in large high-tech firms the internationalization of firm-internal technology acquisition has not progressed as far as might have been expected from previous research findings.

Country- and industry-specific results are summarized in Figure 5.4 where the proportion of respondents who acquire their technology exclusively in their home countries is depicted by country and industry. As might have been expected from the quantitative data previously discussed, internationalization of firm-internal technological sources is much higher among German than Japanese respondents and much higher in the semiconductor industry than in the pharmaceutical industry. However, in the case of external technological sources, differences between respondents from different countries and industries are much smaller. In other words, the internationalization of external sources of technological knowledge appears to be very common for the home country R&D units of high-tech firms. With regard to the internationalization of firm-internal sources of technologies, however, strong differences prevail between firms from different countries and industries.

In addition to the quantitative information on the R&D of business units and the questionnaire data, information on the organizational structure of the international R&D of business units surveyed was gathered in interviews with firm managers.

The impression that most German business units, particularly in the pharmaceutical industry, maintain R&D locations abroad that cover the full vertical range of R&D activities was confirmed by the quantitative data. It turned out that all German business units in the pharmaceutical industry and some in the semiconductor industry maintain R&D activities covering the entire scope from research to product development (in the semiconductor industry), and from research to clinical development (in the pharmaceutical industry), at one or two foreign locations. In contrast, the functions of the foreign R&D locations of Japanese business units are limited in both industries to specific fields such as product development or research. Even business units that cover different R&D stages in the R&D process at overseas sites do not integrate

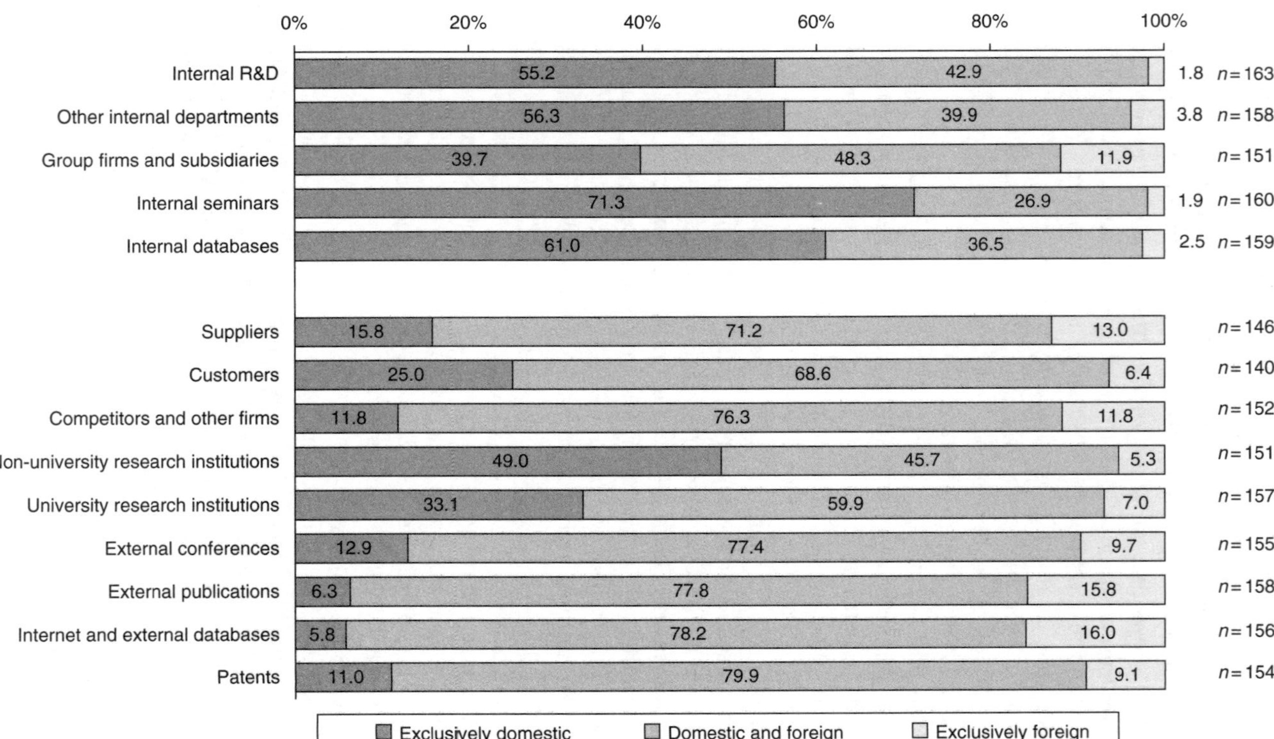

Figure 5.3 Internationalization of the technological sources of questionnaire respondents (distribution of responses)

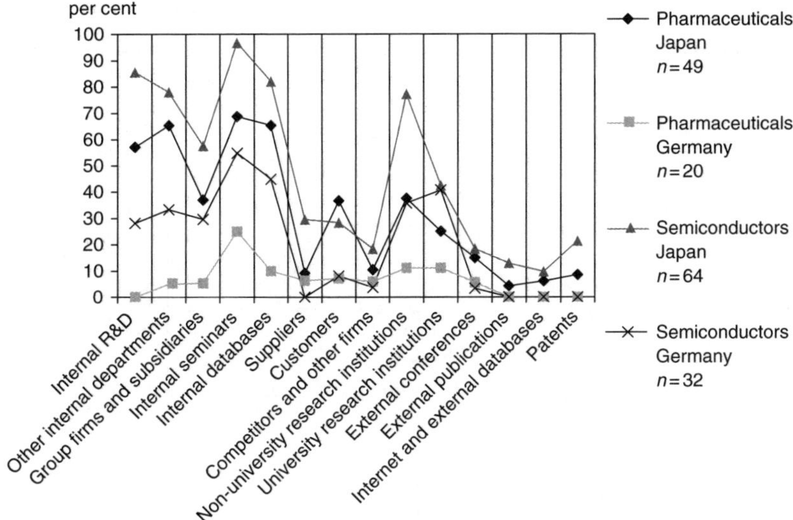

Figure 5.4 Percentage of questionnaire respondents who receive technological information exclusively from domestic sources by country and industry

these activities. Some Japanese semiconductor business units, for instance, maintain research laboratories as well as sites for product development and design in the USA. However, these activities are operated separately with little direct communication between them. In short, foreign locations covering the entire vertical scope of R&D do not exist in the Japanese business units surveyed. The management of only one Japanese pharmaceutical business unit announced during an interview that it is planning to establish integrated R&D activities of this kind in North America in the future.

3.2.2 Technology acquisition performance

Respondents were also asked in the questionnaire to rate technology acquisition performance in their respective technological fields. It was measured on a five-point scale using six performance-specific criteria relative to their competitors. Three of these criteria (low cost of input factors, efficiency of technology acquisition, and speed of technology acquisition) measured the input performance of technology acquisition, while the other three (newness of technologies, market fit of technologies, and transferability of technologies) were indicators of output performance. Additionally, respondents were asked for an overall rating of their technology acquisition performance. The highest rating was

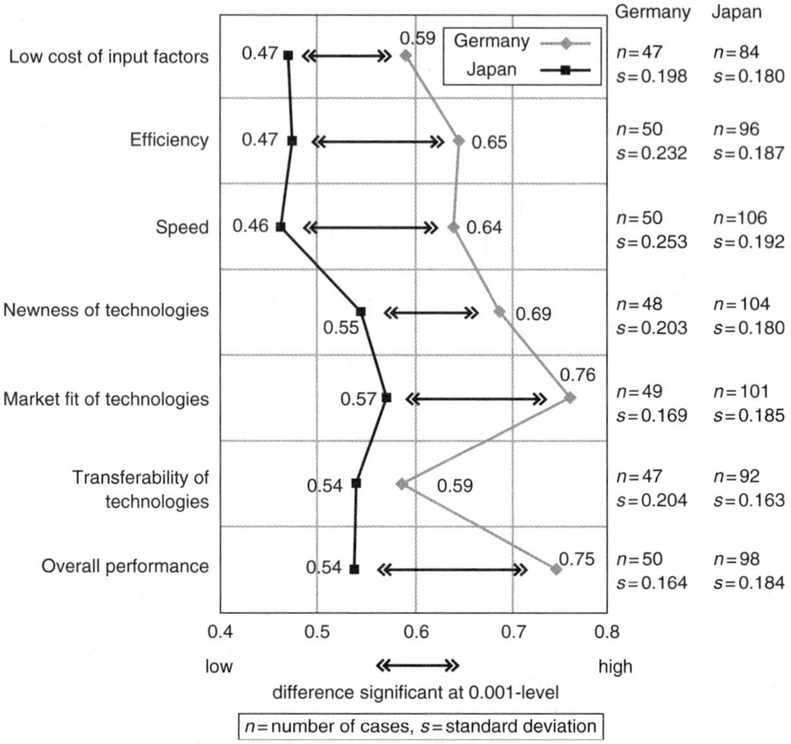

Figure 5.5 Average technology acquisition performance assessments by questionnaire respondents by country

assigned to a much better performance compared to competing firms, the lowest to a much worse performance compared to competing firms. This was treated as interval data and measured on a standardized scale between 0 and 1.

Figure 5.5 shows the country-specific differences in the assessment of technology acquisition performance. The average assessment by German respondents was generally higher than that of Japanese respondents. With the exception of the transferability of new technologies criterion, country-specific differences are significant for all items at the 0.001 level.

Differences between industries in the assessment of technology acquisition performance are much smaller than those between countries. For most items, the average rating is somewhat higher in the semiconductor industry than in the pharmaceutical industry. However, with the exception of the market fit of technologies, where industry-specific difference is significant at a level of 0.05, differences observed between the two industries are quite small. Moreover, the average assessments of overall technology acquisition performance are almost identical in both industries.

The strong country-specific differences in the self-assessment of technology acquisition performance raise the issue of the intercultural validity of the results. However, the differences observed were confirmed in the course of the interviews. Most of the German R&D managers evaluated their current competitive performance in the field of technology acquisition as better than their Japanese counterparts. In order to validate the country-specific findings with exogenous data, a patent analysis was conducted as well.

The growth in the number of US patents granted to the business units surveyed in the respective technological fields between 1995 and 2000 was analysed. It turned out that although there was a substantial volatility between the business units, the overall growth both in the semiconductor and pharmaceutical industry within the five-year period was much stronger in the German business units than those of the Japanese. Therefore, the principal finding of superior technology acquisition performance by German business units compared to Japanese units was confirmed by the patent analysis.

The country-specific findings suggest that a possible explanation lies in the different international organization of R&D activities by the firms located in Germany and Japan, which was discussed in the previous section. Since the questionnaire also covers the internationalization of technological knowledge sources, the statistical relation between internationalization and technology acquisition performance can be analysed. For this purpose, an 'internationalization variable' was created for each technological source by assigning the lowest value for 'exclusively domestic' sourcing, an intermediate value for 'domestic and foreign' sourcing and the highest value for 'exclusively foreign' sourcing. Based on these variables, a correlation analysis of the internationalization of technological sources and technology acquisition performance was conducted. Due to the non-metric input data, Spearman's Rho correlation coefficients were used in the calculation.

All indicators of the internationalization of internal technological sources show a positive correlation with those of technology acquisition performance (Table 5.2). Most correlation coefficients are statistically significant as far as efficiency, speed, newness, market fit, and total performance are concerned. Thus, the supposed positive relation between

Table 5.2 Correlation between internationalization of technological sources and technology acquisition performance assessments of questionnaire respondents

Technological source	Performance indicator							
	Low cost for input factors	Efficiency of technology acquisition	Speed of technology acquisition	Newness of technologies	Market fit of technologies	Transferability of technologies	Total technology acquisition performance	Intervals for numbers of cases n
Internal R&D	0.005	0.077	0.101	0.208**	0.220***	0.049	0.170**	131–155
Other internal departments	0.116	0.241***	0.197**	0.148*	0.204**	0.129	0.261***	127–150
Group firms and subsidiaries	0.097	0.157*	0.111	0.151*	0.123	0.109	0.125	123–145
Internal seminars	0.031	0.243***	0.182**	0.309***	0.238***	0.09	0.316***	129–152
Internal databases	0.039	0.216**	0.160**	0.270***	0.253***	0.119	0.305***	128–152
Suppliers	0.281***	0.058	0.045	−0.059	0.021	0.06	0.104	117–140
Customers	0.073	0.059	0.093	0.134	0.085	0.079	0.078	113–135
Competitors and other firms	−0.033	−0.081	−0.126	−0.048	0.033	−0.026	−0.042	124–146
Non-university research institutions	0.088	0.035	0.042	0.107	0.1	0.031	0.157	122–144
University research institutions	−0.042	−0.014	−0.053	−0.005	−0.049	0.002	0.026	126–149
External conferences	0.127	0.044	0.003	−0.079	−0.094	0.011	0.015	127–148
External publications	0.044	−0.108	−0.194**	−0.122	−0.058	0.015	−0.058	128–152
Internet and external databases	−0.003	−0.103	−0.193**	−0.033	−0.091	0.148*	−0.020	126–149
Patents	0.122	0.042	−0.085	0.065	0.089	0.026	0.043	124–147

*significant at 0.1 level.
**significant at 0.05 level.
***significant at 0.01 level.

the internationalization and performance of technology acquisition is statistically confirmed with regard to *internal* sources of technology. At the same time, the correlation between the internationalization of *external* technological sources and performance indicators is generally very weak and significant in only very few cases. This finding suggests that there is no clear impact between the internationalization of external technology and technology acquisition performance.

3.3   Discussion

The results of the survey of German and Japanese high-tech business units indicate strong country-specific differences in the international organization of R&D. First, the internationalization of R&D (and specifically of technology acquisition) in German business units is much higher than that of Japanese business firms. Second, most German business units have applied a horizontal division of labour between their home country sites and host country sites in Europe and North America. In contrast, the international R&D organization in the Japanese business units is centred much more around the home country sites, which are supported by host country sites with functionally limited tasks such as research or product development.

These findings are reflected in the results of the questionnaire which was conducted on the level of each technological field at the home country sites of the business units. The survey revealed that the main difference between the German and Japanese business units lies in the internationalization of internal technological sources, whereas the internationalization of external sources of technology is (with the exception of research institutions) quite high in both countries. This suggests that under both types of organizational structure, a certain degree of access to international sources of external technology has been achieved. A possible explanation is that host country R&D sites in both German and Japanese business units also function as listening posts in fostering access to external knowledge.

Most German R&D managers, however, have access to both domestic and international sources of internal technology, whereas the majority of the Japanese managers rely exclusively on domestic sources. This result is remarkable considering the predominant organizational patterns of business units in the two countries. Since host country R&D sites of Japanese business units have limited functional tasks, they might be expected to interact more strongly with home country sites rather than the vertically integrated host country sites of German business units. Despite the horizontal division of labour between home country and host country sites established in their business units, German R&D managers have stronger links to their host country business unit sites than their Japanese counterparts do. This suggests that with an organizational structure based on the horizontal division of labour between the different sites, more technological knowledge is absorbed by the home country site than under an ethnocentric organizational structure with host country sites that only fulfil functionally limited tasks.

Furthermore, the findings suggest that stronger absorption of technological knowledge from host country R&D sites, at least from a home country perspective, results in improved technology acquisition performance. This means that compared to the organizational structure chosen by Japanese business units, the organization of international R&D established by German R&D units results in superior competitive performance in the field of technology acquisition.

The matter of path dependency must also be taken into consideration. German manufacturing firms have a track record of strong internationalization in the field of R&D, at least from the 1980s onwards (Brockhoff 1990). In contrast, Japanese business firms are regarded as latecomers to internationalization, particularly in the field of R&D (Pearce and Papanastassiou 1996). Therefore, the difference observed in business units from both countries concerning internationalization of technology acquisition is not just a result of the current firm management, but also of previous history.

From an industry-specific perspective, the higher level of internationalization of technology acquisition in the pharmaceutical industry as distinct from the semiconductor industry can be explained by the relative explicitness of technological knowledge in the pharmaceutical industry, in contrast to the more tacit, implicit knowledge in the semiconductor industry (von Hippel 1994). Since explicit, codified knowledge is easier to transfer than implicit knowledge, a greater organizational and geographical dispersion of technology acquisition might be more feasible in the pharmaceutical industry than in the semiconductor industry. This tendency could be reinforced by the supposedly higher level of continuity in the entire R&D process in the semiconductor industry than in the pharmaceutical industry. It can be expected that discontinuous operations are easier to divide between different organizational units and locations than continuous operations.

It should be mentioned that the empirical research discussed in this chapter has a number of limitations. First of all, only two countries and industries were covered, and therefore, the applicability of results to firms from other countries and industries cannot be assumed automatically.

Second, the results derived from questionnaires and interviews exclusively reflect the assessments of R&D managers based in their home countries; they do not reflect the viewpoint of host country R&D sites. This lies in the design of the research which focused on the perspective of home country R&D sites.

Another aspect possibly limiting the significance of the empirical results stems from the methodological approach of collecting numerous questionnaire responses from each business unit surveyed. Although the project partners in the business units were asked explicitly to assign each questionnaire to an R&D manager responsible for a separate technological field, we cannot exclude the possibility that some responses came from R&D managers with overlapping fields of responsibility, and therefore the underlying assumption that each questionnaire stands for a totally separate area of technology acquisition within each business unit may not be true in all cases.

4   Implications

Finally, some implications of the survey results for research and management in the field of international organization of R&D activities are briefly drawn.

Regarding the first issue, the survey results discussed here reveal some aspects worth considering in future research on this topic: notably, the explicit performance measurement increases the normative value of the findings. The application of multiple methods also contributed to the overall understanding of the results. Furthermore, it appears promising to include firms operating in different countries and industries in order to verify the applicability of the findings in different contexts.

As discussed above, notwithstanding the detailed and multi-method-based approach of the empirical survey, many issues remain open. This adds to the need for more empirical research on the international organization of R&D in business firms.

From the point of view of R&D managers, the results of the empirical research suggest that, at least for large multinational firms operating in high-tech industries, internationalizing technology acquisition appears to be a promising method of improving competitiveness in this field. Notably, however, the organizational mode of this internationalization matters also. An international organization of vertically integrated R&D units based on a horizontal division of labour appears to lead to better results in terms of competitive performance than an ethnocentric organization with vertically specialized host country R&D units.

Finally, it should be noted that, due to contextual barriers, the successful implementation of such an organizational structure may not be easy to achieve in many cases. In the case of many Japanese firms it could be hampered by the generally low level of internationalization of firm operations. Notwithstanding, an increase in the internationalization of R&D accompanied by the international decentralization of the organizational structure appears an urgent task for Japanese high-tech firms if they are to preserve or resume international competitiveness.

Notes

1 In German R&D surveys, industries with an R&D intensity of over 8.5 per cent are defined as high-tech (BMBF 2000).
2 According to Brockhoff (1999, 48), R&D is the combination of productive factors to enable the acquisition of knowledge.
3 Due to internal circumstances, one Japanese semiconductor business unit limited its participation to the first two parts of the survey.

References

Bartlett, C. A. and Goshal, S. (1998), *Managing Across Borders, The Transnational Solution*, 2nd edn (Boston, MA: Harvard Business School Press).

BMBF (2000), *Zur technologischen Leistungsfähigkeit Deutschlands, Zusammenfassender Endbericht 1999* (BMBF: Bonn).

Brockhoff, K. (1990), *Stärken und Schwächen industrieller Forschung und Entwicklung, Umfrageergebnisse aus der Bundesrepublik Deutschland* (Stuttgart: Poeschel).

Brockhoff, K. (1999), *Forschung und Entwicklung, Planung und Kontrolle*, 5th edn (Munich: Oldenbourg).

Brockhoff, K. and Schmaul, B. (1996), 'Organization, Autonomy, and Success of Internationally Dispersed R&D Facilities', *IEEE Transactions on Engineering Management*, 43, 33–40.

Gassmann, O. and von Zedtwitz, M. (1998), 'Organization of Industrial R&D on a Global Scale', *R&D Management*, 28, 147–61.

Gerybadze, A., Meyer-Krahmer, F. and Reger, G. (1997), *Globales Management von Forschung und Innovation* (Stuttgart: Poeschel).

National Science Foundation (2000), *Research and Development in Industry: 1998*, NSF 01–305 (Arlington, VA: National Science Foundation).

OECD (1999), *Globalisation of Industrial R&D: Policy Issues* (Paris: OECD).

Patel, P. (1996), 'Are Large Firms Internationalizing the Generation of Technology: Some New Evidence', *IEEE Transactions on Engineering Management*, 43, 41–7.

Pearce, R. D. and Papanastassiou, M. (1996), *The Technological Competitiveness of Japanese Multinationals: The European Dimension* (Ann Arbor: University of Michigan Press).

Reger, G. (1997), *Koordination und strategisches Management internationaler Innovations-prozesse* (Heidelberg: Physika).

Semiconductor World (1999), *1999-nenpan nihon handôtai nenkan* (*Japanese Semiconductor Yearbook 1999*) (Tokyo: Puresujânaru).

Tsûshô Sangyôshô (2000), *Dai 29-kai 1999-nen kaigai jigyô katsudô kihon chôsa gaiyô* (*Overview of the 29th basic survey of overseas business activities*) (Tokyo: Tsûshô Sangyôshô).

von Hippel, E. (1994), 'Sticky Information and the Locus of Problem Solving: Implications for Innovation', *Management Science*, 40, 429–39.

6

International Trade in Services: A World Trade Organization and Asia-Pacific Economic Cooperation Perspective

Sayeeda Bano

This study examines the nature and growing importance of international trade in services (intangibles) in the world economy, discusses the concept and definition of services drawing upon the literature on this issue, and identifies and measures in detail the size and importance of trade in services of selected countries and regional groups. It examines the relative share of trade in services in the total world trade of selected Asian nations, South Pacific Forum Island economies and OECD countries. The evidence shows that some countries have experienced growth and a reversal in their net service trade. It discusses the goals and strategy for freeing trade in services within the framework of the World Trade Organization (WTO) and APEC nations. Further, using existing theories of trade in goods, such as Hecksher–Ohlin–Samuelson and Linder's demand base model, product differentiation, economies of scale and technological gap models, some of the key determinants of trade in services and sources of comparative advantage are examined. These include the relative levels of development of trading partners, level of trade in goods, degree of product differentiation, human capital, R&D, foreign direct investment, exchange rates, the degree of economic integration and similarity and dissimilarity of culture, religion and languages. Some policy implications are drawn in the context of the changing world economic order, globalization in telecommunication and financial services, and the role of APEC and the WTO in freeing services trade. It is suggested that the research agenda should focus on developing a comprehensive model and databases for estimating the welfare costs and benefits of liberalization of trade in services and for the efficient management of the services sectors in this dynamic world economy.

1   Introduction

There has been a good deal of discussion concerning the role and importance of international trade in services in the development process and as part of the balance of payments. There have, however, been few attempts to develop new databases, theory and empirical analysis to examine such trade and identify its economic determinants.[1] This is probably because, until recently, services trade was assumed to be ancillary to commodity trade rather than a separately identifiable group of commodities.

The post-war period witnessed a major growth in the significance of services. In recent years we have seen the development and rapid growth of the 'service economy' in North America, Western Europe and now in Asia-Pacific nations and newly industrialized countries (NICs). Increased interest in international trade in service has followed from recognition of the importance of the services sector itself, with attention being focused both on the size of the trade in services in national incomes, in total trade and also on the scope for realizing gains from trade in services. There is no doubt about the increasing importance of services in domestic economies as they account for an average of about 70 per cent of OECD nations' GDP. Although a large proportion of services are non-tradable, international trade in services accounts for a large and rapidly growing proportion of world trade. Exports of services constitute an important source of export revenue for many industrialized countries. Trade in services grew faster than trade in merchandise throughout 1980s. In the 1990s, trade in services reached US\$1.2 trillion per year, maintaining about 20 per cent share in world trade (WTO 1996). It is expected that for developed OECD nations such as New Zealand, Australia and the USA, and also the rapidly growing Asian nations, trade in services will grow along with the rapid growth in technological information. One of the important reasons for the rapid growth in services sector is the high-income elasticity of demand for services. As per capita incomes rise people tend to spend a larger proportion of their income on high quality and differentiated goods and services.

Trade in services has received increased attention, in recent years, from economists, the business community and policy makers. One manifestation of this increased interest has been the central role given to services in recent international trade policy negotiations. Liberalization of trade in services was an important feature of the Australia–New Zealand Closer Economic Relations Trade Agreement (ANZCERTA) as well as NAFTA (North America Free Trade Agreement) and it is also an important component of the enlarged EU. United Nations Conference on Trade and Development (UNCTAD) has also entered into a series of negotiations on trade in services to represent the developing countries. The Uruguay Round of General Agreements on Trade and Tariffs (GATT) negotiations acknowledged trade in services as a separate item on its agenda and services were given a prominent place on the international trade policy issues. As a result of all these concerns and negotiations, WTO has now established a set of rules under the New General Agreement on Trade and Services (GATS), which establishes a single set of rules for international trade in services to bring about some kind of effective multilateral discipline.

In order to analyse the growing importance of trade in services in a country's domestic structure and in the international economy, it is important to understand the concept, characteristics and the evolution of determinants of trade in services. A number of questions arise, including these:

1   How does one define a service?
2   How are different services to be classified?
3   Does evidence exist to show that trade in services has grown?
4   Which services have grown or promise to grow most rapidly?
5   What are the sources of comparative advantage in service trade?
6   Can trade theory explain the extent and growth of world trade in services?
7   What kind of policy is needed for fostering and managing world trade in services?

This chapter attempts to address these questions. The plan is as follows: the next section discusses the definition and some facts concerning international trade in services. The following section presents and analyses the available data on trade in services. Then there is a section that offers a brief review of the existing trade theories, followed by a section where the role of WTO and APEC are discussed. Finally, some concluding remarks are presented and some issues are identified for future research and policy.

2   Defining trade in services: some characteristics of goods and services

There has long been a debate amongst economists and practitioners as to the differences between goods and services. An important question arising in any discussion of trade in services is what exactly is traded among nations? There exists no commonly agreed definition of a service activity. International trade in services, like so many other services, consists of a heterogeneous collection of economic activities. Often services were defined as *intangibles*, *invisibles*, perishable, non-storable and non-tradable economic commodities or as a residual category, which included almost everything, whereas goods are *tangible*, visible, tradable and permanent. That goods and services are different is now generally agreed. What is less agreed upon is the various ways in which they differ and to the extent to which these differences are relevant and significance for policy purposes (Bano and Lane 1995).

In everyday language, we make a clear distinction between goods and services. When we refer to services, we tend to think of services rendered to people. Classic examples include Fourastie's much cherished hairdresser, Baumol's singer and Pigou's valet. A more recent use of 'services' (namely, business services) refers to the process of externalizing parts of R&D or management functions. Services are commonly seen as extending to activities such as retailing, banking, insurance and non-market activities linked to public and private administration (*The New Palgrave Dictionary* 1994).

Historically, economists have attempted to define services and their economic roles from different perspectives. For Adam Smith (1776), it is the perishable characteristic of tertiary production which is the real problem: '[they] perish in the very instant of their performance'. This non-material aspect allows for neither storage nor further transaction. Hence, for classical economists, services do not contribute to an increase in the volume of exchange. Services are in this sense unproductive. Simultaneity of the acts of production and consumption nullifies the value of work dispensed: '[services] seldom leave any trace or value behind them' (Smith 1776).[2]

Marx continued this distinction between productive and unproductive labour. However, he placed it in the context of an analysis of the circuit of value in which the worker's labour power, and not his service, determined value. The theoretical concept of unproductive labour was often identified with an evaluation of the social utility of service activities. John Stuart Mill (1848) pointed out that educational and medical provision had a favourable effect upon producers and thus indirectly upon production. The duration of this effect seemed more important to him than the non-material aspect of services (*The New Palgrave Dictionary* 1994).

On a different level, in the national accounts of socialist countries where distinction is made between material and non-material production, services that contribute directly to production (transport, trade, etc.) are classified under activities related to the production of goods, so the distinction advocated by the classical economists does not appear clear-cut. All these propositions are difficult to extend to the case of services (*The New Palgrave Dictionary* 1994).

Some economists argue that goods and services belong in different logical categories and therefore an adequate definition must make a distinction between the process of production and the product of a service. According to Hill (1977), a service represents a transformation of the user (in the case of services to persons) or the user's goods (in the case of services involving goods) as a result of the voluntary intervention by the producer of services. Service utilization therefore does not involve any transferable acquisition but a modification to the characteristics of the agents or their goods. A consequence of this approach is that product and agents are diversified indefinitely. From this viewpoint an operative concept of services has been provided by Hill (1977, 331):

> A service may be defined as a change in the condition of a person, or of a good belonging to some economic unit, which is brought about as the result of the activity of some other economic unit … with the agreement of the former. This definition … is consistent with the underlying idea, which is inherent in the concept of a service; namely that one economic unit performs some activity for the benefit of another … Whatever the producer of the service does must impinge directly on the consumer in such a way as to change the conditions of the latter. Otherwise no service is actually provided.

This distinction between goods and services does not, however, represent a consensus view.[3] It seems to provide some characteristics of services. In the absence of a commonly accepted working definition, the next best approach to characterizing the service industry has led to a direct classification and categorization of the various activities and professions encompassed.

Data classification is a serious problem and there are a number of suggested methods. For example, UNCTAD and OECD studies suggest that there should be five broad categories: financial, information/communication, professional, tourism/travel and social services. The most important source of data for measuring the intensity of trade in services is the balance of payments statistics of a country. A country's total earnings from 'invisibles' are recorded as exports of services (credit) and total 'invisible' payments as a measure of imports of services recorded as (debit). The International Monetary Fund's (IMF's) *Balance of Payments Statistics Yearbook*, Parts 1 and 2, broadly classified services into five categories: shipments, other transportation, travel, other private services, and other official or government services. The IMF has recently added two sub-divisions (passenger services and other services) into the broad classification. This is the classification which has been used for most empirical research: for example, Sapir and Lutz (1980, 1981) and Bano and Lane (1995).

The secretariat of the WTO has divided service activities into the following 12 sectors:

- business (including professional and computer) services
- communication services
- construction and engineering services
- distribution services
- educational services
- environmental services
- financial (insurance and banking) services
- health services
- tourism and travel services
- recreational, cultural and sporting services
- transport services
- other services not included elsewhere

These 12 sectors have been further divided into 155 sub-sectors.

2.1   Four modes of transactions

The different characteristics of goods and services influence the modes in which international transactions take place. While international trade in goods involves the physical movement of goods from one country to another, only a few service transactions entail cross-border movements. Examples of cross-border transactions are services that can be transmitted by telecommunications (e.g., transfer of money through banks) or services embodied in goods (e.g., a consultant's technical report or software on a diskette). In the bulk of service transactions, however, their time and place of consumption cannot be separated, and proximity between the service supplier and the consumer is required. Such proximity can be established through a commercial presence in the importing country (for instance, by setting up a branch of subsidiary company) or the movement of natural persons for temporary periods (e.g., lawyers or architects moving to another country to provide their services). The nature of a few service transactions requires consumers to move to the country where the services are available (e.g., tourists visiting countries of tourist interest or students going to another country for higher education).

Thus, unlike international transactions in goods which require a physical transit across a country's borders, services are supplied internationally according to one or a combination of four modes of supply: (1) cross-border movement of service products; (2) movement of consumers to the country of importation; (3) the establishment of a commercial presence in the country where the service is to be provided; and (4) the temporary movement of natural persons to another country, in order to provide the services in foreign countries.

The total value of services traded through the last two modes is probably much greater than that of the trade in services taking place through the first two modes. However, the lack of statistics makes any concrete estimate difficult.

2.2   The GATS Agreement: WTO

Prior to the Uruguay Round, trade in services was not subject to any discipline at the international level. The GATS, which was negotiated in the Uruguay Round, takes a first major step towards bringing the trade in services gradually under international discipline. The GATS consists of a framework which sets out the general concepts, principles and rules that apply to measures affecting trade in services. Among the important general obligations imposed by the framework text are those relating to:

- transparency of regulations
- rules governing monopolies and exclusive service and other business practices restraining competition
- measures to be taken to liberalize trade, including those securing the greater participation of developing countries
- specific commitments for liberalizing trade within the service sectors and sub-sectors listed in the national schedules of member countries

The objectives of the GATS are similar to those of GATT. It aims to promote the economic growth of all trading partners and to develop developing countries through the expansion of trade in services. It seeks to achieve this by applying to the service trade the rules of GATT, with the modifications necessary to take into account its special features. The GATS applies to government measures affecting services provided on a commercial basis. It thus covers both private-sector enterprises and companies owned (or controlled) by governments if they supply services on a commercial basis. Services obtained by government departments and agencies for their own use are excluded from the purview of the Agreement. The term 'services' covers any service in any service sector, including their production, distribution, marketing, sales and delivery according to the four modes described above.

The obligations, which the framework imposes, can be broadly divided into two categories.

These are: (1) general obligations, which apply to all service sectors; (2) conditional obligations applicable to sectors covered by commitments specified in the national schedules (WTO 1996; APEC 1999).

2.3   WTO and APEC: liberalization of trade in goods and services

Asia-Pacific Economic Cooperation (APEC) was formed in November 1989 in Canberra, in response to the growing interdependence among Asia-Pacific economies. It began as an informal dialogue group with limited participation. The main aim was to participate collectively in the debate for fostering trade liberalization in the Uruguay Round of the GATT negotiations.

The objectives of APEC as expressed in the Seoul Declaration of 1991 are as follows:

- to sustain the growth and development of the region for the common good of its people, and contribute to the growth and development of the world economy
- to enhance the positive gains, both for the region and the economy, resulting from increasing economic integration and interdependence, including encouraging the flow of goods, services, capital and technology
- to develop and strengthen the open multilateral trading system in the interests of Asia-Pacific and all other economies
- to reduce barriers to trade in goods and services and investments, among participants, in a manner consistent with GATT principles, without detriment to other economies

The Declaration also specified that APEC was to encourage private sector participation in APEC activities in order to maximize welfare effects of regional cooperation. APEC supports open regionalism to encourage trade liberalization throughout the world economy. APEC ministers of foreign affairs and ministers of economic affairs meet annually. These meetings are hosted by the APEC chair, which rotates each year.

In the APEC Leader's Meeting hosted by New Zealand in September 1999, the objectives of New Zealand's 'Individual Action Plan' concerning trade in services are two-fold: (1) progressively reducing restrictions on market access for trade in services and (2) progressively providing for most-favoured nation (MFN) and national treatment for trade in services. Various other measures have been committed to further foster telecommunication, education, banking and financial and transport services.

APEC is experiencing the most striking economic growth in the world. It is a major contributor to global prosperity and stability. APEC includes all the major economies of the region and the most dynamic, fastest growing economies in the world. APEC's members account for 46 per cent of the world's total merchandise trade, 38 per cent of world population and about half the world's total annual output. (India is not a member yet.) The fact that half of the world's trade is within these countries clearly reveals the importance of APEC in the promotion of world trade. Moreover, APEC is willing to offer trade relationships to non-members on the basis of reciprocity.

The common goal is to advance Asia-Pacific economic dynamism and to create a zone of free trade and of unrestricted investment by the year 2020 to all nations. Since its creation in 1989, APEC has taken the position that it should build on the principle of a fair, free and open multilateral trading system. The main goal is full and effective implementation of the Uruguay Round outcomes within the agreed time, in a manner consistent with the spirit of the WTO Agreement.

At the 1998 APEC Leaders' Meeting in Kuala Lumpur, the importance of services was recognized. It was noted that 'Knowledge-based industries and tourism have considerable potential to contribute to growth and development in the next (present) century' and there was also a 'need for efforts to maximize the contribution of these sectors'. Korea proposed a new initiative to promote better understanding of the concept of knowledge-based industries and current status and best practice of knowledge-based industries. Korea hosted an expert seminar in June 1999 on the topic of promoting knowledge-based industries in the region which was similar to the workshop on 'Intangibles and Competition/Cooperation Strategy' in New Delhi in December 1999, to promote debate and stimulate research on this area. New Zealand is taking the initiative to promote a knowledge-based economy in this millennium. Much needs to be done. It appears that the common goals and strategy of APEC nations, to foster trade in goods and services and investment through effective regional and multilateral negotiations, are steps in a positive direction. The WTO, and other regional groupings such as NAFTA, EU and CER (Closer Economic Relations), have set up their own strategies for freeing international trade in goods and services.

3   The significance of trade in services

How important is the trade in services in the context the world economy, OECD nations, Asian nations and the developing countries? Which sectors of trade in services are important in absolute terms and in relation to merchandise trade? What is the performance of different categories of services in relation to total trade and as a proportion of total service trade of selected countries? These questions are explained with the help of Tables 6.1–8 and Figures 6.1–4). Table 6.1 reports the data of trade in goods and services for selected years 1970–99. It shows that the total value of exports of services (credit) amounted to US$1,325.7 billion and the total value of imports was US$1,450.2 billion in 1999. The discrepancy of US$124.5 billion (about 8.5 per cent) is statistically high, and relatively very large when compared to the commodity trade discrepancy of only US$44.3 billion (credit, 0.8 per cent). The statistically high discrepancy may suggest that data compilation, recording, aggregation processing and reporting is less reliable for trade in services than for trade in goods. It is also noted that the value of service exports was US$99.47 billion (credit) and the total value of world imports of services (debit) was US$106.43 billion in 1970. The discrepancy was only US$7 billion in services trade (debit) and US$7.5 billion (credit) for the goods trade. It also shows that world trade in goods was in surplus but there was a deficit in service trade for many years. World trade surpluses seem to finance world service trade deficits. Total world trade in goods and services amounted to US$13,920.2 billion in 1999. The data from 1974 to 1986 include other goods and income, so these are not comparable. Data from 1970 to 1973 and 1987 to 1999 are consistent for analysis. These data show that from 1970 to 1973 and from 1987 to 1999 there has been considerable growth in both trade in goods and services. Figure 6.1 shows trade in services increased in every year except in 1987 when there was minor fall. Total trade increased every year except in 1983 when there was a marginal decrease. Total services trade as a percentage of total trade for the sample averaged 25 per cent over the entire period. This percentage fell in 1972–74, 1987–88 and 1994–99, and increased in all the other periods.

Tables 6.2–4 show the absolute value of trade in goods and services by different country and by region as well as its distribution by type of service in 1999 (1996 data in appendix). It can be seen that the USA, Japan and Italy had trade deficits but experienced surpluses in services trade. It also shows that Denmark, France and the Netherlands had surpluses in both trade and services. Most of the other countries had to pay

Table 6.1 World trade in goods and services over time, 1970–99 (in US$ billions)

Year	Xg	Mg	Xg + Mg	Xs	Ms	Xs + Ms	Xg + Xs	Mg + Ms	Xg − Mg	Xs − Ms	Xg − Xs	Mg − Ms	(Xg + Mg) + (Xs + Ms)	(Xg + Mg) − (Xs + Ms)
1970	270.51	262.99	533.50	99.47	106.43	205.90	369.98	369.42	7.52	−6.96	171.04	156.56	739.40	327.60
1971	301.71	292.51	594.22	113.83	118.46	232.29	415.54	410.97	9.20	−4.63	187.88	174.05	826.51	361.93
1972	331.81	319.51	651.32	122.02	126.32	248.34	453.83	445.83	12.30	−4.30	209.79	193.19	899.66	402.98
1973	411.20	394.31	805.51	146.06	150.82	296.88	557.26	545.13	16.89	−4.76	265.14	243.49	1,102.39	508.63
1974	588.92	575.89	1,164.81	183.26	190.83	374.09	772.18	766.72	13.03	−7.57	405.66	385.06	1,538.90	790.72
1975	601.00	588.09	1,189.09	196.33	211.75	408.08	797.33	799.84	12.91	−15.42	404.67	376.34	1,597.17	781.01
1976	716.48	705.94	1,422.42	226.28	243.35	469.63	942.76	949.29	10.54	−17.07	490.20	462.59	1,892.05	952.79
1977	808.30	796.29	1,604.59	258.60	278.12	536.72	1,066.90	1,074.41	12.01	−19.52	549.70	518.17	2,141.31	1,067.87
1978	883.96	856.20	1,740.16	300.12	315.24	615.36	1,184.08	1,171.44	27.76	−15.12	583.84	540.96	2,355.52	1,124.80
1979	1,158.30	1,142.20	2,300.50	401.62	424.82	826.44	1,559.92	1,567.02	16.10	−23.20	756.68	717.38	3,126.94	1,474.06
1980	1,405.20	1,381.90	2,787.10	493.27	531.06	1,024.33	1,898.47	1,912.96	23.30	−37.79	911.93	850.84	3,811.43	1,762.77
1981	1,539.70	1,521.50	3,061.20	592.07	658.34	1,250.41	2,131.77	2,179.84	18.20	−66.27	947.63	863.16	4,311.61	1,810.79
1982	1,513.90	1,517.30	3,031.20	623.78	715.31	1,339.09	2,137.68	2,232.61	−3.40	−91.53	890.12	801.99	4,370.29	1,692.11
1983	1,521.30	1,515.20	3,036.50	607.43	683.29	1,290.72	2,128.73	2,198.49	6.10	−75.86	913.87	831.91	4,327.22	1,745.78
1984	1,777.10	1,764.10	3,541.20	751.86	834.64	1,586.50	2,528.96	2,598.74	13.00	−82.78	1,025.24	929.46	5,127.70	1,954.70
1985	1,789.80	1,779.80	3,569.60	762.72	849.53	1,612.25	2,552.52	2,629.33	10.00	−86.81	1,027.08	930.27	5,181.85	1,957.35
1986	1,955.40	1,948.30	3,903.70	870.92	931.62	1,802.54	2,826.32	2,879.92	7.10	−60.70	1,084.48	1,016.68	5,706.24	2,101.16
1987	2,303.00	2,281.30	4,584.30	557.17	571.73	1,128.90	2,860.17	2,853.03	21.70	−14.56	1,745.83	1,709.57	5,713.20	3,455.40
1988	2,645.50	2,612.60	5,258.10	618.05	643.32	1,261.37	3,263.55	3,255.92	32.90	−25.27	2,027.45	1,969.28	6,519.47	3,996.73
1989	2,855.70	2,839.70	5,695.40	676.39	706.31	1,382.70	3,532.09	3,546.01	16.00	−29.92	2,179.31	2,133.39	7,078.10	4,312.70

1990	3,263.30	3,243.50	6,506.80	818.35	853.20	1,671.55	4,081.65	4,096.70	19.80	−34.85	2,444.95	2,390.30	8,178.35	4,835.25
1991	3,347.80	3,319.30	6,667.10	855.81	894.89	1,750.70	4,203.61	4,214.19	28.50	−39.08	2,491.99	2,424.41	8,417.80	4,916.40
1992	3,585.50	3,553.20	7,138.70	959.88	992.22	1,952.10	4,545.38	4,545.42	32.30	−32.34	2,625.62	2,560.98	9,090.80	5,186.60
1993	3,730.50	3,663.40	7,393.90	919.10	984.00	1,903.10	4,649.60	4,647.40	67.10	−64.90	2,811.40	2,679.40	9,297.00	5,490.80
1994	4,232.60	4,135.10	8,367.70	922.30	993.10	1,915.40	5,154.90	5,128.20	97.50	−70.80	3,310.30	3,142.00	10,283.10	6,452.30
1995	5,086.60	4,969.50	10,056.10	1,110.60	1,189.70	2,300.30	6,197.20	6,159.20	117.10	−79.10	3,976.00	3,779.80	12,356.40	7,755.80
1996	5,335.60	5,234.90	10,570.50	1,175.30	1,251.00	2,426.30	6,510.90	6,485.90	100.70	−75.70	4,160.30	3,983.90	12,996.80	8,144.20
1997	5,543.50	5,423.20	10,966.70	1,234.40	1,296.80	2,531.20	6,777.90	6,720.00	120.30	−62.40	4,309.10	4,126.40	13,497.90	8,435.50
1998	5,429.40	5,350.60	10,780.00	1,319.40	1,415.90	2,735.30	6,748.80	6,766.50	78.80	−96.50	4,110.00	3,934.70	13,515.30	8,044.70
1999	5,594.30	5,550.00	11,144.30	1,325.70	1,450.20	2,775.90	6,920.00	7,000.20	44.30	−124.50	4,268.60	4,099.80	13,920.20	8,368.40

Xg   Exports of Goods
Mg   Imports of Goods
Xs   Export of Services
Ms   Import of Services

Notes

1 In SDRs until 1983, then in US dollars.
2 Services Statistics from 'Services' category 1970–73 and 1987–99, and from 'Other Goods, Services and Income' in 1974–86.
3 Figures from 1993 to 1999 updated.

Source: IMF, *Balance of Payments Statistics Yearbook*, Part 2, various issues (1973–2000).

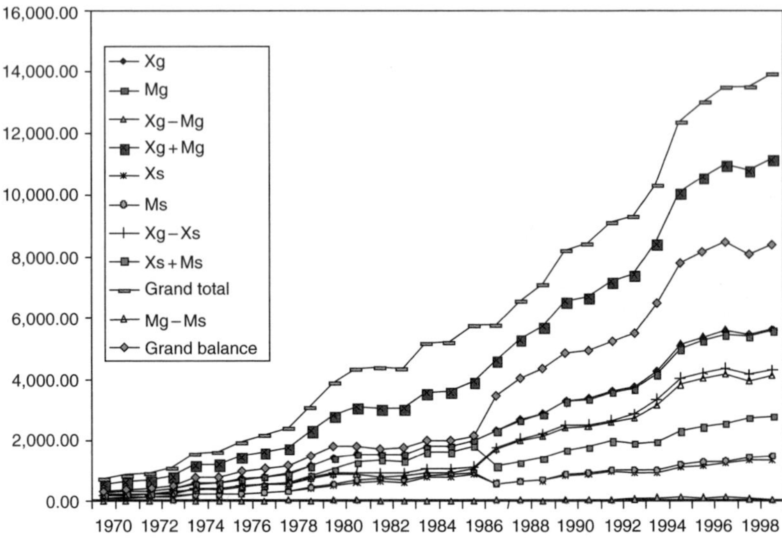

Figure 6.1   World trade in goods and services over time, 1970–99

more for their import of services than they received in export revenue from services trade. Tables 6.5–7 illustrate the geographical and regional distribution of world trade in goods and services and the contribution of each service category in relation to regions and trade areas. In 1999, total world trade was US$13,924.7 billion and total service trade was US$2,780.4 billion (about 20 per cent). In 1996 total world trade was US$13,138.8 billion. Developing countries' share in total world trade was about 33 per cent, Asia's share about 18 per cent, the Middle East only 3 per cent and the Western hemisphere's share about 5 per cent.

All the countries had positive growth in total trade from 1992 to 1999, except the Middle East, which had high negative growth in 1995 but then experienced marginal growth (about 0.8 per cent) between 1996 and 1999, while developing countries experienced marginal negative growth. Though the Western hemisphere had its lowest growth in 1995, it had a relatively high growth rate in 1996 and achieved its highest positive growth in 1999 at about 15 per cent. Europe had about 3.5 per cent growth over the 1996–99 period. The world as whole experienced about 5.5 per cent positive growth during 1996–99. Trade in services as a percentage of total trade for the sample averaged 20 per cent with a marginal variation. The world and the Western hemisphere had different experiences with varying degrees of positive and negative

Table 6.2 International trade in goods and services by country, 1999 (in US$ millions)

Country	Xg	Mg	Xg + Mg	Xs	Ms	Xs + Ms	Xg + Xs	Mg + Ms	(Xg + Mg) + (Xs + Ms)
USA	686,663	1,029,921	1,716,584	269,581	191,297	460,878	956,244	1,221,218	2,177,462
Canada	242,820	220,064	462,884	34,854	38,921	73,775	277,674	258,985	536,659
Australia	56,048	65,828	121,876	17,356	18,395	35,751	73,404	84,223	157,627
Japan	403,694	280,369	684,063	60,998	115,158	176,156	464,692	395,527	860,219
New Zealand	12,618	13,028	25,646	4,308	4,569	8,877	16,926	17,597	34,523
Austria	64,422	68,072	132,494	30,498	27,829	58,327	94,920	95,901	190,821
Belgium/Lux.	162,439	157,659	320,098	22,570	45,672	68,242	185,009	203,331	388,340
Denmark	49,548	43,011	92,559	15,823	15,201	31,024	65,371	58,212	123,583
Finland	41,983	30,328	72,311	6,646	7,682	14,328	48,629	38,010	86,639
France	298,148	278,083	576,231	83,343	64,260	147,603	381,491	342,343	723,834
Germany	542,960	470,961	1,013,921	83,065	134,337	217,402	626,025	605,298	1,231,323
Greece	NA	NA	NA	NA	NA	NA	NA	NA	NA
Iceland	2,009	2,316	4,325	968	1,044	2,012	2,977	3,360	6,337
Ireland	66,989	42,811	109,800	14,683	26,076	40,759	81,672	68,887	150,559
Italy	230,831	210,445	441,276	61,476	58,669	120,145	292,307	269,114	561,421
Netherlands	195,076	177,122	372,198	53,668	49,547	103,215	248,744	226,669	475,413
Norway	NA	NA	NA	NA	NA	NA	NA	NA	NA
Portugal	25,673	39,830	65,503	8,373	6,782	15,155	34,046	46,612	80,658
Spain	111,005	140,213	251,218	53,350	30,427	83,777	164,355	170,640	334,995
Sweden	87,568	71,854	159,422	19,904	22,617	42,521	107,472	94,471	201,943
Switzerland	91,733	91,009	182,742	27,253	15,858	43,111	118,986	106,867	225,853
UK	268,080	311,393	579,473	103,465	84,782	188,247	371,545	396,175	767,720

Xg Exports of Goods
Mg Imports of Goods
Xs Exports of Services
NA Not Available
Ms Imports of Services
Xg + Xs Total Exports of Good and Services
Mg + Ms Total Imports of Goods and Services

Source: IMF, *Balance of Payments Statistics Yearbook*, Part 2 (2000).

Table 6.3 Categories of trade in services by country, 1999 (in US$ millions)

Country	TOTM Xs + Mg Total	TOTS Xs + Ms Total	TOT X + M Total	SH X + M Total	TR X + M Total	OTR X + M Total	PRTRAV X + M Total	GOV X + M Total	OS X + M Total	PS X + M Total
USA	1,716,584	460,878	2,177,462	33,883	102,355	27,290	150,772	36,972	170,779	41,182
Canada	462,884	73,775	536,659	7,954	14,447	2,172	21,525	1,145	36,658	4,321
Australia	121,876	35,751	157,627	3,835	10,350	558	14,061	752	10,588	5,957
Japan	684,063	176,156	860,219	30,948	53,571	11,897	36,203	1,671	84,712	10,725
New Zealand	25,646	8,877	34,523	NA	2,787	NA	3,690	131	2,267	NA
Austria	132,494	58,327	190,821	3,863	7,214	1,038	20,171	543	30,399	2,313
Belgium/Lux.	320,098	68,242	388,340	12,439	19,126	2,027	20,049	1,975	57,092	2,695
Denmark	92,559	31,024	123,583	NA	13,317	NA	8,461	NA	9,245	NA
Finland	72,311	14,328	86,639	2,031	3,938	703	3,555	192	6,642	1,204
France	576,231	147,603	723,834	NA	39,575	NA	50,004	1,907	56,116	NA
Germany	1,013,921	217,402	1,231,323	21,571	44,428	10,302	65,061	5,297	102,617	12,544
Greece	NA	NA	NA	NA	NA	NA	NA	NA	NA	NA
Iceland	4,325	2,012	6,337	107	776	510	656	121	459	159
Ireland	109,800	40,759	150,559	NA	3,755	NA	5,016	294	31,694	NA
Italy	441,276	120,145	561,421	NA	NA	NA	NA	NA	NA	NA

Netherlands	372,198	103,215	475,413	20,175	36,047	5,615	17,676	2,335	47,158	10,258
Norway	NA	NA	NA	NA	NA	NA	NA	NA	NA	NA
Portugal	65,503	15,155	80,658	1,808	3,487	399	7,372	357	3,940	1,279
Spain	251,218	83,777	334,995	7,195	15,263	3,566	37,877	779	29,858	4,502
Sweden	159,422	42,521	201,943	4,448	7,993	1,829	12,154	318	22,057	1,716
Switzerland	182,742	43,111	225,853	2,477	6,653	NA	14,683	1,056	20,719	4,176
UK	579,473	188,247	767,720	12,866	41,188	12,028	59,645	5,644	81,770	16,294

TOTM	Total Merchandise Trade	SH	Shipping	PRTRAV	Private Travel	PS	Passenger Services
TOTS	Total Services Trade	TR	Transport	GOV	Government Services	NA	Data Not Available
TOT	Total Trade, Total Merchandise Trade and Total Services Trade	OTR	Other Transport	OS	Other Services		

Notes

1 The seven categories of trade in service do not sum to equal the TOTS values published in the IMF, *Balance of Payments Statistics Yearbook* figures,
2 Part 2, 2000. The TOTS values expressed above are the IMF Yearbook figures
3 The calculation of proportions SH%, TR%, OTR%, PRTRAV%, GOV%, OS% and PS% used the sum of the seven categories of trade in services as the denominator. This method was used to ensure that SH%, TR%, OTR%, PRTRAV%, GOV%, OS% and PS% summed to 100%, which would not have been the case if TOTS was used as the denominator.

Source: IMF, *Balance of Payments Statistics Yearbook*, Part 2 (2000).

Table 6.4 Categories of trade as a proportion of total trade and trade in services by country, 1999 (TOTM and TOTS in US$ millions)

Country	TOT X + M Total	TOTM X + M Total	TOTS X + M Total	Services %	SH %	TR %	OTR %	PRTRAV %	GOV %	OS %	PS %
USA	2,177,462	1,716,584	460,878	21.17	6.02	18.17	4.85	26.77	6.56	30.32	7.31
Canada	536,659	462,884	73,775	13.75	9.02	16.38	2.46	24.40	1.30	41.55	4.90
Australia	157,627	121,876	35,751	22.68	8.32	22.45	1.21	30.50	1.63	22.97	12.92
Japan	860,219	684,063	176,156	20.48	13.47	23.32	5.18	15.76	0.73	36.88	4.67
New Zealand	34,523	25,646	8,877	25.71	NA	31.40	NA	41.58	1.48	25.54	NA
Austria	190,821	132,494	58,327	30.57	5.89	11.01	1.58	30.78	0.83	46.38	3.53
Belgium/Lux.	388,340	320,098	68,242	17.57	10.78	16.57	1.76	17.37	1.71	49.47	2.34
Denmark	123,583	92,559	31,024	25.10	NA	42.93	NA	27.27	NA	29.80	NA
Finland	86,639	72,311	14,328	16.54	11.12	21.56	3.85	19.46	1.05	36.36	6.59
France	723,834	576,231	147,603	20.39	NA	26.81	NA	33.88	1.29	38.02	NA
Germany	1,231,323	1,013,921	217,402	17.66	8.24	16.97	3.93	24.85	2.02	39.19	4.79
Greece	NA	NA	NA	NA	NA	NA	NA	NA	NA	NA	NA
Iceland	6,337	4,325	2,012	31.75	3.84	27.83	18.29	23.53	4.34	16.46	5.70
Ireland	150,559	109,800	40,759	27.07	NA	9.21	NA	12.31	0.72	77.76	NA
Italy	561,421	441,276	120,145	21.40	NA	NA	NA	NA	NA	NA	NA
Netherlands	475,413	372,198	103,215	21.71	14.49	25.88	4.03	12.69	1.68	33.86	7.37
Norway	NA	NA	NA	NA	NA	NA	NA	NA	NA	NA	NA
Portugal	80,658	65,503	15,155	18.79	9.70	18.71	2.14	39.55	1.92	21.14	6.86
Spain	334,995	251,218	83,777	25.01	7.26	15.41	3.60	38.24	0.79	30.15	4.55
Sweden	201,943	159,422	42,521	21.06	8.81	15.82	3.62	24.06	0.63	43.66	3.40
Switzerland	225,853	182,742	43,111	19.09	4.98	13.37	NA	29.51	2.12	41.63	8.39
UK	767,720	579,473	188,247	24.52	5.61	17.95	5.24	26.00	2.46	35.64	7.10

TOT	Total Trade, Total Merchandise Trade and Total Service Trade	SH	Shipping	PRTRAV	Private Travel	PS	Passenger Services
TOTM	Total Merchandise Trade	TR	Transport	GOV	Government Services	NA	Not Available
TOTS	Total Services Trade	OTR	Other Transport	OS	Other Services

Source: IMF, *Balance of Payments Statistics Yearbook*, Part 2 (2000)

Table 6.5 International trade by regions/areas, 1999 (in US$ millions)

Region/area	Xg	Mg	Xg + Mg	Xs	Ms	Xs + Ms	(Xg + Mg) + (Xs + Ms)
World	5,594,300	5,550,000	11,144,300	1,382,500	1,397,900	2,780,400	13,924,700
Developing Countries	1,910,600	1,758,000	3,668,600	366,711	417,024	783,735	4,452,335
Asia	1,049,937	913,317	1,963,254	184,808	202,067	386,875	2,350,129
Middle East	184,189	153,897	338,086	33,563	59,991	93,554	431,640
Western Hemisphere	306,545	317,795	624,340	53,599	65,118	118,717	743,057
Europe	262,624	272,916	535,540	72,654	58,434	131,088	666,628

Xg   Exports of Goods
Mg   Imports of Goods
Xs   Export of Services
Ms   Imports of Services

Notes: 'World', 'Developing Countries', 'Asia', 'Middle East' and 'Western Hemisphere' regions are those defined in IMF, *Balance of Payments Statistics Yearbook*, Part 2 (2000).

Source: IMF, *Balance of Payments Statistics Yearbook*, Part 2 (2000).

Table 6.6 Categories of trade in services by country, 1999 (in US$ millions)

Region/area	TOTM Xg + Mg Total	TOTS Xs + Ms Total	TOT TOTM + TOTS Total	SH X + M Total	TR X + M Total	OTR X + M Total	PRTRAV X + M Total	GOV X + M Total	OS X + M Total	PS X + M Total
World	1,114,430	2,780,400	13,924,700	324,731	670,267	181,985	835,014	103,887	1,171,228	163,552
Developing Countries	3,668,600	783,735	4,452,335	124,592	207,530	53,757	233,290	35,954	306,959	29,182
Asia	1,963,254	386,875	2,350,129	68,966	105,045	24,691	105,890	6,799	169,143	11,389
Middle East	338,086	93,554	431,640	14,694	22,505	4,386	18,129	17,876	35,045	3,424
Western Hemisphere	624,340·	118,717	743,057	12,913	30,056	9,877	46,587	4,260	37,813	7,266
Europe	535,540	131,088	666,628	17,846	33,329	12,314	46,149	2,193	49,419	3,168
Oil Exporting Countries										
Non-Oil Exporting Countries										

TOT	Total Trade, Total Merchandise Trade and Total Services Trade	OTR	Other Transport
TOTM	Total Merchandise Trade	PRTRAV	Private Travel
TOTS	Total Services Trade	GOV	Government Services
SH	Shipping	OS	Other Services
TR	Transport	PS	Passenger Services

Notes: 'World', 'Developing Countries', 'Asia', 'Middle East', and 'Western Hemisphere' regions are those defined in IMF, *Balance of Payments Statistics Yearbook*, Part 2 (2000). The seven categories of trade do not sum to equal the TOTS values published in IMF, *Balance of Payments Statistics Yearbook*, Part 2 (2000). The TOTS values expressed above are the *IMF Yearbook* figures.

Source: IMF, *Balance of Payments Statistics Yearbook*, Part 2 (2000).

Table 6.7 Categories of trade in services as a proportion of total trade and trade in services by trade areas, 1999

Trade area	TOTM Xg + Mg Total	TOTS Xs + Ms Total	TOTM + TOTS (TOT) X + M Total	Services %	SH %	TR %	OTR %	PRTRAV %	GOV %	OS %	PS %
FTA	2,179,468	534,653	2,714,121	19.70	8.69	24.27	6.12	0.45	7.92	43.10	9.45
CER	147,522	44,628	192,150	23.23	6.98	23.90	1.01	32.29	1.61	23.38	10.84
EEC	3,430,864	890,897	4,321,761	20.61	5.92	19.09	3.00	26.86	1.72	39.45	3.95
EFTA	551,294	160,299	711,593	22.53	6.92	14.22	2.18	27.41	1.19	42.96	5.12
EEA	3,982,158	1,051,196	5,033,354	20.88	6.87	20.20	3.74	19.48	3.45	40.37	5.90
OECD	7,475,700,000	1,985,897	7,477,685,897	20.73	7.50	19.32	3.62	24.86	2.79	36.43	5.47
Average OECD	339,804,545.45	90,268.05	339,894,813.5	20.73	7.50	19.32	3.62	24.86	2.79	36.43	5.47

TOT	Total Trade, Total Merchandise Trade and Total Services Trade	
TOTM	Total Merchandise Trade	
TOTS	Total Services Trade	
TR	Transport	
FTA	Free Trade Area (Canada/USA)	
CER	Closer Economic Relations (Australia/New Zealand)	
EEC	European Economic Community (Belgium/Luxembourg/Denmark/France/Germany/Greece/Ireland/Italy/Portugal/Spain/UK)	
EFTA	European Free Trade Area (Austria/Finland/Iceland/Norway/Sweden/Switzerland)	
EEA	European Economic Area (EEC/EFTA)	

OTR — Other Transport; PRTRAV — Private Travel; GOV — Government Services; OS — Other Services; SH — Shipping; PS — Passenger Services

Notes

1   The seven categories of trade in service do not sum to equal the TOTS values published in the IMF Balance of Payments Statistics Yearbook figures, Part 2, 2000. The TOTS values expressed above are the IMF Yearbook figure.

2   The calculation of proportions – SH%, TR%, OTR%, PRTRAV%, GOV%, OS% and PS% used the sum of the seven categories of trade in services as the denominator. This method was used to ensure that SH%, TR%, OTR%, PRTRAV%, GOV%, OS% and PS% summed to 100%, which would not have been the case if TOTS was used as the denominator.

The OECD was calculated by summing the values of the following members and dividing the sum by the number of member listed (22). The members include: USA/Canada/Australia/Japan/New Zealand/Austria/Belgium/Luxembourg/Denmark/Finland/France/Germany/Greece/Iceland/Ireland/Italy/Netherlands/Norway/Portugal/Spain/Sweden/Switzerland/UK.

Source: IMF, *Balance of Payments Statistics Yearbook*, Part 2 (2000).

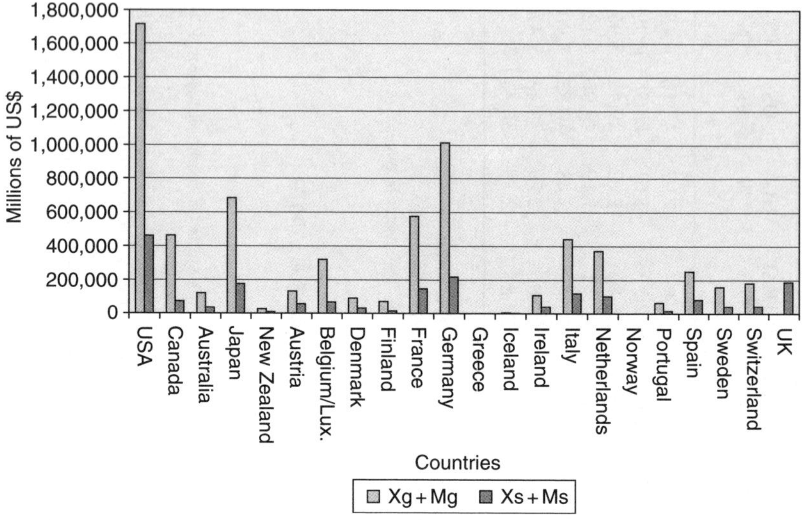

Figure 6.2   Trade in goods and services by country, 1999
Source: Table 6.2.

growth over the decade; only in Asia did this percentage increase every year. Figures 6.2, 6.3 and 6.4 demonstrate these effects.

Tables 6.5–7 show the value of total trade in merchandise and seven service categories (as defined by the IMF) by regions/areas. In 1999 the largest category of trade in services was 'other private services' (OS), equal to US$11,171.23 billion. The world share was 42 per cent, with 39 per cent for developing countries, Asia 44 per cent, the Middle East 38 per cent, the Western hemisphere 32 per cent and Europe about 38 per cent; for the OECD the average was 36 per cent of total services trade. Several countries experienced a decrease in 'shipping' services in 1994 and 1996, and saw positive growth in 1999. In general, the highest growth was in 1994, and there was a marginal positive growth in 1996 and in 1999. All the countries had positive growth in transport services from 1993 to 1996, except France, Germany and Portugal, which experienced negative growth in 1994, and France, Germany, Japan and Switzerland in 1996, which then saw positive growth between 1996 and 1999.

Many countries experienced a decrease in 'other transport services' from 1993 to 1996 but had varying experiences between 1996 and 1999. Australia was the only country to have negative growth over the entire period. Data on 'government services' indicate that many countries

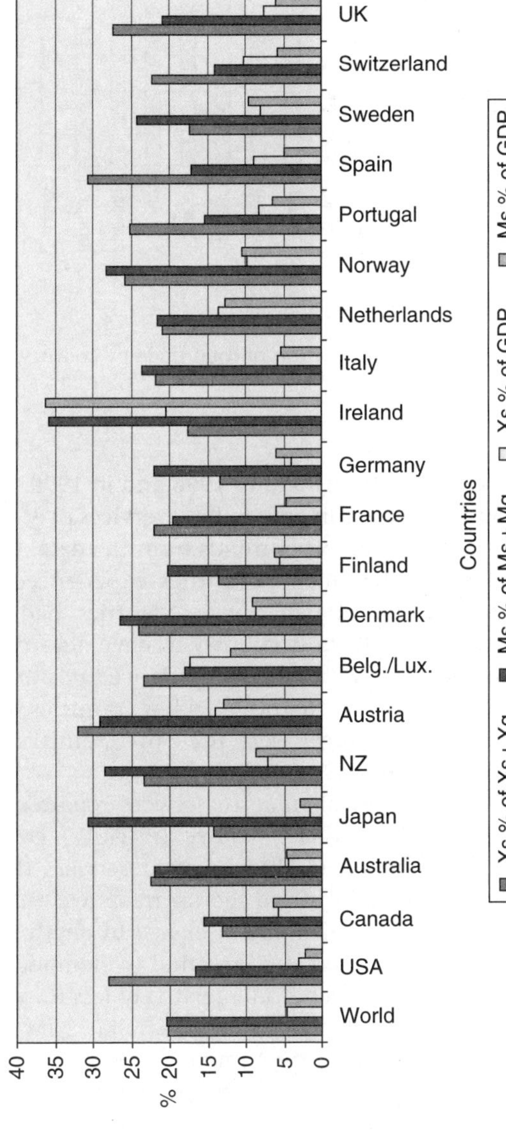

Figure 6.3 International trade in services in relation to total trade and GDP by country, 1998

Source: Table 6.8.

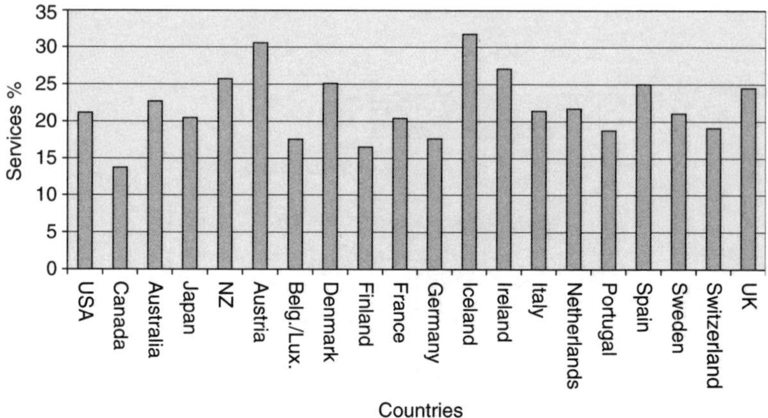

Figure 6.4 Trade in services as a proportion of total trade by country, 1999
Source: Table 6.4.

experienced negative growth from 1993 to 1996 and in 1999. Germany and Spain experienced a decrease in government services over the entire period. It is difficult to draw any other trends from the data. Other private services demonstrate that many countries experienced positive growth from 1993 to 1996, though a few countries had negative growth; the Netherlands was the only country to have negative growth in more than one period. Many countries experienced positive growth in private *services* from 1993 to 1996, though a few countries had reversal in growth. France and Portugal were the only countries to have negative growth in more than one period.

If we consider the categories of trade in services reported in these tables, shipment (SH), transport (TR), Travel (PRTRAV) government (GOV) and other transportation (OTR) passenger services (PS), other services (OS) and total merchandise and service trade, we observe that the tables contain too much detail to be discussed in depth; however, some important points to be noted are, first, that while trade in goods dominates trade in services, it has become relatively less important for some countries. Second, in the cases of Australia, New Zealand, Denmark, Norway, Portugal, Spain, the USA and Greece the most obvious explanation is that the growth of tourism, arising from easier travel facilities and a better information network, has increased their export of services. For only a few countries there has been greater growth in trade in services (New Zealand, the USA, Greece, Australia, Canada, and

France marginally). But there has been an increase in the tradability of services due to technological innovation, advancement, reductions in transaction costs, the reduction in the cost of long distance air tickets, the growth of leisure time in Asia-Pacific regions, the expanded role of multinationals and the integrated world information network. In the case of New Zealand this is the result of growth in tourism, brought about by policy reforms which facilitated improved travel systems, aided by the removal of restrictions on airline operations and a conscious effort to make the tourist centres more attractive to visitors. International travel, passenger transportation and tourism probably explain the growth for Austria and Greece, while France has become increasingly important as a seller of financial and transportation services and Sweden has markedly increased her supply of technical, professional and managerial services. By contrast, the USA, Britain and Norway have not experienced much export growth. The UK and USA have lost much of the monopoly they once held in the provision of financial and freight services as industrial nations such as Germany and Japan have become increasingly important providers of services; Norway experienced her oil boom and most of her growth has gone into oil related industrial expansion (Bano and Lane 1995; Bano 1998).

Table 6.8, which shows the relative importance of trade in services as a proportion of total trade and in relation to GDP and total world trade, produces some interesting results. In some countries, exports of services accounted for quite a large proportion of GDP. The first column indicates that exports in services as a percentage of total trade occupy a relatively important place in many countries such as Belgium, Luxembourg, the USA, Austria, Spain, France, New Zealand and Greece. In the second column the same exercise has been performed for imports in ratio to total trade in goods and services. In the third column the export in services ratio has been expressed as a percentage of imports in services ratio. The countries showing evidence for a strong specialization in services are Switzerland, the USA, Spain, Greece, Austria and Norway. In many OECD countries export of services in relation to import of services occupied an important position in relation to GDP. These countries may be the potential gainers from a liberal trade policy in services. However, much depends on the category of trade in services involved. The ratio of export and import only increased in more than one year in Australia, Canada, Iceland, Spain and the world; for all the other countries the percentage fell in at least one year. Export in services as a percentage of GDP only increased in more than one year for Australia, Italy, New Zealand and Spain; for all the other countries the

Table 6.8 International trade in services in relation to total trade by country, 1998

Country	Xs as % of Xs + Xg	Ms as % of Ms + Mg	Xs/Ms	GDP (US$ bill.)	Xs as % of GDP	Xg as % of GDP	Ms as % of GDP	Mg as % of GDP	Xg + Xs as % of GDP	Mg + Ms as % of GDP
World	20.17	20.42	1.00	28,736,978,000	4.77	18.89	4.78	18.62	23.67	23.40
USA	27.94	16.61	1.43	8,230,397	3.17	8.17	2.22	11.14	11.34	13.36
Canada	13.15	15.54	0.87	580,623	5.67	37.44	6.49	35.24	43.11	41.73
Australia	22.44	22.01	0.94	361,722	4.47	15.44	4.77	16.92	19.91	21.70
Japan	14.30	30.77	0.56	3,782,964	1.65	9.89	2.96	6.65	11.54	9.61
New Zealand	23.40	28.53	0.83	52,845	7.09	23.22	8.56	21.45	30.31	30.01
Austria	31.98	29.03	1.09	211,858	14.05	29.88	12.93	31.62	43.92	44.55
Belgium/Lux.	23.23	17.92	1.43	284,184	17.31	57.21	12.11	55.45	74.52	67.56
Denmark	24.10	26.39	0.96	174,870	8.70	27.40	9.02	25.17	36.10	34.20
Finland	13.48	20.16	0.87	123,502	5.47	35.14	6.32	25.02	40.61	31.34
France	21.90	19.59	1.25	1,426,967	5.95	21.24	4.75	19.49	27.19	24.23
Germany	13.38	21.92	0.64	2,134,205	3.93	25.43	6.10	21.74	29.36	27.84
Greece	0.00	0.00	0.00	120,724	0.00	0.00	0.00	0.00	0.00	0.00
Iceland	32.95	29.73	0.98	NA	NA	NA	NA	NA	NA	NA

Ireland	17.56	35.78	0.56	81,949	20.42	95.87	36.15	64.88	116.29	101.04
Italy	21.78	23.45	1.07	1,171,865	5.76	20.70	5.41	17.66	26.46	23.07
Netherlands	20.90	21.56	1.08	381,819	13.52	51.15	12.56	45.70	64.67	58.26
Norway	25.80	28.23	0.92	145,892	9.69	27.85	10.54	26.78	37.54	37.32
Portugal	25.15	15.34	1.25	106,697	8.12	24.16	6.48	35.79	32.28	42.27
Spain	30.57	17.12	1.80	553,230	8.91	20.24	4.96	23.99	29.15	28.95
Sweden	17.41	24.33	0.83	226,492	7.93	37.61	9.59	29.82	45.53	39.41
Switzerland	22.18	13.98	1.77	263,630	10.14	35.57	5.72	35.22	45.71	40.94
UK	27.22	20.91	1.26	1,357,197	7.49	20.03	5.96	22.53	27.52	28.49

Xg	Export of Goods		Ms	Import of Services
Mg	Import of Goods		Xs + Xg	Total Export of Goods and Services
Xs	Export of Services		Ms + Mg	Total Import of Goods and Services
NA	Not Available		GDP	Gross Domestic Product

Notes: World GDP figure in trillions of US$; GDP figures taken from World Bank, *World Development Indicators* (2003).

Source: IMF, *Balance of Payments Statistics Yearbook*, Part 2 (2000).

percentage fell in at least one year. In general, the highest increase in the percentage was in 1995. The UK, Switzerland, France, Portugal and the USA had high ratios in 1998. The share of services in the world economy remained steady in relation to the world GDP at about 24 per cent in 1998.

The evidence for developing nations shows that export earnings from services are important for a number of developing countries. 'Other private services' is the largest item in generating export revenue for these nations (though a disaggregation in data would probably show that the imports are primarily of high-skilled advisory and managerial skills and exports that of unskilled migrant or semi-migrant labour). As one would expect, developing countries import about 25 per cent more than they export, the only section showing a positive balance being that of trade in travel (tourism): tourists tend to go from the rich to the poor countries rather than in the other direction. The oil-exporting nations, in particular, experience very high deficits in exchange of services.

'Other private services' is an extremely heterogeneous group. This group comprises different items for exports for developed and developing countries. In developed countries, the main components are non-merchandise insurance, professional, technical and banking services, construction, engineering services and royalties and fees from affiliated companies. In low-income countries the principal component has been remittances from the residents working abroad. Some Asian countries, such as India, Singapore and Korea, are beginning to develop significant exports of services in the business categories. It is also observed that, with few exceptions, 'other private services' (OS) have a dominant position in most OECD countries. The total value of 'other private services' exports amounted to US$126 billion in 1985 and increased to US$259.8 billion in 1990, US$37,306.6 billion in 1993 and US$388.7 billion in 1996 which increased to US$2,780.4 billion in 1999 (about 86 per cent increase). The highest absolute values are for travel and other private services for the world, the OECD as a group, South Pacific islands and for most individual countries.

3.1   Pacific Rim island countries

Data concerning trade in goods and services have also been compiled, along with their main categories and their relative share in total trade of selected South Pacific island countries, for the years 1984 and 1992. In 1996 data these countries are put together in the Asian region as defined by the IMF *Balance of Payments Yearbook 1997*. In 1999, we identified selected countries and compiled the relevant data for this group as well. For some island nations consistent data are not available, so those countries have been excluded. A number of interesting points emerge from this information: the total value of South Pacific Forum Island trade amounted to US$77.8 billion in 1984 which increased to US$136.63 billion in 1992. The value of total goods trade was US$60.58 billion in 1984, which increased to US$105.19 billion in 1992. The value of trade in services rose from US$16.35 billion in 1984 to US$30 billion in 1992. The value of world trade increased from US$4,356.14 billion in 1984 to US$9,090.8 billion in 1992. Trade in services rose from US$806.54 billion in 1984 to US$1,952.18 billion in 1992. Average trade in these countries is very similar to the world average and that of OECD nations.

The statistics (Tables 6.9–6.11) show that the share of trade in services as a proportion of total trade is high in most of the island countries. In Fiji the share was 41 per cent in 1992 and this increased to 43.45 per cent in 1999. The Solomon Islands, Fiji, Tonga, Samoa and Vanuatu all show a high proportion of services trade in relation to their total trade. Only Papua New Guinea has less than 20 per cent of its trade in services. However, transport, travel and private services are a larger share of the total trade.

Shipping services seem to dominate in few island countries. One explanation is the establishment of Pacific Forum Line (PFL) in 1977. The PFL's main object was to provide a viable shipping service to promote export earnings and to meet the special conditions of the region. The summary of this information suggests that shipping, transport, travel and private services are important components of trade in services in South Pacific Forum Island nations. Some island countries heavily depend on tourism. These statistics also indicate that Pacific island countries possess a comparative advantage in service trade. It is clear that trade in services by developed countries involves a much wider range of activities, with particular strengths in knowledge-intensive producer services, while most developing countries and Pacific island nations are largely engaged in tourism or provisions of services overseas by their citizens. Most of the Pacific island countries are closely integrated with the functioning of the world economy. Both of these involved movement of persons across national frontiers. Embodied services and trade in factor services may have concentrated in developed economies. However, trade in all services usually makes a much greater contribution to the balance of payments. Trade in services clearly deserves to be high on the agenda of the Forum Island Countries' (FICs') policy-makers. The Asia-Pacific region is one of the most

Table 6.9 Categories of trade in services as a proportion of total services, 1999 (South Pacific Countries)

Country	Goods % of TOT Trade	Services % of TOT Trade	Shipping	Transport	Travel	Off.	PS
Australia	77.32	22.68	10.97	29.61	40.23	2.15	17.04
Fiji	56.55	43.45	12.35	33.41	38.15	4.96	11.14
Kiribati	NA	NA	NA	NA	NA	NA	NA
New Zealand	74.29	25.71	NA	42.18	55.84	1.98	NA
Papua New Guinea	73.59	26.41	43.34	43.34	13.32	NA	NA
Solomon Islands	65.79	34.21	36.23	43.48	9.42	5.07	5.80
Tonga	NA	NA	NA	NA	NA	NA	NA
Vanuatu	37.27	62.73	10.71	29.29	42.14	11.43	6.43
Samoa	92.95	7.05	5.33	6.67	61.33	25.33	1.33
South Pacific	67.23	32.77	21.9	35.29	30.71	5.11	6.99
World	80.03	19.97	15.48	31.96	39.81	4.95	7.80

TOT Trade   Total Trade in Goods and Services   PS   Passenger Services
NA   Not Available   Off.   Official Services

Note: Sum of five categories used as denominator in calculating the proportion.

Source: IMF, *Balance of Payments Statistics Yearbook*, Part 2 (2000).

Table 6.10 Categories of trade in services as a proportion of total services, 1992 (South Pacific Countries)

Country	Goods % of TOT Trade	Services % of TOT Trade	Shipping	Transport	Travel	Off.	PS
Australia	78.42	21.58	13.58	24.98	34.88	3.89	22.76
Fiji	59.30	40.70	14.75	27.58	37.76	10.03	9.88
Kiribati	60.42	39.58	36.84	15.79	10.53	0.00	31.58
New Zealand	74.85	25.15	11.92	28.10	33.31	2.10	24.57
Papua New Guinea	82.17	17.83	34.66	3.47	10.92	6.76	44.19
Solomon Islands	59.92	40.48	15.13	8.40	18.49	24.37	33.61
Tonga	61.90	38.10	30.00	22.50	22.50	17.50	7.50
Vanuatu	41.98	58.02	13.10	8.94	29.27	26.02	22.76
Samoa	55.17	44.83	21.79	8.97	23.08	7.69	39.74
South Pacific	77.50	22.50	13.67	25.06	34.04	3.92	23.31
World	78.53	21.47	13.23	15.10	28.94	6.40	36.34

Off.   Official Services
PS   Passenger Services

Table 6.11 Categories of trade in services as a proportion of total services, 1984 (Pacific island countries)

Country	Goods % of TOT Trade	Services % of TOT Trade	Shipping	Transport	Travel	Off.	PS
Australia	79.55	20.45	19.63	27.52	28.33	5.04	19.49
Fiji	60.45	39.55	13.58	21.48	41.23	14.07	9.63
Kiribati	69.0	30.95	30.77	46.15	7.69	0.00	7.69
New Zealand	76.73	23.27	40.99	6.43	22.40	4.85	25.32
Papua New Guinea	81.72	18.28	32.62	14.76	8.33	7.38	37.14
Solomon Islands	80.50	19.50	33.33	10.26	12.82	25.64	12.82
Tonga	63.49	36.51	21.74	13.04	34.78	30.43	0.00
Vanuatu	52.83	47.17	13.33	17.33	34.67	20.00	14.67
Samoa	75.29	24.71	23.81	19.05	28.57	14.29	19.05
South Pacific	78.75	21.25	24.30	22.52	26.88	5.44	20.84
World	81.49	18.51	17.39	17.89	24.93	10.76	29.02

Off. Official Services
PS   Passenger Services

dynamic regions in the world. Trade in goods has increased in this region very markedly. Trade in services is likely to follow its remarakble growth in manufactured products. Issues in services trade are of importance to this region. It is suggested that for policy implications, some key determinants and the barriers to service trade be clearly investigated and identified.

4   Explaining the growth of international trade in services

What are the major causative factors of trade in services? Is trade in services determined primarily by economic or non-economic factors? Can trade theory explain trade in services? Can certain sectors of service trade be explained by some factors that are less important in explaining others? In the absence of a developed theory of trade in services, the theory of trade in goods has been applied for investigating the causative factors. As a result, a number of hypotheses have been derived from the trade theories, which have evolved over the years. Some of these are listed below:

- the Heckscher–Ohlin–Samuelson, and Ricardo theories
- the demand similarity model (Linder's theory)
- the economies of scale models
- the product differentiation models
- the theory of human/knowledge capital
- the biological trade theory
- the product life cycle, the technological gap, and the flying geese model
- theories of trade barriers

The traditional trade theories of comparative advantage, based on constant returns to scale, perfect competition and the assumptions about technical differences (the essence of Ricardian theory) and the factor endowment differences among nations (the essence of Heckscher–Ohlin–Samuelson theory) and homogeneity of products, provides price/cost as the basis and the unique determinant of the direction, composition and volume of trade. In fact, the past few decades have witnessed a significant trade growth among industrialized nations, whose economies are very similar in factor endowments, demand, tastes and preference patterns, technological advancements and the level of development. They seem to share similar cultural and other socio-institutional attributes.[4] Those developed countries are selling each other similar brand products, such as different makes of television sets, chemicals, wine and beer. In the real world, a large volume of trade consists of differentiated products, which are close (but not perfect) substitutes. Hence price and cost are no longer unique determinants of trade flows. There are a host of factors that determine modern trade flows among countries. One of the main conclusions drawn from this evidence is the fact that there is a theoretical foundation for trade to take place in the absence of different factor endowments between countries as long as the products are differentiated and economies of scale exists.

This body of theory, developed to explain intra-industry trade, seems to provide a more satisfactory set of explanatory determinants of trade in services, since many services are differentiated by quality, may exhibit increasing returns to scale, are associated with exchange between high income level nations and contain high technology inputs. Trade in services has many of the characteristics of this new pattern of trade. Services are not homogeneous but rather highly differentiated, so the law of one price cannot hold across the global economy. Many services are subjected to regulations, and using relative prices may not lead to accurate predictions of trade flows because prices may not capture the regulatory conditions and perceived quality differences. They tend to be sophisticated products both produced and consumed by the wealthier nations and, especially in the growing sector, have a high technological component. Recently international trade theorists have drawn heavily on the area of industrial organization to investigate the causative factors for the basis of trade between similarly endowed countries (Bano and Lane 1995).

5   The role of comparative advantage

The laws of comparative advantage (embodied in the Heckscher–Ohlin–Samuelson, or HOS, model) have long been used for explaining the patterns of trade in tangible goods. Endowments such as strategic locations or raw materials are considered important, and comparative cost advantage is explained in terms of the relative abundance of factor inputs (Hindley and Smith 1984; Daniels 1993) but finance and capital, political and cultural factors, and characteristics of human capital have been less emphasized in the list of consultative factors. These are more dynamic, less fixed national endowments on the important issue of whether the law of comparative advantage applies to trade in intangible services. Recent literature on this subject, Lloyd and Lee (2002) supports the argument that the standard theoretical analysis of distortions and impediments to trade would be applicable to trade in services as well. In addition, contemporary economic literature supports the assertion that countries may realize gains from the liberalization of trade in services. The WTO and APEC can therefore play an important role in fostering trade in services.

6 Changes in technology and comparative advantage

With the rapid development of satellites and Internet services, it has become possible to provide a variety of information, financial and other services, at a minimal cost. Technological innovation and change affect the relative costs and prices of services (and goods) and the resulting pattern of production and trade. Given the fact that technological change is an ongoing process, what is now important is the dynamics of comparative advantage rather than comparative statics, which is the basis for much of the analysis of trade theory. The distinction between statistics and dynamics is well known, and is not unique when applied to trade in services. The difficulty lies in modelling endogenous technological change in a comprehensive and general manner.

6.1 The role of cultural and economic comparative advantage

Riddle (1986) makes a distinction between cultural and economic comparative advantage. The law of comparative advantage as discussed above is a more commonly accepted form of comparative advantage, but a country may also be able to utilize a particular cultural trait as international competitiveness. An example is the adoption by the world's major airlines of the 'etiquette schools' used by Japan Airlines for its customer services personnel (Riddle 1986). A country may also be able to derive cultural comparative advantage because the service provided by some other country with a different cultural is not compatible (e.g., provision of halal meals). Services sourced from countries with extensive colonial history, such as Britain, France and the Netherlands may also generate a form of cultural comparative advantage over countries that have not had such institutional or commonweal or trade ties with host countries before (Daniels 1993).

6.2 The role of dynamic comparative advantage

In a classic economics textbook, C. P. Kindleberger (1958) succinctly summarized two of the three elements of conventional views of the dynamics of development of service industries in modern society. He did so by reference to the work of Fourastie (1952/58). The French statistician, J. Fourastie, who is much interested in productivity, has suggested a model of economic development which combines systematic differences in productivity by sectors with the pattern of income-elasticity of demand implied by Engels' Law. In his exposition, potatoes are chosen as an example of a primary good, bicycles as an example of secondary, and a hotel room of tertiary output. Labour productivity in the first is said to have increased from 100 in 1800 to 130 in 1950. Consumption rose continuously throughout the period to the 1920s, but has recently developed negative income-elasticity with per capita consumption at 250 per cent of the 1800 level. In bicycles productivity increased from 100 in 1800 to 700 in 1950, and is still increasing. Consumption has gone up nine times in the same period, but is beginning to level off. For hotel rooms, labour productivity remained practically unchanged from 1800 to 1950, but demand brought about an increase in consumption from 100 in 1800, to 10,000 in 1950. Fourastie uses these systematic differences in productivity and demand by sectors to project systematic changes in the terms of trade which favour tertiary industry over primary, and both over secondary (*The New Palgrave Dictionary* 1994).

These two elements are, on the one hand, an 'Engels' Law' type of explanation, based on the income-elasticity of demand for services, such that richer people tend to consume more high quality services than poorer; and on the other, a 'productivity gap', such that output per worker in the service industries rises more slowly than elsewhere in the economy. Put these two elements together, and we have a prediction that, when the economy as a whole is growing, the service sector increases its size relative to the rest of the economy. This model was formulated in the early 1950s; more than 20 years later, exactly the same model formed the core of the first substantial description of the trend towards 'post-industrial society' (*The New Palgrave Dictionary* 1994). This explanation can be further linked to Linder's demand-based explanation of trade.

6.2.1   Per capita income

There appears to be a relationship between the levels of development of a country and the propensity to export services or to generate demand for service imports. Linder (1961), in his important contribution, envisioned trade in differentiated products. He argued that patterns of trade in manufactured goods (which vary in quality) are determined by the structure of domestic demand, and the demand structure in turn is determined by income distribution and per capita income. It is expected that the demand for differentiated services will be higher as per capita income of a country rises. The share of services expenditure as a proportion of GDP tends to rise as income rises, which is indicative of high income elasticity for high quality services in rich as compared to poor countries. The countries with highest levels of per capita income and well developed knowledge-based industries have the potential for fostering services trade.

6.2.2   International trade in goods and services

What is the relationship between international trade in goods and trade in services? Do services transactions differ in any fundamental sense from trade in merchandise? Hindley and Smith (1984) do not think so. They argue that there is no need for a new paradigm or theoretical framework for trade in services. The wine and cloth in Ricardo's classic example could easily be replaced by wine and insurance policies without changing the validity of the law of comparative advantage. There seems to be a close link between trade in goods and trade in services. A substantial proportion of the services traded internationally represent intermediate inputs that are related to flows of traded goods. It is expected that trade in services will tend to rise as trade in merchandise rises. For example, transport and freight services are those most affected by total merchandise trade. Countries such as New Zealand, Australia and Canada seem to be dependent on transport to distant markets. Shipping is the next service most influenced by total merchandise trade. The service sectors – travel, other private services and official services – may not be affected by merchandise trade. Perhaps the answer is that the official services are determined by political and non-economic factors rather than economic forces.

6.2.3   Trade in services and foreign direct investment

Foreign direct investment plays an important role in the production and development process in many host countries. This role is more pertinent in the context of trade in services because of the simultaneity of their production and consumption. This has further implications for those services provided by means of foreign direct investment. It is expected that as FDI increases, trading partners' level of development will increase and that the share of trade in services will also tend to increase over time.

6.2.4   Human capital and trade in services

As development proceeds, trading partners invest more in education (secondary and tertiary levels of education, specific skill). A high degree of knowledge capital tends to generate innovation, technological advancement and produce high quality goods and services. The human-capital-abundant and knowledge-based economies will export more educational services. Thus a positive causal relationship is expected.

6.2.5   Research and development expenditure

High levels of research and development activities tend to generate a wide range of innovative outcomes, creating new products or processes. To the extent R&D leads to the creation of high quality differentiated products, it will have positive effects on trade in services. It was intended to examine whether the product life cycle and technological gap existed in the context of service trade.

7   Some observations and conclusions

In the first place, it has been established that trade in services has grown along with merchandise trade. It is surprising to observe that while services form a rapidly increasing proportion of domestic trade, they are not growing as rapidly in international trade. It is expected that with the growth of regionalism, economic integration, trade liberalization, technological innovation, increasing ease of transport, travel, information dissemination and financial transfers, many hitherto 'non-traded' services should be more readily available across national borders.[5]

This is a surprising result, as one would expect that growth in internationally traded services would follow the same pattern as growth in domestically provided services, which constitutes about 60 per cent of the GDP of the high-income OECD nations. The explanation probably lies in the inadequacy of a comprehensive database for service trade. A comprehensive database is available to examine merchandise trade data, such as the United Nations Standard International Trade Organization. Comprehensive disaggregated data are compiled at different levels of aggregation. At the 3-digit level, we can define over 700 separate 'industries' or goods categories. For services, there are just a few categories – only five, recently extended to seven (by the IMF) – each containing a wide range of services. For example, 'other private services' includes business consultancy, migrant labour, entertainment, sport, communications and other quite disparate services, whose incidence in trade may be moving in opposite directions and whose growth or decline are determined by quite different factors. The data seem to underestimate the extent of trade in services. So, until data on service trade are disaggregated in a manner similar to data on merchandise trade, it will be difficult to analyse it with any degree of confidence. In addition, there exist many barriers to trade in services which are under negotiation.

Evidence suggests that most of the Pacific island countries are closely integrated with the functioning of the world economy. Empirical results of trade in services (travel, transportation, other services) show that income-elasticity of demand for imports (exports) of services is greater than unity. Other determinants which suggest themselves as worthy of study are relative levels of technology and human capital, degree of economic integration, trade creation and diversion effects, relative capital : labour ratios in the production of services, the presence of tariff and non-tariff barriers, economies of scale in production and the presence of transnational corporations. The effects of government procurement policies and barriers to labour movement may well be significant factors.

It has been observed that differences in factor endowments and technology have a major influence on the relative prices of services and returns to factors in developed and developing countries. Evidence suggest that many services are more expensive in rich than poor countries, and the price of services relative to goods tends to rise with higher levels of per capita income. This suggests that developing countries have a comparative advantage, especially in the provision of labour-intensive services.

The developing countries need to focus on the expansion of both trade in goods and services. The mix between a country's actual and potential comparative advantage in goods and services is important in planning future development strategy. Trade in services seem to contribute to economic integration: for example, the reduction in transport costs has reduced the distance between nations. Further, phenomenal growth in IT services, telecommunication, business, banking and insurance are promoting linkages and growth in many countries.

Perhaps the most important message that comes through is the urgent need for the development of a comprehensive database on a consistent basis for all IMF member countries and for all Pacific Island Forum countries to facilitate analysis of the growing roles of trade in services. The IMF should redefine and expand the categories of services consistent with their WTO classification. Reductions and phasing out the barriers to trade in services would appear to be a positive step towards fostering such trade in the world economy. For example, residential and visa restrictions prevent the movement of natural persons across national boundaries, government procurement insists on the use of local consultancy and financial services, national carriers are given preference over foreigners in freight contracts, and foreign companies are frequently forbidden to operate in domestic banking, insurance, internal freight and communications, although foreign involvement in manufacturing may be welcomed. The GATS brings the international trade in services under internationally agreed rules for the first time. The prospect of future liberalization contained in the GATS is reasonably favourable for the Asian nations and for the South Pacific island countries and the integrated world economy.

8   Implications for research

Several issues relating to the international aspects of services deserve further study from both theoretical and policy perspectives:

1 Is there evidence to suggest that comparative advantage has shifted in recent years to service industries?
2 What is the relationship between international trade in goods and trade in services?
3 What is the effect of technological innovations and globalization on trade in services?
4 Given the fact that many services are labour-intensive, will labour-abundant developing countries become major exporters of services?
5 If trade negotiations deal foster liberalization of services trade, will it be beneficial?
6 Growth of producer services, which are relatively capital-intensive, is due to various types of capital (physical, human, and knowledge). Given the fact that OECD countries are well endowed with such capital, they have a comparative advantage in goods that intensively embody the producer services, so will these countries foster human-capital-intensive exports in services as capital further accumulates in these economies?
7 Which international forum is appropriate for dealing with issues related to trade in services?

Appendix: the definition of trade in services and data used

In this study the concept of trade in services as defined by the IMF has been used. According to the IMF Balance of Payments classification, trade in services consists of the following five categories: (1) Shipment, (2) Other Transportation, (3) Travel, (4) Other Private Services and (5) Other Official Services (now extended to passenger services, government and other services).

Here, 'shipment' covers freight, insurance and port and related services involved in distributing merchandise items on the basis of f.o.b. valuation. 'Other transportation' includes services performed by carriers, chiefly the transport of passengers that are not included in 'shipment' or travel and port services. 'Travel' covers goods and services acquired from a country by non-resident travellers (both tourists and business) for their own use during their stay in the host country. It excludes international passenger services (which are included in other transportation services). 'Other private services' includes labour income, property income not included elsewhere (i.e., royalties, licence fees and other goods and services). 'Other goods and services' covers such items as non-merchandise insurance, communications, advertising, brokerage, professional and technical services, processing and repair, periodicals bought through subscription, operational leasing, and management. 'Other official services' includes expenditures incurred by official entities located abroad, embassies and consulates, military units for goods and services.

The sources of data are the IMF *Balance of Payments Yearbook* Parts 1 and 2 (2000, and various issues), *World Development Report* (various issues) and the OECD *Economic Outlook, International Financial Statistics*, IMF (various issues), and the *Direction of Trade Statistics*, IMF (various issues), New Zealand Statistics Department.

Notes

1　Earlier attempts have been made by Baldwin (1979), Sapir and Lutz (1980, 1981), Kierzkowski (1989) and Bano and Lane (1995).
2　Adam Smith viewed services as unproductive activity. He wrote: 'The Labour of a menial servant … adds to the value of nothing … the labour of some of the most respectable orders in society is like that of menial servants, unproductive of any value, and does not fix or realize itself in any permanent subject or vendible commodity which endures after that labour is past …. In the same class must be ranked … churchmen, lawyers, players, buffoons, musicians, opera singers etc.'
3　Bhagwati (1984) agrees with Hill's view that the production of a service cannot generally be distinguished from that of a good by means of the technology used but by the fact that the producer unit operates directly on goods which already belong to the consumer of the services. The fact that services must be acquired by consumers as they are produced means that they cannot be put into stock by producers. Bhagwati sets up categories and classes of services to describe the characteristics of services as distinct from goods.
4　Intra-industry trade is defined as the simultaneous exports and imports of trade within the same industry (similar products not homogeneous, differentiated products, e.g., different models of cars). This became evident in Western Europe after the formation of the European Economic Community (EEC), and virtually all OECD nations have experienced rapid growth in such trade. See for detail Grubel and Lloyd (1975), Helpman and Krugman (1985), Bano (1991) and Tharakan (1989).
5　As noted earlier (cf. Bano and Lane 1995).

References

Asia Pacific Economic Cooperation (1999), Assessing APEC Trade Liberalization and Facilitation – 1999 Update; Report by the Economic Committee, September (Singapore: APEC Secretariat).

Baldwin, R. B. (1979), 'Determinants of trade and foreign investment: further evidence', *Review of Economics and Statistics*, February.

Bano, S. (1991) *Intra-Industry International Trade: The Canadian Experience* (London: Avebury Academic Publishing Company).

Bano, S. (1998), 'International Trade in Services: Their Important Role in New Zealand, Asian Nations and the World Economy', 15th Annual Conference of Euro-Asia Mangement Studies Association, *Proceedings* (Taipei, Taiwan), 185–220.

Bano, S. and Lane, P. (1995), 'The Significance and Determinants of Trade in Services: Canada and the World Economy', in R. Moncarz (ed.), *International Trade and the New World Order* (Oxford: Pergamon, Elsevier Science), 129–50.

Bhagwati, M. N. (1984), 'Splintering and Disembodiment of Services and Developing Nations', *The World Economy*, 7, 133–43.

Campbell R. H. and Skinner A. S. (eds) (1976) Adam Smith *An Inquiry into the Nature and Causes of the Wealth of Nations*, Vol 1, pp. 330–4 (Oxford: Clarendon Press).

Daniels, P. W. (1993), *Service Industries in the World Economy* (Oxford: Basil Blackwell).

Fourastie, J. (1952/58), *Le grand espoir du XXème siècle* 4th edn (Paris: PUF).

Grubel, H. G. and Lloyd, P. J. (1975), *Intra-Industry Trade, The Theory and Measurement of International Trade in Differentiated Products* (London: Macmillan).

Helpman, E. and Krugman, P. R. (1985), *Market Structure and Foreign Trade: Increasing Returns, Imperfect Competition and the International Economy* (Cambridge, MA: MIT Press).

Hill, T. P. (1977), 'On goods and services', *Review of Income and Wealth*, 23 (4) (December), 315–38.

Hindley, B. and Smith, A. (1984), 'Comparative Advantage and Trade in Services', *The World Economy*, 7, 377–81.

International Monetary Fund (2000), Balance of Payments Statistics Yearbook (Washington, DC: International Monetary Fund); Various Years and 2000.

Kierzkowski, H. (1989), 'Intra-industry Trade in Transportation Services', in P. K. M. Tharakan and J. Kol (ed.), *Intra-Industry Trade: Theory, Evidence and Extensions* (London: Macmillan).

Kindleberger, C. P. (1958), *Economic Development* (New York: McGraw-Hill).

Linder, S. B. (1961), *An Essay on Trade and Transformation* (New York: John Wiley).

Lloyd, P. J. and Lee, H. H. (eds) (2002) *Frontiers of Research in Intra-Industry Trade* (Great Britain: Palgrave Macmillan).

Mill, J. S. (1965), *Principles of Political Economy*, reprinted, ed. W. Ashley (New York: Kelley).

The New Palgrave: A Dictionary of Economics (1994), edited by John Eatwell, Murray Migate, Peter Newman, Volume 4 (London: Macmillan, 1987, reprinted in 1991 and 1994).

Riddle, D. I. (1986), *Service-led Growth: The Role of Service Sector in World Development* (New York: Praeger).

Sapir, A. and Lutz, E. (1980), 'Trade in Non-Factor Services: Past Trends and Current Issues', *World Bank Staff Working Paper*, No. 410 (Washington, DC: World Bank, August).

Sapir, A. and Lutz, E. (1981), 'Trade in Services: Economic Determinants and Development Related Issues', *World Bank Staff Working Paper*, No. 480 (Washington, DC: World Bank).

Smith, A. (1979), *An Inquiry into the Nature and Causes of the Wealth of Nations* (Harmondsworth: Penguin).

Tharakan, P.K.M. and Kol, J. (eds) (1989), *Intra-Industry Trade: Empirical and Methodological Aspects* (Amsterdam: North Holland Publishing Company).

World Development Report (Washington, DC: World Bank) Various years and 2000.

World Trade Organization (1996), *Special Topic: Trade and Foreign Direct Investment, Annual Report Vol 1 and Vol II* (Geneva: WTO).

World Trade Organization (2000), *World Development and World Trade in 1999*, World Trade Organization, Press Release 175, April.

7
Students' Perceptions of Choice Criteria in the Selection of Tertiary Institutions: A Regional Comparison

Zahiruddin Ghazali and Mohamad Hanapi Mohamad

The issue of tertiary institution choice criteria has without doubt been widely researched. This is due to intense competition for full fee-paying foreign students in tertiary education. The identification of the criteria considered important to future customers is a prerequisite for the development of strategies, especially at a time when Malaysia has projected the image of being a centre of excellence in education. This chapter examines regional differences in current customer choice criteria. A questionnaire containing four factors with 19 variables was used in a sample of 721 foreign students to gain insight into Malaysian tertiary education and develop relevant strategies.

1   Introduction

Over the years, tertiary education reforms have taken place in several countries around the globe. As a result of the Asian financial crisis in 1997, Asian students in particular have become more selective in their choice of tertiary institutions. The fact that traditional tertiary education destinations such as Australia reported a 45 per cent decrease in student visas issued to some Asian countries (Maslen 1998), and an 80 per cent decrease in visas issued to Malaysian students (Illing 1998) confirms this view. However, foreign student enrolments in Malaysia, amounting to a mere 2.0 per cent but climbing annually, seem not to be affected by the crisis (Mohamad, Zahiruddin and Kassim 2001). As a result of these environmental factors, tertiary institutions need to develop strategic options that work with the changes facing this sector.

In line with Vision 2020, the Malaysian government liberalized its higher education policy as part of the plan to make Malaysia 'a centre of academic excellence'. Local education administrators such as Kamarudin (1997), Sulaiman (1997) and Ramaiah (1996) believe that characteristics related to choice of courses and selection of the institution are key factors in determining the choice of location. However, no empirical research or evidence has been brought forth to substantiate their claims.

In line with what has emerged, this study focuses on the identification of choice attributes considered relevant by foreign students to their chosen destination. As Griffin and Hauser (1993) point out, 'the knowledge of what is important to the customer can provide insight into what assets and skills are needed to compete and can form the basis of sustainable advantages'.

2   Literature review

Studies that look at the variables influencing student selection of tertiary institution (Houston 1979; Krone *et al.* 1983; Webb 1993) point to a wide range of choice variables. Without doubt, most traditional tertiary education institutions have extensively researched the issue of tertiary institution choice criteria (Chapman 1981; Lay 1981; Murphy 1981; Steadman and Dagwell 1990; Lawley 1993, 1997; Joseph and Joseph 1998) with varied results, most of which are due to the different perspectives with regard to the attributes.

With the abundance of literature on attributes in the selection of tertiary institutions, one could lose sight of what to look for. However, past studies have addressed the issue of student choice criteria and identified several determinants. Several studies (Blaug and Woodhall 1985; Austin 1988; Wu 1989; Lawley 1993, 1997) confirm the importance of course characteristics in the choice of destination. Blaug and Woodhall (1985) suggest that standard of courses is the main reason for overseas students choosing the UK as their destination. This coincides with an earlier study by Bower and Pugh (1972) concluding that first-rate faculties and high academic standards were what students looked for.

Studies on the influence of family and friends on choice of destination were put forward by Rao (1979) and AGB (1992). Moreover, Harris and Rhall (1993), later confirmed by Lawley (1993, 1997), stress family and friends as the key source of advice for overseas students. Although Houston (1979) found it to be at the bottom of the scale, Joseph and Joseph (1998) confirmed it as one of the most important elements in selecting tertiary institutions.

Nevertheless, Chapman (1981) found that the influence of both groups differed, and Joseph and Joseph (2000) found that Indonesian students did not refer to it as the most important source of advice.

Previous research by Rao (1979), Hill, Romm and Patterson (1992), and Joseph and Joseph (2000) stresses ease of entry as a major influential variable in selecting education institutions. Moreover, ease of gaining exemptions (Austin 1988) and ease of obtaining visas (Hill, Romm and Patterson 1992) were put forth as influencing choice variables in tertiary institution selection.

Possibly the one factor that most researchers agree on as an influential variable in tertiary institution selection is cost. Financial cost has been hypothesized by several researchers (Throsby 1986; Chandler 1989) as being a major contributing factor to choice of destination. Variables contributing to the cost factor should also cover both financial (physical) and psychological cost, as was realized by Lawley (1997), who also included the level of racial discrimination as a variable.

The question arises as to whether a model could be produced from this abundance of factors and variables. It is a major challenge, especially with the use of multicultural background respondents. As Joseph and Joseph (2000) pointed out, most research uses US samples and Joseph and Joseph (1998) use a New Zealand sample. Furthermore, Joseph and Joseph (2000) also use the single sample of Indonesia in their study. It can be argued that there is very little cultural distance between these samples. Therefore, this study will try to extend the boundaries of literature on choice criteria for tertiary institutions with a multicultural framework.

3 Methodology

The first stage in the process involved an assessment of the appropriateness of the questionnaire. A preliminary study to assess the appropriateness of the attributes was carried out from October to December 2000, and involved a series of focus groups using 55 foreign students attending local public universities. The initial attribute model was based on research by Lawley (1997) but adjusted to local conditions. Although the study was done retrospectively, the results of initial focus groups indicate that these attributes are globally accepted. The questionnaire contained four sections:

- demographic information on the respondents
- ranking of perceived most important attributes

- evaluation of the perceived attributes
- student perception of Malaysian tertiary institutions

The 19 item, Likert scale questionnaire had response categories of 1 – strongly disagree, 2 – disagree, 3 – undecided, 4 – agree, 5 – strongly agree.

The second stage involved a survey of random samples from tertiary institutions (public and private) identified throughout Malaysia. In order for the institutions to be included in this study, they had to have at least 500 registered full-time students and a minimum of 20 foreign students enrolled in their colleges. The final outcome of this exercise was the participation in this study of 721 respondents from 15 countries. The first mailing of the questionnaire was completed in March 2001. Follow-up mailings were completed in May 2001.

4 Findings

In the second part of the questionnaires, respondents were asked to rank the different dimensions in order of importance (Table 7.1). The rank order shows that 87.50 per cent of the respondents indicated that 'Course characteristics' was the most important dimension followed by 'Administrative processes', 'Cost characteristics', and 'Country characteristics'.

The mean comparison (Table 7.2) shows that there is no significant difference among respondents in perceived importance of choice criteria

Table 7.1   Summary of factor importance

Rank	Factor	Percentage
1	Course characteristics	87.50
2	Administrative processes	71.50
3	Cost characteristics	61.80
4	Country characteristics	52.00

Table 7.2   Comparison of importance

Factor	SEA	Asia	Africa	Europe	Others	*F*	Sig.
Course	87.5	85.3	86.8	98.0	100.0	1.793	0.128
Administration	71.1	69.6	79.2	67.3	75.0	0.689	0.599
Cost	57.4	59.4	79.2	59.2	75.0	3.127	0.015
Country	56.7	46.5	52.8	53.1	37.5	1.203	0.308

SEA = Southeast Asia.
Sig. = Significance.

in destination selection, with the exception of cost attributes. Although it emerged as the third influencing factor overall, not all respondents have the same perception of cost.

The comparison of importance (Table 7.2) shows that respondents attach great importance to all variables in the four factors, especially variables in course attributes. All three course characteristic variables, 'Standard of courses' (4.3138), 'Recognition of qualification' (4.4364), and 'Standard of teaching facilities' (4.2163), score highest in the assessment of the most important variables influencing choice destination (see Table 7.3). Furthermore, most of the other variables had a mean score above 3.5 except for the following items: 'Possibility of immigrating' (3.4149), 'Friends' opinion' (2.7052), 'Climate of the place of study' (3.0821), 'Distance from home' (2.9847), and 'Exemptions' (3.2757).

As shown in Table 7.4, the regional mean comparison reveals deviations in several variables, including 'Recognition of qualification' in course characteristics, 'Safety of place of study' and 'Friends' opinion' in

Table 7.3 Summary of means

Variables	Importance
Course characteristics	
The standard of courses	4.3138
Recognition of qualification	4.3464
Standard of teaching facilities	4.2163
Administrative processes	
Obtaining information about studying	4.0504
Process of obtaining a student visa	3.8808
Possibility of legally working part-time	3.5517
Entry to universities/institutions	3.9300
Exemptions	**3.2757**
Cost characteristics	
Cost of study	4.096
Climate of the place of study	**3.0821**
Distance from home	**2.9847**
Favourable levels of racial discrimination	3.7361
Availability of scholarships	3.6667
Time to complete course	4.1306
Country characteristics	
Safety of place of study	4.1148
Family opinion	3.6393
Possibility of immigrating	**3.4149**
Friends' opinion	**2.7052**
Way of living	3.6805

Table 7.4 Comparison of means

Factors/variables	Mean SEA	Mean Asia	Mean Africa	Mean Europe	Mean others	F	Sig.
Course characteristics	4.2716	4.2506	4.3491	4.3537	4.5833	0.916	0.454
The standard of courses	4.2748	4.3053	4.2571	4.6122	4.6250	1.971	0.097
Recognition of qualification	**4.3053**	**4.2847**	**4.5810**	**4.4082**	**4.5000**	**2.692**	**0.030**
Standard of teaching facilities	4.2442	4.1979	4.2358	4.0408	4.6250	0.972	0.422
Administrative processes	3.7561	3.7408	3.7892	3.6422	3.9188	0.629	0.642
Obtaining information about studying	3.9809	4.0954	4.1524	3.9167	4.3750	1.524	0.194
Process of obtaining a student visa	**4.0229**	**3.8363**	**3.8113**	**3.5625**	**4.0000**	**2.676**	**0.031**
Possibility of legally working part-time	**3.4809**	**3.4648**	**3.9528**	**3.5306**	**3.5000**	**3.198**	**0.013**
Entry to universities/ institutions	3.9538	3.8975	3.9811	3.8367	4.1250	0.424	0.792
Exemptions	**3.3235**	**3.3307**	**2.9195**	**3.3265**	**3.5714**	**2.882**	**0.022**
Costs characteristics	3.4642	3.5099	3.7005	3.4558	3.5000	2.169	0.071
Cost of study	4.0649	4.0245	4.2830	4.2245	4.1250	1.591	0.175
Climate of place of study	**3.0451**	**3.1226**	**3.3750**	**2.5714**	**2.7500**	**3.840**	**0.004**
Distance from home	2.9668	3.0309	2.7273	3.1667	2.7500	1.235	0.295
Favourable levels of racial discrimination	**3.6240**	**3.6614**	**4.2159**	**3.8367**	**4.3750**	**4.960**	**0.001**
Availability of scholarships	3.6119	3.6142	3.8140	3.8085	4.0000	0.943	0.439
Time to complete course	4.1182	4.1333	4.2299	4.0000	4.1667	0.466	0.761

Table 7.4   continued

Factors/variables	Mean SEA	Mean Asia	Mean Africa	Mean Europe	Mean others	*F*	Sig.
Country characteristics	3.5431	3.4916	3.5458	3.5633	3.3750	0.452	0.771
Safety of place of study	**4.2328**	**3.9717**	**4.0192**	**4.4286**	**4.2500**	**4.926**	**0.001**
Family opinion	3.6489	3.6175	3.5755	3.8367	3.7500	0.555	0.695
Possibility of immigration	3.3038	3.4823	3.5288	3.2857	3.7500	1.095	0.358
Friends' opinion	**2.8724**	**2.6374**	**2.6250**	**2.4082**	**1.8750**	**3.571**	**0.007**
Way of living	3.6349	3.6420	3.8409	3.8571	3.2500	1.474	0.209

SEA = Southeast Asia.
Sig. = Significance.

country characteristics, 'Process of obtaining student visas' and 'Possibility of legally working part-time' in administrative process characteristics, and 'Climate of the place of study' and 'Favourable level of racial discrimination' in cost characteristics. These findings suggest, however, that although respondents generally agree on what is important and what influences their choices, they react differently with regard to specific variables, depending on their region of origin.

5 Discussion

Tertiary institution administrators and investors, especially in Malaysia, should note that almost all attributes identified in this study are considered important by foreign students studying in Malaysia. More significantly, course attributes should be taken more seriously as these influence students greatly in determining their choice of destination. This finding aligns with other tertiary education scholars such as Baird (1967), Bower and Pugh (1972), and Murphy (1981), whose findings suggest that what students look for are first-rate faculties with high academic standards. Results in Table 7.4 also suggest that foreign students perceive Malaysian course standards and teaching facilities as high and are influenced by them in their choice of destination. Although qualification recognition attributes are high on the scale of factors influencing choice of destination, they somehow fail to capture the 'mind-set' of Southeast Asian (SEA) and Asian students.

As mentioned earlier, some SEA and Asian students regard Malaysian tertiary education qualifications as limited or not on a par with their counterparts in the traditional choice of destination tertiary institutions. Much of this misconception is due to lack of information about qualification recognition. Malaysian tertiary institution qualifications, especially those from public universities, are accepted and on a par with Commonwealth countries and most European and American universities. Malaysian tertiary institutions lack the benefits provided by Australian IDPs (International education and development Australia), MACEEs (Malaysian-American Commission on Educational Exchange) and British Councils. Furthermore, despite increased acceptance of web-based information on the recognition of Malaysian tertiary education, admission requirements tend to be severe.

The mean comparison in Table 7.4 clearly shows that there are regional differences in the perception of what is important, and what influences student choice destinations. In 'Administrative processes', regional differences in influential variables of choice destination are clear and definite. The 'Process of obtaining a student visa' is placed as a high influencing factor by SEA students as well as students from 'Other regions'. Much of this is due to the intense scrutiny prior to granting student visas, as a result of the influx of foreign nationals who work illegally after entering the country on student visas. African students in particular positioned 'possibility of legally working part-time' as a high influencing factor in selecting Malaysia as their choice of destination. It is currently illegal for any foreign student to hold a job in Malaysia, be it full- or part-time.

This issue ought to be considered by the government if Malaysia is to become more attractive for foreign students. As the Australian Industry Commission (1991) pointed out, 'work rights for students make Australia a more attractive place … as they appear to be more generous than in other competitor countries'. Nevertheless, considering the recent economic slowdown and severe layoffs in the electronic and banking sectors, the Malaysian government should only consider granting part-time work permits to these foreign students.

There are significant regional differences in the perception of the 'Climate of the place of study' and 'Level of racial discrimination' variables in the 'Cost' sector. Although the 'Climate of the place of study' variable does not gain a high position on the scale of influencing attributes, it is interesting (albeit not surprising) to learn that there are significant regional differences when it comes to placing it as an influencing attribute of choice of destination. European students obviously do not select Malaysia as a destination because of its climate, whereas students from SEA, Asia, and Africa are indifferent towards it. With average temperatures of 32 degrees Celsius throughout the year, it is not surprising that these weather conditions hold no appeal for students of temperate climates. There is a highly significant regional difference with regard to the 'Favourable level of racial discrimination' variable, fortunately in favour of Malaysia. This variable was put forward by Lawley (1997) to identify foreign, especially Asian, student perceptions of the level of racism in Australia. This study finds that students from Africa and 'Other regions' think highly of Malaysia as a result of its 'Favourable level of racial discrimination'. This is mostly due to a policy of tolerance towards the different races living in Malaysia, which is already a multiracial country.

In the 'Country characteristic' section, European students attach great importance to the 'Safety of place of study' variable, whereas Asian students, although recognizing its importance, do not place it as high as students from other regions. This is due mainly to the fact that Asia and most European countries have experienced political and military calm in recent years, with no outbreak of major conflict, although this might not justify students selecting Malaysia for security reasons. Thus, SEA students (almost 70 per cent were Indonesian) attached great importance to 'Safety of place of study'. Political peace and safety of the country could also be an important attribute in marketing Malaysian tertiary institutions internationally. With its multiracial, tolerant way of life, Malaysia is one of the most hospitable places to live.

The 'Friends' opinion' variable in the 'Country' sector is not only placed as the most insignificant factor in influencing choice of destination, but also indicates regional differences. This rebuts findings by Lay (1991) but coincides with Lawley (1997) and Chapman (1981). It appears that Malaysia is not 'a happening place' for young people (a minus) when compared to other traditionally chosen destinations but does provide excellent courses (a plus from parents' point of view). This coincides with the mean comparisons on 'The standard of course' and 'Family opinions' variables, which show only minimal differences and indicate that this variable is a very influential choice destination attribute.

6   Conclusion

Expanding Malaysian tertiary institutions globally would serve government aims to position Malaysia as a centre of excellence in education. However, in order to succeed, administrators must understand the need of potential overseas students to consider carefully their choice of tertiary institution. The primary purpose of this study was to identify and verify attributes contributing to the selection of destination for tertiary education in Malaysia. Although this study successfully identified these attributes, caution should be applied, nevertheless, in promoting tertiary education in Malaysia. The results of this study suggest that it should be done selectively with respect to region and attribute. Moreover, apart from having ascertained the attributes students look for in their choice destination, tertiary administrators are also urged to understand what foreign students themselves feel. This assessment is essential if Malaysian competitive advantages in the world market are to be measured and assets ascertained that need to be enhanced.

References

AGB (1992), *International Competitiveness Study* (Canberra: Department of Employment, Education and Training).

Austin, M. (1988), 'Asian Electrical and Computing Engineers at a California University: Why are They Here? Why Might They Stay?', *Research Report* (University of California, Santa Barbara).

Australia Industry Commission (1991), *Exports of Education Services*, Report No. 12 (Canberra).

Baird, L. (1967), *The Educational Tools of College Bound Youth*, American College Testing Program Research Report (Iowa).

Blaug, M. and Woodhall, M. (1985), 'A Survey of Overseas Students in British Higher Education 1980', P. Williams (London: Heinemann).

Bower, T. and Pugh, R. (1972), 'A Comparison of Factors Underlying College Choice by Students and Parents', American Educational Research Association Annual Meeting.

Chandler, A. (1989), *Obligation or Opportunity?* IIE Research Report No. 18, August (New York).

Chapman, D. W. (1981), 'A Model of Student College Choice', *Journal of Higher Education*, 52 (5), 490–505.

Griffin, A. and Hauser, J. (1993), 'The Voice of the Customer', *Marketing Science*, Winter, 1–27.

Harris, D. R. and Rhall, T. M. (1993), *Survey of International Students* (Canberra: Department of Employment Education and Training).

Hill, C., Romm, T. and Patterson, P. (1992), 'The Pre-Purchase Decision Making Process Experienced by Overseas Students in Australia', Paper presented at the ANZAM (Australian and New Zealand Academy of Management) Conference, University of Western Sydney (Sydney).

Houston, M. (1979), 'Cognitive Structure and Information Search Patterns of Prospective Graduate Business Students', *Advances in Consumer Research*, VII (October), 552–7.

Illing, D. (1998), 'Malaysian visas drop 80 per cent', *The Australian*, 1 July.

Joseph, M. and Joseph, B. (1998), 'Identifying Need of Potential Students in Tertiary Education for Strategy Development', *Quality Assurance in Education*, 6 (2), 90–6.

Joseph, M. and Joseph, B. (2000), 'Indonesian Students' Perceptions of Choice Criteria in the Selection of a Tertiary Institution: Strategic Implications', *The International Journal of Education Management*, 14 (1), 40–4.

Kamarudin, K. (1997), *Internationalizing Post-graduate Education* (Universiti Teknologi Malaysia, Johor Bahru, Post-Graduate Education Regional Seminar).

Krone, F., Gilly, M., Zeithaml, V. and Lamb, C. (1983), 'Factor Influencing the Graduate Business School Decision', American Marketing Association Educators' Proceedings, Chicago.

Lawley, M. A. (1993), 'Factor Influencing the Choice of Destination', *International: The Case of Hong Kong*, MBus thesis (University of Southern Queensland).

Lawley, M. A. (1997), 'International Students: Reasons for Choice of an Overseas Study Destination', 11th Australian International Education Conference (Melbourne).

Lay, L. (1981), 'Marketing Higher Education', *Journal of Higher Education*, 51 (4), 40–59.

Maslen, G. (1998), 'AIEF points to grow in new market', *Campus Review*, 8 (11), 25–31.

Mohamad, H. M., Zahiruddin, G. and Kassim, Mohammad Shah (2001), 'The Development of Global Education in Malaysia: Strategies for Internationalization' (unpublished).

Murphy, P. (1981), 'Consumer Buying Roles in College Choice', *College and University*, 56, 140–50.

Ramaiah, A. L. (1996), 'Emerging Trends in the Development of Higher Education', National Seminar on Internationalizing Higher Education (University of Malaya, Kuala Lumpur).

Rao, G. L. (1979), *Brain Drain and Foreign Students* (Brisbane: University of Queensland).

Steadman, G. T. and Dagwell, R. H. (1990), 'A Survey of Overseas Students in Queensland', *Australian Universities Review*, Vols 1 and 2, 59–63.

Sulaiman, Y. (1997), 'Government Policy and its Effects on Postgraduate Education', Post-Graduate Education Regional Seminar (Universiti Teknologi Malaysia, Johor Bahru).

Throsby, C. D. (1986), 'Economic Aspects of the Foreign Student Question', *Economic Record*, December, 400–14.

Webb, M. (1993), 'Variables Influencing Graduate Business Students', *College and University*, Vol. 12, 38–46.

Wu, W. C. (1989), 'Strategy Formulation in the International Service Sector: Factors Influencing Students' Perceptions of College Recruiting Activities', PhD Thesis (University of Mississippi).

8
Revisit the Impact of the Single European Market Programme on the Reorganization of Japanese Subsidiaries in the Region: Case Studies of Canon, YKK and Mitsui OSK Lines

Romdej Phisalaphong

1 Introduction

In 1985 the European Commission introduced the single European market programme with the intention of eliminating a wide range of non-tariff barriers to the internal movement of goods, services, assets and labour in the European Community by January 1993.

This chapter aims to clarify the impact of the programme on the operation of Japanese companies in the region and their responses to it by introducing case studies on three Japanese companies with substantial operations in Europe: Canon, YKK and Mitsui OSK Lines. First, the methodology used will be introduced. The chapter will then analyse the potential impact of the economic integration on foreign direct investment. The analysis is used in subsequent sections to categorize the results of the investigation into the impact of the programme on the Canon, YKK and Mitsui OSK Lines organizations in Europe. This is followed by the summary of the investigation with the aim of extracting common elements from all three case studies.

2 Methodology

This chapter uses case studies as a way to demonstrate how the single European market programme has affected Japanese direct investment in the region. The three companies used in this study were selected carefully in order to represent the bulk of investment. Canon was selected for its substantial production activities in the region and its characteristic high scale economies production which is commonly found in Japanese direct investment there. YKK was also selected for its sizeable investment as well as the characteristic low-volume, high-variety and extensive customer-orientation of its products. It is therefore useful to give an insight into the impact of the programme on the investment of a non-Canon type enterprise. In addition to its similar substantial operations in the region, Mitsui OSK Lines is in the transport service business, which faced an immediate business environment change as a result of liberalization of trade and service flows.

In order to understand the impact of the single market programme on the three companies, three data collection methods were used. First, existing literature was reviewed in order to acquire first-hand information about the firms in question. The main works used in this process are A. Kudo, *Taioushu chokusetsu toushi no genjo* (in Japanese, 1993) and R. Strange, *Japanese Manufacturing Investment in Europe: its impact on the UK economy* (1993). Kudo (1993) is particularly useful for its substantial description and analysis of the changing circumstances faced by Canon and YKK and their responses to them in the late 1980s and early 1990s. Although less detailed on individual company information, Strange (1993) provides a comprehensive comparison of Japanese subsidiaries in several business sectors and a description of anti-dumping cases targeted on them.

Second, published documents from the three companies were used for general information, including annual business reports, company handbooks, publicized news, and websites.

Finally, sequential interviews were conducted with the management of the three firms at their European headquarters, distribution centres, and production and sales subsidiaries. The interviews, in combination with the published documents, helped to acquire additional information, explore new ways of analysis, and confirm and compare firm strategies in a long run with those in a relatively short run described in the existing literature.

3   The categorization of the impact of the single market programme on foreign direct investment

The impact of the single market programme can be divided into the impact on *the locational advantages of the EU* and those on *the internalization advantages of foreign investors.* The former can be further divided into *production factors* and *market factors* which only applies when a firm supplies the local market.

The impact on *the internalization advantages of foreign investors* can be illustrated by three factors: (1) the utilization of cross-border production technology, (2) the preferential treatment of member governments as a result of intensified internal competition for foreign direct investment, and (3) the restriction of regional FDI regulations. However, due to difficulties in apprehending the second and third factors at firm level, analysis here will concentrate on the first factor only.

The *production factors* of the single market programme impact on the benefit of the European location consists of (1) the possibility of more efficient production through reorganization, and (2) the expansion of part procurement scope.

There are two additional *market factors* for firms that provide local markets with their products: (1) the reshaping of final product markets and the increase of competition, and (2) the increase and fear of external trade barriers.

3.1   The internalization advantages of foreign investors

3.1.1   The utilization of cross-border production technology

Market integration enables foreign firms (particularly multinationals) to utilize their skills and experience on cross-border production, to combine efficiently a wider scale of production factors and manufacturing technology. Furthermore, since these skills are often intangible and difficult to transfer to local firms, foreign prefer direct investment to other modes of utilization.

3.2   Production factors of European location

3.2.1   The possibility of more efficient production through reorganization

Due to the reduction of internal non-tariff trade barriers, the cost of cross-border production has declined. This enhances the benefits of scale economies and specialization firms can gain from the reorganization of their production.

Production can be reorganized in several ways: for example, vertical integration of production or product specialization; horizontal integration of production or specialization of production process; construction of regionally integrated functions such as regional headquarters and regional distribution centres in place of national functions; and the increase of production scale through mergers and acquisitions. The evidence suggests that compared with their local counterparts, foreign firms are likely to obtain more benefits from the possibility of reorganizing production. This is because of their concentration on sensitive sectors (e.g., high scale economy sectors) and their superiority in cross-border production (Dunning 1998).

Foreign firms can conduct *reorganization investment* or *rationalized investment* to reorganize their production. When foreign firms have already been producing in the integrated region, production facilities could be regrouped in fewer locations with more favourable costs. This *reorganization investment* may not entail a net increase in foreign direct investment in the integrated region. On the other hand, *rationalized investment* is the new direct investment that responds to lower production costs. This results directly in the increase of foreign direct investment in the region (Yannopoulos 1990). The rapid increase in Japanese firms in the late 1980s has partly been explained as a result of being relative outsiders (Clegg and Scott-Green 1999).

The reorganization of production in Japanese affiliates from national to regional base is evident from the change in sales and production figures. Since 1986, the distribution of sales of Japanese affiliates between the host country and the rest of the EC has altered significantly. While the overall share of sales in Europe (both local and intra-EC) has remained almost constant at 95 per cent, the share of sales directed to other EC countries has increased regularly, rising from 4 per cent in 1988 to 22 per cent in 1990 and then 24 per cent in 1991 (MITI 1992).

3.2.2   The expansion of part procurement scope

The reduction of internal trade barriers enables firms to obtain parts from a wider range of sources, enhancing competition among part suppliers. This increases the opportunity of acquiring better quality parts at a lower price. However, this effect should be partly offset by the increase in competition among producers for production factors, e.g., labour.

3.3   Market factors

3.3.1   The reshaping of final product markets and the increase of competition

The single market programme enables foreign firms to access the integrated European market, whose 340 million customers make it almost as large as the US and Japanese markets combined. The integrated market encourages market-seeking foreign direct investment in two different ways: *the increase in the optimal size of market-servicing investment* and the *strategic investment reaction of oligopoly.*

Increasing the optimal size of market-servicing investment results from the inadequacy of initially fragmented markets to achieve minimum optimal scale economies. Market integration increases the efficiency, and consequently, the profitability of investment, thus enhancing incentives for foreign direct investment.

However, the prospect of a unified, less fragmented market with increased sale opportunities might also encourage some firms to invest in excessive capacity they do not intend to use, in order to deter potential competitors from the expanded future market (Helpman and Krugman 1989). This is called *strategic investment reaction of oligopoly*.

In summary, the integration of the internal market induces more foreign direct investment. Aristotelous and Fountas (1996) found strong evidence in favour of a single market effect where anticipation of a larger market due to a barrier-free European market leads to an increase in the inflow of foreign direct investment. Furthermore, the fact that the share of small-market countries like Belgium, Luxembourg and the Netherlands hosting foreign direct investment has increased significantly since the latter half of the 1980s confirms a shift in foreign firms' marketing strategies from a national basis into a regional basis.

Nonetheless, the enhanced possibility of firms in one country to penetrate markets in other countries also results in higher competition. The new competitive environment increasingly requires more market orientation and speedy decision-making. Furthermore, it intensifies the downward pressure on product prices, and therefore reduces the attractiveness of the market. This effect could be substantial in industries that previously had a monopolistic situation.

3.3.2   *The increase and fear of external trade barriers*

Three factors lead to the expectation of external trade barriers against third countries in the case of market unification. First, member states may have to compensate their national local industries due to the reduction of internal trade barriers (Bhagwati 1993). Second, the European Community has often *communitarized* its members' respective policies, for instance in the case of voluntary export restraints (VERs) on import of Japanese cars. In addition, the European Community has suffered from the *restaurant bill* problem, as each member has often been successful in having the Commission add its restrictive measure to those adopted at Community level (Winters 1993). Winters claimed that the gradually increased use of European Community non-tariff barriers compared to other countries is a result of this problem.

Third, the expectation of an increase in trade barriers may escalate due to *the uncertainty of policy-making*. The external trade policy of the European Commission is based on a variety of policy instruments whose application is not always specified with clarity and certainty. In addition, the Commission has fluctuated between protectionism and a more liberal policy (Abe 1999). This uncertainty may encourage unnecessarily high levels of foreign direct investment in expectation of restrictions on future access to the enlarged market. New foreign direct investment stimulated by uncertainty can raise problems with surplus capacity and does not correspond to an efficient worldwide distribution of investment resources (Yannopoulos 1990).

Additionally, according to the Heckscher-Ohlin theory, the increase in external barriers in the EC may enhance the income of import-competing industries. As the return on capital improves, inward foreign direct investment is expected to increase (Hansen, Heinrich and Nielsen 1992).

Barrell and Pain (1999) found that Japanese direct investment, controlling market prices and relative labour costs, was induced by trade protection measures and in particular by the level of anti-dumping actions initiated in the 1980s. Belderbos (1997), using firm-level data for the Japanese electronics sector, found that anti-dumping duties in the EU had a substantial effect on the probability of Japanese firms setting up manufacturing plants in Europe.

4   The impact of the single market programme on Canon

In Europe, Canon is a US$7.0 billion company that employs 12,500 people in research, manufacturing, marketing, sales, service and recycling, accounting for more than 25 per cent of its world-wide business. It has production bases in Giessen, Germany and Bretagne, France. Based in London and Amsterdam, Canon Europe Ltd and Canon Europa NV are the headquarters for sales, marketing and distribution operations in Europe, Africa and the Middle East (Figure 8.1). Canon Europa NV imports more than 1,100 ocean containers on a monthly basis and more than 230 trucks serve the European market, 25 per cent of which is distributed via Canon's central distribution centre in the Netherlands. A Canon subsidiary has been established in each European country to represent Canon in the supply and service of its products.

4.1   History

Canon started with a representative office for overall European business in Switzerland in 1963. Switzerland was selected for its flexible tax system which was beneficial to reinvestment. In 1968, the company established a distribution centre in Amsterdam, the Netherlands, which was suitable because of its generous visa system regarding foreign labour, its

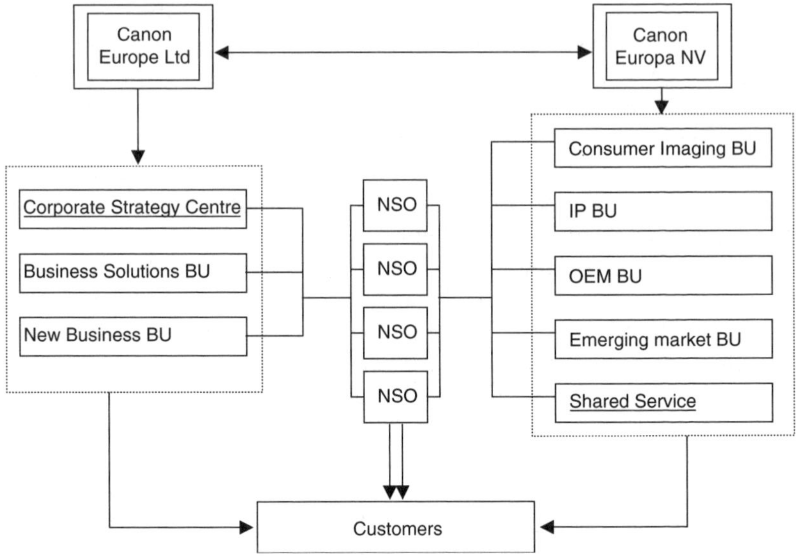

Figure 8.1   Canon organization in Europe

good labour pool with the added advantage of high English language ability, and the country's geographical advantage for distribution. In 1982, the company expanded the functions of the centre and renamed it Canon Europa. Invoice-related works carried out in Switzerland were moved to the new subsidiary. Later, with the improvement of the Dutch tax system, tax-related works were also moved here (Kudo 1993).

Around this time, rising export figures to the UK, France and Germany called for Canon subsidiaries in each of these countries. The function of Canon Europa changed from being a mere distribution centre to being a decision-making centre for European business (Kudo 1993). Canon Europa was reorganized in 2000, while the regional strategic planning function was transferred to Canon Europe Ltd in London. The reason for dispersing the European headquarters was the availability of information technology and the gradual need for European personnel in a customer-oriented business approach. Furthermore, the booming economy in the Netherlands led to a labour deficit. The UK was selected in response to the need for an English-speaking base.

4.2   Impacts and responses

In contrast to Western companies, Canon used a pragmatic, incremental approach in response to the single market, a process which took over ten years to complete. This approach is quite common among Japanese companies in Europe, and arises from a lack of clear business concepts, cooperative management style (unlike the US top-down style), and time-consuming information transmission to the parent firms in Japan. In 2001, Canon experienced a final decisive reorganization, the reasons for which were more availability of information from EU and American counterparts, the use of consulting firms, the switch from executive personnel to an EU-experienced group, the increase of pan-EU customers (e.g., pan-EU retailers and wholesalers), enhanced product diversification by competitors, availability of information technology, stagnation of the market combined with increasing competition, product characteristics that increase the need for a customer-oriented approach, preparation for the European monetary union, and the increased importance of management competition due to a reduced technological advantage.

4.2.1   The reorganization of the manufacturing function

In Europe, Canon produces mainly copying machines. Even within this seemingly narrow range of products, the company has chosen to produce different products at separate production bases and identical products at one production base only in order to reap scale economies. Since the production system was initially in line with economic integration, the changes here were less dramatic than those of YKK. The factory in Giessen, Germany specializes in the manufacturing of high-grade, high-speed copying machines, photosensitive drums, refilling of toner cartridges for copying machines and ink cartridges for bubble-jet printers. The French factory in Bretagne manufactures desktop copying machines, laser printers, and fax machines. Low-speed copying machines were previously produced at the Canon factory in Italy. However, with increased competition from Asia and probably a decline in anti-dumping threats, the factory ceased production in 2000.

The main markets for Canon copying machines in Europe are the UK (25 per cent), France (25 per cent), and Germany (25 per cent), with 25 per cent for the rest of Europe. Coordinated by Canon Europa in the Netherlands, products from both factories are transported directly to the sales subsidiaries in each European country, with the exception of the Nordic and Benelux countries which go through Canon Europa.

4.2.2   The reorganization of distribution and sales functions

Up to the middle of the 1990s, Canon had two sales systems: direct sales (with the one-country, one-agency system) and dealers. From the late 1980s, the ratio of direct sales increased and was consolidated (Canonized) in order to strengthen technical and financial support for the sale of new products in preparation for business diversification, as well as in response to government and national purchasing. In addition, it was concerned that dealers would be more likely to concentrate on short-term profit maximization than long-term planning (Kudo 1993). Today, with the exception of Portugal, most of the EU NSOs (National Sales Organizations) are 100 per cent Canon stock-holding companies.

With the reorganization of the sales function, transactions currently pass via two main routes: traditional NSOs and direct dealing at Canon Europa to increase big-lot or pan-European customers. The traditional NSO one-country, one-agency system has been under pressure from the proliferation of cross-border trade by independent distributors and dealers who utilize the decrease in border procedures and the fluctuation of European currencies to transport Canon goods to other countries at the lowest price in one particular country. This has brought about the greater comparability of prices between countries, and consequently the need for closer NSO coordination by the European headquarters.

Pan-European transactions have taken place in two ways. First, American competitors responded to market unification by increasing low-profit, large-amount sales, or so-called 'warehouse sales'. In addition, customers Europe-wide started to order through a 'pan-European account', which covers the whole of Europe and where negotiations cannot be carried out at the individual country level. This need for Europe-wide treatment also appeared in the after-service provision.

With regard to the distribution function, Canon has planned to redirect the flow and stock of goods to reduce transport and warehouse costs. This plan, however, was still in progress in 2001.

4.2.3   *The reorganization of the headquarters function*

Two subsidiaries share the function of headquarters: Canon Europe Ltd in the UK as the pan-EU strategic planning centre and Canon Europa NV as the logistics and distribution centre. Canon Europe Ltd consists of Corporate Strategy Centre, Business Solutions BU, and New Business BU. The Corporate Strategy Centre controls the pan-EU management, IT, and financial and human resource strategies. In Europe, it has the important task of loosely controlling the sector's operation as well as assisting communication between product-based departments in Japan and country-based sales subsidiaries in the EU. Business Unit (BU) is a division with a mandate over a particular business sector. Business Solutions BU is a business unit dealing with customer service for IT solutions products. New Business BU researches markets for new products. Because of the novelty of the markets, the headquarters controls these two product sectors.

Canon Europa NV comprises Consumer Imaging BU, Imaging Products (IP) BU, OEM BU, Emerging Market BU, and Shared Services. Consumer Imaging BU is the centre for pan-EU marketing support for camera, video, bubble-jet printer, scanner, fax and POP products. IP BU has the same mandate for semiconductor sales and service. OEM BU deals with the sales of OEM (Original Equipment Manufacturer) products to other manufacturers. Emerging Market BU takes care of marketing, servicing, and selling strategies in emerging markets such as Africa, Russia, Eastern Europe, and the Middle East. Shared Services is the back office for pan-Europe functions such as training and administration.

Missions for the new organization as described by Canon management are an efficient pan-EU logistics structure (pan-EU marketing approach in response to pan-EU scale customers, speeded-up collection and distribution of information between the parent firm, subsidiaries and customers, and reduce production stock); more information-sharing among an increasing number of employees (using IT to improve marketing research); the creation and provision of new values (with more local R&D for the diversification of products and promotion of business solutions); and the enhancement of the problem-solving ability of pan-EU organization (tax, labour, finance, training, benchmarking-related works) by regionalizing functions through shared services.

Concerning the new headquarters function, local subsidiaries accept the need for expert support in the fields of finance, tax, laws, and advertising. In the field of law, for example, support from EU law experts is indispensable. In addition, the production plan must be carried out on a global scale. However, they insisted that decisions on marketing, sales and service functions should be taken independently by the local subsidiaries; thus the independence of local subsidiaries is required to a certain extent.

Although important decisions are still taken in the parent company, particularly as regards production and research, the role of the Canon European headquarters has expanded from pure coordination and exchange of information to co-decision-making on important issues and full decisions on less important ones. It also has the authority to seek and control new businesses independently.

4.2.4   The expansion of part procurement scope

The expansion of part procurement scope is not apparent in the case of Canon. In 2000, 30–40 per cent of parts used in manufacturing at Canon Giessen were imported from Japan, 60–70 per cent from EU countries. However, 90 per cent of the latter come from Germany and only 10 per cent from other EU countries such as the Netherlands, Denmark,

Spain, or Italy. This can be explained partly by its manufacturing system which requires fast delivery, close quality control, the development of part suppliers in the country, and the increasing possibility of importing cheap parts from outside the region, especially from Asian countries.

4.2.5   *The reshaping of markets: new business, R&D*

Canon has two R&D centres, one in the UK for software development and one in France for research on telecommunication. With the reshaping of the European markets, Canon transferred management of the two centres to Canon European headquarters. With the new organization, the centres can buy, sell and cooperate with non-Canon firms in order to increase the efficiency of production and capital. In addition, Canon established Criteria, a 100 per cent Canon Europe Ltd share-holding company in the UK, in order to expand business fields in solutions technology.

4.2.6   *The increase of competition*

The company was not particularly aware of the increase in competition in the region. This is because the integration of the markets coincided with their high growth. However, with the more liberal development of the programme in later stages imported goods became cheaper and, therefore, the need for further cost reduction in the production processes increased. The benefit of being in the region has less to do with cost reduction than with market and service information, the reduction of production time, as well as more flexibility in production.

4.2.7   *The increase and fear of external trade barriers*

Both the fear of, and the increase in, external trade barriers apparently influenced Canon's decision to establish production bases and, at a later stage, introduce localization policies. The Bretagne factory in France was established in 1983 for the production of electronic typewriters, copying machines and facsimile machines, just one year before the anti-dumping case on electronic typewriters imported from Japan, which resulted in a 35 per cent definitive duty being imposed on imported electric typewriters from the Canon parent company in 1985. The anti-dumping duty on typewriters was later extended to typewriters assembled in the Community by Canon Bretagne, resulting in the definitive duty of 44 ECU. The duties were lifted accordingly, however, after Canon Bretagne offered the Community acceptable undertakings on the future procurement of parts and materials.

An anti-dumping case on plain paper photocopiers imported from Japan was also initiated in 1985 which led to 20 per cent of definitive duty imposed on Canon Inc. in 1987. In the same year (1987) Canon decided to participate with an Italian photocopy manufacturer, Olivetti, in Olivetti-Canon Industriale SpA in Italy for the production of photocopiers, laser printers, and facsimile machines. The duty on plain paper photocopiers was extended to a few Japanese companies in 1988 but was terminated without extension of duty to Canon Giessen, Olivetti-Canon Industrial SpA, and Canon Bretagne. The reasons were Canon Geissen and Olivetti-Canon Industrial both used less than 60 per cent of imported Japanese parts in finished plain paper photocopiers, while Canon Bretagne offered undertakings on the future sourcing of parts and materials (Strange 1993).

However, following the upsurge of Japanese investment in the late 1980s, European production of photocopiers diminished substantially as a result of the termination of production and the serial capital acquisitions of Japanese companies. This reduced the threats of external trade barriers for Japanese companies (Bourke 1996).

5   The impact of the single market programme on YKK

Besides having sales subsidiaries in every European country, YKK has 15 factories scattered around Europe (Figure. 8.2). The five in France, Germany, Italy, the UK, and Spain are main factories, accompanied by ten small assembling factories. The production of YKK in Europe is limited to the fastener sector, which alone has global sales of over US$1.7 billion. It consists of Slide Fastener Division which currently produces 80 per cent of the profits, Snap Fastener and Button Division (15 per cent), and Textile and Plastic Products Division (5 per cent).

5.1   History

YKK was among the first Japanese investors in Europe. Its first production site dates back to 1964. The investment incentive was to compete with local firms that enjoyed the decrease in internal tariffs and external common tariffs, due to the 1958 common market programme. In addition, the company had suffered from its late response to notices. It had initially regarded the European market as unified and intended to supply it from one production site. The company later realized the different market demand in individual countries. It therefore expanded its production to several countries. The second factory was built in neighbouring Germany in 1972 to serve this different demand and fast delivery.

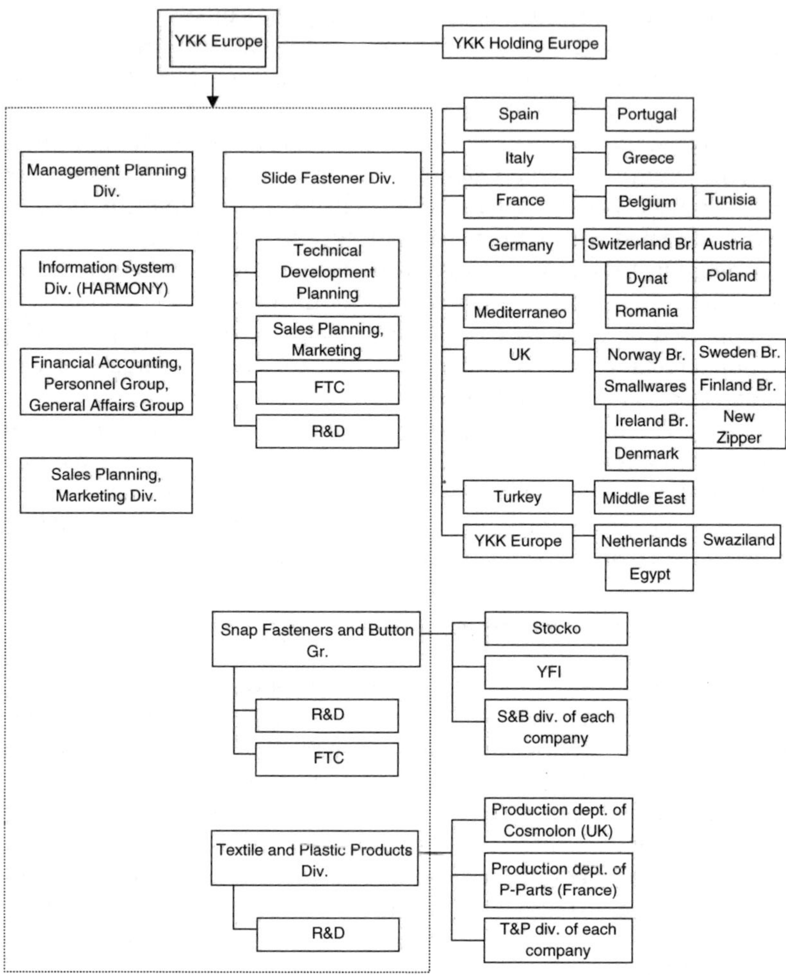

Figure 8.2   YKK organization in Europe, and Middle and East Africa (EMEA)

Before this, the country had to import YKK products from the Dutch factory. This was also the case in France in 1972. Thereafter, more than ten factories were established around Europe for the same reason. In 1977, YKK established a company in Italy, YKK Mediterraneo SpA, in order to manufacture zip-fastener parts for supply to other European factories (Kudo 1993).

In 1988, the company planned the establishment of its European headquarters, which came into full effect in 1990. The YKK Holding

Company, the stockowner, was established in Amsterdam in 1988. Two years later, the European management centre, YKK Europe Ltd, was built in London. The change of organization was not only the result of a long-term strategy towards market unification but also short-term strategies for the stagnation of demand due to the depression in 1993 (Kudo 1993).

5.2 Impacts and responses

5.2.1 The reorganization of the manufacturing function

As previously mentioned, the decision to establish YKK production bases was the result of the high quality orientation and strict delivery demands of European clothing manufacturers. In response to these, YKK adopted a one-country, one-factory production system for low-volume production of a large variety of products.

In order to increase production efficiency and remain in close proximity to customers, YKK has divided its production into upstream and downstream. The production of upstream goods was shifted to main factories in five countries in order to polarize production. However, downstream goods continued to be produced in all factories of the region. These assembling factories acquired raw materials from the main factories. The reduction of work meant that assembling factories would have vacant capacity which could be used for the diversification of products or even business. Furthermore, the main factories allocated the production of different kinds of zippers, including magic tape in the UK, plastic notions (small garments) in France, and metal notions in Italy. Factories in France and the Netherlands also altered production processes to suit diversification of production, so that machines that cut spesa (long zippers) according to usage and previously stood in a horizontal line, for example, were partly regrouped vertically in order to increase flexibility of ordered production (Kudo 1993).

However, the dual system of production allocation is facing a serious new problem: the moving of customers, apparel manufacturers, into Southern Europe, Eastern Europe and Turkey to cut production costs in response to the single market programme. In the early years, these apparel manufacturers purchased raw materials, including zippers, in the northern parts and had them sent to southern parts for the production of final goods. However, with the accumulation of experience and development of systems, they began to require raw materials be produced in the southern parts. The decline of demand in the north has pressured the shifting of YKK's downstream production to those regions and may result in the closure of a number of factories in the north.

In order to sustain subsidiary businesses in the northern part, gaining new business and new customers, particularly those with a high concern for delivery dates and quality, is essential.

5.2.2   The reorganization of distribution and sales functions

YKK uses a direct sales system in all European markets, with the partial exception of the UK where the ratio of direct sales is relatively low. It has established a sales subsidiary in each country with direct connection to the factories there. The sales of three business sectors, slide fastener, snap fastener and button, and textile and plastic products, operate in one unit. This one-country, one-agency system has enabled YKK to adapt quality, price and colour of its products to the demand and preference of individual European markets.

This 'market-in' strategy, however, will have to change. Market unification has popularized cross-border trade, which utilizes the price difference (has been up to 15 per cent) between countries. Under the EU law, refusal to sell to cross-border trade dealers is not allowed. This has changed the territory awareness of sales subsidiaries drastically. Furthermore, another type of transaction has prospered as a result of market unification: the pan-European account. As in the case of Canon, the pan-European account has created the need for deals at a regional level. Large companies (e.g., Hallmark), which have their production bases in several EU countries, started to order goods in one regional price, quality and currency. The percentage of pan-European accounts increased to 20 per cent of overall sales in 2001.

5.2.3   The reorganization of the headquarters function

In 1990, the European headquarters of YKK was established in London. Its function includes coordinating between the subsidiaries and the parent company, planning regional strategies, purchasing common parts and services (e.g., insurance, air cargo fares), and managing financial and reinvestment plans for all subsidiaries in Europe.

With the polarization of production and the inflexibility of delivery dates, the need for close coordination between YKK subsidiaries by the European headquarters has substantially increased. Moreover, the headquarters produces simulations to indicate the best site for production. Criteria include labour costs, labour quality, the convenience of part procurement, transportation network, currency exchange, and financial institutions.

The parts procurement of YKK factories in Europe can be divided into three main categories. A large part of the raw materials are purchased directly by each factory from YKK material factories in several regions: for instance, wires from Japan, some final products from Asia, and sliders from YKK Mediterraneo in Italy. Each factory also purchases specific parts for individual factory production needs from outside sources. However, common parts from outside sources (such as threads) are purchased at headquarters. In 2001, the purchase of common parts amounts to 10 per cent of overall purchases. In addition, for purchases of the first two sorts, the European headquarters also has responsibility for checking, contracting, and coordinating the flows. The demand for particular final products and their parts rises and falls rapidly in the fashion world. Therefore, appropriate coordination can hedge the production risk and cost of YKK material production bases.

Financial decisions such as those on reinvestment are among the decisions previously prepared on a national basis and proposed directly to the parent company. Under the new organization, dividends are first collected at YKK Holdings in the Netherlands before being redistributed to the subsidiaries according to the need for additional finance. The national-based decision-making pattern was beneficial in the first investment stage when there was a great need and an opportunity for domestic reinvestment. However, due to the saturation of several European markets, especially in the north, chances for business expansion in the same sector have diminished. In order to improve the returns on investment, subsidiaries have to reinvest beyond their traditional boundaries in other fields of business requiring new expertise, or in other European countries, even in Africa or Asia. This enhances the benefits of the regionalization of financial decisions.

All the same, regionalizing all works in the European headquarters is not the best solution for the management of YKK. Additional decision-making procedures can be costly and time-consuming. At YKK European headquarters, attempts to shorten these procedures are regulated by some executives holding more than one position. This speeds up decision processes and reduces administrative costs.

In addition, the importance of the European headquarters function is weakened by a number of factors that enhance the benefits of management centralization to the overall YKK headquarters in Japan, such as the development of information technology and the globalization of business. The return of employees with European experience to the parent company has further enhanced its ability to analyse and make decisions. In 2001, the directors of the three product divisions in Japan all had European experience. This enables each sector in the local subsidiaries to report directly to Japanese headquarters. The return of more management works to Japan is now a matter of time and depends on the development of technology for data collection.

5.2.4   *The reorganization of business systems*

Besides the reorganization of sales and production functions, YKK has integrated several business systems in its subsidiaries in Europe to be controlled by specialists at the European headquarters. These include year of depreciation, accounting systems and paper administration systems. The company has developed a new programme called 'Harmony' to be used for the integration of accounting in common European sales management. With the introduction of this software, customers, orders, stocks, and sales amount can be aggregated and shown punctually. This is part of the standardization and sharing of information. The system also enables the calculation of productivity and its comparison in the different countries, which was not possible in the past. The setting of common currency among subsidiaries was also a topic for discussion. However, after a try with ECU the plan was cancelled because of currency fluctuation (Kudo 1993).

5.2.5   *The expansion of part procurement scope*

YKK's factories in Europe are all fairly small-scale and have little contact with outside parts makers. Most raw materials and all machinery are produced internally. Therefore the influence of the market unification programme on the scope of YKK's parts procurement is extremely limited. Nevertheless, some common materials are purchased regionally by the headquarters. For specific parts from outside producers, the high specification of some European customers (e.g., requests for particular domestic parts) obstructs the regionalization of part procurement.

5.2.6   *The reshaping of markets: new business, R&D*

In 1994, YKK acquired Stocko, a European company specializing in specific snap fasteners, in order to acquire new technology and explore new markets. However, the acquisition was not successful mainly due to the lack of experience in the YKK business. In contrast, the acquisition of a German company, Dynat, and a UK company, New Zipper, have brought YKK large profits because the company already had experience in the business prior to the acquisitions.

6   The impact of the single market programme on Mitsui OSK Lines

Mitsui OSK Lines is the eleventh largest liner (marine-shipping) company in the world, with 16,000 employees worldwide. With its 'three-key

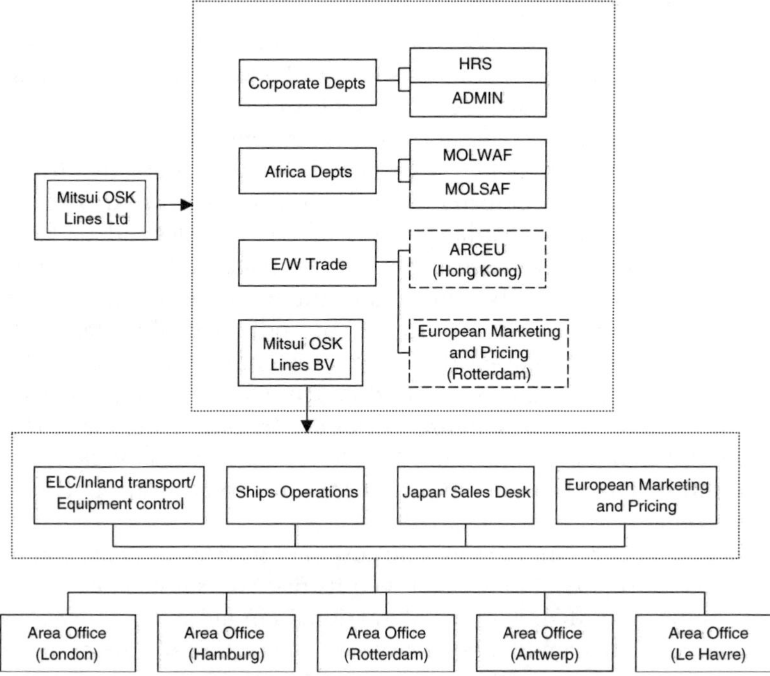

Figure 8.3 Mitsui OSK Lines organization for liner business in Europe

regions' concept, the company increased its investment in Europe by establishing a European headquarters with both area and trade functions, and a number of subsidiaries in its two major businesses: liners and logistics (Figure 8.3). For the liner business, the company established European headquarters in London and Rotterdam and area offices in London, Hamburg, Rotterdam, Antwerp and Le Havre. For the logistics business, the Netherlands is the stronghold of the company with the service area covering all of Europe. Recently renamed MOL Logistics Netherlands, it is the European core of the company's global logistics network, offering services that include freight forwarding, warehousing, truck transportation and supply chain management. It comprises Wassing BV and Hermex in Tilburg and MO Express International in Rotterdam. Wassing has a turnover of 53 million guilders, 28,000 square metres of warehouse, and 295 employees. MO Express International was established in 1989 to service the logistic needs, including air and ocean freight, of Japanese companies in the Netherlands. The company has 25 employees and an annual turnover of 14 million guilders.

6.1 History

Up to the middle of the 1980s, Mitsui OSK Lines had established several representative offices for liner business in London, Milan, Rotterdam, Paris, Hamburg and Duisburg. These offices merely had reporting tasks, while actual works were outsourced to independent local agencies through contracts. The responsibilities of branch offices were later extended and they became limited companies as of 1990 with their own departments for tax procedures, vessel arrangements, unloading, sales and marketing, mainly because of increased competition, changing business patterns (work does not stop at the ports), and the need for speedy (a shorter chain) and interconnected services. As of April 2000 all container ship services from Asia to Europe (trade management function) were unified at Mitsui OSK Lines (Europe) in London. This replaces a system whereby Europe-bound space was controlled jointly by offices in Tokyo, Hong Kong and London. In addition, the Rotterdam subsidiary gained the function of European area management with some strategic controls from London.

For non-liner business, to expand customer services and raise competitiveness Mitsui OSK Lines established its first two subsidiaries in logistics, Amtex and MOL Express International (an air and sea-forwarding service) in Rotterdam in 1988. In 1990 at the request of Fuji Photofilm, Mitsui OSK Lines acquired Wassing, a Dutch logistics company, and positioned it as the hub of its European distribution network. Apart from obvious business relations with Fuji Photofilm, what was decisive for the Wassing acquisition was its ideal location as a distribution centre close to Rotterdam, European's busiest port, as well as its position at the centre of Europe. Hermex, an affiliate of Wassing, thus became the sole distributor for Fuji Photofilm subsidiaries in Europe. The company distributes Fuji products to all EU countries as well as to the USA and Asia. The three subsidiaries merged under the name of MOL Logistics Netherlands in 2000, in order to eliminate redundancies and become a single source of comprehensive services under a unified brand.

6.2 Impacts and responses

The single European market programme of 1992 eliminated import duties, unified documentation for customs requirements at national borders, and abolished customs and border quarantines for animals and plants within Europe. However, from the point of view of Mitsui OSK Lines management, it is difficult to outline benefits and costs of the single market programme on the company's business since the decrease in check-points coincided with increase in traffic, and the slight reduction in paper works was accompanied by a more price-cut customer demand.

6.2.1 *The reorganization of the headquarters function of the liner operation*

The functions of Mitsui OSK Lines (Europe) Ltd in London can be classified in three groups. First, the E/W Trade department has the trade management function for the arrangement of price, profits and container space on the route from Asia to Europe. Second, the Africa department and the European Marketing and Pricing division are the overall strategic planning centres for liner business in Africa and Europe. Third, the Corporate department supports all European subsidiaries with a HRS division for regional human resource management strategies and ADMIN for dealing with customer claims and contracts with independent agencies.

Mitsui OSK Lines (Europe) BV has an area management function covering maintenance, customer services (except the UK and France), business systems, and the arrangement of prices and container space in the trade all over Europe. In practice, the subsidiary organizes EU operational works such as meetings, alliance-related works dealing with large cargoes, as well as visiting global-account customers. It has five departments: Ships Operation, ELC/Inland Transport/Equipment Control, European Marketing and Pricing, Japan Sales Desk (to deal with Japanese and Japanese companies' customers) and Area Offices. There are Area Offices in Hamburg, Rotterdam, London, Antwerp, and Le Havre. Each has its own functions such as sales and marketing, which contact directly to relevant departments in Rotterdam. However, their directors are affiliated to the Area Offices department.

This new structure of European operations results from an accumulation of several factors. First, the trade between Japan and other countries, which was almost all of the trade in 1970s, dropped to a mere 18 per cent in 1990s. With the shift in business turnovers from Japan to abroad, the Mitsui OSK Lines' global operation was highly localized. Works related to international trade coordination, which used to be carried out in Tokyo, are currently done in London and works usually related to the European headquarters, previously done in London, were shifted to Rotterdam. Second, the containerization of shipping increased container services and consequently the importance of Rotterdam port, which at the same time decreased the importance of the UK as a shipping centre. Compared to the relatively small size of Mitsui OSK Lines (Europe) Ltd,

Mitsui OSK Lines (Europe) BV has more than 100 employees for its responsibility over all day-to-day works.

6.2.2   *The reshaping of markets: business expansion and increased competition*

As a response to the decrease of border control, MOL Netherlands group has expanded its logistic operation to destinations in other European countries. Of the 75 per cent of 4,920 Hermex shipments to European destinations in 2000, only 8 per cent were domestic. The UK, Germany and France are the main destinations. For MOL Netherlands, around 30 per cent of MOL Logistics Netherlands land shipments in 2001 go to destinations in the Netherlands, while the rest heads for other EU countries (40–50 per cent of which go to Germany). The company uses its own trucks for shipments within the Benelux countries and hires trucks from external local firms for shipments outside the region. Mounting competition forced the company to withdraw from long-distance service and specialize in service inside the Benelux countries. Nevertheless, competition from other countries is restrained to some extent by regulations that reserve domestic shipments for domestic firms only.

6.2.3   *The expansion of service procurement scope*

The single market programme has expanded the range of subcontracting companies that subsidiaries of Mitsui OSK Lines can use. However, the subsidiaries cannot freely go for lower price and better quality offered by transport companies in different countries. The selection must also consider reliability, which gives an advantage to domestic companies that have had a long relationship with the subsidiaries. Additionally, there is a limitation from customers, who prefer transport companies of their own nationality as convenient contacts. This is particularly the case with Hermex.

7   Summary of the results

This chapter has clarified how the single European market programme affected the European operations of Canon, YKK and Mitsui OSK Lines. Although details differ with regard to reorganization or market reshaping, the case studies show some common elements in the impacts of the programme and responses to them.

First, the final product markets of all three companies have been reshaped as a result of several phenomena including cross-border trade, warehouse sales of competitors, pan-European account trade with customers, relocation of customers, and redefinition (vertical and horizontal) of business boundaries. Nevertheless, market reshaping was limited by the different quality, price, and delivery time preferences of the customers in various EU countries.

Second, the parts and service procurement scope of all three companies has expanded as a result of the programme. However, domestic suppliers still enjoy advantages over procurement due to the need for close quality control, customer specification for particular domestic materials, customer preference for domestic service suppliers as convenient contacts, restrictive national regulations.

Third, there are common strategies for business reorganization:

1 *The polarization and concentration of manufacturing*: companies polarized and concentrated the production of similar products in one production base in order to exploit the benefits of scale economies. Nevertheless, they have endeavoured to maintain their 'market-in' by introducing a few minute changes to similar products such as colour, price, and manual.
2 *Coordination of sales*: sales functions in all three companies were loosely integrated due to the collapse of nationally based sales territories. However, as locals are best suited for local sales and for responding to the demand of sales subsidiaries for independence, reorganization took the form of enhanced coordination of sales subsidiaries through regional headquarters.
3 *Integration of business systems*: business systems such as those for accounting, productivity calculation, cost calculation and ordering were regionally integrated to enable the timely transmission of information for regional strategic planning and coordination.
4 *Regionalization of marketing, finance and overall strategies*: strategic planning for several functions, mainly marketing, finance and overall strategies, have been moved to the authority of the regional strategic planners to increase efficiency and effectiveness.
5 *Sharing supporting facilities such as technical and legal services*: due to the integration of legal systems, the increasing need for professional support and transnational service, sharing of support facilities was introduced to increase efficiency and reduce maintenance costs.
6 *Exploration and development of new markets*: with the reshaping of market environments, the exploration and development of new markets has become more essential in order to survive and grow.

The final point to note here is that the impact of the single European market programme and the respective strategic company responses cannot be considered independently of the surrounding business circumstances. On the contrary, changes in information technology, globalization, and competition from imported goods and other business environments have affected them considerably and must therefore be taken into account.

Acknowledgements

This research proceeded under the supervision of Joop Stam, Leo Sleuwaegen, and Akira Kudo. The author is greatly indebted to the management of Canon, YKK and Mitsui OSK Lines who all kindly gave up their precious time for the interviews. In particular, I would like to thank H. Tsuruoka (President, Canon Europa), M. Ito (President, Canon Giessen), T. Nakamasu (Manager, Canon Europa); M. Fujimori (Company Secretary, YKK Europe); D. Carr (GM, MOL Europe), H. Miyazaki (President, Hermex), T. Yamada (Senior Manager, Fuji Photofilm NL), Y. Sawada (GM, MOL Logistics), T. Tomoda (Manager, MOL Netherlands), and N. Everett (Manager, MOL Europe). Last but not least, I am grateful to Masato Shinohara who kindly introduced me to the management of MOL. Without his help, this chapter could not have been completed.

References

Abe, A. (1999), *Japan and the European Union: Domestic Politics and Transnational Relations* (London: Athlone Press).

Aristotelous, K. and Fountas, S. (1996), 'An Empirical Analysis of Inward Foreign Direct Investment Flows in the EU with Emphasis on the Market Enlargement Hypothesis', *Journal of Common Market Studies*, 34 (4), 571–83.

Barrell, R. and Pain, N. (1999), 'Trade Restraints and Japanese Direct Investment Flows', *European Economic Review*, 43, 29–45.

Belderbos, R. (1997), *Japanese Electronics Multinationals and Strategic Trade Policies* (Oxford: Clarendon Press).

Bhagwati, J. (1993), 'Regionalism and Multilateralism: An Overview' in Melo, J. D. and Panagariya, A. (eds), *New Dimensions in Regional Integration* (New York: Cambridge University Press).

Bourke, T. (1996), *Japan and the Globalisation of European Integration* (Aldershot: Dartmouth).

Canon (several years), *Canon Fact Book* (Tokyo: Canon).

Clegg, J. and Scott-Green, S. (1999), 'The Determinants of New FDI Capital Flows into the EC: A Statistical Comparison of the USA and Japan', *Journal of Common Market Studies*, 37 (4), 597–616.

Dunning, J. (1988), *Explaining International Production* (London: Unwin Hyman).

Hansen, J., Heinrich, H. and Nielsen, J. (1992), *An Economic Analysis of the EC* (London: McGraw-Hill).

Helpman, E. and Krugman, P. R. (1989), *Trade Policy and Market Structure* (Cambridge MA: The MIT Press).

Kudo, A. (1993), *Taioushu chokusetsu toushi no genjo* (Tokyo: Japan Centre for International Finance).

MITI (1992), *Dainijunichikai – Wakaguni Kigyo no kaigai jigyo katsuyo* (Tokyo: Tsusho sangyosho sangyo seisaku kyoku kokusai sangyo ka).

Mitsui OSK Lines (1999), *A Guide to Total Logistics* (Tokyo: MOL).

Mistui OSK Lines (several years), *Annual Report* (Tokyo: MOL).

Strange, R. (1993), *Japanese Manufacturing Investment in Europe: Its Impact on the UK Economy* (London: Routledge).

Winters, A. (1993), 'The European Community: A Case of Successful Integration?' in Melo, J. D. and Panagariya, A. (eds), *New Dimensions in Regional Integration* (New York: Cambridge University Press).

Yannopoulos, G. N. (1990), 'Foreign Direct Investment and European Integration: The Evidence from the Formative Years of the European Community', *Journal of Common Market Studies*, 28 (3), 235–59.

9
Japanese Businesses in China: Performance, Control, Trust and their Relations in Japanese–Chinese Joint Ventures

Tadamasa Imaguchi and Xinjian Li

A great many Japanese companies have established business operations in China since the 1980s, and particularly since 1992. According to several surveys, however, the performance of these enterprises is not satisfactory. After a brief review of the above points, this chapter will focus on joint ventures and examine the relationship between performance, control and trust. It will conduct an empirical study on the control pattern employed by Japanese headquarters for joint ventures in China and its relationship to the achievement of joint-venture objectives, using 14 joint-venture decision-making categories: profit disposal, upper management positioning, strategic priority setting, product pricing, training and development policies, reward and incentive policies, financial control, reinvestment policy, purchasing policies, production planning, sales and distribution, technology innovation, quality control, and recruitment policies. The effect of mutual trust on performance will also be examined. Data were collected from a questionnaire survey conducted in February/March 2001 that involved 215 respondents from 1,015 Japanese companies with joint ventures in the manufacturing industry in China.[1]

1 Development of Japanese direct investments in China: an introduction

Japanese firms have established a vast number of businesses in China since the introduction of the open-door policy in 1979 that allowed FDI. Three investment booms involving Japanese firms in China (see Table 9.1) have occurred up to now. In the early 1980s, Chinese policy

Table 9.1 Trends of Japanese FDI

	Japanese FDI contracts in China				Japanese FDI values in China			
	Amount	To previous year (%)	Share in Japanese world FDI (%)	Share in Japanese Asia FDI (%)	Amount (US$ mil.)	To previous year (%)	Share in Japanese world FDI (%)	Share in Japanese Asia FDI (%)
1983	5		0.2	0.6	3		0	0.2
1984	66	1,320	2.6	9.8	114	3,800	1.1	7.0
1985	118	178.8	4.5	17.2	100	87.7	0.8	7.0
1986	85	72.0	2.7	10.4	226	226.0	1	9.7
1987	101	118.8	2.2	7.5	1,226	542.5	3.7	25.2
1988	171	169.3	2.8	12.5	296	24.1	0.6	5.3
1989	126	73.7	1.9	7.4	438	148.0	0.6	5.3
1990	165	131.0	2.8	11.0	349	79.7	0.6	4.9
1991	246	149.1	5.4	19.3	579	165.9	1.4	9.8
1992	490	199.2	13.1	38.6	1,070	184.8	3.13	16.7
1993	700	142.9	20.1	47.4	1,691	158.0	4.7	25.5
1994	636	90.9	25.7	48.7	2,565	151.7	6.2	26.4
1995	770	121.1	26.9	47.3	4,485	174.9	8.7	36.2
1996	365	47.4	14.6	29.6	2,515	56.1	5.3	21.6
1997	258	70.7	10.4	22.4	1,989	79.1	3.7	16.3
1998	112	43.4	7.0	20.9	1,063	53.4	2.6	16.3
1999	76	67.9	4.4	14.4	751	70.7	1.1	10.5
2000	102	134.2	6.1	22.8	995	132.5	2	16.8

Note: Amounts measured in Japanese yen since 1995 have been changed into US dollars with the following percentages: 96.3 (1995), 112.46 (1996), 122.59 (1997), 128.25 (1998), 111.56 (1999), 110.45 (2000).

Sources: Japan Bank for International Cooperation (formerly the Export–Import Bank of Japan), 'Japanese FDI Trends' in the *Journals of the Research Institute for International Investment and Development* (1982–99) and the *Research Institute for Development and Finance* (2000–1).

and legislation on foreign investment were neither clear nor systematic, while the hard infrastructure left much to be desired. But its mass of cheap labour resources and market potential continued to attract certain companies. Sanyo Electric Company, for example, took its audio-visual production there in 1983. With open areas extending to 14 coastal cities in 1984, investments by Japanese hotels and appliance firms (televisions, refrigerators, etc.) increased vastly, causing the first investment boom in China. However, the total investment amount was very limited until 1986 when Japanese firms, stimulated at the time by the strengthening of the Japanese yen, reactivated their efforts at internationalization and sought opportunities in China, now a fast-growing economy with steady progress in open-door practices. There were even trends to transfer export bases from newly-industrializing economies (NIEs) and ASEAN countries to China in order to take advantage of cheap labour and the huge market potential. In 1988, Japanese firms launched a second investment boom in China, a 70 per cent increase in the amount of FDI contracts compared to the previous year. Although the value of Japanese direct investment fluctuated greatly up to 1992, the annual amount generally remained above US$300 million, peaking in 1987 due to a big oil exploration project involving US$933 million of Japanese FDI.

Japanese investments in China soared from 1992 to 1995. A number of Japanese firms had become dissatisfied with the performance (sales and profits, etc.) of their investments in developed countries (Tejima 1994), whereas China's open-door policies, stimulated by Deng Xiaoping's Southern-survey Speech in 1992, had in the meantime become encouragingly market-oriented. The combined effects of China-specific advantages (low cost, market potential) and Japanese globalization motives persuaded almost all manufacturing industries to make a rush for China, encompassing the food, textile, cosmetic, pharmaceutical, cement, kiln, appliance, electronics and automobile industries. The manufacturing move extended even to supplier firms. Moreover, firms in the wholesale, retail and financial services, restaurant, and cleaning industries were also found riding the crest of the wave (Inagaki 2000). From 1992 to 1995, annual investment growth rates exceeded 50 per cent. This investment volume peaked in 1995, with US$4.5 billion accounting for 36.2 per cent of Japan's Asian FDI and 8.7 per cent of its world FDI. The proportion of Japanese FDI in China compared to its FDI contracts worldwide spiralled: 13.1 per cent in 1992, 20.1 per cent in 1993, 25.7 per cent in 1994, and 26.9 per cent in 1995. On Japan's worldwide FDI scale, its investment shares in China ranked sixth in 1992, fifth in 1993, and second in 1994 and 1995. In Asian areas they ranked second in 1992 and topped the scale in the three successive years 1993, 1994 and 1995 (Export–Import Bank of Japan, 'Japanese FDI Trends', *Journal of the Research Institute for International Investment and Development*, 1992–96).

The year 1996, however, saw a turning point in Japanese investments in China. Both contracts and investment values began losing ground and this continued up to 1999. Although the tax imposed on capital goods in China and the deteriorating performance of Japanese firms at home are considered the main reasons (Ma 2000, 79), rumours of operational difficulties and low business performance in China are major contributing factors. Two questionnaire surveys dealing with this aspect are presented below:

1 Questionnaire surveys by the Japan–China Investment Promotion Organization. This organization has been carrying out questionnaire surveys with Japanese expatriates in China almost every two years since its foundation in 1990. The results (Table 9.2) show that appraisals on growth aspects of Japanese enterprises in China are above the median point each year, indicating a fairly satisfactory annual increase in sales revenue; but respondents harbour doubts about the profitability of their Chinese businesses. The general degree of satisfaction was evaluated as mediocre in 1996 and 1997, dropping below this in 1999.
2 The questionnaire survey carried out by the Japan Bank for International Cooperation (formerly the Export–Import Bank of Japan). Investigations of this kind have been implemented annually in Japan since 1989. Results show that managers in Japan were far from

Table 9.2 Performance evaluation by Japanese expatriates in China

	1996		1997		1999	
	Mean	**Respondents**	**Mean**	**Respondents**	**Mean**	**Respondents**
Profitability	2.8	393	2.9	277	2.6	420
Growth	3.6	398	3.4	277	3.4	419
General satisfaction	3.1	395	3.1	276	2.8	419

Note: The evaluation score rating is as follows: 1 = 'low', 2 = 'fairly low', 3 = 'moderate', 4 = 'fairly high', 5 = 'high'.

Sources: Calculated from Japan–China Investment Promotion Organization, Summary and Analysis of the Sixth Questionnaire Survey on Japanese FDI in China, 37.

Table 9.3 Performance evaluation by managers in the manufacturing industry in Japan

		1996	1997	1998	1999	2000	*(Respondents)*
NIEs	Profitability	3.24	3.31	3.29	3.07	3.11	*(311)*
	Sales	3.29	3.42	3.3	3.12	3.27	
ASEAN	Profitability	3.2	3.21	2.76	2.74	2.99	*(626)*
	Sales	3.31	3.28	2.89	2.89	3.25	
China	Profitability	2.55	2.65	2.67	2.61	2.73	*(250)*
	Sales	2.72	2.7	2.74	2.59	2.93	
North America	Profitability	2.88	3.07	3.14	2.97	3.04	*(338)*
	Sales	3.22	3.35	3.5	3.21	3.39	
EU	Profitability	2.81	2.99	2.99	2.78	2.75	*(247)*
	Sales	3.01	3.23	3.2	3	3.03	

Note: 1 = 'poor', 2 = 'farily poor', 3 = 'moderate', 4 = 'fairly satisfactory', 5 = 'satisfactory'.
Source: Tekigi, Ikehara and Izushi (2001), 23.

happy about the profitability and sales of their Chinese operations, although the year 2000 did show some improvement (see Table 9.3).

2   Japan–China joint ventures: hypotheses

According to a series of surveys by the Japan Bank for International Cooperation, Japanese firms have in recent years annually ranked China as their 'most promising' host country for future middle- and long-term overseas investment (cf. Tekigi, Ikehara and Izushi 2001). In addition to its enormous market potential and abundant cheap labour, China's acceptance as a formal member of WTO was to serve as further encouragement for foreign investment. After a successive decline that began in 1996, Japanese firms set about increasing their investments in China in 2000, indicating a fresh round of active establishments. Although various survey results paint a gloomy picture as far as performance is concerned, not all enterprises show a deficit. High-profit and stable-profit groups still exist (Summary and Analysis on the Sixth Questionnaire Survey on Japanese FDI in China by the Japan–China Investment Promotion Organization, 4). The fact that different Japanese firms exhibit divergent performances in China draws attention to the organizational aspects of internal management. Since most Japanese investments in China took the form of joint ventures, we will focus on this type of organization. We first relate Japanese–Chinese joint-venture performances to the issue of control and go on to examine the relationship between performance and partner trust.

Research has shown that Japanese companies tend to hold the reins in their overseas operations (Bartlett and Ghoshal 1989; Sakakibara 1997). In accordance with this assumption, our first hypothesis is as follows:

H1: *Japanese firms tend to play a larger role than their Chinese partners in most decision-making areas of Japanese–Chinese joint ventures.*

Research results on the effects of control patterns on joint-venture performance are mixed. Killing (1983) found dominant control by one partner to be more successful than shared control due to easier operation. However, based on data from alliances between developed and developing countries, Beamish (1988) concluded that shared control leads to improved performance where local partners contribute resources. Child and Yan (1998) argue that there is no consistent link between the relative level of joint-venture control held by the parent companies and assessments of their performance. Considering that Japanese management style is difficult to transfer overseas, some scholars assume it is best not to rush into localization (Kagono 1997, 286). In line with this argument, our second hypothesis is as follows:

H2: *Dominant control by Japanese companies is positively related to performance achievements.*

A mutual trust relationship between partners was considered important for a number of reasons: to lower transaction costs (Gulati 1995) and hence create a competitive advantage to induce cooperative behaviour (Madhok 1995), to reduce the extent of formal contracts (Larson 1992), to reduce harmful conflicts and facilitate dispute resolution (Ring and Van de Ven 1994), and to promote effective responses to crisis. Accordingly, we propose a third hypothesis:

H3: *Good trust relationships in Japanese–Chinese joint ventures are positively related to performance achievements.*

3   Methods: data collection and measures of variables

3.1   Data collection

A list of 1,015 Japanese firms with joint ventures was drawn up using the Japanese publication, *The List of Japanese Invested Enterprises in China (2001–2002 version)*. In January 2001, a questionnaire was mailed to the department responsible for business in China. It was asked to choose a Japanese–Chinese joint venture for the questionnaire. In all, we received 215 answers from CEOs (36), board members (31) and heads of international departments (74), as well as section heads of international departments (74). The basic characteristics of the sample are as shown below.

Duration of joint ventures

	< 5 years	*5–8 years*	*>= 8 years*	*n.a.*	*Total*
Respondents	67	87	53	8	215
(ratio)	31%	41%	25%	4%	100%

Capital ratios of Japanese firms in joint ventures

	< 50	*50*	*50–75*	*75–95*	*n.a.*	*Total*
Firms	52	34	84	44	1	215
(ratio)	24.3%	15.9%	39.3%	20.6%	0.5%	100%

Scale of Japanese firms (capital: 100 million Japanese yen)

	< 3	*3–10*	*>= 10*	*n.a.*	*Total*
Firms	90	47	71	7	215
(ratio)	42%	22%	33%	3%	100%

3.2   Measures of variables

Following Yan and Gray (1994), *performance* of joint ventures was measured by manager satisfaction rating with various aspects of objective achievements. Judgement was rated on a 5-point scale ranging from 1, 'very dissatisfied', to 5, 'very satisfied'. The main objectives and their mean values are shown in Table 9.4.

Table 9.4   Joint-venture performances evaluated by managers in Japan

		Mean	**s.d.**	**Respondents**
A	Profit	3.00	1.17	208
B	Exploration of China's local market	2.82	0.99	192
C	Export (including Japan)	3.28	1.00	196
D	To ensure local raw materials	3.02	0.91	192
E	To get cheap local labour	3.45	0.79	207
F	To get and retain local talent	2.98	0.86	200
G	The spillover effects on Japanese headquarters or other foreign operations	3.23	0.81	184
H	General achievement of objectives	3.23	0.93	213

s.d. = standard deviation.

According to Table 9.4, there is some frustration with the 'Exploration of China's local market' (average score 2.82) and 'To get and retain local talent' also encountered some obstacles (average score 2.98). A mediocre level of satisfaction was expressed with 'Profit' and 'To ensure local raw materials' (average score 3 and 3.02 respectively). Assessment of the objectives 'To get cheap local labor', 'Exports to foreign markets', and 'Spillover effects on Japanese headquarters or other foreign operations' fared better than the median level (average score 3.45, 3.28, and 3.23 respectively). The general evaluation is also above the moderate level (score 3.23) and, although not very bright, the general picture in Table 9.4 indicates progress compared to previous surveys.

Adapted from Kale, Singh and Perlmutter (2000), *trust* was measured by assessing four aspects of mutual relations between Japanese firms and Chinese partners on a 5-point scale. The contents and mean values are shown in Table 9.5. The figures show a relatively smooth relationship between the partners.

In accordance with Lee and Beamish (1995) and Child, Yan and Lu (1998), we measured *control* by assessing the relative degree of influence of Japanese and Chinese partners in 14 areas of joint-venture decision-making: profit disposal, upper management positioning, strategic priority setting, product pricing, training and development policies, reward and incentive policies, financial control, reinvestment policy, purchasing policies, production planning, sales and distribution, technology innovation, quality control, and recruitment policies. A 5-point scale was employed, where the evaluation score 1 stands for 'Totally controlled by

Table 9.5   Mutual trust between Japanese firms and Chinese partners

	Mean	s.d.	Respondents
There is close, personal interaction between the partners at multiple levels	3.10	1.08	211
The joint venture is characterized by mutual reliance between the partners at multiple levels	3.29	0.96	210
The joint venture is characterized by personal friendship between the partners at multiple levels	3.14	1.04	210
The joint venture is characterized by reciprocity among the partners	3.42	1.03	209

s.d. = standard deviation.

Note: 1 = 'Totally Disagree', 5 = 'Totally Agree'.

Chinese partner', 3 for 'To make decision by mutual consensus', and 5 for 'Totally controlled by Japanese firms'.

The Cronbach alphas for the multi-item measures of control and trust, as well as the seven specific performance items (A–G) are 0.95, 0.89 and 0.7 respectively, passing the 0.7 cut-off level. These constructs can, therefore, be considered reliable.

4   Results

According to Table 9.6, Japanese firms usually exert strong control over 'technology innovation' (average 3.88), 'quality control' (average 3.79), and 'strategic priority-setting' (average 3.67). With the exception of 'recruitment policies' (average 2.79) and 'reward and incentive policies' (2.95), all decision-making areas in Japanese–Chinese joint ventures seem to be more influenced by Japanese firms than Chinese partners, thus giving general support to Hypothesis 1. In the minority-ownership cases, Japanese firms still maintain a relatively strong influence on 'technology innovation' (average 3.15) and 'quality control' (average 3.11), leaving other areas of decision mainly in the hands of Chinese firms. Where they own joint ventures to 50 per cent, Japanese firms

Table 9.6   The mean value of control by parent firms

Decision making	Total	Capital ratio of Japanese firms			
		5–50	50	50–75	75–95
(General sample)	(215)	(52)	(34)	(84)	(44)
Profit disposal	3.19	2.67	2.91	3.30	3.80
Upper management positioning	3.12	2.27	2.76	3.29	4.14
Strategic priority-setting	3.67	2.82	3.44	3.83	4.51
Product pricing	3.37	2.45	3.24	3.49	4.33
Training and development policies	3.22	2.35	3.24	3.32	4.05
Reward and incentive policies	2.95	2.25	2.71	3.06	3.79
Financial control	3.09	2.21	2.82	3.24	4.07
Reinvestment policy	3.35	2.71	2.97	3.57	4.02
Purchasing policies	3.08	2.10	2.85	3.27	4.05
Production planning	3.33	2.48	3.06	3.44	4.33
Sales and distribution	3.34	2.50	3.00	3.56	4.23
Technology innovation	3.88	3.15	3.68	4.13	4.45
Quality control	3.79	3.11	3.74	3.95	4.36
Recruitment policies	2.79	2.02	2.41	2.95	3.67

tend to pay more attention to 'quality control' (average 3.74), 'technology innovation' (average 3.68), 'strategic priority-setting' (average 3.44), and 'product pricing' (average 3.24), 'training and development policies' (average 3.24), and 'production planning' (average 3.06). With the majority-ownership joint ventures, Japanese firms take almost all major decisions, with the exception of the 50–75 per cent ownership group, where some localization in the area of 'recruitment policies' (average 2.95) is visible. Thus Hypothesis 1 is fairly well supported, but attention should be paid to ownership type and decision-making areas.

Hypotheses 2 and 3 were tested with Pearson correlation analyses. With regard to overall performance we used one question item to assess the degree of satisfaction with the 'general achievement of objectives' (item 'H' in Table 9.4). To enhance the reliability of the performance measure, we devised a weighted average formula to calculate the overall perform-ance for each respondent, based on his/her answers to the seven specific items (A–G). The weights represent the 'importance degree' attached to items A–G, already dealt with separately in the questionnaire. The calcu-lated performance and direct answer to item H are significantly related (coefficient 0.75, $p < 0.0001$), so that we can take the calculated figure as the overall performance of the joint ventures concerned.

Apart from control of 'upper management positioning', as Table 9.7 shows, all other areas of control exhibit a positive and significant rela-tionship to overall performance, thus strongly supporting Hypothesis 2. This means that from the Japanese point of view, control contributes to satisfaction with the total achievement of joint ventures. In addition, Table 9.7 indicates that all four aspects of trust are positively and signif-icantly related to the general performance, thus strongly supporting Hypothesis 3. These results promote our confidence in the important role of trust in joint-venture management.

5 Conclusions

Based on a sample of Japanese–Chinese joint ventures, this study confirms that Japanese companies have a tendency to maintain strong control over their Chinese establishments. However, some qualifications need to be added: the extent of control varies with the ownership ratio and different dimensions of decision-making. Contrary to Child and Yan (1998) and Beamish (1988), dominant control by Japanese firms is found to have significant and positive relevance to joint-venture per-formances as perceived by them. This conclusion is in line with Killing (1983), but the logic is more probably connected to the characteristics

Table 9.7   Correlation analyses on control, trust and general performance

Items of control and trust	Correlation to performance	
	Coefficient	Sample
Control of decision-making		
Profit disposal	0.16**	214
Upper management positioning	0.085	213
Strategic priority setting	0.194***	212
Product pricing	0.216***	211
Training and development policies	0.196***	211
Reward and incentive policies	0.16**	213
Financial control	0.155**	212
Reinvestment policy	0.165**	211
Purchasing policies	0.138**	212
Production planning	0.248***	212
Sales and distribution	0.224***	210
Technology innovation	0.173***	208
Quality control	0.133**	211
Recruit policies	0.116*	212
Trust relations		
There is close, personal interaction between the partners at multiple levels	0.284***	211
The joint venture is characterized by mutual reliance between the partners at multiple levels	0.419***	210
The joint venture is characterized by personal friendship between the partners at multiple levels	0.352***	210
The joint venture is characterized by reciprocity among the partners	0.442***	209

* $p < 0.1$.
** $p < 0.05$.
*** $p < 0.01$.

of Japanese management style. The finding that trust is closely related to performance highlights its importance in joint-venture cooperation, and this corresponds to a number of theoretical propositions. Yet there are several limitations to this study, beginning with the fact that data was collected from Japanese managers only. Future research should take the opinion of Chinese managers into account, and closely examine the factors influencing control and trust.

Note

1 This chapter is a preliminary analysis of the survey result. More detailed examination is now under way.

References

Bartlett, C. A. and Ghoshal, S. (1989), *Managing Across Boards: The Transnational Solution* (Boston, MA: Harvard Business School Press).

Beamish, P. W. (1988), *Multinational Joint Ventures in Developing Countries* (London: Routledge).

Child, J. and Yan, Y. (1998), 'Predictors of Performance in Sino-Foreign Joint Ventures', cited in J. Child and D. Faulkner, *Strategies of Cooperation* (Oxford: Oxford University Press), 207.

Child, J., Yan, Y. and Lu, Y. (1998), 'Ownership and control in Sino–foreign joint ventures', in J. Child and D. Faulkner, *Strategies of Cooperation* (Oxford: Oxford University Press), 188.

Gulati, R. (1995), 'Does familiarity breed trust? The implication of repeated ties for contractual choice in alliances', *Academy of Management Journal*, 38, 85–112.

Inagaki, K. (2000), 'Trends of Japanese investments in China and the business chances in the future', Mitsubishi Research Institute (ed.), *The List of Japanese Invested Enterprises in China (2001–2002 version)* (Tokyo: Sososha), 7–12.

Kagono, T. (1997), *Rehabilitation of Japanese Style Management* (Tokyo: PHP Research Institute).

Kale, P., Singh, H. and Perlmutter, H. (2000), 'Learning and protection of proprietary assets in strategic alliances: Building relational capital', *Strategic Management Journal*, 21, 217–37.

Killing, J. P. (1983), *Strategies for Joint Venture Success* (New York: Praeger).

Larson, A. (1992), 'Network dyads in entrepreneurial settings: A study of the governance of exchange relationships', *Administrative Science Quarterly*, 37, 76–104.

Lee, C. and Beamish, P. W. (1995), 'The characteristics and performance of Korean joint ventures', *Journal of International Business Studies*, Third Quarter, 637–54.

Ma, C. (2000), *Labor Problems of Japanese Enterprises in China* (Tokyo: JETRO).

Madhok, A. (1995), 'Revisiting multinational firms' tolerance for joint ventures: A trust-based approach', *Journal of International Business Studies*, 26, 117–37.

Mitsubishi Research Institute (2000), *The List of Japanese Invested Enterprises in China (2001–2002 version)* (Tokyo: Sososha).

Ring, P. S. and Van de Ven, A. H. (1994), 'Developmental processes of cooperative interorganizational relationships', *Academy of Management Review*, 19, 90–118.

Sakakibara, K. (1997), 'Implications of internationalization in Japanese firms', *Organization Science, Japan*, 31 (1), 4–9.

Tejima, S. (1994), 'Japanese FDI turning to be active', in *Comprehensive Lists of Japanese Overseas Enterprises (by country)* (Weekly Toyo Keizai), 10–17.

Tekigi, S., Ikehara, G. and Izushi, U. (2001), 'The gesture of Japanese manufacturing companies to deepen management reform at home and abroad and expand overseas businesses: report of the questionnaire survey on Japanese FDI in 2000', *Journal of Research Institute for Development and Finance*, January, 23.

Yan, A. and Gray, B. (1994), 'Bargaining power, management control, and performance in United States–China joint ventures: a comparative case study', *Academy of Management Journal*, 37 (6), 1,478–1,517.

10
The Impact of European Union and Middle East Partnership: Agreements on Developing the Level of Environmentalism in Jordan

Dieter Beschorner and Thoraiya Younes

1 Introduction

Environmental problems such as global warming are threatening the entire globe and by nature do not stop at national boundaries. There is no connection between the release of a pollutant in the USA, for example, and a specific effect on some area on the other side of the world.

The international nature of globalization itself is another factor that brings environmental problems to a global level. While globalization links people of all societies together, it also affects their lives. A project outlining this problem was conducted at the University of Ulm with young Japanese and German scientists from different faculties (Beschorner and Stehling 1997).

Although not all environmental problems or forms of pollution are global in scale (depending on local geology and geography), one must bear in mind that, side by side with international trade, the impact of most forms of pollution is spreading worldwide.

As globalization reaches all aspects and processes of our lives, people all over the world view themselves more and more as participants in a small, limited globe. This creates a new level of awareness of our planet, and the belief that its problems must be seen in the same way in scene and effect.

Governments and politicians have become more aware of environmental problems, and globalization has gradually shown that many practices and policies of past industries harmful to the globe are no longer acceptable or appropriate for globalization. The emergence of global environmental change was evident on the international political agenda of the late 1980s and in the press release of the World Commission on Environment and Development 1987 that stated: 'the challenge faced by all is to achieve a sustainable world economy where the needs of all the world's people are met without compromising the ability of future generations to meet their need' (Mada 1999).

A form of trade globalization was expressed in the EU partnership agreements with some Middle East (ME) countries, including Jordan. Environment protection has been seriously taken into account in these agreements and is expected to affect the level of environmental consciousness of ME citizens.

No previous surveys have been conducted on how the EU partnership agreement affects the environmental awareness of ME citizens. This study takes Jordan as a representative example of ME countries that are in a phase of transition towards trade liberalization.

2   Environmental consciousness

'Environmentally conscious describes those who have an understanding, and appreciation of the effect their actions have on the earth, air, water … as well as people' (Cooper 1995). Humanity faces the challenge of protecting the earth as a whole system, and of acting worldwide within a limited period of time.

A pattern shift in environmentally conscious behaviour is required. It starts with changing the way people think, perceive, and value the environmental problems they now face, as coming generations will in the future, and consequently, convincing them to act in a desired way.

This environmental pattern shift is emerging on a global level. In a stereotypical manner, Western developed nations are probably considered to be environmentally more aware than developing nations. Nevertheless, the latter actually show the same level of consciousness and concern for the environment. The differences between these nations involve social, cultural, economic, political and geographical variables that affect the desired environmental behaviour (Dunlap and Gallup 1993).

3   Indicators of a shift in global environmental consciousness

The way people think, value and behave has changed over the last 20 to 30 years, as indicated by Peter Drucker (1993). These changes have different origins. Although there are still some deficits, one outstanding source is education (Beschorner, Lesko and Schweinbenz 1995), which led to a shift in people's level of consciousness, culture and beliefs on a global level.

Indicators of change are essential to understand people's values, needs, concern and expectations. This understanding guides development decisions, evaluates progress, makes revisions and gains support for desired action (Kline 2000). Indicators of a global environmental consciousness shift can be identified by the following.

3.1   Global environmental consciousness and the communication evolution

Considerable shifts in culture and consciousness are gained through satellite television channels and the ability to browse on the Internet. New global consciousness and culture are redefining people's sociological, economic, political and cultural structure. The rapid growth of communications enabled people to present themselves as being more aware of global environmental issues.

3.2   Global ecological awareness and concern

An international survey of attitudes towards global environment conducted in 1993 by Dunlap and Gallup, aimed at surveying citizens in a wide range of 24 nations[1] which varied in geographical location and level of economic development, showed:

- people living in developed and developing nations have similar levels of concern
- there is a widespread tendency among rich and poor nations to accept mutual responsibility for environmental problems
- there is little evidence of the poor blaming the rich for environmental problems
- both poor and rich citizens see the health of the planet as a serious problem
- the majority of developed nations and half of the developing nations surveyed indicated a willingness to pay more to protect the environment
- citizens of developed nations consider that responsibility for solving environmental problems must be carried by institutions, while developing nations are more likely to think citizens themselves are responsible for environmental protection
- majorities in all 24 countries believe that environmental problems will affect the health of their children and grandchildren over the next 25 years

- majorities claimed that environmental protection should be given priority even at the risk of slowing down economic growth
- environmental problems are salient and important issues in both poor and wealthy nations

But the debate concerns the action differential between these nations. A considerable gap between aspiration and reality indicates that a certain level of environmental concern has not been translated into environmental behaviour at the same level (Diekmann and Preisendorfer 1998).

3.3   Sustainable way of living

Most people are now looking for more sustainable ways of living on the earth, indicating a tendency to subordinate economic growth to environmental sustainability (i.e., maximizing economic growth to maximize survival and well-being), supporting priority for environmental health rather than economic growth. People are showing a desire for more sense of balance in their lives, fewer working hours, more time for the family, less stressful lives, more involvement in their communities, new dietary patterns, less meat-eating, increased demand for organic food, vegetarianism, recycling and willingness to pay more for packaging that could be recycled (Duane and Ledrew 2000).

3.4   Legal and policy changes

After the Earth Summit in Rio 1992, where Agenda 21 called on governments to adopt and implement laws and policies that successfully guide both private and government divisions for sustainable development, most countries now have laws and legislation in place that support administrative authorities in dealing with environmental issues, protecting national resources, and controlling air, soil and water pollution.

Developing countries are also putting similar laws and legislation into effect but in varying degrees. The variation refers to the different environmental issues facing developing countries. Health care, clean drinking water, deforestation, overgrazing, population growth, and the status of women are priority concerns in many developing countries, while the environmental challenges of developed countries mainly include urban overpopulation, minority unemployment and greenhouse gases that cause global warming (Dernbach 1989).

Political laws and legislation are used to encourage more environment-friendly behaviour in the individual. Environmental policies such as monetary incentives and condign policies (paying for damage caused by certain industries, raising prices of harmful products) force respondents to take opportunity costs into account or avoid monetary disincentives used to counter undesirable behaviour (Santopietro 1995). These actions could open up new business opportunities if environmental policies were applied to technologies. One example of many similar cases is given by Beschorner *et al.* for the People's Republic of China (Beschorner, Lesko and Schweinbenz 1995).

4   Bases of environmentalism

Environmentalism as an expression of concern for environmental influence and ecological problems has become a worldwide interest, with substantial growth of public concern in both developed and developing countries for environment protection, international resources protection, environmental quality of life, health risks and other environmental issues.

Although Dunlap's 1991 survey shows that both developed and developing countries indicate similar levels of concern for the environment (Dunlap 1991), major differences in environmental attitudes and activism exist between developed and developing countries. These differences can be referred to and explained through socio-cultural, socio-political, and socio-economic context differentials.

4.1   Socio-cultural attitude bases

Socio-cultural attitude bases, beliefs, and values concerning the environment are considered to have an effect on individual environmental behaviour (Adeola 1998). A study conducted by McCarty and Shrum (2001) on the influence of individualism, collectivism, and locus of control on environmental beliefs and behaviour indicated that:

(a) as basic beliefs, people who are individualistic tend to believe that recycling is more inconvenient than those who are less individualistic;
(b) people who are collectivistic are more concerned with the good of the group, and focus on goals, sharing and duty.

Another indicator of different beliefs, values, and pattern effects is realized through public opinion of government involvement in environmental protection in the industrialized nations themselves. For example, while individual American citizens have been found to take part in voluntary efforts to achieve goals, Canadian and Japanese citizens are more likely to welcome state intervention in this case (Seymour 1995). Public opinion in industrialized countries has also been found to vary with regard to supporting more government expenditures on the environment (Skrentny 1989).

Knowledge and social experience as expressed in everyday practice are significant factors for measuring environmental consciousness and explaining individual variations (Adeola 1998). Social factors associated with the level of environmental consciousness such as age, formal education, gender and place of residence are positively or negatively associated (Engel and Potschke 1998):

1 Younger people show more concern for the environment than older age groups, which are negatively associated.
2 Women show more concern and are more likely to behave in an environmentally-conscious manner than men.
3 Individuals with higher formal education are positively associated: the higher the level of individual formal education, the greater the environmental concern.
4 People who were raised or currently live in urban areas worry more about the environment than those who live in non-urban areas.

4.2   Socio-political attitude bases

Socio-political attitude bases also play a significant role in shaping the individual's level of environmentalism. Developed countries are characterized by cultures of democracy, liberty, civil and political rights, and freedom of expression, including the right to object to the environmental behaviour of others. Developing countries, on the other hand, are generally characterized by varying levels of authoritarianism, traditionalism and paternalism, and a lower level of civil and political rights and freedom, which has been found to be inversely related to environmentalism (Adeola 1998).

It should be remembered that there is a noticeable variation in the developing countries themselves. In general, the environment is gaining more attention. This is obvious from the change in attitude towards environmental issues in developing countries and the growing number of national environmental agencies that concentrate on increasing environmental awareness. The number of agencies in developing countries increased from 11 to 102 between 1972 and 1980 (Williams 1993). In addition, the establishment of government departments to take responsibility for environment protection aspects such as conveying surveys, and training and education programmes, contributed to raising the level of environmental awareness.

Another factor is the role played by non-governmental organizations (NGOs) and international agencies, such as Greenpeace and the UN. They also recognize a shift in the attitude of developing countries towards environment protection. The World Bank, for example, has a big direct impact on the environmental debate in developing countries through linking financial resources and knowledge coordination to international policy. The World Bank also played a significant role in designing and implementing Sustainable Development policies. Another example is loans attached to 'green' conditionality introduced from multilateral development institutions (Williams 1993).

4.3   Socio-economic attitude bases

Socio-economic circumstances influence people to make the correct choices about environmental matters including pollution and acceptable industrial waste levels, as well as how to behave rationally towards protecting the environment. If people's understanding, perception and response to environmental issues is to be explained, their socio-economic circumstances must be taken into account (Buttel and Taylor 1992; Vaughan 1995).

Developed countries with their economic prosperity, advanced communication technology, advanced production technology, high level of expenditures on R&D, advanced transportation networks, growth in the services sector, and high level of individual income and education are characterized accordingly as being capable of more concern for national resources and an acceptable level of pollution released by industry, more capable of protecting the environment, and supporting it via job opportunities and income development (Inglehart 1977; Dake 1991).

On the other hand, most developing countries are characterized by weak economic situations, economic crises, high debt to income ratio, a low Human Development Index score, low level of technology, poor R&D expenditures, low quality of education and individual income, low life-expectancy rates, low quality of health care and environment, high unemployment indicators, and overurbanization. According to the economic Contingency Theory, societies with these characteristics are unable to give priority to environmental goals over economic goals, especially during economic crises (Dunlap 1992; Yearley 1996).

5   Cross-cultural differences in risk perception

Risk means different things to different people (Slovic 1997). The Cultural Theory of Risk Perception assumes that individuals pick the risks they fear would affect their favourite lifestyle. So the same risk size is perceived differently in different societies according to the particular lifestyle (Wildavsky 1987).

Assuming that cultural biases and backgrounds, religion and timing (Weber and Hsee 1998) can affect individual choices and risk perception, and that people's perception of environmental risks can be used as an indicator for environmental awareness, understanding these perceptions and biases helps legislators and businesses to formulate and implement specific environmental strategies and plans.

Variability in socio-cultural and socio-economic circumstances explains the differences in response to environmental risks. The interaction between the structural features of the socio-physical environment and the variables at the personal level, such as outcome feedback from previous risky decisions, level of individual beliefs and aspirations, expectations and loss gain function on the individual level, alters and limits individual attitudes and responses to environmental risks (Engel and Potschke 1998).

Socio-economic circumstances make rich people more willing to accept the societal risk of technology, as explained by Wildavsky and Dake (1990), who proposed an economic theory of risk perception. First of all, they benefit from it, and second, they are protected from adverse consequences because they can afford to leave a polluted area and live somewhere else. Poor people are also prepared to accept these risks because of the benefits, but the small difference is they cannot afford to escape the harmful consequences.

6   Development versus environment protection

Development was often seen as a synonym for economic development or economic growth, while no attention was paid to environment protection. This resulted in economic development with adverse consequences for the environment, which in turn even reversed the course of the development attained. Most developing countries increased their exports at the expense of exhausting their natural resources in the form of water pollution and soil deployment. The UNICEF report from 1990 (UN 1991) indicated that half a million children die annually in developing countries due to water-related diseases, and five to six million from water-borne diseases and air pollution (World Bank 2001).

This failure of the old development model led to world realization of the linkages between economic development and environment protection.

This occurred in several stages. The Founex report, Switzerland, June 1971 (Williams 1993), found that there is a distinct link between development and the environment, and argued that environmental problems play a role in poverty and industrialization. Economic development goals that ignore the environment lead to degradation of the natural resources system, and thus limit the duration of development in all sectors so that people will eventually no longer be able to earn their living. The Founex report was a message and a turning-point for developing countries; it stated that environmentalism should not be viewed as a barrier for development but a requirement.

Linkages between the environment and economic development are not single links but 'linkages between linkages' (Mayers 1993). The ozone layer depletion, for example, and its effect on global warming combined with reduced soil moisture leads to an inability to grow several types of crop, with the result that people are unable to earn their living and thus unable to achieve development. More sophisticated linkages are those between human nature and needs, cultural evolution and biological dynamics, which have been adequately described by Timothy (Timothy 2000), and show that microeconomic policy and free trade alone do not improve development prospects for the world's poor, and that environmental degradation accompanied by chronic impoverishment create increasingly unstable economic, social and ecological systems leading to a negative feedback on development.

The UN conference on the human environment in 1972 raised environmental consciousness worldwide, and reinforced national responsibility for protecting it. This conference also led to cooperation and the adaptation of environment laws in many countries, but it did not achieve a method of reconciling development and environment.

Another turning-point came with the United Nations conference on environment and development (UNCED) in Rio de Janeiro in 1992 and gave new meaning to sustainable development[2] (development that meets the needs of the present without compromising the ability of future generations to meet their own needs: Dernbach 1989). The conference introduced a strategy for achieving development and protecting the environment at the same time, thus clarifying the linkage between environment and development. The conference gained international attention by shaping the meaning of sustainable development as a framework for national governments. The new meaning modified the purpose of conventional development by adding a wide range of environmental protection goals to Agenda 21, which declared that countries should make progress towards achieving both goals.

7 Attaining sustainable development

Sustainable development can be achieved through the participation and commitment of nations on global and local levels. International agreements and laws are significant for the process at the global level. As the framework for attaining sustainable development goals, they ensure that the meaning of sustainable development will evolve and change (Dernbach 1998) under continuous monitoring and modification of the process. The role and responsibility of national governments are crucial to achieving sustainable development goals. National governments and their authorities must introduce environment protection laws and establish institutions to assure and control implementation of plans towards sustainable development. Raising public environmental consciousness will make the mission easier for governments, while motivating and energizing public participation at all levels of society will support process implementation.

From the traditional business point of view, environmental laws are usually attacked and resisted as harmful to the economy. Although it is true that sustainable development is not free of costs in the short run, most research findings show that environmental laws have not had any measurable impact on national economic performance. On the regional industrial level, a survey conducted in southern Germany showed that environmental laws are the real reason behind a change of business or location. Successful firm performance was seen as neutral or positive in the long run, in some cases even in the short run (Beschorner 1994).

A study conducted by Meyer (1995) shows that relaxing standards of environmental protection does not produce economic gain. Although the results of the study show that there is no systematic positive or negative relationship between environmental policies and economic performance, it does show that individual businesses and industries gained specific benefits, and strong environmental policies seem to be associated with better economic performance during periods of economic growth. On the other hand, they seem to be associated with weaker economic performance during recessions. In general, and from his study conducted in the USA, Meyer argued that there are three to four years of strong economy for each year of recession, and he implied that during the course of the decade (1982–91), states with stronger environmental policies enjoyed a small net economic gain.

The European Commission White Paper issued in February 2001 proposed a new community policy for chemicals, making sustainable development the overriding goal of the Commission proposals, as the

White Paper addresses the economic and social dimensions of development as well as ecological consequences.

In 1992, the World Business Council for Sustainable Development (WBCSD) promoted eco-efficiency as the 'delivery of competitively priced goods and services that satisfy human needs and bring quality of life, while progressively reducing ecological impacts and resources intensity throughout the life cycle, to a level in line with the earth's estimated capacity' (Boswell 2001). Examples could be mentioned here to support this idea such as the fact that multinational corporations operating in a global economy in developing countries have succeeded in attaining economic gain and protecting the environment at the same time by transferring technology and implementing environmental health and safety policies and practices in developing countries (for instance, Occidental Chemicals and Xerox: Starik 1995).

Other companies were involved in voluntary programmes (McDonald's made a public commitment to reduce its harmful effect on the environment). Such programmes attained sustainable development at a lower business cost (Cairncross 1992; Ludwiszewski 1992).

Developing countries that begin to realize the links between environment and development can attain economic growth and environment protection concurrently without going through the same history as developed countries, since science and technology inventions could be imported from developed countries (Beschorner 1995). Products such as cars which now produce less pollution than before could also be imported. Installing new technology-based plants with much cleaner machinery will save developing countries that initiate new plants a lot of time and money which could be invested in a cleaner environment.

Plans for national environmental protection should be carried out and implemented with continuous control and re-examination during the process in order to monitor the environmental impact of development. Governments must also initiate policies and national laws in combination with raising the environmental consciousness of the population.

Participation and cooperation with developed countries through international agreements is crucial to helping developing countries achieve their goals, by providing financial resources and the required technology transfer.

8   European Union–Jordan partnership agreement

8.1   Facts about Jordan

The Hashemite Kingdom of Jordan is located in the heart of the ME region with a very sensitive geographical and political position. Table 10.1 shows

Table 10.1   Major facts about Jordan

Area	89,342 sq. km, of which 92% is classified as desert or semi-desert
Capital	Amman
Population	4.9 million, 78% living in urban areas; 31% are under 15 years, 54% are over 15. The highest projected population growth among all middle-income Arab states
Currency	Jordanian Dinar (JD) 0.708 JD = $1.00
GDP per capita	$1,490. One of two Arab countries whose human development ranking is higher than its per capita income, indicating efficient investment of resources
Current population growth rate	2.6%, the highest among middle-income Arab states
Economic environment	Jordan's economy is service-oriented and comprises financial services, trade, transportation, communication, construction and education; it contributes 81% to the GDP and the remaining 19% is contributed by the agriculture and industrial sectors
Poverty	27% of families live on a monthly income of less than $170
Unemployment (2000)	13.2%
Literacy	88%. Doubled from 47% in 1960 to 88.6% in 1995. The highest female literacy and overall literacy of all Arab states
Child mortality	29 per 1000 births
Life expectancy	68 years for men, 70 years for women (the highest in Arab countries)
Human development ranking	92 on a list of 174 countries (one of the highest among medium-ranked Arab states)

Source: United Nations Human Development Program (2001).

the most significant facts that are relevant to Jordan's position among ME countries. A closer look to the table reveals the basic reasons for considering Jordan as an example of ME countries.

8.2   Jordan's economic environment

Jordan's economy is differentiated as a free economy. It is service-oriented and comprises financial services, trade, transportation, communication, construction and education; this contributes 81 per cent to the GDP and two-thirds of the labour force. Businesses are largely private-owned, while the public sector is involved in several industries, including the mining industry.

Jordan plays a major role in the economic development of the region and has promoted itself as its business hub. With 121 per cent GNP growth in the decade 1985–95, Jordan's GNP per capita in 1995 was US$1,595 which positioned the country at a take-off stage on the emerging market scale.

On April 1997, the Hashemite Kingdom of Jordan and the EU initiated a partnership agreement that paves the way for a free zone area by the year 2010. The partnership agreement comprises three major parts (and a number of protocols and annexes that are considered part of the original agreement):

- political and security partnership
- partnership in social and human affairs
- economic and financial partnership (this component is aimed at establishing an EU–Jordanian trade area, liberalizing trade progressively by the year 2010)

The areas of cooperation cover trade in agriculture and industrial products, right of establishment and services, payment and capital movement, competition, intellectual property rights, and financial and economic cooperation.

The new partnership will encourage more direct European investments in the area, facilitate technology transfer, and provide free access to the markets of both parties. The agreement will create specific trade and investment opportunities for the Middle East but also bring many challenges with it to the area. Jordan has experienced many changes as a result of the partnership agreement requirements, some of which have had an effect on the environment.

8.3 Environmental trends in Jordan

Jordan possesses very limited cultivable land, limited access to water resources, and has few natural resources to draw from. Current environmental problems in the country include the following:

1 Limited natural fresh water. Fresh water resources in Jordan come mainly from the Jordan River and dams, but are not sufficient to satisfy increased usage and further demand for water.
2 Deforestation. Much-needed irrigation and intensive agricultural cultivation in fertile areas result in land-clearing and deforestation.
3 Desertification. A semi-desert landscape is the main characteristic of the country. The desert area is increasing annually due to lack of water and the intensive use of the remaining wood resources.

4 Fuel wood exploitation.
5 Overgrazing.
6 Soil erosion.

Jordan's successive economic and social development plans put great emphasis on environmental protection. Several governmental organizations were established to organize and control the process of attaining sustainable development. International and non-governmental organizations also play a significant role. Educational activities and programmes concerning environmental issues are being created in Jordanian universities and schools.

8.4 International environmental agreements

The country is party to the following agreements: Bio-diversity, Climate Change, Desertification, Endangered Species, Hazardous Waste, Law of the Sea, Marine Dumping, Nuclear Test Ban and Ozone Layer Protection.

9 The case of Jordan

As a result of the EU–Jordan partnership agreement, a number of economic and legal changes have recently been observed in Jordan. These changes are believed to have had an effect on the level of environmentalism among Jordanian citizens.

A field study was conducted to investigate these changes and verify the following hypotheses:

> **H1**: *In general, there is a correlation between social and economic factors and the level of environmentalism.*

> **H2**: *There is a correlation between social and economic factors and attitudes to risk perception among Jordanian citizens.*

> **H3**: *Jordanian citizens predict an environmental effect from the EU–Jordan partnership agreement.*

> **H4**: *The social and economic situation of Jordanian citizens affects their opinion on giving priority to economic development or environmental protection.*

9.1 Method and data

A questionnaire containing 33 questions was drawn up in English and translated into Arabic by one of the authors. The questionnaire was distributed to a sample of 350 individuals aged 18 and over, picked at random in the rural and urban areas of Jordan over a two-month period in June and July. The questionnaire was grouped in parts and sub-parts,

Table 10.2   Study sample characteristics

Characteristic	Frequency	Percentage
Age (years)		
18–28	164	54.5
29–39	68	22.6
40–50	39	13.0
51–61	25	8.3
Over 62	5	1.7
Gender		
Male	161	53.5
Female	140	46.5
Education		
Preparatory	6	2.0
Elementary	14	4.7
Secondary	73	24.3
Diploma	49	16.3
BSc	159	52.8
Job		
Student	88	29.2
Retired	13	4.3
Employee	116	38.5
Self-employed	37	12.3
Housewife	29	9.6
Unemployed	18	6.0
Monthly family income (JD)		
Less than 100	20	6.6
100–150	45	15.0
151–200	34	11.3
201–250	36	12.0
251–300	27	9.0
301–350	18	6.0
351 and over	121	40.2
Home location		
Big city	71	23.6
Town	157	52.2
Village	73	24.3

and linked to the above-mentioned hypotheses to facilitate analysis. It was distributed and collected by hand. Some 301 completed questionnaires were picked up. Table 10.2 shows the main characteristics of the sample.

The percentage distribution of the parameters shown in Table 10.2 agrees with the characteristics of Jordanian society (see Table 10.1): for example, 54.5 per cent of the sample are aged between 18 and 28, which corresponds to the present age structure of Jordanian society.

9.2   Variable measures

Part 1 of the questionnaire measured the current environmental knowledge of Jordanians. Risk perception was evaluated by a number of questions in Part 2. A group of questions in Part 3 compared European and Jordanian environmentalism from the respondents' point of view. Respondents' perception of economic development versus environment protection in Jordan was covered by the questions in Part 4. Finally, Part 5 was conducted to verify the effects of the EU–Jordan partnership agreement on the level of environmentalism among respondents.

10   Findings

The general environmental knowledge of Jordanian citizens was measured by a 4-question group. The results of the survey show that 48.25 per cent of respondents have no idea of whether the EU–Jordan partnership agreement contains passages dealing with environmental protection. Answers from remaining sample respondents ranged from having little to having excellent information.

The environmental information of respondents covered quite a range, with 26.6 per cent of respondents in possession of average knowledge, 28.9 per cent good, 26.6 per cent very good, and 9.8 per cent excellent. Only 8.6 per cent had no information about global environmental problems. The answers indicated a negative correlation with age indicating that the younger the respondent, the more knowledge was available on global environmental issues. Some 27.9 per cent had participated in activities related to environment protection in Jordan, and this showed a positive correlation with respondents' level of education. The higher the level of education, the more positively the question was answered. Roughly 65.8 per cent of respondents answered the question referring to the Kyoto agreement correctly, describing it as an agreement on the environment.

In the second group of questions, respondents were asked for their opinion on the European environment and environmental attitudes. Some 44.2 per cent of respondents regard the environment in Europe as more polluted than in Jordan, while 38.2 per cent disagreed and 17.6 per cent were not able to decide. A high percentage (75.1 per cent) consider Europeans more environmentally aware than their Jordanian counterparts. At the same time, respondents were equally divided in their opinion on

Europeans giving environment protection priority over economic development. Around 37.5 per cent agreed that Europeans give priority to environment protection via prices and job opportunities, while the same percentage state the opposite and 25.2 per cent were undecided.

Approximately 26.2 per cent of respondents have been to a European country. Results also indicate a correlation between experience in a European country and answers to the above-mentioned questions. Those who have been to a European country tend to disagree that the environment in Europe is more polluted than the environment in Jordan ($p = 0.027$), and they also consider Europeans to be environmentally more aware ($p = 0.025$).

The questions in Part 3 are related to the Jordanian risk perception: 79.4 per cent feel that the environment in Jordan was healthier ten years ago; 59.5 per cent also feel that it will be more polluted in the next ten years, and 87.4 per cent feel that there will be a large increase in ill-health as a result of pollution in the country. Results also indicate that gender is correlated with answers, with men showing a higher risk perception than women. This high risk perception was also indicated by the 63.5 per cent who think that global environmental problems such as the greenhouse effect have consequences for the environment in Jordan.

Respondents were equally divided in evaluating the role of new technology in these perceived risks: 47.5 per cent agreed that new technology is harmful to the environment, while 47.2 per cent disagreed.

As for economic development versus environmental protection, the relation between the current need for economic growth in Jordan and environmental protection was investigated by a number of cause and effect questions. In response to the question of who is to blame for global environmental problems, 5.3 per cent blamed developing countries only, 7.6 per cent blamed others, 7.0 per cent didn't know, while the remainder were almost equally divided between blaming industrial countries only or both parties, with 39.9 per cent and 40.2 per cent, respectively. While 55.5 per cent agreed that economic growth generally influences the environment negatively, 37.2 per cent disagreed.

Roughly 33.9 per cent see a static contradiction between economic growth and environment protection, while 56.8 per cent are not aware of this contradiction. Age, job, education, and income were found to correlate to answers. Age was found to be negatively correlated, but education was positively correlated. While the retired, the unemployed and housewives were aware of this contradiction, students and employees saw no contradiction. The results also show that there is a correlation between income and answers to previous questions. Medium-income people see a contradiction between economic development and environment protection.

On specific questions that priority is to be given to economic growth as against environmental protection in Jordan, respondents were biased (48.8 per cent) towards protecting the environment rather than attaining economic growth. At the same time, they see that protecting the environment in Jordan requires the achievement of economic growth (with 67.8 per cent agreed).

Legal and economic changes in Jordan were a prerequisite for the EU–Jordan partnership agreement signed in 1997. The estimated effect on the level of environmentalism generated by recent economic and legal changes that accompanied the EU–Jordan partnership agreement was the subject of the fifth group of questions. About one-third of the respondents (34.9 per cent) have noticed gradual changes in work places, with evidence of improved environment protection measures. A considerable percentage (58.1 per cent) agree that international environmental agreements guarantee harmony between economic, social and environmental objectives. While almost half of the respondents (49.8 per cent) believe that local environmental laws and legislation are adequate, 39.9 per cent demand stricter legislative local measures. On the subject of industries that harm the environment, 83.4 per cent supported the idea of demanding financial compensation from these industries. Almost half of the respondents (49.5 per cent) consider Jordan to be a suitable place for foreign industries trying to escape strict environmental laws in their home countries, while 34.9 per cent do not agree that Jordan is a suitable place for these industries. Analysis of results showed little correlation with the effect of economic and social attitudes on attained results.

Willingness to pay for the environment was relatively low: 66.4 per cent of the respondents rejected the idea of imposing higher diesel prices in order to reduce its consumption. Here, the place of residence was seen to affect answers. Most of those who disagreed lived in villages. While 13.6 per cent of respondents considered the decrease in natural resources to be the most significant effect of export increase, the remainder saw its economic effect. Considering Jordan's economic structure, mining industries are a vital component of its exports and a candidate for further expansion as a result of the EU–Jordan partnership agreement. Environmental effects of this expansion were the subject of some direct questions. The answers showed a considerable level of awareness towards dangers such as the threats concerning the Dead Sea.

There was, however, less awareness for other cases such as that of phosphate mining and the announcement that Aqaba was to become a special trade zone which could accommodate chemical industries, thus compromising the value of the harbour as a tourist attraction.

Separate questions were asked in order to evaluate and assess environmental education in Jordan. Although 93.7 per cent stressed that systematic environmental education in schools and universities is very important in the current stage, 80.4 per cent indicated the media as their main source of information. In another question, the respondents were asked to indicate the best method of increasing environmental awareness in Jordan, and here the respondents were allowed to choose more than one option in the list provided. In the analysis each option was treated as a separate question.

Some 71.1 per cent chose strict government regulations and legislation as the best method, followed by enlightenment campaigns sponsored by government or non-government bodies, and education programmes in the work place, with approximately 50 per cent for each, and finally enlightenment campaigns carried out by international agencies with 34.9 per cent. Age was found to be positively correlated with the tendency of respondents to favour more environmental legislation. Income was found negatively correlated with government regulations and education programmes.

11   Discussion

For Hypothesis 1, age, education and income were generally noticed to have an effect in correlation with the level of environmental consciousness, which is supported by Engel's findings (Engel and Potschke 1998).

For Hypothesis 2, our analysis did not reveal a correlation between risk perception and social and economic attitudes. A correlation between gender and risk perception was observed, with men showing higher risk perception than women. Level of income also showed a correlation. The acceptance of risks from technology was correlated to the level of income such that medium-level income respondents showed less acceptance of these risks than others of low- or high-level income. An acceptance pattern of this kind was proposed by Wildavsky and Dake (1990).

For Hypothesis 3, the respondents felt the economic effects of the agreement and some of the environmental effects. An explanation of this partially-felt effect is that, normally, environmental effects (if existent) cannot be seen in a short time span, so timing here is believed to be the main factor affecting ability to judge (Weber and Hsee 1998).

Hypothesis 4 was supported by observations from the results. The socio-economic situation was related to respondents' priorities for economic development versus environment protection. Answers were negatively related to age and positively correlated to education concerning the question of whether there is always a contradiction between economic development and environment protection. The younger the respondents, the more they disagreed. Jobs were also related, so that retired respondents agreed most, while students and employees disagreed most. Results also showed that middle-level income respondents tend to agree with the contradiction assumption.

The disapproval by Dunlap and Gallup (1993) of stereotyping the level of environmentalism in developing countries as low is supported by this study.

According to the results, our main findings were as follows:

- people in Jordan show a remarkable level of environmental consciousness and concern
- they show adequate levels of information and knowledge about local and global environmental issues
- people are biased towards blaming industrial countries for global environmental problems
- people see the environment in Europe as more polluted than the environment in Jordan, but they believe that Europeans care more about the environment

Major indicating results on risk perception are:

- people in Jordan see that the environment in Jordan is degrading with time
- global environmental problems are seen to be affecting the environment in Jordan
- modern technology was not seen as harmful to the environment
- people anticipated that ill-health situations would increase in the future as a result of environmental pollution

For economic development and growth versus environment protection, results indicate that few people blamed developing countries for environmental problems; the majority were divided between blaming industrial countries only and blaming both parties. In general, economic growth and environment protection were not strictly seen to be in contradiction. People could see that economic growth is needed in order to protect the environment in Jordan, but tended not to sacrifice their environment for the sake of economic growth.

For the effect of recent legal and economic changes related to the EU–Jordan partnership agreement, results indicate that:

- in spite of the need for economic growth in Jordan, people seem not to ignore the environmental dimension of the process
- people expressed concern for the environment by asking for more local environmental legislations and measures
- people believe in a strong government role in environment protection
- people expressed confidence in international agreements for environment protection
- in spite of the apparent concern for the environment, this did not translate into willingness to pay for the environment: individuals felt that industries have to take that burden

12 Conclusions

This study investigated the impact of the EU–Jordan partnership agreement on developing environmentalism among Jordanians. The findings of the study show that there is a new pattern of environmental concern related to the current economic changes in Jordan. There is some evidence pointing to the role of the agreement in forming this new pattern.

The new pattern being formed shows that Jordanian citizens have a considerable level of environmental awareness. Foreign and local businesses attempting to exploit the opportunities created by the agreement must consider this element when building their plans and strategies.

In order to evaluate the EU partnership agreements at the level of environmentalism, a future comparative study will include other developing nations (members and non-members in the partnership agreements).

Notes

1 Industrialized nations (Switzerland, Portugal, USA, Germany, Denmark, the Netherlands, Canada, Ireland, Norway, Japan, Finland, Russia and Great Britain) and developing nations (Brazil, Mexico, Philippines, Uruguay, Chile, India, South Korea, Hungary, Turkey, Nigeria and Poland).
2 A very early example of sustainable development is German forestry, which was invented in the nineteenth century with the *Nachhaltigkeitsprinzip* (Sustainability).

References

Adeola, F. O. (1998), 'Cross-national Environmentalism Differentials', *Society and Natural Resources*, 11 (4) (June).

Beschorner, D. (1994), 'Anmerkungen zum Stand des "Öko-Controlling" in der Praxis', in G. Ebert (ed.), *Controlling-Managementfunktion und Führungskonzeption*, Moderne Industrie, Justus, Landsberg/Lech 1990, 15, Nachlieferung (September), 1–22.

Beschorner, D. (1995) 'The Lack of Integrated Ecological and Business (Management) Studies in Academic Education', in J. Höhn and U. Schiewer (eds), *The Future of the Baltic Sea: Ecology, Economics, Administration, and Teaching* (Marburg: Metropolis), 241–55.

Beschorner, D., Lesko, M. and Schweinbenz, A. (1995), 'Marketing German Environmental Technologies in the PRC', *Management International Review*, Wiesbaden (January), 53–63.

Beschorner, D. and Stehling, F. (eds) (1997), *Umweltschutz und Krisenmanagement*, DJAB (Deutsche Japanische Akademische Burse), January, Workshop I.

Boswell, C. (2001), 'Sustainability and Eco-Efficiency', *Chemical Market Report*, New York, 259 (13) (March).

Buttel, F. H. and Taylor, P. J. (1992), 'Environmental Sociology and Global Environmental Change, a Critical Assessment', *Society and Natural Resources*, 57, 211–30.

Caircross, F. (1992), 'Environmentalism and Beyond', *Columbia Journal of World Business*, 27 (3/4) (Fall/Winter), 12.

Cooper, R. B. Jr (1995), 'Defining Environmentally Conscious Facility', *Grand Rapid Business Journal*, 13 (23) (May), 2.

Dake, K. O. (1991), 'Dispositions in the Perception of Risk', *Journal of Cross-Cultural Psychology*, 61–82.

Dernbach, J. C. (1989), 'Sustainable Development as a Framework for National Governance', *Case Western Reserve Law Review*, 49 (1) (Fall), 340.

Diekmann, A. and Preisendorfer, P. (1998), 'Environmental Behavior', *Rationality and Society*, 10 (1) (February), 79.

Drucker, P. (1993), *The Post Capitalist Society* (New York: Harper Business, 1993).

Duane, E. and Ledrew, C. (1997), *Global Consciousness Change* (Seattel: New Horizons For Learning).

Dunlap, R. E. and Scarce, R. (1991), 'The Polls – Poll Trends: Environmental Problems and Protection', *Public Opinion Quarterly*, 55, 651–72.

Dunlap, R. E. (1992), 'The Social Bases of Environmental Concern: Have They Changed Overtime', *Rural Sociology*, 57, 28–47.

Dunlap, R. E. and Gallup, G. A. H. (1993), 'Of Global Concern', *Environment*, 35 (9), (November), 33–9.

Engel, U. and Potschke, M. (1998), 'Willingness to Pay for the Environment', *The European Journal of Social Sciences*, 11 (3) (September), 315.

Inglehart, R. (1977), *The Silent Revolution: Changing Values and Political Styles Among Western Publics* (Princeton, NJ: Princeton University Press).

Kline, E. (2000), 'Planning and Creating Ecocities: Indicators as a Tool', *Local Environment*, 5 (3) (August), 343.

Ludwiszewski, R. B. (1992), 'The Interdependence of Economic Development and Environmental Protection', *Economic Development Review*, 10 (3) (Summer), 5.

Mada, C. N. (1999), 'A Decision Support Framework for Environmental Planning in Developing Countries', *Journal of Environmental Planning and Management*, Abigdon, 42 (3) (May), 287.

Mayers, N. (1993), 'The Question of Linkages in Environment and Development', *Bioscience*, 43 (5) (May), 302.

McCarty, J. and Shrum, A. (2001), 'The Influence of Individualism, Collectivism', *Journal of Public Policy and Marketing*, 20 (1) (Spring), 93–105.

Meyer, S. M. (1995), 'The Economic Impact of Environmental Regulation', *Journal of Environmental Law and Practice*, 3 (2) (September), 4.

Santopietro, G. D. (1995), 'Raising Environmental Consciousness Versus Creating Economic Incentives as Alternative Policies', *Journal of Economic Issues*, 92 (2) (June), 17.

Seymour, L. (1995), *Canada and the U.S: The Cultural Dimensions in Canada and the U.S.* (Englewood Cliffs, NJ: Prentice-Hall).

Skrentny, J. D. (1989), 'Concern for the Environment: A Cross-National Perspective', *International Journal of Public Opinion Research*, 5, 335–52.

Slovic, P. (1997), 'Public Perception of Risk', *Journal of Environmental Health*, 95 (9) (May), 22.

Starik, M. (1995), 'Corporate Environmentalism in a Global Economy: Social Values in International Technology Transfer', *Academy of Management Review*, Mississippi State, 20 (4) (October), 1105.

Timothy, J. D. (2000), 'Changing the Culture of Underdevelopment and Unsustainability', *Journal of Environmental Planning and Management*, Abingdon, 43 (5) (September).

UN (1991), *Human Development Report*, Human Development Program.

UN (2000), *Human Development Report*, Human Development Program.

UN (2001), *Human Development Program*, Human Development Program.

Vaughan, E. (1995), 'The Socioeconomic Context of Exposure and Response to Environmental Risk', *Environment and Behavior*, 27 (4), (July), 454.

Weber, E. and Hsee, C. (1998), 'Cross-Cultural Differences in Risk Perception', *Management Science*, 44 (9) (September), 12–18.

Wildavsky, A. (1987), 'Choosing Preferences by Constructing Institutions, A Cultural Theory of Performance Formation', *American Political Science Review*, 81, 3–21.

Wildavsky, A. and Dake, K. (1990), 'Theories of Risk Perception', *Daedalus*, 119, 41–60.

Williams, M. (1993), Rearticulating the Third World', *Third World Quarterly*, 14 (1), 7.

World Bank (2001), *World Bank Launches New Environment Strategy*, M2 communications.

Yearley, S. (1996), *Sociology, Environmentalism, Globalization: Reinventing the Globe* (London: Sage).

11
The Development of Global Education in Malaysia: Strategies for Internationalization

Mohamad Hanapi Mohamad and Zahiruddin Ghazali

The globalization of society and the economy has had an impact on research and education and been influenced by them. In the case of Malaysia, a liberalized democratic education policy brought a sudden upsurge of foreign students to Malaysia in 1966, when the government introduced the Higher Education Act. Terms such as international education and global education were an expression of this development. To become a major player, however, Malaysia essentially needs to acquire global competencies, in curriculum, administrative ease or pricing, in order to make its location a strategic choice for post-secondary education. The globalization of markets and competition, rapid technological changes and changing relationships between states and firms require different approaches from those traditionally assumed. This chapter proposes the development of a coherent global education model of higher education, based on an eclectic-locational rather than a multi-disciplinary approach.

1 Introduction

Although the first university was established in 1962, foreign student enrolments in Malaysia have only increased rapidly in the last 25 years. The total number increased from 32 in 1970 to 12,605 in 1999. While foreign students still represent less than 2 per cent of higher education enrolments in Malaysia, this proportion is likely to grow over the next decade as university enrolments increase and the government policy of liberalizing higher education continues. One consequence to date has been that many colleges and universities depend on students for a major part of their tuition revenues or enrolment-determined budget, a dependence that is likely to grow over the next decade. A further consequence of larger flows of foreign students is a probable increase in the number of private colleges and foreign university campuses in Malaysia. Anuwar (1997) argued that the rapid expansion of Malaysian higher education, involving extensive growth, relied principally on the liberalization of government education policies. Whilst Kamarudin (1997), Sulaiman (1997) and Ramaiah (1996) agreed that more openness contributed to this growth, they also believed that characteristics related to choice of course and selection of institution were deciding factors in determining the choice of location.

The growing influence of foreign students as consumers of Malaysian higher education services highlights the importance of understanding the nature of this phenomenon more clearly. This study empirically identifies which of the above factors have made a significant contribution to the growth of foreign student enrolments in the last decade. It applies the model of foreign student demand for Malaysian higher education and takes the view that liberalization of higher education improves growth prospects for the internationalization of Malaysian higher education. Section 2 examines the openness to foreign student enrolments. The received theory and data employed in the analysis are described in section 3. Estimation procedures are discussed in section 4, and regression results are also reported there. Concluding comments are provided in section 5.

2 Foreign student performance

Comparatively speaking, the number of foreign students in Malaysian universities is insignificant. In any one of the years between the 1986–87 and 1989–90 academic sessions, foreign students numbered no more than 466 (or 0.8 per cent) of the country's university population. This low inflow of students from abroad could be influenced by factors such as university admissions policy, the local demand for higher education, the language issue, provision of learning, teaching and research facilities, student accommodation, and student welfare services. Table 11.1 shows the growth of student admission and foreign student enrolment in Malaysia from 1996 to 1999, which ranged from 0.08 per cent to 2.0 per cent per annum. However, this pattern is not uniform across the countries of the region. During this period, ASEAN as a group reported a growth of close to 2.5 per cent per annum. An interesting

Table 11.1 Public and private universities offering degree programmes

(a) Public	Universiti Malaya
	Universiti Kebangsaan Malaysia
	Universiti Sains Malaysia
	Universiti Putra Malaysia
	Universiti Teknologi Malaysia
	Universiti Islam Antarabangsa
	Universiti Utara Malaysia
	Universiti Malaysia Sarawak
	Universiti Malaysia Sabah
	Universiti Institut Teknologi Mara
	Universiti Pendidikan Sultan Idris
	Kolej Islam Sultan Zainal Abidin
	Institut Teknologi Tun Hussein Onn
	Kolej Universiti Islam Malaysia
	Kolej Universiti Islam Malaysia
	Kolej Universiti Sains & Teknologi Terengganu
	Kolej Tun Abdul Rahman
	Kolej Universiti Teknikal Melaka
(b) Private	Universiti Petronas Malaysia
	Universiti Multimedia Malaysia
	Universiti Tun Abdul Razak
	Universiti Tenaga Malaysia
	Universiti Terbuka Malaysia

Table 11.2 Post-secondary enrolment

Year	No. institutions	Enrolment
1965	48	12,965
1970	22	16,404
1980	26	48,851
1985	34	74,607
1990	38	122,340
1995	42	189,020
2000	55	264,690

feature of this student enrolment was that it did not seem to be affected by the economic crisis that attacked the region.

Table 11.2 shows a number of new institutions (public and private), a proxy for openness, and firm-level data of the institutions as an indicator of market performance. Historically, the first university was established in 1962 when the division of the University of Malaya in Kuala Lumpur was upgraded to full university status. Eight other universities were established between 1969 and 1995: the University of Science Malaysia 1969, the National University of Malaysia 1970, the University of Agriculture Malaysia 1971, the University of Technology Malaysia 1972, the International Islamic University 1982, the Northern University of Malaysia 1984, the University Malaysia of Sarawak 1994, the University Malaysia of Sabah 1995, and the University MARA Insitute of Technology 1997.

3   Received theory and data

Malaysian private and public educational institutions have emerged as important avenues to meet the increasing demand for higher education among both Malaysians and foreigners. The large student demand for higher education has remained constant. This enormous demand for higher education in the case of Malaysian students is a complex interaction of three main sets of social, political and economic factors operating at both personal and societal levels. At the personal level, higher education is seen as a key to jobs with good salaries, as conferring social status and prestige, and as an avenue to social mobility. At the societal level, the Malaysian government uses higher education programmes to restructure Malaysian society, so that more of the indigenous population can pursue higher education and later on improve their living standards. As for foreign students, selecting Malaysia as their preferred location for higher education implies that it provides greater benefits, both tangible and intangible, and that these override the cost. From the student point of view, Malaysia offers a unique advantage and by selecting it students will be able to study at reasonable cost. The resource-based view of the firm (Penrose 1959; Barney 1991) proposes that its ability to create wealth is largely determined by its unique capabilities. Firm success or failure is not entirely dependent on industry structure, but rather on the function of the resources and capabilities controlled by the firm, deployed by managers, and developed and extended by the organization (Schendel 1994). A basic premise of this theory is that firm capabilities that are rare, inimitable and difficult to trade form the basis of a sustainable competitive advantage (Barney 1991). Subsequent researchers have highlighted the importance of intangible resources such as knowledge and scientific capabilities to competitive advantage (Kogut and Zander 1992; Petraff 1993; Henderson and Cockburn 1994; Deeds, DeCarolis and Coombs 1997).

During the last few decades, dozens of studies have examined various aspects of tertiary school internationalization. Some have focused on the internationalization of curriculum (Kubin 1973; Mintz 1980; Burns 1990). Some have examined internationalization at different degree levels, such as the masters' level (Ball and McCulloch 1988; Nehrt 1987) or the doctoral level (Kuhne 1990). Some have focused on a particular region or country, such as Europe (Luostarinen and Pulkkinen 1991), the USA (Terpestra 1969), and Japan (Cummings and Kobayashi 1985). Major strands that explain the rapid inflow of foreign student enrolments concern course characteristics, country characteristics, administrative processes, and cost factors (Lawley and Blight 1997). Several studies highlight the importance of course characteristics (Austin 1988; Wu 1989; Steadmena and Dagwell 1990) and confirm that course characteristics which refer to standard or quality of course, recognition of qualifications, and time taken to complete a course are important determinants for selecting a place of study. On the other hand, Harris and Rhall (1993), Smart and Ang (1992), and Hill, Romm and Patterson (1992) confirm country characteristics as the most significant contributing factor to the choice of location. Variables contributing to country characteristics include the level of personal safety, lifestyle, the potential to emigrate, the opinion of family and friends and their presence in a destination country. The second most important determinant for choice of destination is the administrative process, which includes ease of admission to institutions, ease of obtaining a visa, ease of gaining exemptions, availability of information about a destination, and being able to work part-time legally. These variables have been found to be of central importance in influencing the choice of destination as confirmed by Hill, Romm and Patterson (1992) and Rao (1997). The other factor of importance is cost characteristics. The variables that influence cost are comparative financial cost, availability of scholarship, distance from home, and psychological costs such as racial discrimination and the presence of students from other countries. Studies that reflect the importance of this criterion can be seen in Hill, Romm and Patterson (1992), and Purdy (1992).

Hence, the measure of Malaysia's unique advantages as a destination for higher education stems from both financial and non-financial benefits. The rising cost of tertiary education overseas in the traditional places, with the imposition of full fees beginning in the mid-1980s for foreign students, and the upsurge in demand for higher education, has led to the expansion and provision of various forms of higher education. The variables that influence cost are comparative financial costs, such as tuition fees, accommodation, transportation, living expenses, entertainment and recreation expenses, amongst others. In the case of non-financial benefits, prospective students scrutinize specific areas of organizations that offer tertiary education, including the overall strength of the institution, such as curricula, language of instruction, availability of qualified lecturers, and teaching facilities.

One type of pecuniary benefit is the possibility of converting student visas to a different status, one that would permit employment or permanent residence. Hence, this benefit is measurable and might explain the flow of foreign students to Malaysia. Some students may enrol in Malaysian institutions of higher education with the intention of eventually having their visa status adjusted. For these students, status adjustment may be an easier method of immigration than directly applying for an immigrant visa in their country of origin. Other students, especially those receiving Malaysian or home government financial aid, may find it very difficult to get their status adjusted while still in Malaysia but could establish contacts that later permit direct immigration. Most foreign students, however, probably enrol in Malaysian institutions, simply knowing that there is a possibility of immigration. The potential benefits of immigration would obviously influence their enrolment decision.

Students incur costs whether they attend college at home or abroad, but the amount may differ and thus influence student enrolment decisions. Normal costs include out-of-state tuition fees, board and lodging, food and entertainment, and travel and transportation. Malaysian institutions may want to introduce residential accommodation in order to attract foreign students to enrol for higher education at their colleges and, at the same time, reduce other restrictions that make a distinction between foreign and local students. In addition, the cost of room and board in Malaysia might normally exceed the cost of room and board in the home country, where students probably live at home. Hence, students might find it attractive to study in Malaysia if institutions were able to arrange some kind of financial assistance such as part-time work or internships that would reduce their tuition fees. Students view differences in tuition and living costs between the home country and Malaysia as part of the cost of Malaysian higher education. Hence, in summation, it is also implied that the availability of institutional or governmental financial aid and family income play an important role in student decisions about where to attend college.

Curriculum, medium of instruction, exemptions and duration of study are key components in the internationalization of the Malaysian tertiary programme. Students are keen to know what level of education can be achieved should they choose to study in Malaysia. In the case of the curriculum, for example, students will be interested to know whether the Malaysian system follows the practice of infusion or integration of core and general subjects. For some students, integration of a larger percentage of core subjects in junior and senior years will certainly give them added advantage, particularly those who are thinking of pursuing post-graduate studies at a later stage. The implementation of exemptions and credit transfers is another area with a strong bearing on the decision to study in Malaysia. It is a very common practice for universities to accept credit transfers and give exemptions for work done previously in other institutions of post-secondary education. These provisions would enable students to finish their schooling earlier, and cut expenses. Hence the availability of exemptions and credit transfers could be decisive for these students in choosing Malaysia as their location for tertiary education.

Finally, the last issue governing a student's decision to study in Malaysia is related to administrative processes that include ease of admission to institutions, obtaining visas, and gaining exemptions. Malaysian universities normally commence the academic year in late May. Potential students must be fully informed of such issues as student visas and other related areas in time. Students also want to know whether they are allowed to work part-time, particularly during the long vacation. Choosing Malaysia as the destination of post-secondary education seems greatly influenced by the ready availability of this information, either at Malaysian embassies or through information channels of the potential colleges, as well as rapid administrative implementation by the respective institutions.

The theory thus implies that foreign student demand for higher education in Malaysia relates directly to market and organizational conditions such as course characteristics, country characteristics, administrative processes and costs. Demand is thus expected to vary directly with expected income differentials attributed to higher education, family income, and financial aid inversely with tuition, books and supply expenses, and opportunity costs. The demand model postulated above assumes that the supply of places to foreign students is exogenous. In Malaysia, where foreign students represent a small proportion of all college students, and where (according to Table 11.1) no country, apart from Iran, supplies a large proportion of all foreign students, and where an abundance of enrolment-hungry institutions exists with low admission standards, this assumption is not a strong one. While some elite colleges and universities may impose constraints on the number and composition of foreign students, and some graduate programmes may also face capacity constraints, foreign students wishing to study in Malaysia can usually do so with little difficulty.

A model of foreign student demand for Malaysian higher education would ideally include variables representing each of the costs and benefits listed above. Unfortunately, much of the desired information either does not exist or does not exist in cross-section data. Time-series data on income differentials associated with having been educated in different countries is not available for use either in this study or by prospective students. Given the absence of such information, it is unlikely that year-to-year variations in foreign student enrolments in Malaysia reflect changes in current income differentials, especially since the appropriate benefit measure is future income differentials as perceived by students.

3.1   Specification of the model

The theory of foreign students' demand and the data limitations discussed above result in an empirical model which postulates that the individual decision to attend college in Malaysia is affected by the unique characteristic of the course offered by the institutions in the country (*C*), the price (*P*) or cost of Malaysian higher education to the student, the host administrative ease (*A*) for higher education in the host country, and the expected benefits (*Y*) in the host country such as climatic conditions, short distance from home, and tolerance and liberal attitude among the residents. While this model explains individual decisions, the number of students (*F*) from a particular country enrolling in Malaysian institutions depends in part on the size of the college-eligible population (*N*) in the country of origin. The model of foreign student demand can thus be summarized as:

$$F = f(C,\ P,\ A,\ Y) \tag{11.1}$$

This equation represents demand for Malaysian higher education by residents of a given country. In fact, the measure of educational opportunities applies only to undergraduates. No satisfactory measure exists to describe such opportunities for graduate students, and in most developing countries the graduate education offered is not a good substitute for that offered by industrialized nations, including Malaysia.

3.2   Research methodology

3.2.1   Questionnaire

The survey questionnaire consisted of two separate parts. Part A was addressed to the head of the organization (the dean or equivalent administrator). It asked questions about the role of internationalization in the mission of the college, the organizational structure, the programme offered, the structure of the academic staff and administrators, and the level of student and staff satisfaction with various internationalization efforts, particularly with respect to student and staff facilities and welfare.

Part B of the questionnaire was considerably longer and was addressed to students currently pursuing tertiary education in the college. These students had to be from outside Malaysia and registered in a bachelor degree course. It asked questions about programme and faculty internationalization and the international linkages between the institution surveyed and foreign institutions, and the level of satisfaction with internationalization efforts and progress.

3.2.2　The sample

The sample was designed to focus on an educational institution with post-secondary business degree programmes and foreign student enrolments. The sample was taken from several sources, including the Malaysian Ministry of Education listings for institutions granting degrees, institutional subscribers to the *Journal of Education Malaysia*, and from the Student Visa Division of the Department of Immigration, Malaysia. The resultant sample consisted of 563 institutions and 25,000 importers of Malaysian higher education, 80 per cent of whom were located in Kuala Lumpur and the remaining 20 per cent outside the capital. Institutions included in this study had to have no fewer than 500 full-time students registered and a minimum of 20 foreign students enrolled in their colleges. Countries with fewer than 50 students were excluded because their presence was minimal. The final outcome of the exercise was that 721 respondents from 15 countries participated in this study. A further reason for selecting the 15 nations was the growing increase in foreign students originating from these institutions. The first mailing of the questionnaire was completed in March 2001. Follow-up mailings were completed in May 2001.

4　Major findings

Hierarchical regression analysis was used to determine the factors that contributed most to predicting the intention of foreign students to study in Malaysia. The analysis proceeded in two stages. In the first stage, a correlation analysis of intention was conducted. The objective of this analysis is to choose a destination with the perceptions of that destination on each factor. In the second stage it was regressed on the study's four independent variables. The estimated results are given in Table 11.3. These results are acceptable as it is generally acknowledged in behavioural science that $R2$ values of between 20 per cent and 30 per cent are satisfactory. The adjusted $R2$ also appear acceptable as they dropped minimally in the equations, indicating the adequacy of the sample size. The results in Table 11.3 also showed an F value, indicating the significance of the equations at the alpha level of 0.05. Finally, Table 11.3 also gave estimates of regression coefficients which are normally greater than 0 at the alpha level of 0.05, as indicated by t values. In general, the other estimated coefficients have the expected signs, and educational opportunity is significantly related to the place of offering. The estimated coefficients are typically of the expected sign. The statistically significant estimates of course characteristics, price elasticity and country characteristics are positive, and range in size from 0.098 to 0.271. The exponents associated with obtaining student visas, information about studying in Malaysia, and working part-time are consistently negative. The estimated coefficients for the respective countries are almost similar on course characteristics, country characteristics, administrative process and price.

Table 11.3   Model summary

Model	R	R square	Adjusted R square	Std error of the estimate
1	0.554	0.306	0.283	0.5558

ANOVA

Model		Sum of squares	df	Mean square	F	Sig.
1	Regression	76.559	19	4.029	13.043	0.000
	Residual	173.307	561	0.309		
	Total	249.866	580			

Notes: Predictors: (constant); courses are quicker to complete; difficult to obtain information about studying; the climate is not very good; my friends think it is a good place to study; short distance from home; comparatively cheap place to study; a safe place to study; easy to gain entry to universities/institutions; there are high levels of racial discrimination; difficult to get a student visa; my family think it is a good place to study; I would like to immigrate here; recognized qualification; there are scholarships available; teaching facilities are of a good standard; possible to work part-time legally; favourable way of living; easy to gain exemptions; standard of courses available in Malaysia is high.

Cont. overleaf

Model		Non-standardized coefficients B	Std error	Standardized coefficients Beta	t	Sig.
1	(Constant)	1.577	0.200		7.870	0.000
	Standard of courses available in Malaysia is high	0.166	0.030	0.271	5.576	0.000
	A safe place to study	1.119E-02	0.030	0.016	0.376	0.707
	Comparatively cheap place to study	6.032E-02	0.027	0.098	2.243	0.025
	Difficult to obtain information about studying	−7.039E-02	0.027	−0.108	−2.563	0.011
	Recognized qualification	1.869E-02	0.028	0.030	0.662	0.509
	My family think it is a good place to study	8.840E-02	0.031	0.122	2.862	0.004
	I would like to immigrate here	−1.019E-02	0.022	−0.021	−0.470	0.639
	Difficult to get a student visa	−6.582E-02	0.022	−0.132	−2.967	0.003
	Teaching facilities are of a good standard	9.856E-02	0.034	0.132	2.927	0.004
	Possible to work part-time legally	−3.293E-02	0.020	−0.074	−1.614	0.107
	Easy to gain entry to universities/institutions	3.811E-02	0.030	0.053	1.282	0.201
	My friends think it is a good place to study	3.840E-02	0.031	0.056	1.222	0.222
	The climate is not very good	−1.545E-02	0.024	−0.027	−0.642	0.521
	Easy to gain exemptions	7.344E-02	0.028	0.122	2.626	0.009
	Short distance from home	2.133E-02	0.019	0.047	1.103	0.271
	Favourable way of living	7.336E-02	0.033	0.102	2.255	0.025
	There are high levels of racial discrimination	2.725E-02	0.022	0.052	1.219	0.223
	There are scholarships available	−1.441E-02	0.026	−0.025	−0.565	0.573
	Courses are quicker to complete	1.628E-03	0.027	0.003	0.061	0.951

Dependent variable: overall evaluate Malaysia for tertiary education.

4.1 Discussion

As stated earlier, the goal of this study is to introduce and justify the use of firm-specific capabilities and location characteristics to develop the internationalization of higher education in Malaysia. In particular, we suggested that the internationalization development undertaken by the institutions is accurately captured when the processes are fully implemented in the implementation of the model. The inclusion of course characteristics, country characteristics, administrative processes, and costs in the process creates a more realistic representation of the model. How the decision to study in Malaysia was developed in our model of firm-specific capabilities and destination choice for post-secondary education.

The results provide strong evidence for the underlying premise that course characteristics, country characteristics, administrative processes, and costs are important determinants of locational decisions to pursue post-secondary education in Malaysia. Four of our 19 variables received support at the 0.05 level or higher. We were able to explain over a third of our variation in the absolute extent of internationalization development in our sample.

Though for most countries the number of foreign students in Malaysia has increased over time, the size of the eligible pool or population has increased even more rapidly. Participation in secondary education has risen above a minority of the population over the past 30 years for most of the countries in the study. Although a very small proportion of secondary school graduates gain access to higher education, the number of college students often increased more rapidly than secondary school enrolments (UNESCO). The assumption made here is that, *ceteris paribus*, a percentage increase in the eligible population results in the same percentage increase in foreigners from that country studying in Malaysia. In fact, the proportion of all college students who elect to study in Malaysia has been increasing for most of the countries of origin. While other factors offer potential explanations for this phenomenon, we see the relationship of income, price, educational opportunity and immigration benefits as the most relevant factors favouring post-secondary education in Malaysia.

The income-elasticity of demand is readily used in normal quantitative analysis to estimate the influence of price on demand. In this study, however, we used the minimal (but statistically significant) cross-section data. The coefficient for variable price is 0.098 and its *t*-value is 2.243. As noted earlier, per capita income may be a poor measure of income for the eligible population, but in this study it does explain its strong predictive power. Studies on domestic demand for higher education usually find large, statistically significant, income-elasticity. This study revealed a trend towards price increase which, however, does not affect the desire of foreign students to attend Malaysian colleges and universities. Tuition (plus room and board) has increased from $1,155 in 1970 to $30,542 in 2000. According to the regression results, this increase has not reduced the number of undergraduate and graduate foreign students in Malaysia. Other items in this sub-group were availability of scholarships, racial discrimination and duration of study, all of which seemed to be insignificant in determining Malaysia as a location for post-secondary education.

The reasons for prediction are not easily ascertained, but the principal explanation seems fairly straightforward. Although one cannot obtain precise numbers, both Indonesia and Thailand greatly increased financial aid to students studying abroad during this period. Such financial aid appears to be part of an overall strategy of investment in human capital, consistent with the ambitious development plans of both countries. Their fulfilment was, of course, financed to a large extent by the rapid growth in revenues from the oil exports of both countries.

In fact, both Southeast Asian countries and the Asian region increased educational expenditure at a much more rapid rate than the growth of GNP. GNP increased at an annual rate of 11.1 per cent in the Asian region and 15.3 per cent in the Southeast Asian region between 1990 and 1996, while educational expenditures increased annually by 57.8 per cent and 77.0 per cent, respectively, in the same time period. The elasticity of educational expenditures with respect to GNP is higher in general for Southeast Asian countries than for other developing countries. In addition, this elasticity was higher after the 1970s for Southeast Asian countries than beforehand.

The course characteristics variable showed a significantly positive relation to the choice of location. The course characteristics variable in our study, which was measured by the item standard of course offered, was positive and significantly related to location at a 0.05 level, with its coefficient at 0.271 and its *t*-value at 5.576. The standard of course recorded the highest coefficients among the variables of sub-groups comprising the course structure. The other item in this sub-group which registered a positive relationship was teaching facilities. Teaching facilities recorded a fairly significant relationship with choice of location. The coefficient value for teaching facilities was 0.132 and its *t*-value was 2.927. The only item of insignificance in this group was recognition.

Administrative ease is an important determinant for the decision to study in Malaysia. Five items measured administrative ease. In the case of Malaysia, the exemptions item seemed to have a strong influence on the choice of location. Ease in gaining exemptions was significantly related to destination. This item registered a coefficient of 0.122 and its *t*-value was 2.626. The other item which registered a positive but not significant relationship was ease of entry with a *t*-value of 1.282. The other items in this sub-group seemed to behave negatively in relation to the choice of location. Difficulty in obtaining a student visa, difficulty in obtaining information about studying in Malaysia, and legally working part-time registered at -2.967, -2.563 and -1.614 respectively.

Country attributes were also important determinants for the choice of location for post-secondary education. In the case of Malaysia, attributes such as a favourable way of living and opinions of family and friends were important dimensions for the suitability of the location. These three items seemed to have exerted a strong influence in the choice of country with two of these factors (favourable way of living and family opinion) recording *t*-values of 2.255 and 2.862 respectively. Climate, potential to immigrate, and safety seemed to be insignificant in determining the location.

Several explanations can be offered for the progress of internationalization in Malaysian post-secondary education. First, the tremendous growth in human capital investment in Asian countries, apart from reflecting the growth in GNP, may have resulted from the relative ease with which such an investment could be made relative to time-consuming physical investment. Furthermore, the enormous rise in secondary school enrolments over the previous decade in most Asian countries meant that human capital investment via higher education abroad was one that could be undertaken with almost no time-lag. This highly-educated manpower would be viewed as essential to successful implementation of development plans and future staffing of national institutions of higher education.

Second, with the gradual integration of the world economy, the method of conducting international trade is converging under common methodology, criteria and practices, and in particular Anglo–American rules. The education sector is no exception, where transactions are conducted at arm's length rather than on the basis of personal relationships. Transparency, administrative credibility and solid systems for evaluating programme performance are regarded as paramount.

Third, the rules of the game in the global economy are usually set by the dominant power, while the weak have no choice but to acquiesce. The strong seek to restrain the advance of competitive forces in order to defend their position, meaning that the leadership of a late-industrializing country must have the vision and strategic thinking necessary to elevate it to the ranks of advanced economies.

Fourth, there is no denying that Malaysia has taken a huge leap in economic development over the past 30 years, which was only possible because of the country's unique strengths. Specific conditions related to Malaysia's socio-political importance also played a major role, but there is no doubt that the nation's economic development would not have been possible if Malaysia had not had a strong institutional and structural foundation. After all, Malaysia's privatization policy includes a number of positive features. The existence of numerous affiliated firms within the programme has enabled them to overcome problems related to immature markets, and pursue bold investments in new areas.

Finally, to progress further and succeed as a centre for educational excellence, Malaysia needs to internationalize its education system and reform its public sector in ways that ensure government policies are formulated and implemented by professionals who are familiar with international practices and have a global perspective. In short, Malaysia will have to attain a level of globalization equal to that of Singapore and Hong Kong. But globalization does not mean recklessly opening up markets that are still immature; it must be supported by strategic thinking and vision. Malaysia has a record of having successfully achieved economic development with its own strategy and vision, but this was in the 1970s. Circumstances surrounding Malaysia and the world have changed markedly since then, and the new environment demands that Malaysia develop a new strategy and vision to adopt open and internationalized systems and norms.

5 Conclusion

The number of foreign students in Malaysia has increased for the most part because eligible populations have increased, especially in the non-industrialized countries of the world. Enrolment for secondary and higher education in these countries has grown even more rapidly than the number of foreign students in Malaysia. A conceptual analysis of the factors that seem to attract foreign students pursuing post-secondary education in Malaysia exhibits an interesting scenario on the process of internationalization. While Malaysian higher education enjoys comfortable location advantages to some extent, its institutions seemed to be losing balance in their quest for well-measured unique firm-specific advantages. The empirical section of this study reveals that course attributes, country characteristics, cost and administrative ease are significant predictors in influencing the decision to attend post-secondary education in Malaysia. While Malaysia enjoys significant advantages in areas pertaining to the quality of the course and country attractiveness, the other two factors of cost and administrative ease seem to be on the decline and need to be improved. To continue successfully, Malaysia needs to streamline its internationalization strategy. Greater improvement of courses and quality of student services, such as accommodation and recreation facilities, as well as teaching resources (in particular, well-qualified lecturers and capable administrators), are needed immediately. Apart from this, Malaysia also needs to contain its costs in order to allow the programmes to enjoy cost competitiveness. Once this is carried out, the eligible population will increase significantly over time as a result of two primary factors: a rise in the actual cost of Malaysian higher education and improved higher education opportunities in the host country. For most countries, the elasticity associated with these variables is relatively large. The projected demand model for post-secondary education indicates that if UNESCO projections of growth in secondary and higher education enrolment are accurate, the total number of foreign students in Malaysia will increase substantially by 2005.

References

Anuwar, A. (1997), *Postgraduate Education in Malaysia: Future Scenario and Policy Implications* (Universiti Teknologi Malaysia, Johor Bahru, Post-Graduate Education Regional Seminar).

Ball, D. A. and McCulloch, W. H. Jr (1988), 'International business education program in American and non-American schools', *Journal of International Business Studies*, 19 (2).

Burns, J. O. (1979), 'A study of international accounting education in the US', *International Journal of Accounting Education and Research*, (Fall).

Deeds, D., DeCarolis, D. and Coombs, J. (1997), 'The impact of firm specific capabilities on the amount of capital raised in an initial public offering', *Journal of Business Venturing*, 12 (1).

Henderson, R. and Cockburn, I. M. (1994), 'Measuring competence? Exploring from effects in pharmaceutical research', *Strategic Management Journal*, 15.

Jaffe, A. (1986), 'Technological opportunity and spillovers of R7D: Evidence from firm's patents, profits and market value', *American Economic Review*, 75 (5).

Kamarudin, K. (1997), *Internationalizing Post-Graduate Education* (Universiti Teknologi Malaysia, Johor Bahru, Post-Graduate Education Regional Seminar).

Kogut, B. and Zander, U. (1992), 'Knowledge of firm, combinative capabilities and replication of technology', *Organization Science*, 3 (3).

Krugman, P. (1991), *Geography and Trade* (Cambridge, MA: MIT Press).

Kuhne, R. (1990), 'Comparative analysis of US doctoral program in international business', *Journal of Teaching in International Business*, 1 (3/4).

Luostarinen, R. and Pulkkinen, T. (1991), *International Business Education in European Universities in 1990* (Brussels, Belgium: European International Business Association).

Nehrt, L. C. (1987), 'The ranking of masters' programs in international business', *Journal of International Business Studies*, 18 (3).

Penrose, E. (1959), *The Theory of the Growth of the Firm* (Oxford: Basil Blackwell).

Petraff, M. (1993), 'The cornerstone of competitive advantage: A resource-based view', *Strategic Management Journal*, 14 (3).

Prime Minister's Department (2000), *Eighth Malaysia Plan* (Kuala Lumpur: National Printing Corporation).

Ramaiah, A. L. (1996), 'Emerging Trends in the Development of Higher Education', National Seminar on Internationalizing Higher Education (University of Malaya, Kuala Lumpur).

Schendel, D. (1994), 'Introduction to competitive organizational behavior: Toward an organizational based theory of competitive advantage', *Strategic Management Journal*, 15.

Terpestra, V. (1969), *University Education for International Business* (Bowling Green, OH: Association for Education in International Business).

12

The Determinants of Share Market Response to Employee Share Option Plans Announcements and Implementations: A Review of the Malaysian Bourse

Zahiruddin Ghazali, Norlida Abdul Manab,
Rusmawati Ismail, Nurwati Ashikkin Ahmad Zaluki,
Habibah Tolos and Munauwar Mustaffa

Many employee ownership arrangements, such as employee share option plans (ESOP), aim to create a better management–employee situation. Moreover, agency theory proves such plans ease agency problems, although at the expense of current shareholders. This chapter intends to verify the effect of firms' announcement and implementation of ESOP on share prices using the Single Index Market Model (SIMM). In addition, tests to examine the relationship between cumulative abnormal returns (CAR) and several firms' variables were carried out. Findings reveal that announcement of such plans does not create significant abnormal returns to shareholders. However, firms' specific variables contribute to share market response in an ESOP announcement. Furthermore, significant negative abnormal returns were found before and after the implementation of the plan and firms' variables provide some insight on the determinant factors surrounding it.

1 Introduction[1]

Market reaction to news events such as ESOP are not only well documented (e.g., Hite and Long 1982; Miller and Scholes 1982; Brickley, Bhagat and Lease 1985; Mehran 1992; Cuny and Jorion 1995; Yermack 1997) but also diverse in scope, ranging from shareholder tax effect (Smith and Watts 1982, 1983; Aitken and Brown 1995) to the magnitude of price effect on shares (Brickley, Bhagat and Lease 1985; Murphy

1985; Tehranian and Waegelein 1985). However, many of these studies are concentrated on well-developed markets. Only the study done by Yeo, Chen, Ho and Lee (1999) emphasizes emerging capital markets. A comparison of findings from a study of emerging markets relative to the findings documented in developed markets can provide useful conclusions about the form of market efficiencies, which is known to have institutional deficiencies (Cheng, Ariff and Shamsher 2001). This study tries to explore the market reaction to ESOP announcements and implementations in the Malaysian bourse and provide some insight into the relationship between firm-specific variables and market reaction.

ESOP in the Malaysian market is unique due to some differences in how it is implemented or orchestrated. ESOP in Malaysia permits full voting rights for employees at the company's meeting and thus creates a full transfer of ownership control. Second, it represents a short-term compensation plan rather than a long-term pension plan for most employees. Third, in Malaysia ESOP does not have any means of financial support from the employer or the financial institution. Lastly, ESOP shareholders do not enjoy any tax advantages compared to the UK and USA.

This chapter is divided into five sections. Section 2 deals with perceived theory and evidence from past research. Section 3 describes research design, hypotheses, data and variables. Findings and discussion are presented in section 4, while section 5 concludes the study.

2   Theory and evidence

Executive compensation schemes such as ESOP are frequently associated with motivational factors in an organization. Brickley, Bhagat and Lease (1985) quote economists such as Smith and Watts (1982) in stressing the importance of these incentives whereby such alternative schemes (not only salary) are seen as important contracts. They have the ability to reconcile or align interests between the management team and the company's shareholders. Smith and Watts also believe that by initiating such profit-sharing and ownership schemes, agency cost could be decreased and thus the work force would be better motivated.

Research by Brickley, Bhagat and Lease (1985) shows that, on average, the stock prices increase by about 11 per cent on the announcement of the executive's compensation plans. Furthermore, their research also indicates that such plans produce a moderate increase of 2.4 per cent in share prices soon after announcement. In addition to that, Stulz (1988), Chang and Mayer (1992) and Yeo *et al.* (1999) also found that firms establishing ESOP experience, on average, a positive stock price reaction of 0.73 per cent, 1.22 per cent and 2.34 per cent respectively, when such announcements are made.

There are few studies in the literature on the magnitude of ESOP implementation. This is due to acceptance of implemented ESOP shares as issuance of new shares. Stigler (1970) Shaw (1971), and McCornell and Servaes (1990) found that market-adjusted returns upon issuance of new shares were negative. Nevertheless, McCornell and Servaes (1990) found that average raw returns were positive in all 12 months after these new shares were issued, except for the first month. On the local front, Sufar (1993) also found that 36 per cent of newly issued shares recorded negative average excess returns in the first week of trading. In reviewing literature of market behaviour to an anticipated announcement, research by Kim and Verrecchia (1991) on anticipated forthcoming public announcement is relevant to this study as employees (and the general public) know exactly when and how many shares are to be issued.

Due to the scarcity of literature about local conditions, this exploratory study embarks on the usage of literature in related areas. Based on previous empirical research, many factors have been taken into consideration in determining stock returns. Each researcher tries to provide evidence that some of the variables do affect share returns.

Numerous studies have examined the size effect on firm's value. However, to date, there is no formal definition of firm size. Previous empirical studies used various means to measure firm size. Market value of equity (number of shares outstanding times price per share) is one of the common ways used by Banz (1981), Reinganum (1981, 1992), Fouse (1989), Ball and Kothari (1989), Fama and French (1992), Fant and Peterson (1995), Kim (1995, 1997) and Berk (1997). Other ways to measure firm size are current assets, book value of assets and value of annual sales (Berk 1997).

According to Banz (1981) and Reinganum (1981), market value or size of the firm has an important role in explaining stock returns. They cited the fact that small firms have greater returns while large firms have smaller returns. Pertaining to the size effect, Berk (1997) suggest that firms with low market value earned higher returns due to having higher discount rates than the other firms, presumably because they are riskier.

Chopra, Lakonishok and Ritter (1992) find that the full spread between market returns and the risk-free rate does not compensate for beta risk. Jegadeesh (1992) argues that beta does not explain the cross-sectional differences in average returns when the test portfolios are constructed.

A study by Fant and Peterson (1995), by using simple regression, confirms the findings of Fama and French (1992). Their results show that there is a significantly negative relation between returns and size, but no relation between returns and prior earnings, and beta.

Traditional agency theory suggests that highly concentrated ownership should induce corporate management to be more attuned to the preferences of owners, with consequent higher performance level. The degree of owner's control of a particular firm is usually measured by the percentage of stock held by either a strongly related group or by a single dominant power. Morck, Vishny and Shleifer (1988) find a significant relationship between ownership structure and a firm's market value.

3 Methodology

3.1 Research design

This study employs the use of standard event study method to identify the direction and magnitude of share price upon ESOP announcements and implementations. Sharpe's (1963) Market Model was used as a standard equilibrium model to estimate abnormal returns (*AR*):

$$AR_{f,t} = R_{f,t} - (\alpha_i + \beta_i R_{m,t}) \tag{12.1}$$

where $R_{f,t} = (P_f - P_{f-1})/P_{f-1}$ and $R_{m,t} = (CI_t - CI_{t-1})/CI_{t-1}$, P is the company end of the day closing price and CI refers to market's composite index. The market parameters α and β are estimated by ordinary least square over the trading period -120 days to $+120$ days, omitting -6 days to $+6$ days (estimation period) relative to the announcement or implementation date. The returns were adjusted for thin trading bias using Scholes–Williams's method, primarily due to its ease of use. The resulting risk-adjusted abnormal returns of each observation is then added and averaged across all the observations to obtain the AAR_t as the simple arithmetic average. Next, the average returns over $t = 1, \ldots, T$ is calculated as:

$$CAR = \sum_{t=1}^{T} AAR_t \tag{12.2}$$

The cumulating is done over a price reaction window consistent with other studies and tested for statistical significance.

With a notion that share prices are not solely determined by news events but also due to other sources of information, this study looks at the relation between returns and other information to control the effect of left-out variables. In ESOP announcements, two variables were identified, which are firm-specific beta (Ball and Kothari 1989; Chopra, Lakonistok and Ritter 1992) and firm's size in the form of market capitalization. In this study, tests of the relation between CAR, firm beta, and firm's size were done using the following formula:

$$CAR = a_i + a_2\beta_f + Size_i + \varepsilon_1 \tag{12.3}$$

where CAR_i = cumulative abnormal returns over a specified window; β_f = firm-specific beta; and $Size_i$ = market value of the firm.

In ESOP implementations, four variables were identified, which are beta (Ball and Kothari 1989; Chopra, Lakonistok and Ritter 1992); firm size (Reinganum 1992; Fant and Peterson 1995; Kim 1997; Berk 1997); firm's total assets (Loughran and Ritter 1995; Johnson and Rao 1997; Lee *et al.* 1999); and growth in revenue. This study tests the relation between cumulative abnormal returns, firm size, firm-specific beta, firm's total assets, and growth in revenue by using the following formula:

$$CAR = a_i + a_2\beta_f + Size_i + TA_i + R_g + \varepsilon_1 \tag{12.4}$$

where CAR_i = cumulative abnormal returns over a specified window, β_f = firm-specific beta; $Size_i$ = market value of the firm; TA_i = firm's total assets; and R_g = growth in revenue, $Ln\ (R_t/R_{t-1})$

3.2. Hypotheses

The main hypothesis in this study is the existence of the sign of the relationship as well as the magnitude existing between risk-adjusted abnormal returns, which represents adjusted price change, and ESOP news event. The appropriate hypotheses for this study are:

> **H1**: *There is no significant relation between share price changes and ESOP announcement;*

> **H2**: *There is no significant relation between share price changes and ESOP implementation.*

If ESOP announcements and its implementation in the emerging market are to be consistent with what has been documented in the developed markets, null hypotheses are to be rejected.

3.3 Data

In this study, the data set relating to the period 1989 to 1997 came from the daily closing prices; and companies' financial information from the following sources: Securities Clearing Automated Network Services (SCANS) and ESOP announcements; and implementations in *The Investor Digest*, Kuala Lumpur Stock Exchange (KLSE) official monthly publication. In this study, the sample used consists of companies from

Table 12.1   Selected ESOP announcements and
ESOP implementation events

Year	Announcement	Implementation
1989	4	8
1990	6	13
1991	6	5
1992	7	9
1993	16	11
1994	14	12
1995	5	9
1996	1	7
1997	0	3
Total	59	77

listed and traded companies over the test period and covers a wide
range of industries.

These companies are subject to the following criteria: the companies
are traded in Malaysian-domiciled and not foreign companies; for ESOP
announcements, the selected event should have an announcement of at
least 1 per cent of total share outstanding and not shared announcements; for ESOP implementation, 500,000 shares are to be issued at any
selected event; selected events should not have more than 10 continuous non-trading days.

Daily closing prices of selected stocks traded from January 1989 to
December 1997 were extracted. Daily changes of more than 5 per cent
were checked for errors. Initially, for ESOP announcements, 87 events
were identified and 59 events were finally selected for analysis, while for
ESOP implementation 92 events were identified and 77 events selected
for analysis (see Table 12.1).

During the test period, no major significant economic or financial
event occurred which might affect market direction.

4   Findings

This section summarizes the results on both ESOP announcements and
implementations. First, results about the direction of the announcements and the implementation are presented, followed by controls for
firm-specific variables. In this study, price variations over -40 to $+40$
days were observed.

4.1   CAR and ESOP announcements

The cumulative abnormal returns over −40 to +40 (referred to as long window CAR) and from −1 to +1 days (short window CAR) are summarized. From Table 12.2, the mean over the long window (−40 to +40) is −7.266 with a standard deviation of 0.054837, with returns ranging from −1.01157 to 0.994. Moreover, mean over the short window is −2.229 with a standard deviation of 0.0049427 and returns ranging from −1.157 to −0.458.

From Figure 12.1, it is clear that markets had reacted as far away as day −39. Abnormal returns at day one before, zero day, and one day after are −0.614, −0.458, and −1.1157 per cent respectively; however, none is

Table 12.2   Test of significance on CAR over different cumulating periods ($n = 59$)

Observation window	CAR	*t*-test
−40 to +40	−0.07266	−1.20455
−40 to 0	−0.03192	−0.56461
−20 to 0	−0.00659	−0.11185
−5 to 0	−0.03308	−1.25027
−1 to 0	−0.01072	−0.88347
−5 to +5	−0.07517	−2.63456*
−5 to +1	−0.04465	−5.32032**
−1 to +1	−0.02229	−0.55226

Note: Significant at the * 0.05 or ** 0.01 level.

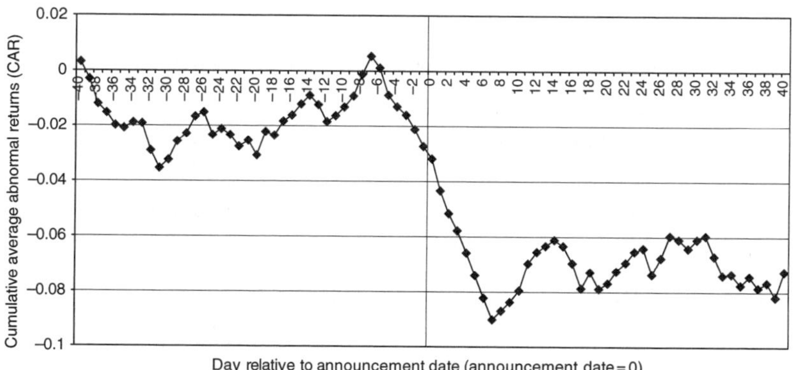

Figure 12.1   Risk-adjusted CAR around ESOP announcement on KLSE, 1989–97 ($n = 59$)

significant. Nevertheless, it is clear that the markets reacted drastically from −5 days to +5 days of the announcement and subsequently. Although none of the daily returns recorded is significant, the largest daily average excess returns occurred at +1 day after the announcements with $AAR = -1.157$.

The daily average excess returns started −50 days prior to the announcement, and levelled off from +8 days after the announcement. During the post-announcement period there are no abnormal returns. The market appears to have anticipated the announcement, and reacted negatively, by means of other information.

4.2   CAR and ESOP implementation

For ESOP implementation, the mean over the long window (−40 to +40) is −13.48 with a standard deviation of 0.05534 with returns ranging from −1.348 to 0.966. Moreover, the mean over the short window is −1.3670 with a standard deviation of 0.002505 and returns ranging from −0.755 to −0.281. Results for 77 events are as summarized in Table 12.3.

From Figure 12.2, with its gradually downward slope, it is clear that the markets had reacted as far away as day −38. Abnormal returns at day one before, zero day, and one day after are −0.281, −0.331, and −0.774 per cent respectively. However, none of these daily returns tested significant. Although no daily returns recorded were significant, the largest daily average excess returns occurred at +2 days after the announcements with $AAR = -1.348$.

The daily average excess returns started −50 days prior to the announcement, and levelled off from +28 days after the announcement. During the post-announcement period there were still abnormal

Table 12.3   Test of significance on CAR over different cumulating periods ($n = 77$)

Observation window	CAR	*t*-test
−40–+40	−0.13352	−2.15460*
−40–0	−0.08795	−2.68133*
−20–0	−0.04997	−2.20358*
−5–0	−0.02491	−4.31658**
−1–0	−0.00612	−12.24000**
−5–+5	−0.05494	−3.69093**
−5–+1	−0.03246	−4.89768**
−1–+1	−0.01367	−3.03048

Note: Significant at * 0.05 and ** 0.01 level.

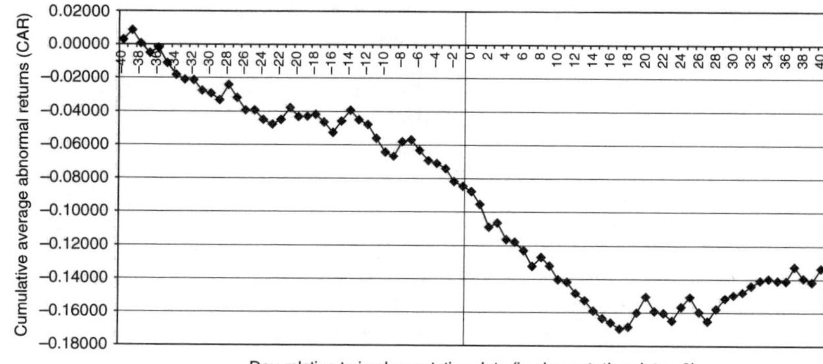

Figure 12.2   Risk-adjusted CAR around ESOP implementation on KLSE, 1989–97 ($n = 77$)

Table 12.4   Results of ESOP announcement model regression for beta, and firm size for long window ($n = 59$)

	Standard error	Standardized coefficients beta	t	Significance
(Constant)	0.027		−3.396	0.001
Beta	0.118	−0.273	−2.140	0.037
Size	0.000	−0.242	−1.897	0.043

Model summary: Adjusted $r^2 = 0.092$, standard error = 0.02888542, $F = 3.834$, Sig. = 0.028.

returns recorded. The market appears to have anticipated the announcement, and reacted negatively gradually, by means of other information as were to ESOP announcement.

4.3   Controlling for firm-specific variables

In ESOP announcements, Table 12.4 shows the results of firm-specific variables in explaining the behaviour of share returns. By using Spearman Correlation Rank, it is found that correlations amongst variables were low and insignificant. Apart from constants being significant at the 0.001 level, it is also found that firm beta and market capitalization were also recorded as being significant at the 0.05 level. These results imply that, apart from the announcement, firm's beta and firm's size could also influence share returns.

Table 12.5   Results of ESOP implementation model regression for beta, firm size, firm's assets, and turnover for long window ($n = 77$)

	Standard error	Standardized coefficients beta	t	Significance
(Constant)	0.093		−1.997	0.050
Beta	0.392	−0.689	−5.624	0.000
Size	0.000	0.310	2.733	0.008
Total assets	0.000	0.273	2.364	0.021
Turnover	0.061	0.246	2.576	0.012

Model summary: Adjusted $r^2 = 0.338$, standard error $= 0.30426873$, $F = 10.585$, Sig. $= 0.000$.

The regression results lead to acceptance of the null hypothesis; therefore, there is no significant relationship between abnormal returns and ESOP announcements. However, it is found that beta and size variables have a significant influence on share returns.

Furthermore, similar to what had been employed in ESOP announcements, Spearman Correlation Rank shows that correlations amongst variables in ESOP implementation were low and insignificant. In ESOP implementation, apart from constants being significant at the 0.05 level, it is also found that firm beta, market capitalization, firm's assets, and turnover were also recorded as being significant at the 0.05 level. These results show that, apart from the announcement, a firm's specific variables would also influence share returns.

The regression results in Table 12.5 lead to acceptance of the null hypothesis; therefore, there is no significant relationship between abnormal returns and ESOP implementations. This aligns with findings that other variables also have a significant influence on share returns.

5   Conclusions

Some pertinent highlights of the findings are identified. This research addressed the issue of the effect on share prices of ESOP announcements, and implementations in an institutionally emerging market, namely the Kuala Lumpur Stock Market in Malaysia. The research design is adapted from ESOP announcements, and other related literature. It is, however, unlikely that these findings could be generalized to all emerging markets until findings of other emerging markets are documented.

Nevertheless, the findings in this chapter suggest that ESOP announcement has a contemporaneous impact on share prices, and the effect is more visible over the short window than the long window. The lack of a strong announcement effect during the period immediately prior to the announcement is not surprising given the emerging nature of the market, which suggests that either pre-announcement information dissemination or speculative trading over a short period are being corrected over a longer period.

It is also found that the magnitude of the risk-adjusted price change and announcements is quite robust over the long window. Moreover, shorter window results are not only smaller in magnitude but also contradict those documented in developed market. While the developed market recorded a small positive abnormal returns, Brickley, Bhagat and Lease (1985), Stulz (1988) and Chang and Mayer (1992) show an average of 2.4 per cent, 0.73 per cent, and 1.22 per cent in share prices at the early stage of announcement respectively. However, the Malaysian market reacted significantly negatively with CAR for the -5 to $+1$ day window at -4.465 per cent.

The incremental information affected by firm-specific variables (beta and market value of the firm) beyond the value from ESOP announcements was checked. The results support evidence of these variables having an influential value ahead of the value from ESOP announcements. This indicates that firm-specific variables also have an impact on share prices in the emerging market.

In ESOP implementation, a long-standing impact on share prices is noted. This effect is visible over the long window rather than the short window. The lack of a strong implementation effect during the period immediately adjacent to the issuance is not surprising given the emerging nature of the market. Hence, it suggests that either pre-implementation dissemination of information or speculative trading in longer period is uncorrected.

Furthermore, it is also found that a shorter observation window produces a small but negative significant, return similar to what has been documented in developed markets. Malaysian markets reacted significantly negatively at $\alpha = 0.05$ with CAR for -5 to $+1$ days and -5 to $+5$ window are -3.246 per cent and 5.494 per cent respectively.

The incremental information affected by firm-specific variables (beta, market value of the firm, firm assets, and turnover) beyond the value from ESOP announcements was tested. The results support evidence of these variables having an effectual value ahead of the value from ESOP implementations. This indicates that firm-specific variables also have an impact on share prices in the emerging market, which is speculative in nature and constrained by differences in firm-related variables. Investors react not only to the implementations but also to firm-specific variables. The overall result seems to be consistent with the theory and evidence from the developed markets.

Finally, while ESOP news events are value-relevant, the speed and strength of the impact from these releases are more subdued (but negative in returns) in this emerging market.

Appendix

Table A12.1   Risk-adjusted average abnormal returns on ESOP announcements of the KLSE listed firms, 1989–97 ($n = 59$)

	AR	*t*-test	CAR		AR	*t*-test	CAR
−40	0.00317	0.01123	0.00317	1	−0.01157	−0.03194	−0.04349
−39	−0.00619	−0.02128	−0.00302	2	−0.00816	−0.03804	−0.05166
−38	−0.00918	−0.02486	−0.0122	3	−0.00615	−0.02203	−0.05781
−37	−0.00311	−0.01154	−0.01532	4	−0.00808	−0.03016	−0.06589
−36	−0.00448	−0.01025	−0.0198	5	−0.00813	−0.03455	−0.07402
−35	−0.00109	−0.00435	−0.02089	6	−0.00817	−0.02638	−0.08219
−34	0.00214	0.00656	−0.01875	7	−0.00787	−0.02949	−0.09006
−33	−0.00047	−0.00124	−0.01922	8	0.00316	0.01214	−0.0869
−32	−0.0098	−0.02067	−0.02902	9	0.00313	0.01436	−0.08377
−31	−0.00644	−0.01871	−0.03546	10	0.00416	0.0161	−0.07961
−30	0.00313	0.01432	−0.03233	11	0.00994	0.04142	−0.06967
−29	0.00664	0.02173	−0.02569	12	0.00411	0.00997	−0.06555
−28	0.00287	0.006	−0.02282	13	0.00218	0.01082	−0.06338
−27	0.00612	0.01811	−0.01671	14	0.00213	0.01005	−0.06124
−26	0.00157	0.00556	−0.01513	15	−0.00214	−0.00891	−0.06338
−25	−0.00816	−0.04045	−0.0233	16	−0.00612	−0.02286	−0.0695
−24	0.00214	0.01117	−0.02116	17	−0.00926	−0.0296	−0.07877
−23	−0.00213	−0.01006	−0.02329	18	0.00592	0.01755	−0.07285
−22	−0.00418	−0.01334	−0.02747	19	−0.00613	−0.02189	−0.07898
−21	0.00212	0.01031	−0.02535	20	0.00214	0.00704	−0.07684
−20	−0.00543	−0.02093	−0.03078	21	0.00428	0.00538	−0.07255
−19	0.0086	0.03276	−0.02218	22	0.00313	0.01262	−0.06943
−18	−0.00128	−0.00531	−0.02346	23	0.0041	0.0165	−0.06533
−17	0.00511	0.02316	−0.01835	24	0.00108	0.00218	−0.06425
−16	0.00215	0.00906	−0.0162	25	−0.00952	−0.02788	−0.07377
−15	0.00411	0.016	−0.01208	26	0.00614	0.01993	−0.06764
−14	0.00313	0.01117	−0.00895	27	0.00804	0.02236	−0.0596
−13	−0.00336	−0.01822	−0.01232	28	−0.00145	−0.00659	−0.06104

Table A12.1   continued

	AR	*t*-test	CAR		AR	*t*-test	CAR
−12	−0.00614	−0.0263	−0.01846	29	−0.0031	−0.0096	−0.06414
−11	0.00214	0.00804	−0.01632	30	0.0032	0.01133	−0.06094
−10	0.00313	0.01393	−0.01319	31	0.00127	0.00527	−0.05967
−9	0.00415	0.01821	−0.00904	32	−0.00739	−0.02393	−0.06706
−8	0.00783	0.02898	−0.00121	33	−0.00699	−0.00956	−0.07406
−7	0.00653	0.02635	0.00532	34	0.00048	0.00127	−0.07358
−6	−0.00418	−0.01328	0.00114	35	−0.00401	−0.00749	−0.07759
−5	−0.00997	−0.04372	−0.00882	36	0.00313	0.01048	−0.07445
−4	−0.00412	−0.01193	−0.01294	37	−0.00412	−0.01578	−0.07857
−3	−0.00312	−0.01165	−0.01606	38	0.00181	0.00571	−0.07676
−2	−0.00515	−0.01999	−0.02121	39	−0.00514	−0.01762	−0.0819
−1	−0.00614	−0.01951	−0.02735	40	0.00923	0.03042	−0.07267
0	−0.00458	−0.00934	−0.03193				

Table A12.2   Risk-adjusted average abnormal returns on ESOP implementations of the KLSE listed firms, 1989–97 ($n = 77$)

	AR	*t*-test	CAR		AR	*t*-test	CAR
−40	0.00262	0.01031	0.00262	1	−0.00755	−0.02769	−0.09546
−39	0.00567	0.02105	0.00828	2	−0.01348	−0.05810	−0.10894
−38	−0.00774	−0.03245	0.00054	3	0.00230	0.00902	−0.10664
−37	−0.00567	−0.01510	−0.00513	4	−0.00994	−0.04151	−0.11657
−36	0.00296	0.01577	−0.00217	5	−0.00136	−0.00619	−0.11793
−35	−0.00892	−0.04756	−0.01108	6	−0.00505	−0.01735	−0.12298
−34	−0.00715	−0.02659	−0.01823	7	−0.00925	−0.03242	−0.13224
−33	−0.00295	−0.01639	−0.02118	8	0.00522	0.01965	−0.12702
−32	−0.00036	−0.00115	−0.02154	9	−0.00508	−0.01233	−0.13210
−31	−0.00620	−0.01938	−0.02774	10	−0.00806	−0.03258	−0.14015
−30	−0.00155	−0.00475	−0.02929	11	−0.00157	−0.00637	−0.14172
−29	−0.00400	−0.01873	−0.03329	12	−0.00694	−0.02652	−0.14865
−28	0.00907	0.04331	−0.02421	13	−0.00413	−0.01466	−0.15278
−27	−0.00760	−0.03867	−0.03181	14	−0.00628	−0.02642	−0.15906
−26	−0.00760	−0.02928	−0.03941	15	−0.00444	−0.01397	−0.16350
−25	0.00005	0.00018	−0.03936	16	−0.00257	−0.00814	−0.16607
−24	−0.00554	−0.02563	−0.04489	17	−0.00376	−0.01445	−0.16983
−23	−0.00294	−0.01237	−0.04783	18	0.00124	0.00533	−0.16859
−22	0.00298	0.01215	−0.04485	19	0.00849	0.02577	−0.16010
−21	0.00689	0.02923	−0.03795	20	0.00966	0.04741	−0.15045
−20	−0.00522	−0.02139	−0.04317	21	−0.00871	−0.03032	−0.15915
−19	0.00032	0.00097	−0.04285	22	−0.00125	−0.00390	−0.16041
−18	0.00113	0.00552	−0.04173	23	−0.00468	−0.02098	−0.16508

Table A12.2   continued

	AR	*t*-test	CAR		AR	*t*-test	CAR
−17	−0.00462	−0.01925	−0.04635	24	0.00832	0.03427	−0.15677
−16	−0.00629	−0.02468	−0.05264	25	0.00611	0.02334	−0.15065
−15	0.00695	0.03966	−0.04569	26	−0.00917	−0.04423	−0.15982
−14	0.00639	0.02466	−0.03930	27	−0.00530	−0.01835	−0.16512
−13	−0.00565	−0.02165	−0.04495	28	0.00719	0.03350	−0.15793
−12	−0.00300	−0.01284	−0.04794	29	0.00620	0.03367	−0.15173
−11	−0.00808	−0.04647	−0.05602	30	0.00212	0.00708	−0.14961
−10	−0.00831	−0.03481	−0.06433	31	0.00164	0.00755	−0.14797
−9	−0.00251	−0.00946	−0.06683	32	0.00411	0.01585	−0.14387
−8	0.00881	0.03242	−0.05802	33	0.00311	0.01626	−0.14076
−7	0.00120	0.00361	−0.05682	34	0.00091	0.00374	−0.13985
−6	−0.00618	−0.02756	−0.06300	35	−0.00094	−0.00457	−0.14079
−5	−0.00640	−0.02740	−0.06940	36	−0.00030	−0.00129	−0.14108
−4	−0.00176	−0.00434	−0.07116	37	0.00843	0.04339	−0.13265
−3	−0.00289	−0.00948	−0.07406	38	−0.00684	−0.03124	−0.13949
−2	−0.00774	−0.03315	−0.08179	39	−0.00212	−0.00836	−0.14161
−1	−0.00281	−0.01044	−0.08460	40	0.00815	0.02958	−0.13347
0	−0.00331	−0.00933	−0.08791				

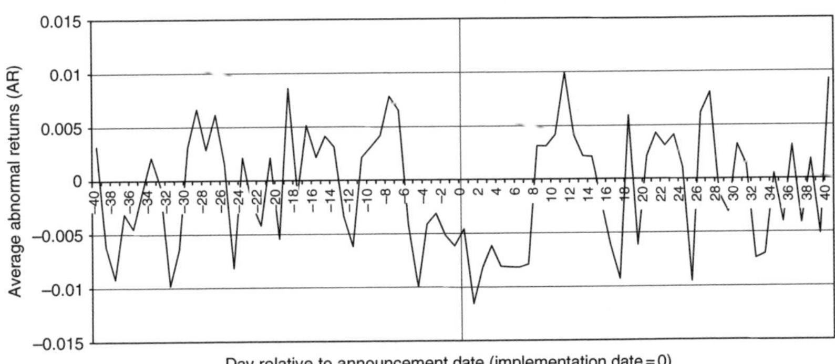

Figure A12.1   Daily risk-adjusted abnormal returns on ESOP announcements of the KLSE listed firms, 1989–97 ($n = 59$)

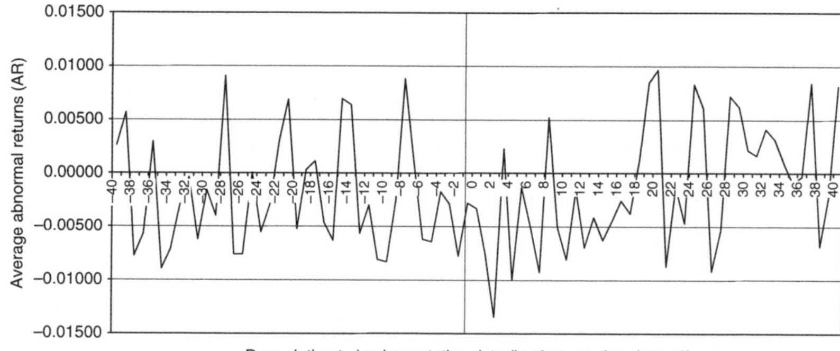

Figure A12.2   Daily risk-adjusted abnormal returns on ESOP implementations of the KLSE listed firms, 1989–97 (*n* = 77)

Note

1 We record our appreciation for the helpful comments of fellow colleagues and participants at the School of Finance and Banking Monthly Seminar in Universiti Utara Malaysia. We also would like to extend our gratitude to Associate Professor Dr Che Ani Mad and Associate Professor Dr Merouane for their insights. We also thank Madam Wan Sofiza Wan Azmi for preparing this chapter.

References

Aitken, M. and Brown, P. (1995), 'An intraday analysis of the probability of trading on the ASX at the asking price', *Australian Journal of Management*, 20 (2), 115–55.

Ball, R. and Kothari, S. P. (1989), 'Non-stationary expected returns: implications for test of market efficiency and serial correlation in returns', *Journal of Financial Economics*, 25, 51–74.

Banz, R. W. (1981), 'The relationship between returns and market value of common stocks', *Journal of Financial Economics*, 9, 3–18.

Berk, J. B. (1997), 'Does size really matter?', *Financial Analysts Journal* (September/October), 12–18.

Brickley, J. A., Bhagat, S. and Lease, R. C. (1985), 'The impact of long-range managerial compensation plans on shareholder wealth', *Journal of Accounting and Economics*, 7, 115–29.

Brown, S. and Warner, J. B. (1985), 'Using daily stock returns: The case of event studies', *Journal of Financial Economics*, 14, 3–32.

Chan, L. K. C., Hamoa, Y. and Lakonishok, J. (1991), 'Fundamentals and stock returns in Japan', *Journal of Finance*, 46, 1739–89.

Chang, S. and Mayers, D. (1992), 'Managerial vote ownership and shareholder wealth', *Journal of Financial Economics*, 32, 103–31.

Cheng, F., Ariff, M. and Shamsher, M. (2001), 'Accounting earnings and share market revaluation', *MFA 2001 Conference Proceedings* (Kuala Lumpur).

Chopra, N., Lakonishok, J. and Ritter, J. R. (1992), 'Measuring abnormal performance', *Journal of Financial Economics*, 31 (2), 235–69.

Cuny, C. and Jorion, P. (1995), 'Valuing executive stock options with endogenous departure', *Journal of Accounting and Economics*, 20, 193–205.

Davis, J. L. (1994), 'The cross-section of realized stock returns: The Pre-COMPUSTAT Evidence', *Journal of Finance*, 49, 1,579–93.

Fama, E. F. and French, K. R. (1992), 'The cross section of expected stock returns', *Journal of Finance*, 47, 427–65.

Fant, L. F. and Peterson, D. R. (1995), 'The effect of size, book-to-market equity, prior returns, and beta on stock returns: January versus the remainder of the year', *The Journal of Financial Research*, XVIII (2) (Summer), 129–42.

Fouse, W. L. (1989), 'The "small stocks" hoax', *Financial Analyst Journal*, 45 (4), 12–15.

French, K. R., Schwert, G. W. and Stambaugh, R. F. (1987), 'Expected stock returns and stock market volatility', *Journal of Financial Economics*, 19, 3–30.

Hite, G. L. and Long, M. S. (1982), 'Taxes and executives stock options', *Journal of Accounting and Economics*, 4, 3–14.

Jain, B. A. and Kini, O. (1994), 'The post-issue operating performance of IPO firms', *Journal of Finance*, 49 (5), 1,699–727.

Jegadeesh, N. (1992), 'Does market risk really explain the size effect?', *Journal of Financial and Quantitative Analysis*, 27, 337–51.

Johnson, R. S. and Rao, R. M. (1997), 'Take me out to the boardroom', *Fortune*, 136 (2), 42–8.

Kim, D. (1995), 'The errors-in-variables problem in the cross-section of expected stock returns', *Journal of Finance*, 50, 1,605–34.

Kim, D. (1997), 'A re-examination of firm size, book-to-market, and earning price in the cross-section of expected stock returns', *Journal of Financial and Quantitative Analysis*, 32 (4), 463–89.

Kim, O. and Verrecchia, R. E. (1991), 'Market reaction to anticipated announcement', *Journal of Financial Economics*, 30, 273–309.

Kumar, R. and Sopariwala, P. R. (1992), 'The effect of adopting of long-term performance plans on stock prices and accounting numbers', *Journal of Financial and Quantitative Analysis*, 27, 561–95.

Lambert, R. A. and Lacker, D. F. (1985), 'Executive compensation, corporate decision-making and shareholder wealth: An overview of evidence', *Journal of Accounting and Economics*, 7, 287–309.

Lee, C. F., Yeo, G. H., Chen, S. S. and Ho, K. W. (1999), 'Effect of executive share option plans on shareholder wealth and firm performance: The Singapore evidence', *The Financial Review*, 34, 1–20.

Loughran, T. and Ritter, J. R. (1995), 'The new issues puzzle', *Journal of Finance*, 50 (1), 23–53.

McCornell, J. J. and Servaes, H. (1990), 'Additional evidence on equity ownership and corporate value', *Journal of Financial Economics*, 27, 595–612.

Mehran, H. (1992), 'Executive incentives plan, corporate control and capital structure', *Journal of Financial and Quantitative Analysis*, 27 (4), 539–60.

Miller, M. and Scholes, M. (1982), *Executive Compensation, Taxes and Incentives, Financial Economics: Essays in Honour of Paul Cooper* (Englewood Cliffs, NJ: Prentice-Hall).

Morck, R., Vishny, R. and Shleifer, A. (1988), 'Management ownership and market valuation', *Journal of Financial Economics*, 20, 293–315.

Poterba, J. M. and Summers, L. H. (1988), 'Means reversion in stock prices: Evidence and implications', *Journal of Financial Economics*, 22, 27–59.

Reinganum, M. (1981), 'Misspecification of capital asset pricing: Empirical anomalies based on earnings yields and market values', *Journal of Financial Economics*, 9, 19–46.

Reinganum, M. (1992), 'A revival of the small-firm effect', *Journal of Portfolio Management*, 18 (3), 55–62.

Rosenbergs, B., Reid, K. and Lanstein, R. (1995), 'Persuasive evidence of market inefficiency', *Journal of Portfolio Management*, 11, 9–17.

Scholes, M. and Wolfson, M. A. (1990), 'Employee stock ownership plan and corporate restructuring: Myths and realities', *Financial Management*, 19, 12–28.

Sharpe, W. F. (1993), 'A simplified model for portfolio analysis', *Management Science*, January, 277–93.

Shaw, D. (1971), 'The performance of primary common stock offerings: A Canadian comparison', *Journal of Finance*, 26, 1,103–13.

Smith, C. W. and Watts, R. L. (1982), 'Incentives and tax effect on US executives compensation plans', *Australian Journal of Management*, 7, 139–57.

Stigler, C. P. Jr, (1970), 'A study of the relationship of accounting principles and common stock prices of firms going public', unpublished PhD dissertation (Tallahasse: Florida State University).

Stulz, R. M. (1988), 'Managerial control of voting rights, financial policies, and the market for corporate control', *Journal of Financial Economics*, 20, 25–54.

Sufar, S. B. (1993), 'Performance of new issues: The Malaysian case', *Jurnal Pengurusan*, 8, 17–28.

Tehranian, H. and Waegelein, J. F. (1985), 'Market reaction to short-term executives compensation plan adoption', *Journal of Accounting and Economics*, 7, 133–44.

Warner, J. B. (1985), 'Stock market reaction to incentives plan adoption', *Journal of Accounting and Economics*, 7, 145–9.

Yeo, G., Chen, S., Ho, K. and Lee, C. (1999), 'Effects of executives share option plans on shareholder wealth and firm performance: The Singapore evidence', *The Financial Review*, 34, 1–20.

Yermack, D. (1997), 'Good timing: CEO stock option awards and company news announcements', *Journal of Finance*, 52, 449–76.

13
Technology Transfer in Asia

Akira Kuroda

A less developed country achieves industrialization in a flying geese pattern, step by step, assisted by technology carriers and characterized by cooperation between industrialized and less developed countries. In Southeast Asia, however, it is frequently argued that Japanese firms and expatriates hide technology from the local people. It is also argued that Japanese expatriates stay for decades, thus denying local staff the opportunity of acquainting themselves with technology. Local staff with higher education prefer a Western-style hierarchy and want to be promoted even before they have learnt how to manufacture. They are interested in typically American paper contracts, job descriptions and manuals. Japanese management, on the contrary, tends to train people from scratch within the firm, mainly through on-the-job training, work experience and learning by mistakes.

1 Why don't they trust the management authority?

1.1 Two nationalities in a firm

This section treats the sensitive and controversial issue of nationalities. First of all, it is essential to understand that ownership and management are separate issues. Once a firm is established, management comes first, not ownership. Management requires cooperation between the parent company in Japan and the Thai partner. Management intends to achieve the best for the firm and is not motivated purely by personal promotion. Nevertheless, it is also true that local people feel ambivalent about what they experience as Japanese domination. It is argued that even in the case of minority ownership Japanese expatriates dominate the management of subsidiaries. The first question to the 16 Thai–Japanese joint ventures

Table 13.1 Which side takes responsibility for management of the following?

	Japanese side	Thai side	Total
Manufacturing	16		16
Sales	15	1	16
Finance	15	1	16
Labour management	12	4	16
R&D	16		16
Government procedures	10	6	16

Source: The author's survey (*Survey A*). Figures denote the number of firms.

(JVs) (among the 23 firms surveyed: see Table A13.1 in the Appendix) was: 'Which side takes responsibility for the following management matters, the Japanese investor or the Thai partner?' (see Table 13.1).

This question is in fact improper because management of the six categories is carried out in cooperation, not separately. However, the understanding of the Japanese expatriates is at least expressed. The Japanese side bears full responsibility for all management matters in ten JVs. In six others, certain tasks are shared by the Thai side; in six firms, 'government procedures' are carried out by the Thai side; 'sales' and 'financing' are run by the Thai side in one firm each respectively, while in four firms, 'labour management' is carried out by the Thai side. On average, the number of tasks carried out by the Thai side is limited. Management responsibility is mostly taken over by the Japanese side regardless of whether the capital shares are majority or minority.

The second issue is the transfer of responsibility from headquarters (HQ) to the local management side. This is important from the technology transfer point of view. If local management is entrusted with a wider range of management matters, Thai staff will have the opportunity of increasing their management skills. Management by a Japanese minority is the result of government restrictions on foreign capital shares. Very often, Japanese firms accept these restrictions and work under Thai majority (but silent) shareholders. These silent shareholders retain the right to take over management but, as a result of their short history of industrialization, usually lack experience and skill. The second issue addressed was 'Which side has the real authority, the parent company (HQ) or the local management side, which includes both expatriates and local staff?' (see Table 13.2).

Table 13.2   Which side has the real authority, the parent company or local management? Or is a transfer to local management planned?

		HQ	Local	Planned	Total
1	Directors' appointment/personnel	**20**	3		23
2	Staff personnel	2	**21**	2	25
3	Volume of stocks and production	1	**22**	4	27
4	The purchase of parts and raw materials	5	**22**	1	28
5	Methods of manufacturing	10	14	1	25
6	Planning of equipment investments	14	10	3	27
7	Product items and composition	11	11	1	23
8	R&D	**15**	5	3	23
9	Marketing	13	10	3	26
10	Financing	**17**	7		24
11	Settlements of yearly accounts	5	**17**	1	23
	Average per firm (total exceeds 23)[a]	10.3	12.9	1.7	24.9
	Share	44.8%	56.1%		

[a] Total exceeds 23 because a few firms answered both 'HQ' and 'local side', dividing each category into several parts.

Source: The author's survey.

In most cases, the tasks of 'directors' appointment and personnel' (20 firms), 'R&D' (15 firms) and 'financing' (17 firms) remain in the hands of the HQ, whereas 'volume of stocks and production' (22 firms), 'the purchase of parts and raw materials' (22 firms), 'staff personnel' (21 firms) and 'settlement of yearly accounts' (17 firms) are usually transferred to local management. In about half the firms, the local side was entrusted with responsibility for the remaining four categories (i.e., 'methods of manufacturing', 'planning of equipment investment', 'product items and composition' and 'marketing').

What follows are the least advanced cases of entrusting responsibility to the local side. Management is still in the hands of HQs (J-7, 14, 20; see Table A13.1)[1] in the case of three firms. The reasons are explained below.

1 *The first overseas investment.* Since all companies are small- and medium-sized industries in Japan and investments in Thailand were the first FDI, expatriates lack experience and know-how in overseas manufacturing. In the case of J-7, for example, the post of Managing Director (MD) is held by the deputy MD in Japan who makes decisions as a Japanese, not as a resident of Thailand. The senior expatriates are technicians in press works and mould-making. They do not speak English or Thai. They are skilled workers, but are not trained as managers. One adviser who speaks English is a retired ex-salaried

man from a *sogo shosha* (general trading company). He has just started working for the firm and does not have full knowledge of the firm's business and technology. Therefore, all eleven categories depend on HQ. The other two firms also lack capable staff due to their short history in overseas operations. This leads to strong direct involvement by the parent companies in FDI operations, at least until they begin to make profits.

2 *A production base for the parent, no marketing function.* They are defined as production bases, with no marketing function attached. All products are sold to Japanese parent companies (J-14, 20), or to both the parent company and the *oya kojo* (parent workshop) in Thailand in the case of J-7.

3 *No opportunity for R&D learning, dies and moulds are provided.* Since the subsidiary is defined as carrying out easy processes such as manual assembly tasks, moulds and dies are provided by parent companies or customers and the level of technology is still low. Opportunities for improvement or acquisition of R&D technologies are rare. In the case of J-20, the process is complicated: it not only covers press works but also machining, heat treatment, electroplating and assembly. But they concentrate on 'brake hose sockets', producing 150,000 pieces per month. There is no time to work on improvement and R&D technologies yet.

Because the HQ holds major responsibility, Thai staff in the above three cases are not provided with the opportunity to learn the whole process of technology and management know-how. The subsidiary firms are only partial production bases of the parent companies. The replacement of expatriates by trained local staff would seem to be easier in this type of subsidiary firm, with the exception of a few difficult technological matters.

1.2 The role of expatriates: the worker–expatriate ratio

The next question is staff localization from expatriates to Thai staff. This question intends to investigate whether the replacement of local staff means the completion of technology transfer. The author calculated the number of employees, expatriates and the worker–expatriate ratio of each firm.

Table 13.3 clearly demonstrates that Japanese firms have a higher average of expatriates than Western firms both in number and ratio. At the time of start-up, a Japanese firm had 4.1 expatriates (*b*) on average and the worker–expatriate ratio (*a/b*) was 23.3 (i.e., one expatriate for every 23.3 persons). At present, a Japanese firm has 6.0 expatriates (*d*)

Table 13.3   Worker–expatriate ratio (*a/b*, *c/d*) (Japanese and Western firms)

	Start-up year			Present (1994)			Years of operation
	Employee (*a*)	Expatriate (*b*)	Ratio (*a/b*)	Employee (*c*)	Expatriate (*d*)	Ratio (*c/d*)	
23 Japanese firms	95.3	4.1	23.3	521.8	6.0	86.3	7.4
13 Western firms	n.a.	n.a.	n.a.	325.6	1.4	232.5	6.2

n.a. = not available.

Sources: Table A13.1, A13.2 (see Appendix).

and the worker–expatriate ratio (*c/d*) is 86.3. Meanwhile, a Western firm has 1.4 persons per firm (*d*) and the worker–expatriate ratio (*c/d*) is 235.2. The reasons for the gaps are as set out below.

1 The claims are that Japanese expatriates do not normally speak English or the local language, while Western expatriates and many of the local staff in developing countries speak English. Consequently, as a result of the language barrier, Japanese expatriates are less efficient in technology transfer in comparison with Western expatriates. As a result, they have to come in large numbers and stay longer in Thailand.
2 Japanese firms do not generally have good systems of technology transfer such as job descriptions and manuals. Consequently, Japanese firms are less efficient in technology transfer and have to send more staff for longer periods.
3 Japanese firms pay expatriates lower salaries, hence Japanese firms can afford to send more staff for a longer period.
4 Japanese firms invest in a riskier, more competitive market. Therefore, they have to stay longer and send more staff, who struggle to survive and take full responsibility.
5 Japanese firms invest in more difficult processes than Western firms. Therefore, technology transfer takes longer and requires more energy.

The first three reasons all seem to be true to a great extent from the viewpoint of Western standards. The fourth comes from the issue of *desideratum*. The survey found that Western firms concentrate on assembly with regard to the fifth. Even where they are involved in metal-working, the sample shows that Western firms seem to have easier jobs to tackle than Japanese firms, as below.

As shown in Table A13.4, Western firms in the survey make aircraft goods, electric motors, and electric appliances such as toasters, cookers and hot pots. As a Western plant manager explained,[2] these processes are normally easier than engineering plastics (J-10, 14, 19) or precision press parts for microwave ovens, video tape recorders (VTRs) or air conditioners (J-7, 11, 13). Rubber injection is another case in point. There are two rubber injection firms in the surveyed samples, one Japanese (J-5) and the other a US firm (W-1, Table A13.2). The former makes silicone rubber parts (defect ratio 5–10 per cent, claim ratio 0 per cent) and the latter produces windshield wipers (defect ratio 2.5 per cent). The former has two expatriates and plans to add another soon, while the latter has no expatriates at all. The Japanese president (a skilled expert) teaches technologies for making moulds, dies and machines to Thai staff. In contrast, local management staff at the Western firm say that they can manage without expatriates. Moulds are supplied by the parent company in the USA and the technologies are not very difficult for them (W-1).

1.3   High turnover ratios

Training loss (high turnover ratio) is a serious problem for both Japanese and Thai firms. At J-1, for example, the training loss is as high as 49/50. It means that of the 50 Thai workers that J-1 sent to Japan for two or three years' training, only one worker is still currently with the firm; the other 49 have all left. The president of J-1 regretted that the firm had sent them to Japan for such a long period of training. Since they had learned Japanese, they were in a position to leave and utilize their language ability to advantage in other firms. The firm therefore changed its policy and has so far sent about 20 workers to Japan, each for less than one year. In the interviews, many other firms also raised the problem of the high turnover ratio (Table 13.4).

Even in the case of a large Thai firm, 8–10 per cent quit every year (T-19, Table A13.3). In the case of small firms, over 30 per cent quit within two years (T-5, J-22). This means that trained staff might have to be replaced completely within six to ten years. Recruiting workers for a small firm (T-5) is difficult. T-5 operates a five-day technical training course regularly for this purpose.

1.4   Towards good teamwork

There are some successful cases of local staff leadership. After two years of unsuccessful management, J-21 changed the management method from direct control to indirect control. Japanese expatriates explained management policies and targets only to Mr A, a Thai graduate from a university in Japan, asking him to implement them. Japanese expatriates trusted him (J-21), and the result was successful management.

Table 13.4   Training loss

Year of start	Loss ratio	Period of training
J-1 (1966)	49/50	2–3 years in Japan
J-5 (1990)	3/4	1 year 2–8 months in Japan
J-7 (1991)	2/11	6 months to 1 year in Japan
J-14 (1988)	8/10 ·	2 or 3 months in Japan
J-19 (1992)	4/8	3–6 months in Japan
J-22 (1989)	45/50	3 months in Japan
T-6 (1990)	2/10	2 months in Japan
T-1 (1981)	4/5	In the past 12 years
T-5 (1991)	14/42	2 years
T-19 (1967)	16–20/200	Every year 8–10% quit

Note: 49/50 means that of the 50 people trained, 49 resigned.

Source: The author's survey (*Survey A*).

In the preparation stage, the parent company of J-11 recruited three Thai students in Kobe who, after returning to Thailand, worked for J-11 in Thailand. They formed the core of the Thai staff and helped the successful start-up in Thailand. In some cases, the leadership of the MDs succeeded in creating strong teamwork among the entire staff (J-8, 12, 16). Mr Prasartsilp (T-14), the son of a farmer in the northeast (*isarn*), was educated at a technical college and worked for Isuzu for 13 years, which included training in Japan. With this background, he succeeded in achieving good teamwork by employing people from *isarn*, his native area. The management concept of these firms looks similar to that of the teamwork spirit in Japan. The concept differs from the elitism of Thai university graduates.

Our findings suggests that fewer expatriates or lower ratios do not always mean the completion of technology transfer. Technology transfer depends more on products and processes, and cultural aspects, namely, the characteristics of management systems and management philosophies of FDI.

2   Indirect secondary diffusion of technology

Diffusion of technology is carried out through many routes such as inside technology transfer among corporations, *shitauke* (sub-contracting), technical assistance, indirect secondary diffusion and indigenous efforts. What follows are examples of indirect secondary diffusion (spin-off, secondary sub-contracting, JVs) and indigenous efforts (learning-by-doing, reverse engineering).

2.1   Spin-off

There are many spin-off entrepreneurs in the survey. They acquired technologies through work experience and then became independent. Most of them were trained in Japanese firms, either in Thailand or in Japan. Because they understand Japanese businesses and have many friends in Japanese firms, they are likely to receive orders from them.

T-14 is a die and press specialist with 65 employees. Mr Prasartsilp, the MD of T-14, worked at Isuzu for 17 years from 1973 to 1990. He then established his own factory in 1990, using his experience. He was born into a farming family at Ubon, in northeastern Thailand, and educated there at a technical high school (MS6), followed by technical college (diploma) in Bangkok. In 1973 he began working at Isuzu, and the company sent him to Japan for seven months on a two-month language course followed by five months of technical training. He has worked in the die-making and press section of Isuzu since 1977 and accumulated experience of die and press work technology. He mentioned that he knew most of the people in the die sections of automobile firms such as Isuzu, Summitr Motors Manufacturing, SAB and Thairung. He has since established two other factories apart from T-14. One factory caters for the CNC lathe process (6 CNC lathe machines and 24 employees in Thonburi), while the other produces pressed parts for air conditioners in Cholburi.

Next there is the case of T-6, a mould and die-maker with 50 employees. In 1978, Thai Kawasaki (established in 1966, 100 per cent Thai-owned) established a die maintenance section composed of four people, where the MD of T-6 (Mr Banpot) was chief of the section from the beginning. Mr Banpot and his staff were trained as the staff of Thai Kawasaki and received technical training in mould-making. In the late 1980s, mould and die-making orders had increased so much that Thai Kawasaki split the die section in 1990 to make it an independent die and tool factory. This is how T-6 began. It received technical assistance from Tatsuno Chemical in Kobe when it was still a section of Thai Kawasaki. T-6 makes injection moulds and aluminium die cast moulds for motorcycles (e.g., dust covers), sanitary units (toilet lids) and chairs (seat parts made of plastic). From 1985 to 1988, ten people were trained in Japan for one or two months. Of the ten people originally trained on the staff, eight are still with the firm. This is a very low training loss ratio compared to other cases in Tables 13.1–4. This low ratio is probably the result of the firm's independence from Thai Kawasaki. The new company is small and has to stand on its own feet. The entire staff are conscious that the future of the firm is in their hands.

T-9, a mould base maker, is also a case of spin-off. Mr Verasak, the MD of T-9, worked for a Japanese firm in Thailand and was trained in Japan. He established T-9, using his work experience at a Japanese firm. The MD's father was a plastic injection machinery dealer and the MD and his brother had helped their father when they were young. Later, the MD worked for the Kawaguchi Company in Thailand (two years of office work in Thailand, three years' training in Japan, five years' factory work in Thailand). The two sons inherited the business when their father died in 1986, and set up a trading company with the assets of their father's company. In 1990, the MD set up a JV in Thailand with a Japanese company from Kakegawa, Shizuoka. The products of the JV were for the international market only. Hence, the MD established T-9 in 1994 for the domestic market. T-9 produces guide-pins and guide-bushes for moulds, the technology for which the MD was able to acquire at the JV with Japan. T-9's largest customer is Srithai Miyagawa (8 per cent). T-9 has 17 employees, including three vocational-school graduates. Two CNC Mori Seiki injection machines and a Toshiba grinding machine are brand new and were expensive. The seller of the machines, Yamazen, a Japanese machine tools dealer in Bangkok, provides training and maintenance service.

2.2   Secondary sub-contracting

Metalworking jobs are likely to be sub-contracted and tend to produce spin-off entrepreneurs. Both J-1 and J-8 sub-contract to spin-off entrepreneurs who are former employees. In addition, two other firms sub-contract to local firms.

In the case of J-1, subcontracting was a result of the change in government policy. When the government banned J-1 electroplating to stop pollution, J-1 helped the electroplating section to become an independent local firm in 1967. The chief of the electroplating section set up a small firm (EZP Company Ltd) which became a subcontractor to J-1. The owner of the subcontracting firm was one of the first 50 trainees sent to Japan. President Aoyama claims that EZP has achieved satisfactory results over the past 20 years. In the case of the machining process at J-8, one worker who had received training in Japan was interested in starting his own business and now has a factory with 10 workers. J-8 subcontracts the machining of brass rods to his factory.

2.3   Joint ventures

Among the 23 Japanese subsidiary firms in this survey, 16 are Thai–Japanese JVs, and among the 20 Thai firms, one is a Thai–Japanese

JV (Table A13.1, Table A13.3). From the local partner point of view, these JVs are a means of acquiring technology. First, the JV itself is the subject that acquires technology. Second, the JV is a route through which technology can be acquired. In the latter case, the final technology users could be any firm or people outside the JV. This section introduces a case of the former (a JV as the technology recipient, J-18) and a case of the latter (a JV as the route for technology diffusion, T-17).

When J-18 was established, learning a new technology looked so easy that the Thai side took over the entire management responsibility. However, the technology proved to be very difficult and the JV became unprofitable. A few years later, the HQ of the technology supplier decided to invest an additional amount of capital to take over full management and technology responsibility.

T-17 is a JV with a Japanese firm, while T-10 is a 100 per cent Thai-owned firm. Both T-17 and T-10 are owned by the Siam Cement group. Therefore, technologies acquired by the left hand (T-17) could possibly be transferred to the right hand (T-10). For example, before the start of T-10, about 90 young people were newly recruited and trained at T-17 where the technology was provided by Japan. When training was completed, the plant manager and two senior technicians were transferred to lead the T-10 operation.

2.4   Learning-by-doing

T-5 is a case of 'learning-by-doing' (i.e., indigenous technological development). A Chinese immigrant set up a trading business in agricultural products. The immigrant's son, Mr Tanapol, the MD of T-5, was in the same business and established a factory to make agricultural machinery with several simple press machines in 1971. Twenty years later, stimulated by technical training and seminars by MIDI (a metalworking institute), the MD decided to set up a separate factory for tools and die-making. He visited factories in Thailand and Japan in order to learn operational technology and collect designing data for his own tool and die factory. This factory is a typical case of learning-by-doing.

T-5 invested in equipment, a mixture of second-hand and new machines, a computer numeric control lathe, a wire cut electro discharge machine, a machining centre and computer aided design. However, due to lack of experience and skilled technical staff, the managerial and technical capability of the firm is still quite low. The design capability of the firm is especially weak. In addition, the flow of production lags behind schedule so that the firm is often unable to complete products in the required delivery time.

T-11, a mould maker, is the second case of 'learning-by-doing' and at the same time an example of a 'spin-off'. Mr Prasit, the MD, developed his technology through learning-by-doing at foreign firms from the age of 16 to 22. He thus accumulated knowledge and experience in mould-making at four firms:

- a Thai firm, Imperial Thai Toys, for 2 years
- a Hong Kong firm, Ying Mee, for 1 year
- a Taiwanese firm, Power Mould, for 1 year
- a Japanese firm, Bandai, for 2 years

In 1991, at the age of 22, he established a small injection mould shop at Sukhumvit with his father's financial assistance. His firm has 12 employees, seven for mould-making and five for injections. The firm has 15 customers, two of which are Japanese firms.

2.5   Reverse engineering

T-4 is a case of 'reverse engineering'. The founder, the son of a Thai farmer in Cholburi, was born in the late 1920s. This case involves a manager of local origin, not a Chinese immigrant. After the Second World War he engaged in sugarcane and cassava plantations. At that time farmers had to rely on manpower or animal power, using simple farm equipment. Returning from a study tour of looking at the manufacture of agricultural machinery in Europe, the founder began the production of Thai-made 'disc ploughs' in 1958.

As an agricultural country, Thailand uses many types of agricultural machinery. Machines made by Massey Ferguson, Ford, John Deere and Kubota are popular and need spare parts such as 'disc ploughs' or 'front blades'. Due to the expansion of agricultural production, the demand for spare parts has increased. At present, T-4 has over 400 dealers in Thailand and occupies 30 per cent of the after-sales market for spare parts such as disc ploughs for agricultural machines.

T-4 has developed some original brand products by reverse engineering. It is able to reproduce copies of a sample if there is an original available to disassemble and analyse. The MD says that it may take a year or two to start commercial production of a new product after importing a sample model. The retail price is less than half or a third of the original price of the imported part or equipment. Thus, reverse engineering helps a developing country to accumulate not only capital but also technological capability.

T-20 is also a case of 'reverse engineering'. The founder, who is the son of a Chinese immigrant in Cholburi, established a small workshop in

1972 at the age of 27 with only three people. Observing the potential market for hydraulic pumps, the founder worked hard to acquire technologies for manufacturing hydraulic systems. His firm is an example of successful indigenous in-house technology development. He has not made any specific technical licence agreements so far.

It is very important for a developing country to be able to make machines on its own. T-20 is a good example of indigenous machine-making in Thailand, which is why it has received several government prizes. It produces mainly large equipment manufactured in the batch production system. The strength of this firm lies in its ability to design and in marketing. However, the range of metalworking technologies is limited. The firm has to purchase critical parts from outside or import them from foreign countries, which demonstrates the limits of indigenous efforts.

The founder of T-20 sent his sons to study overseas with a view to the future development of the firm. One is studying in the USA and the other in Japan. They will challenge higher technologies to strengthen the industrial base, hopefully meeting the father's expectations.

2.6   Summing-up

The above observations on technology levels (the highest = 10, the lowest = 0) at 20 Thai firms are summarized in Table 13.5. Four firms in sub-contracting or *shitauke* presented the highest levels in four items of operational technologies on average (point 6.9). Five firms in technical assistance (TA) showed the second highest technology levels (point 6.6). Six firms which acquired technology through the 'diffusion route' seem to remain at low levels (point 5.1). Indigenous development of technologies is effective only for a limited market and of which technology levels are lowest (point 4.5). These figures demonstrate that the parent–child relationship or *shitauke* provides the highest levels of technology. Sub-contracting in Thailand seems to be practised in the same manner as in Japan. There is no capital relationship apart from some major suppliers. However, they cooperate for their common aim to upgrade technological capability, based on mutual trust and interest.

The lowest level of technology in indigenous development suggests that learning through human contact is important. In particular, what is learnt from competitors in industrialized countries proves indispensable to enabling a firm to compete in international markets. Thailand developed a three-wheeled car (*tuktuk*), a four-wheeled car (*see-lo*), a country car (*ee-than*) and a long-tail boat (*rua-harn-yao*). However, these products cannot earn foreign currencies as the international market

Table 13.5 Learning levels of technologies at local firms

		Present (1994, at the survey time)					Future (3 years later)				
	No. of firms	Operation	Maintenance	QC	PC	Average	Operation	Maintenance	QC	PC	Average
Sub-contracting	4	7.3	6.5	6.8	6.8	6.9	8.3	8.3	8.8	8.5	8.6
TA	5	6.8	7.2	6.4	6.0	6.6	8.1	8.4	7.6	7.6	7.9
Diffusion	6	5.7	4.2	4.8	5.5	5.1	7.8	6.0	6.8	7.8	7.1
Indigenous	5	5.2	4.2	4.4	4.2	4.5	6.2	6.0	5.4	5.6	5.8
Total	20	6.2	5.4	5.5	5.6	5.7	7.6	7.1	7.1	7.4	7.3

Note: QC = quality control; PC = production control; average = average of operation, maintenance, QC and PC.

Source: The author's survey.

prefers more sophisticated products. This is the reason why FDI is considered the best way to develop modern industrial technology.

3   Conclusion

East Asian economies today are specifically set within a culture where labour and management cooperate, and where large industry and small–medium industries cooperate. In this culture, technology spreads from more developed to less developed countries and facilitates speedier industrialization. It will not happen in a culture where rich and poor are divided, or the exempt and the non-exempt. Learning technology means learning manufacturing techniques, *gijutsu*, on the shop floor. Technology diffuses through human contact, and accumulates. Thus, developing countries will catch up with developed countries. It occurs among grassroots people only through grassroots people. This inevitable path of economic development is akin to Akamatsu's flying geese theory (Akamatsu, 1935/6, 1937, 1962).

Appendix: profiles of the surveyed firms (October 1994–March 1995)

Table A13.1 Profile of the surveyed firms (23 Japanese subsidiaries)

	Holding company		Thai investment							
	Capital	Employees	Start-up	Capital	Ratio		Employees	Expatriates	Products and processes
Firm no.	(mil. yen)			(mil. baht)	Thai	Japan			
J-1	14	980	1966	4	0	100	280	4	Bolts and nuts (auto)
J-2	898	65	1989	100	19	62 (USA 19)	209	5	Press, assembly (auto)
J-3	2,000	1,100	1989	26	5	90 (Singapore 5)	270	2	Uninterrupted power supply, bar code readers
J-4	4,170	778	1990	60	51	49	210	5	Clutches
J-5	80	160	1990	48	0	100	110	2	Silicone rubber
J-6	2,506	1,200	1974	17	73	27	450	6	Steel wheel
J-7	365	215	1991	24	19	81	62	5	Metal press
J-8	21,207	1,500	1988	200	20	80	263	4	Valves (brass and bronze)
J-9	40,000	5,000	1991	500	0	100	1,350	9	Electric wires
J-10	30	180	1989	20	0	100	1,500	4	Precision mould
J-11	80	600	1987	220	33	67	3,800	40	Components assembly
J-12	780	1,000	1989	100	51	49	303	5	Engine parts
J-13	160	350	1988	12	20	80	130	4	Timers
J-14	2,600	280	1988	40	0	100	700	6	VTR parts
J-15	2,500	700	1979	20	51	49	140	1	Super hard dies
J-16	339	240	1989	5	10	90	159	3	Anchor bolts
J-17	200	350	1989	80	51	49	270	7	Dies and tools
J-18	2,008	700	1980	10	27	73	1,165	8	Condenser
J-19	400	120	1992	90	0	100	215	4	Precision mould and die
J-20	104	340	1989	40	10	90	64	3	Brake hose sockets
J-21	38	230	1987	19	0	100	230	3	Microwave oven parts
J-22	14,220	3,200	1989	60	30	70	85	4	Dump trucks units
J-23	108	620	1989	50	69	31	37	5	Heat treatment
Average	4,122.0	865.6	86.6	75.9	23.4	75.5	521.8 86.3	6.0	←worker–expatriate ratio

Notes: capital = capital amount; employees = number of employees including foreign expatriates; start-up = the year of start-up; ratio = capital ratio between countries; expatriates = number of foreign expatriates; worker–expatriate ratio = the number of workers divided by the number of expatriates.

Source: The author's survey (*Survey A*).

Table A13.2 Profile of the surveyed firms (13 Western subsidiaries)

Holding company			Thai investment					
Firm no.	Start-up	Capital (mil. baht)	Ratio			Employees	Expatriates	Products and processes
			Thai	West	Japan			
W-1	1989	n.a.	0	100	0	300	0	Rubber parts (auto)
W-2	1988	500	98	2	0	1,059	5	Telephone
W-3[a]	1986	2	0	100	0	70	2	UPS
W-4	1987	20	2.5	97.5	0	350	3	Aircraft goods
W-5	1988	145	51	5 (Taiwan 44)	0	250	0	Electric wire
W-6	1990	100	95	5	0	450	0	Printed circuit board
W-7	1989	80	66.5	33.5	0	300	0	Hermetic compressors
W-8	1989	60	90	10	0	200	1	Electric motor
W-9	1989	5	2	98	0	200	2	Hard disk drive
W-10	1990	15	70	30	0	220	0	Electrical appliances
W-11	1989	152	0	100	0	156	1	Electric control board
W-12	1989	113	51	49	0	450	2	Integrated circuit
W-13[a]	1979	150	24.5	51	24.5	228	2	Engine valves (auto)
Average	87.8	103.2	42.3	52.4	1.9	325.6	1.4	

Notes: [a] denotes the *Survey A*. Capital = capital amount; employees = number of employees including foreign expatriates; expatriates = number of foreign expatriates; start-up = the year of start-up; ratio = capital ratio between countries.

Source: The author's survey (2 *Survey A* and 11 *Survey B*).

Table A13.3 Profile of the surveyed firms (20 Thai firms)

Firm no.	Start-up year	Capital (mil. baht)	Ratio		Employees	Expatriates	Product
			Thai	Japan			
T-1	1981	30	100	0	280	3	Core stamping
T-2	1974	120	100	0	360	1[a]	Radiators
T-3	1986	50	100	0	240	0	Radiators, press
T-4	1953	0.3	100	0	450	0	Agricultural machinery
T-5	1991	20	100	0	42	1	Die making
T-6	1990	5	100	0	50	0	Mould and die
T-7	1989	150	100	0	503	1	Bolts and nuts (auto)
T-8	1975	0.1	100	0	25	0	Repairing
T-9	1994	1	100	0	17	0	Mould base
T-10	1992	170	100	0	170	0	Casting
T-11	1991	0.5	100	0	12	0	Mould making
T-12	1988	5	100	0	25	0	Mould and die
T-13	1986	50	100	0	1,329	5	Auto body press
T-14	1990	10	100	0	65	0	Die and press
T-15	1972	100	100	0	1,739	3[a]	Auto seats
T-16	1977	37	100	0	117	1	Forging parts (auto)
T-17	1977	108	90	10	590	3	Casting
T-18	1986	85	100	0	520	1	Diecast, machining
T-19	1967	85	100	0	1,300	0	Car body assembly
T-20	1972	10	100	0	350	0	Hydraulic machines
Average	81.55	51.8	99.5	0.5	409	0.95	

Note: [a] denotes employees with Japanese background, not expatriates from specific Japanese firms.

Source: Survey A.

Table A13.4   The production processes and products of surveyed firms (56 firms)

			Japanese firms (J)			Western firms (W)			Thai firms (T)			
			Auto	Electrical	General	Auto	Electrical	General	Auto	Electrical	General	
Plastic, rubber	1	Assembly		3, 9			3, 5, 11, 12					6
	2	Injection/ Assembly		10, 13, 14, 19*			2					5
	3	Injection		5*	1							2
Metal (change in the shape)	4	Press/ Assembly		7, 11, 21*								3
	5	Sheet works-welding Press Machining	2, 6, 20				7, 9, 10	4	2, 3, 13, 14, 15, 19	1*	4, 8, 20	17
	6	Mould and die	17						5, 6	9, 11, 12*		6
Metal (change in the nature)	7	Forging Casting Press, Machining	1, 4, 12, 22		8, 16	13	8		7, 10, 16, 17, 18			13
	8	Special product/ process		15, 18, 23			6					4

Table A13.4   continued

	Japanese firms (J)			Western firms (W)			Thai firms (T)		
	Auto	Electrical	General	Auto	Electrical	General	Auto	Electrical	General
Number of firms (sub-total)	8	13	2	2	10	1	13	4	3
Number of firms (total)		23			13			20	56

Notes: auto = auto parts industry; electrical = electrical parts industry; general = general parts industry.

Each figure from 1 to 23 in the columns of Japanese firms denotes the code number of 23 Japanese firms. The same is applicable to Western and Thai firms.

The classification depended on the *main* processes. For example, J-2 has not only 'Press/Assembly' but also 'heat treatment'; it was classified in 'Press/Assembly (No. 4)'. J-11 and W-7 have 'Injection' additionally, but were classified in 'No. 4' and 'No. 5' respectively.

The symbol *, in the electrical parts industry denotes that the firm makes moulds and dies in-house. In the case of the auto parts industries, most of the surveyed firms make moulds, dies and jigs in-house.

Source: The author's survey (*Survey A* and *Survey B*).

Notes

1 J-7, 14 and 20 denote Japanese firms (No. 7, 14 and 20) in Table A13.1.
2 An anonymous plant manager of a Western firm said: 'Technological capabilities of Thai people; I think they are reasonable. Our production processes don't require high technological skills, so that was no problem to us. To find Thai people with good organizing capacities is more difficult. On top of that, the level of English speaking is rather low. Training the organizational skill according to European standards becomes therefore very difficult.' (Interview by Kuroda Akira, December 1994, in Bangkok.)

References

Akamatsu, K. (1935, 1936), 'Wagakuni Yomo-kogyo-hin no Boueki Susei (Japan's International Trade in Wool Industry)', *Shogyo Keizai Ronso*, 13 (I, II) (June), 129–212.

Akamatsu, K. (1937), 'Wagakuni Keizai Hatten no Sogo Bensho-ho (Dialectic in the Development of Japanese Economy)', *Shogyo Keizai Ronso*, 15 (July), 179–210.

Akamatsu, K. (1962), 'A Historical Pattern of Economic Growth in Developing Countries', *The Developing Economies* (March–August), 3–25.

Kuroda, A. (2001), *Technology Transfer in Asia* (Tokyo: Maruzen Planet).

14

Limitations and Potentials of Intercultural Communication in Unethical Business Conventions: A Theoretical Scrutiny of Intercultural Communication, Business Ethics, Habermasian Discourse Ethics and Foucaultian Aesthetics

Nobuyuki Chikudate

The purpose of this study is to provide a reflexive argument regarding business ethics in intercultural communication. Cultural relativist positions (which give priority to cultural idiosyncrasy) in intercultural communication have traditionally dominated the underlying assumptions of conducting and practising communication across cultures. On the other hand, universalist positions such as the integrative social contracts theory of Donaldson and Dunfee (1994) have been discussed in international business ethics. In reality, both positions have pros and cons when discussing the praxis of business communication across cultures. Can intercultural communication scholars advocate the phrase 'respect other cultures, traditions, and customs', for example, when people from cultures with high legal and ethical standards are confronted with corruption, scandal, bribery, embezzlement, fraud, and the severe working conditions in Asian work places? Universalist positions, on the other hand, have been criticized for the imperialism of their economic rationality and Christian-based morality. This study postulates a third way and incorporates apects of both praxis and theory in the light of Habermasian projects on the theory of communicative actions (1984, 1990). Since the latter would unfortunately come to a deadlock on the soil of the Far East, an alternative methodology is proposed.

As the scope of our practice and research expands across nation-states, we speak and hear daily of adjectives such as comparative, cross-cultural, cross-national, global, intercultural, transcultural and transnational. We also play with business words such as communication, collaboration, cooperation, negotiation and understanding in work places and class-rooms. However, the fundamental question, 'Has our knowledge to improve substantial practices in international management advanced?', must be raised if we are to use this vocabulary in practice and research. This question can be asked in current environments where new trends, legitimacies and stakeholders have begun to challenge, intervene, block and disturb (or even condemn) the operations of multinational corporations (MNCs). These trends, legitimacies and stakeholders emerged from concepts of business ethics, corporate citizenship, corporate social responsibility (or responsiveness) and corporate social performance. These concepts are no longer being digested in the conventional naive logic of cross-cultural or cross-national differences in organizational behaviour and human resource development/management, where inter-cultural communication used to intervene.

Some ethical positions in intercultural communication overlap with those of business ethics, but most ethical standards in intercultural com-munication contradict international business ethics. The discussions sur-rounding this issue could be interpreted as a debate on relativist and universalist ethical positions. Donaldson and Dunfee (1994), for exam-ple, introduced the discussion from an international business ethics point of view. However, no one has discussed the issue from the perspective of intercultural communication. An understanding of the intricate nature of intercultural business ethics seems necessary, even in the corrupt coun-tries of the Far East, and especially Japan, if MNCs are to operate without damaging fairness and integrity. On the other hand, MNC host countries must try to deconstruct the unscrupulous nature of historically inherited conventions in business communities, otherwise the social reality of corrupt business communities will be constructed in global communities and reputations will be lost for ever. This scenario is quite evident in the case of Japan. Considering the endless scandals and corruption here, the author believes that business ethicists need to take a step forward from the debating stage of justifying either relativist or universalist ethical positions. Autonomous academicians must assume the duty of prob-lematizing historical inheritance and cleansing it of its unscrupulous nature, even in corrupt countries. The assumption of this study is that oriental (certainly Japanese) intellectuality has not been effective and that the simple adoption of occidental intellectuality is not the solution either. The aim of this study is to scrutinize the use of occidental method-ologies of problematizing and deconstructing theoretically (such as the Habermasian critical theory) in the context of corruption in the Far East. Finally, alternative methodologies will be proposed.

1 Overviews of current status of intercultural communication in management

Before opening the debate on business ethics, it is necessary to gain an overview of the current status of intercultural communication. As contact between strangers increases with face-to-face communication, practitioners are forced to confront the struggles that result from cultural differences, and which were unknown in previous experience. Competencies, confidence, integrity and pride, accumulated in previous education, experience, accomplishments and recognition, become frag-ile in the course of these struggles (Chikudate 1995). In many cases, those who used to be admired in their home countries turn out to be incompetent in overseas assignments. Under these circumstances, the phrase 'intercultural communication' sounds attractive to both interna-tional business practitioners and researchers. In reality, however, there is relatively little convergence between intercultural communication and international management, apart from a few limited topics. This is sim-ply due to the split in traditions where the logic of legitimacy dominates in studies. Originally, intercultural communication evolved as a practical necessity for US servicemen and the Peace Corps overseas after the war, for people whose mental health had deteriorated due to failure in *sojourner adjustment*. This refers to the accommodation to new environ-ments, overcoming psychological and psychosomatic problems during temporary stays in other countries. The various symptoms were caused by *culture shock* (e.g., Oberg 1960), which refers to psychological and psychosomatic reactions triggered by the violation of sojourners' social reality by unfamiliar social norms, values and mores. The symptoms manifest themselves as psychosomatic disorders, a sense of loss, rejec-tion by the host nationals, and a feeling of impotence. Although many of the factors that cause culture shock have been studied in the past, intercultural communication scholars have stressed that communication difficulties with host nationals should be conceived as the most critical factor of culture shock. Communication difficulties are not purely the result of poor competence in local languages but also involve non-verbal aspects of communication (e.g., Gudykunst 1994). Hall (1960), for example, has disseminated the significance of non-verbal aspects of communication across cultures. An underlying assumption in investigating non-verbal aspects of communication is that with recognition and understanding of the hidden dimensions of host cultures, sojourners can accommodate themselves more easily to them and reduce the psychological and psychosomatic discomfort of culture shock.

International business areas simply adopted research and training topics surrounding sojourner adjustment from intercultural communication. Sojourner adjustment was translated into business language as expatriate selection and training (Mendanhall and Oddou 1986; Kobrin 1988; Inkson *et al.* 1997). Varner (2000) even tried to establish a domain of research, training and practice in the overlapping areas of intercultural communication and international business, calling it *intercultural business communication*. This field is, however, at a premature stage. He said that authors in international business might discuss communication issues, including negotiation and conflict resolution, but the emphasis would not typically be on communication. On the other hand, intercultural communication literature does not traditionally examine communication in a business context but in a more general cultural context. Furthermore, so-called 'how to effectively communicate (or negotiate) with foreigners' books are also very common in intercultural communication (e.g., Gao and Ting-Toomey 1998). This research might be helpful for those who need to manage 'the first base' of intercultural encounters in the business scene. The first base includes one-shot overseas travel and/or negotiation. However, as Lovitt (1999) summarized, imported research may not provide sufficient answers to questions at the heart of intercultural business communication. After all, how and why has such an unsatisfactory combination of intercultural communication and business/management continued?

2 Unrealistic expectations of intercultural communication studies

Intercultural communication studies first appeared as the hybrid area between cultural anthropology, communication, social psychology and sociology. Yet, as a degree accreditation, intercultural communication is located in the discipline of human or speech communication, thus hindering the potential of diversifying intercultural communication topics. Conventionally, intercultural communication was a mere extension of interpersonal communication across cultures, and virtually the same interpersonal communication models and methodologies have been mimicked by intercultural communication researchers. Models and theories in interpersonal communication include various kinds of human relations, information processing and speech/rhetoric. The legitimacy of methodologies in interpersonal communication is identical to that of US social psychology and/or behavioural science, where authorized methods of conducting research are based on Popperian quantitative approaches combined with statistical tests. Thus, the goal of intercultural communication studies in the discipline of human communication has been to enhance communication effectiveness by reducing the 'noise' multiplied by cultural differences during the process of communication. Communication researchers believed that there would be no misunderstandings if the noise were reduced. Thus, identification of noise sources caused by cultural differences became the research priority and were to be measured by convenient cross-cultural variability measures. Although there are many variations, the most widely used measures include the individualism versus collectivism of Triandis, Brislin and Hui (1988) and Hofstede's (1980) four dimensions. Intercultural communication researchers combined various human communication models such as the uncertainty reduction theory (Berger and Calabrese 1975) with cross-cultural variability measures to examine the level of cultural noises in human communication. They tended to believe that cultural noises during the communication process could be explained by the metrical distances in cross-cultural variability scales.

Apart from the interpersonal communication research with cross-cultural variability, some intercultural communication researchers took other directions with a sociological flavour. Rogers and Kincaid (1981), for example, advocated the convergence model of communication. This model seems to appeal to those interested in intercultural cooperation because its original thesis was to establish networks or ties across cultures. The assumption among advocates of the convergence model is that the increase in information exchange across different nations will eventually lead to shared meaning systems.

Having reviewed the publications of intercultural communication studies and conversed with the researchers, the author claims that the potential contribution of previous intercultural communication studies to the domain of business ethics is minimal. First of all, these studies are mere extensions of human relations across cultures. This means that the level of enquiry does not meet the demand of practitioners concerned with topics such as business ethics, corporate citizenship and social responsibility/responsiveness. Although ideas surrounding business ethics have gradually gained some recognition in the mainstream of managerial topics, few have touched this intricate sensitive area across cultures in the field of intercultural communication.

Second, the majority of previous studies, especially those dealing with the convergence model of communication, are based purely on American ideas, not because most researchers are Americans or have been trained in the USA but because the basic assumptions taken for granted are American. The fundamental goal here is the possible creation of sytems of shared meaning. However, the researchers' view of these systems is a replica of the US melting-pot view of society, where immigrants from various cultural and ethnic backgrounds are forced to surrender and conform to the legitimacy of the first immigrants from England (Sowell 1981). The final critical pitfall of intercultural communication studies involves the issues of ethics, which will be discussed separately in the following section.

3   Ethics surrounding intercultural communication

Apart from the limitations of previous intercultural communication studies and the ensuing dissatisfaction, there are some dangers for those who blindly swallow a certain type of ethics in intercultural communication. The criteria for good and bad stem from *cultural relativism*, which condemns an ethnocentric attitude towards other cultures but facilitates tolerance towards differences (e.g., Casmir 1997). It also suggests evaluation must be 'relative to the cultural background out of which they arise' (Herskovits 1973, 14). As Renteln (1988, 37) put it, 'cultural relativism was introduced in part to combat… racist, Eurocentric notions of progress'. Eurocentric notations of progress view people from other parts of the world as savage and primitive, and this view was strengthened by the propagation of Christianity. The strategy of colonization was in fact symbiotically related to mission propaganda in non-European countries. Pope John Paul spoke of the sins committed by Christians and publicly begged God's forgiveness on 12 March 2000 (*Los Angeles Times*, 13 March 2000). Intercultural communication has condemned imperialism and the incumbent Eurocentric legitimacies since its foundation.

The cultural relativism thesis has been translated to international human resource consultation and training programmes, and emphasizes the significance (among other things) of business etiquette, customs, patterns of social interaction, greetings and taboos in individual cultures (e.g., *Los Angeles Times*, 14 February 2000). This position has also been advocated in the field of international business, especially negotiations (e.g., Adler 1997). A cultural relativist attitude is a fundamental necessity and should be welcomed by those who need to open their eyes and develop pluralistic world views. When the Japanese economy and its corporations overwhelmed the rest of the world in the 1980s, both Western practitioners and academics partially swallowed this argument. As a result, many business schools opened new courses relating to intercultural management. However, cultural relativism must be challenged in the new stages where the notion of business ethics is involved.

Even intercultural researchers have cautioned the simple introduction of cultural relativism. Barnsley (1972), for example, suggested the necessity of drawing a distinction between the evaluative and descriptive aspects of ethical relativity. Whereas cultural relativism asserts the factual diversity of customs, moral beliefs and practices, ethical relativism is an evaluative thesis affirming that the value of actions and validity of moral judgements depend on the socio-cultural context. Gudykunst (1994) interpreted this as follows: saying that ethics develop out of culture and vary across cultures (cultural relativism) is different from saying that valid moral judgements can only be made within a particular cultural context (ethical relativism). What these researchers advocated was that people cannot avoid making ethical judgements in intercultural interaction, and that cultural universals can be used. Bidney (1968, 545), for instance, provided a very simple example, saying that universals could be used where forbidden activities (such as treason, murder rape or incest) are involved because 'in all cultures the perpetuation of society takes precedence over the life of the individual'.

This view of ethics seems the most compatible with business ethics in the field of intercultural communication. Unfortunately, judging ethical issues in intercultural communication is far more simple than doing so in the field of business. This is due to the limited scope of the latter to discuss matters of communication or attitudes towards intercultural interaction in general socio-cultural contexts. When a debate turns to ethics in international management, it is essential to elaborate on examples from the more subtle grey zones of business operations.

4   Business ethics across cultures

Realistically, the business world does not engage in overt criminal activities. It prefers to dabble in white-collar crimes and/or unethical practices including corruption, embezzlement, fraud, bribery and political contributions, violating anti-trust legislation, deceiving stakeholders, harming customers or clients, and allowing hazardous working conditions. Many of these practices are not only embedded in the company logic of economic optimization but also in the conventions of certain economic systems. Chikudate (1999b), for example, discussed the nature of unethical practices in Japanese business that have been scandal-ridden since 1997 as a mechanism of institutionalization. Since Japanese business people are accustomed to the ongoing conventions upheld by their predecessors, they no longer understand that what they did was wrong. They live in a state of *collective myopia* (Chikudate 1999a, 2000, 2002a) where members of certain communities or systems are able to make sense of the context in which they live, but are not able to monitor the institution created by themselves as a whole.

This situation in Japan raises the fundamental issue of intercultural business cooperation. *If we swallow the logic of cultural relativism blindly, it may already be a violation of business ethics to accommodate the business customs, greetings and value systems of host societies, where unethical behaviour gains the status of being taken-for-granted or common sense.* This thesis is examined for cases between the Far East and Western countries where relatively high ethical standards exist (e.g., Enderle 1997), as well as for cases involving intra-Asian countries. The real crime of MNCs is to claim 'we are adjusting to other cultures' (e.g., Ginwala 1998), knowing full well that what they are doing in other countries is illegal in their own. In 1996, for example, the criminality of US and German pharmaceutical companies was disclosed when Japanese haemophilic patients were given blood transfusions contaminated with AIDS. They could have said that they were simply accommodating their marketing practices to Japanese standards along with Green-Cross, a Japanese pharmaceutical company, under the Japanese authorization system led by the Ministry of Public Health and the authority in Japanese medical societies.

There are several cases of unethical cooperation where Western MNCs did some of the 'dirty' work for unethical companies in the Far East. Credit Suisse First Boston, for example, helped troublesome Japanese financial institutions with window-dressing settlements. These dirty jobs carried out by a US and a European financial institution were disclosed in the summer of 1999. ING Barlings reversed this pattern. It construed a worse-than-actual-status scenario of Japanese financial institutions. In May 2001, ING Barlings issued its analyst report on Daiwa Bank. Daiwa Bank's capital ratio was deliberately described in the analyst report as lower than the actual status, and there was a suggestion of selling Daiwa Bank stock. When the report was finally issued, the price of Daiwa Bank stock fell dramatically. In August 2001, the Financial Services Agency in Japan issued an administrative disposition on ING Barings. The logic of these Western MNCs is strategic and aims at economic optimization in a corrupt country. At the same time, although they publicly criticized Japanese market problems, they also engaged in their own underground activities. There are also intra-Asian cases of corruption, as seen in the Mitsui Corporation bribery case in Beijing, June 2000.

Even under these circumstances, if we still insist on cultural relativism, MNCs would rely on the following rhetoric, 'one must adapt to the corruption belonging to the cultures of certain regions in order to survive in international competition' (Lay 1995) as well as 'When in Rome, do as the Romans do.' In conclusion, cultural relativism can be conveniently manipulated by the economic optimization logic of MNCs, and unfairness justified in international business operations.

What should we do? It must continue to be assumed that corruption is by no means an integral part of non-Western cultures, and that anything else would be an unacceptable distortion of the (moral) principles of open market competition (Löher and Steinmann 1998). Moreover, the author suggests that some incorporation of universalist business ethics, such as the integrative social contracts theory (ISCT) of Donaldson and Dunfee (1994), is necessary. Even though the universalist ethics position has been criticized as cultural imperialism, it is essential in a society like Japan's, whose own ethical judgements are no longer functional. ISCT, which is based on the hierarchy of ethics and value judgements, advocates that globally operating companies must, to some extent, judge their ethical standards by hypernorms that operate above the normative and legal systems of each individual country. Donaldson and Dunfee also assumed the eligibility and/or consent of corporations to operate globally. Corporations that want to operate globally must engage in contracts with hypernorms, and only then will they receive citizenships of global communities in return. Reading their argument as a purely hypothetical and philosophical normative theory, the authors make sense. However, its advocacy to companies originating in the Far East, and especially Japan, could meet with difficulties.

5 Which comes first, normative theory or a theory of norms?

There is a major difficulty in institutionalizing ISCT when discussing business ethics in the context of companies originating in the Far East. Although Hasnas (1998) pointed out the difficulty of institutionalizing normative business ethic theories on US soil, it would certainly be harder to penetrate the soil of the Far East in this respect. One plausible reason is that normative ethic theories go beyond the comprehension of those who were neither born nor trained in Western societies, both at the sense-fulfilling level and the level of conceptual capacities.

As discussed previously, ISCT belongs to the normative theories in philosophy based on deontology, such as Kant's *Groundwork of the Metaphysic of Morals*. Although the idea of social contracts was mentioned by Hobbes, Locke and Rousseau, its legitimacy and philology can be traced back to the very foundation of ancient Greek civilization. One significant theme of ISCT, the duality of governance by the police of Athens and responsible citizens, had already been conceptualized by Plato in *The Republic*. Although the slavery generated by wars is undeniable, this duality of governance (a fundamental form of democracy) first appeared in ancient history. The idea was recovered in the age of enlightenment and with the creation of civic society which was to be governed by responsible citizens rather than authoritative churches and aristocracies. Even in post-modernism, European intellectuals once again recalled this enlightened idea, as seen in Foucault's (1994) *Technologies of the Self.*

Although Donaldson and Dunfee (1994) do not enter into a discussion on the dualistic nature of ethics, it seems to the author, a Japanese, that they introduced these ideas implicitly in the context of international business ethics. They view corporations as citizens and the police of Athens as global communities. In their logic, corporations that cannot assume their duty as responsible members of communities have no possibility of gaining recognition and membership of global communities. To use language derived from ancient Greek, violating corporations should be *ostracized* by global communities.

The idea sounds sublime to those born and educated in Western societies and whose intellectual roots can be traced back to the era of Plato and Aristotle. They are both formally and informally socialized to become responsible citizens, and are taught that this is the essential virtue apart from their religious beliefs. However, for non-Westerners, in particular for Far East Asians, this idea is indigestible. Although some codes of moral guidance and 'appropriate' behaviour exist, the idea of dual governance by police and responsible citizens has been historically and politically marginalized and extinguished. How then could the ideas of ISCT take root in Asian soil? The assumption of this study is that *the protection and disturbance of existing normative systems conveniently serve the interests of those in power in individual societies.*

For Far East Asians, there is no equivalent idea of business ethics, but there are ideas related to work ethics and morals in the work place (Taka 1994; Ang 2000; Chikudate 2000, 2002). High levels of work ethics and work place morals were first observed among the Japanese by Westerners, and myths about Japanese management were created during the 1970s. Westerners were surprised by the high standard of commitment to jobs and loyalty to organizations, even among non-manual blue-collar workers. In fact, from the Korean War up to the 1980s, these characteristics of the Japanese work force were particularly well-suited to the developmental economy environment of manufacturing. Since Japanese labourers conformed to these value systems, the companies they belonged to grew; and they believed that the growth of their companies was a symbol of contributing to greater societal good (i.e., to the economic development of Japan and the enhancement of its status in global communities). On the other hand, Japanese companies believed that business ethics exhausted themselves in the maintenance of full employment and the award of various fringe benefits. In fact, this view was mentioned by the Minister of Finance in a press conference on 28 August 2001: '[regarding the figure of 5 per cent unemployment], twelve thousand layoffs by Fujitsu, then fifteen thousand by Toshiba, [finally,] twenty thousand by Hitachi…I am slightly concerned about the deterioration of employer ethics. Pursuing profits is necessary, but the social responsibility of corporations should centre on the stability of the lives of Japanese people' (Ministry of Finance, Japan 2001). Thus, the value judgement system for Japanese workers is based purely on commitment to jobs and loyalty to organizations, while the maintenance of full employment and the unspoken consent between employees and employers is the ultimate in business ethics for Japanese companies. Furthermore, the Finance Minister's statement infers that the scope of business ethics (societal good) does not extend to hypernorms but remains enclosed in Japanese society. They have some idea of stakeholder relations but, for them, stakeholders were Japanese bureaucrats and politicians. Being responsible to these stakeholders was interpreted as buying favours from them, which is why bribery has long been established as the legitimate way to do business in Japan.

This pattern is not exclusive to Japan but prevails in South Korea and China as well. Work ethics and work place morals are high in both countries, and there is a shared feeling of belonging to particular social organizations (e.g., Chung 1991). The similarities between the three nations may stem from the fact that they share similar unseen Confucianist value systems which teach people the necessity to reconcile themselves to their environment under the respective ruling powers. While many Korean and some Chinese scholars stressed the positive aspects of Confucianism in management, they ignored the aspect of political genocide, the impossibility of producing autonomous citizens under Confucianist socialization. Confucianism was conveniently adopted as a political strategy and encouraged by those who seized power in the Far East. Singapore and ASEAN countries interpreted this as Asian values and utilized the latter as sources of economic development. For the men in power, Confucianism works perfectly to create a status quo for those who are dominated but still form an efficient work force. In this sense, the idea of business ethics does not exist in the Asian mind.

Due to their limited comprehension of business ethics, Far East Asians cannot perform the duties generated by them. This is obvious in the Japanese business community, for example, which first encountered a similar but not identical idea of business ethics during the 1980s when the expansionism and hegemony of Japanese firms was severely criticized by the rest of the world. These ideas centred on corporate social responsibility and corporate citizenship and were put into practice at the time in the form of philanthropic activities. Japanese companies considered them as purely strategic, handling them with public relations and charity. However, when the economy was hit by recession in the 1990s philanthropy declined and, to make matters worse, the demonic side of Japanese business communities involving bureaucrats and politicians broke open in 1997 and 1998. Major players in Japanese financial institutions, including banks, security brokerages, the Bank of Japan (BOJ), and the Ministry of Finance (MoF), were targets of criticism and lost respect in global communities. They were engaged in all kinds of criminal activities including bribery, window-dressing settlements and racketeer payments. More than 200 executives of security brokerages, bankers from BOJ, bureaucrats from MoF and the police were penalized.

Furthermore, similar to the Chinese, *Quanxi*'s logic facilitated the continuation of unethical behaviour behind the scenes. *Quanxi* refers to social networks and/or social capital (or immediate stakeholders: Ang 2000). Fulfilling their obligations to *Quanxi* means trust, and they cultivate social networks in order to receive favours from others. As a result, bribery is justified as a means of cultivating these networks and the idea of integrity beyond immediate stakeholders does not exist in their value or ethical judgements. The Japanese bankers who were penalized did exactly the same thing. They bought favours from BOJ and MoF through university alumni networks, which included leaking information regarding market operations by BOJ and ignoring huge losses and/or window-dressing settlements during inspection by MoF. With the practice of *amakudari* in Japan, whereby companies hire former bureaucrats from their supervising ministries as highly-paid executives, buying favours was institutionalized. Here, the double-dealing by Western financial institutions in Japan became transparent when they criticized the bureaucratic control of Japanese economic systems, although many of them, especially US firms, themselves practised *amakudari*.

Ironically, these unprincipled features were also found elsewhere. In 2000, the criminal behaviour of Japanese manufacturers such as Snow Brand Milk, Mitsubishi Motors and Bridgestone began to surface when the lives of consumers were damaged by deficient products.

The strange thing, at least for Westerners, is that even under these dismal circumstances in the Japanese business world, the Japanese work force scene remains the same: workers are committed to their current jobs and work hard. They have to do the same things as their predecessors did because they do not want to deviate from the perceived normality of Japanese society (Chikudate 1999b). Furthermore, the companies that conducted unethical operations are still the major players in Japanese economic systems, although they have been socially penalized and humiliated by the media. The worst scenario was when exactly the same companies that had committed crimes in the past became the target of public criticism several years later. In the light of these historical facts, can one still claim that Japanese business people make sense of business ethics and social responsibility? Conventional and allergic reactions to this question by those who glorified Japanese business, business management and the economy were as follows: (1) 'Yes, but what is the measure of corporate performance? [not asking a question but condemning the author who brought the antithesis of glorified Japanese companies]'; (2) 'They are just exceptions, but the majority is good'; and (3) 'Yes, but Japanese MNCs still dominate world markets and we [Westerners] have learned a lot from Japanese factories, such as the just-in-time system, total quality control, knowledge-creations, and so on.' These reactions are not hypothetical but the concrete experience of the author in the past. The first was an intervention during the author's presentation by a business/economics professor at the Jesuit University in Tokyo, which has a high reputation for international education. The second was expressed by various people on many occasions. The final one was given by an expert from a leading US management journal during a private meeting. These three representative reactions can, however, be dismissed. With regard to the first one, the professor's knowledge of corporate performance was limited to Friedman's logic of firms. He had no idea of corporate social performance as developed by Wood (1991), or other stakeholder theories. The second reaction cannot be sustained in empirical reality where similar patterns of corporate crime have been repeated in all sectors of the economy. The final one is simply due to the limitation of sources and research on various Japanese companies. The few qualitative studies examining contemporary Japanese companies from the inside, published in leading international academic journals (e.g., Chikudate 1999a,b, 2000, 2002), could also contribute to this blindness of non-Japanese and even Japanese scholars to different aspects of Japanese management. Both Japanese and non-Japanese scholars have little in-depth access to Japanese work places and might be satisfied with factory visits and interviews on a superficial level.

What should be done next? As the author discussed, the mere initiative of introducing ISCT could end up as a desk theory. He suggests that a reinforcing methodology should be adopted: the introduction of critical theory and/or post-modernism in an attempt to deconstruct unprincipled conventions (Chikudate 1999b). While a main theme of Habermasian discourse ethics (critical theory) is the recovery of a linguistically-agreed intersubjective lifeworld, the transformation of norms established as conventions is a step towards mutual agreement. The theme of creating mutual agreement is repeated in ISCT. Hypernorms in ISCT are not a replica of a certain deontology but the result of a convergence of religious, cultural and philosophical beliefs (Donaldson and Dunfee 1994). Donaldson and Dunfee (1994, 265–6) further argued that, 'interestingly enough, a consensus appears to be growing among scholars that such a convergence exists … their concepts reflect a broad commonality of opinion'.

What, then, should the companies that want to gain recognition and membership in the ethical spaces of global communities do in Habermasian logic? They must free themselves of *the spell-binding power of normative control* (Habermas 1987) within their own societies. Interpreting this in the Japanese context, *these companies must condemn what Japanese business communities have conventionally done, legitimized and glorified in the past.* A Habermasian translation to Japanese business would be similar to culture shock, where practitioners experience feelings of rejection and abandonment as a result of having to deny their competencies, accomplishments, integrity and pride, successfully accumulated in previous experience. However, strongly influenced by the myth of Japanese management, economy and culture, they are deaf to this argument. Furthermore, politicians, bureaucrats, the business community and leading academics in Japan have always dismissed (and even extinguished) the possibility of social transformation in Japan by manipulating the fear and insecurity of the people, who have been brainwashed by this myth. They continue to caution (or threaten) that the transformation of

Japanese society would result in turmoil and a Japanese identity crisis. They also carefully programmed and implemented the project of extinguishing social transformation, as will be discussed below.

6 A diagnostic theory for diagnostic theory

As Glasser (1995) said, Habermasian methodology is diagnostic: 'the spellbinding power of the holy is sublimated into the binding/bonding forces of criticizable validity claims and at the same time turned into an everyday occurrence' (Habermas 1987, 77). This is indeed a most challenging statement for the Japanese. As mentioned earlier, the idea of criticizable validity claims is the technology and intellectuality that stems from the civilization of ancient Greece. Binding/bonding forces can only be created by responsible citizens with mature autonomy. *Unfortunately, for Far East Asians who have been brainwashed with the dogma of Confucianism and taught that the status quo is the desired view of society (the opposite of criticizable validity claims), this technology/intellectuality to evolve society is extremely difficult to comprehend and put into practice.* In Japan, governance by responsible citizens was first politically extinguished by the ruling imperial family when Japan was founded, then by Ieyasu Tokugawa (Shogun, General of the samurais) up to the end of the nineteenth century, followed by the military during the war, and the bureaucrats and Liberal Democratic Party after the war. In contrast to Europeans, who retain some memory of Greek civilization and confidence in returning to the era of ancient Greece and enlightenment (e.g., Gadamer 1991; Heidegger 1991; Foucault 1994), Far East Asians, certainly the Japanese, have no history of having experienced ideal forms of governance by autonomous citizens, and thus no intellectual foundation. Under these circumstances, the memory and intellectuality of Far East Asians does not allow them to visualize an image of society alternative to their current one. Thus, in the face of threats by those in power of an identity crisis should social transformation occur, the very first initiative for social transformation has been blocked by a hesitant majority that believes status quo conditions are preferable to an identity crisis and turmoil.

How did the men in power programme the extinction of a potential for communicative rationality in the Habermasian social transformation project? First of all, dialogue and discursive methods that facilitate conceptualization and logic are traditionally extinguished in the classrooms of the Far East. Under Confucianism, there is no concept of learning for the sake of enlightenment and/or empowerment but only one of mastering and following the teachings of the teachers. Thus, the definition of education in the Far East is permitting students to master and follow what their predecessors have said, in a one-way communication between teachers and students. There is no potential for them to develop intellectual skills of criticizable validity claims.

Second, the legitimacy of intellectuality prevailing in the Far East hinders the potential to engage in communicative rationality (Chikudate 2000b). Due to having inherited the legitimacy and definition of intellectuality from ancient China, where *kanji* or the use of Chinese-derived hieroglyphics was invented as a written system, all knowledge must be expressed in *kanji*, the proliferations of which are endless and can only be mastered by rote. Since all knowledge is written in *kanji*, the more one can read it, the more knowledge is gained or, the more *kanji* one can write, the more knowledge can be demonstrated in public. It is the style of writing, the expressions used or the calligraphy that make a difference, not the ideas expressed, so that under this system, the extent of *kanji* knowledge defines intellectuality and the source of admiration. Thus, the banking of knowledge becomes the priority of learning. In fact, the purpose of all tests in the Far East is to measure memorized knowledge. At the same time, embedded in this type of intellectuality, people have no opportunity of mastering academic skills of abstraction, conceptualization and logic.

Finally, the original meanings and nuances of ideas on citizens, ethics, morals and governance from Europe were extinguished or distorted in the process of translation. Whereas the idea of the citizen originally stemmed from the dualistic nature of governance by both police and responsible citizens, the *kanji* translation refers to the humble people of the city governed by the Emperor. The word citizen is expressed as 市民; 市 refers to city, and 民 [also pronounced *tami*] means humble people whose existence was legitimated as a parallel to its counter-concept of 君 which refers to the Emperor. This implies the invisible but significant state of the politically premature Asian mind, especially the Japanese, which is often ridiculed by Westerners. However, as long as Far East Asians continue to be educated in *kanji*-dominated language systems, they have no possibility of grasping the idea of autonomous responsible citizens governing their own society with intellectuality and ethics.

In sum, institutionalizing Habermasian methodology on Far East soil would not be fruitful, although the spirit would be admired. Habermas himself may not even be aware of the many invisible but essential conditions shaping intellectuality based on language and history that are required for his projects to work. Although Habermas advocated the universality of discourse ethics, the author claims that there is much room for speculation and investigation if the project of the former is to be idealized.

7 Technology of the self and intercultural communication

The author explored the possible answer to this question by re-reading the fundamental goal and spirit of intercultural communication. Intercultural communication also involves the aspect of learning (e.g., Gudykunst and Kim 1984). Although experiencing culture shock involves tremendous pain and sacrifice, it also paves the way for reflexivity towards the self (Chikudate 1999a). By encountering unfamiliar settings, many people develop the skill of learning about their own culture as well as about others. In fact, Chikudate (1999a) has already demonstrated theoretically and empirically the successful case of eroding the spellbinding power of normative control in a Japanese company that opened its door to intercultural business ethics.

What, then, is the difference when compared to Habermas, whose methodology is also based on the utilization of reflexivity? As discussed in a previous section, a purely Habermasian methodology that relies on the possibility of criticizable validity claims through discourse cannot be used. The reason is that Far East Asians are shaped as a people incapable of recognizing the necessity. *In their own cultural and language systems where discursive methods are still primitive and the state of the status quo is desired, the moment of asking questions simply does not arise.* On the other hand, if their *smooth, routinized, and concerted actions are disrupted* (Garfinkel 1963), this moment can occur (Chikudate 1999a). The author suggests that although it cannot occur within their current circles, comparative and critical experience can trigger this moment. Comparative and critical experience refers to culture shock. Borrowing Foucault's (1994) idea of *technology of the self,* which permits individuals to effect by their own means or with the help of others a certain number of operations on their own bodies and souls, thoughts, conduct and way of being, so as to transform themselves in order to attain a certain state of happiness, purity, wisdom, perfection or immorality, the first moment of asking questions, breaking ritualized common sense, is to make contact with other cultures (the help of others). Thus, methodologies for institutionalizing business ethics may no longer be the domain of normative theories but of aesthetics.

This thesis was verified in the case of Japanese business people (Chikudate 1999a). Unlike Europeans, the majority of Japanese business people has little opportunity of encountering other cultures (perhaps after finishing college or on their honeymoon). Most of the Japanese people are monolingual (i.e., they have no foreign language skills whatsoever). Contact with other cultures, where value systems differ from those of Japanese business communities, can facilitate the reflexivity of their own assumptions. Thus the possibility of generating reflexivity still remains in the domains of phenomenology, existentialism and hermeneutics, although Habermas dismissed this as Frankfurt critical theory, whereby Heidegger and his followers were politically marginalized by the mainstream of German intellectuals. The theme of reflexivity is indeed the fundamental goal and spirit of intercultural communication. It has often been neglected by international business, which has taught that intercultural communication is the means of overcoming difficulties generated by cultural differences, through coordination, communication, conflict resolution and negotiation.

8   Summary and conclusion

This study theoretically scrutinized the role of intercultural communication in international business from the perspective of business ethics. The potential of institutionalizing a universalist business ethics position, the integrative social contracts theory, was examined for the situation in the Far East. The limitation of critical theory, the Habermasian discourse of ethics, was then discussed. Finally, the reflexivity and aesthetic project of Foucault was discussed in the light of intercultural communication. The main features of the arguments are set out below:

1 Intercultural communication has been misunderstood by international business, where its contributions were limited to overseas assignments and negotiations.
2 The mere introduction of intercultural communication to business may induce moral hazards by MNCs that manipulate the logic of cultural relativism.
3 In the area of business ethics, a universalist thesis such as ISCT is needed to counter MNCs' exploitation of corrupt business communities.
4 However, non-Westerners are unable to comprehend the idea of ISCT as a result of fundamental differences when compared to civilizations where the concept of ethics first appeared in history.
5 Furthermore, those in power conveniently manipulate existing normative structures (such as Confucianism) to block the intrusion of a universalist thesis of ethics in their own countries.

6 Therefore, the indoctrination of different ideas would not be fruitful without the accompaniment of critical theory and/or post-modernism, whose goals are the deconstruction of old power and the recovery of true consensus.
7 Sadly, Habermasian methodologies (critical theory) could not be actualized due to the lack of training and legitimacy of European intellectuality in the Far East.
8 Thus, alternative methodologies that generate reflexivity are required, and the idea of Foucault's technology of the self was interpreted.
9 Finally, self-learning as the further goal of intercultural communication was interpreted in the light of technology of the self.

The potential of intercultural communication accompanying the Foucaultian aesthetics methodology in the area of intercultural business ethics still produces a paradox and a danger. Transformation should be self-initiated and not the result of seduction by MNCs. Otherwise, notorious MNCs boasting new opportunities will trap the local people of the individual countries. The MNCs would, of course, say that they are in the business of educating. It is easy for them to trap people who are dissatisfied with current economic systems. Ginwala (1998) and the author discussed this scenario. Thus, future research should address topics surrounding reflexivity, learning and educating (not international education) in the light of globalization.

References

Adler, N. J. (1997), *International Dimensions of Organizational Behaviour*, 3rd edn (Cincinnati, OH: South-Western College).

Ang, S. H. (2000), 'Out of the mouths, babes: Business ethics and youths in Asia', *Journal of Business Ethics*, 28 (2), 129–44.

Barnsley, J. (1972), *The Social Reality of Ethics* (London: Routledge & Kegan Paul).

Berger, C. R. and Calabrese, R. (1975), 'Some explorations in initial interactions and beyond: Toward a development theory of interpersonal communication', *Human Communication Research*, 1, 99–112.

Bidney, D. (1968), 'Cultural relativism', in D. Sills (ed.), *International Encyclopedia of the Social Sciences*, 3 (New York: Free Press).

Casmir, F. (ed.) (1997), *Ethics in Intercultural and International Communication* (Mahwah, NJ: Lawrence Erlbaum).

Chikudate, N. (1995), 'Communication network liaison as cultural interpreters for organizational adaptation in Japan–Europe business environments', *Management International Review*, 35, Special issue 2, 27–38.

Chikudate, N. (1999a), 'Generating reflexivity from partnership formation: A phenomenological reasoning on the partnership between a Japanese pharmaceutical corporation and Western laboratories', *Journal of Applied Behavioural Science*, 35, 287–305.

Chikudate, N. (1999b), 'The state of collective myopia in Japanese business communities: A phenomenological study for exploring blocking mechanisms for change', *Journal of Management Studies*, 36 (1), 69–86.
Chikudate, N. (2000), 'A phenomenological approach to inquiring into an ethically bankrupted organization: A case study of a Japanese company', *Journal of Business Ethics*, 28 (1) (November), 59–71.
Chikudate, N. (2002a), 'Collective myopia and disciplinary power behind the scenes of unethical practices: A diagnostic theory on Japanese organization', *Journal of Management Studies*, 39 (May), 289–307.
Chikudate, N. (2002b), 'Collective myopia and defective higher educations behind the scenes of ethically bankrupted economic systems: A reflexive note from a Japanese university and taking a step toward transcultural dialogues', *Journal of Business Ethics*, 38 (3) (July), 205–25.
Chung, T. Z. (1991), 'Culture: A key to management communication between the Asian-Pacific area and Europe', *European Management Journal*, 9 (4), 419–24.
Donaldson, T. and Dunfee, T. W. (1994), 'Toward a unified conception of business ethics: Integrative social contracts theory', *Academy of Management Review*, 19 (2), 252–84.
Enderle, G. (1997), 'A worldwide survey of business ethics in the 1990s', *Journal of Business Ethics*, 16, 1475–83.
Foucault, M. (1994), *Michel Foucault: Ethics Subjectivity and Truth*, P. Rabinow (ed.) (New York: Free Press).
Gadamer, H. G. (1991), *Plato's Dialectical Ethics: Phenomenological Interpretations relating to the Philebus* (New Haven, CT: Yale University Press).
Gao, G. and Ting-Toomey, S. (1998), *Communicating Effectively with the Chinese* (Thousand Oaks, CA: Sage).
Garfinkel, H. (1963), 'A concept of, and experiments with "trust" as a condition of stable concerted actions', in O. J. Harvy (ed.), *Motivation and Social Interaction* (New York: Ronald Press), 187–238.
Ginwala, F. (1998), 'The role of governments in international corruption', in H. Lange, A. Löher and H. Steinmann (eds), *Working across Cultures: Ethical Perspectives for Intercultural Management* (Dordrecht: Kluwer Academic), 7–19.
Glasser, T. L. (1995), 'Communication ethics and the aim of accountability in journalism', *Social Responsibilities: Business, Journalism, Law, Medicine*, 21, 31–51.
Gudykunst, W. B. (1994), *Bridging Differences: Effective Intergroup Communication* 2nd edn (Thousand Oaks, CA: Sage).
Gudykunst, W. B. and Kim, Y. Y. (1984), *Communicating with Strangers: An Approach to Intercultural Communication* (Reading, MA: Addison-Wesley).
Habermas, J. (1984), *The Theory of Communicative Action, Volume 1: Reason and the Rationalization of Society* (Oxford: Polity Press).
Habermas, J. (1987), *The Theory of Communicative Action, Volume 2: The Critique of Functionalist Reason* (Oxford: Polity Press).
Habermas, J. (1990), *The Philosophical Discourse of Modernity* (Cambridge, MA: MIT Press).
Hall, E. T. (1960), *The Silent Language* (Greenwich, CT: Fawcett).
Hasnas, J. (1998), 'The normative theories of business ethics: A guide for the perplexed', *Business Ethics Quarterly*, 8 (1), 19–42.
Heidegger, M. (1991), *Sein und Zeit* (Tübingen: Max Niemeyer).
Herskovits, M. J. (1973), *Cultural Relativism* (New York: Random House).

Hofstede, G. (1980), *Culture's Consequences* (Thousand Oaks, CA: Sage).

Inkson, K., Pringle, J., Arthur, M. B. and Barry, S. (1997), 'Expatriate assignment versus experience: Contrasting models of international human resource development', *Journal of World Business*, 32, 351–68.

Kobrin, S. J. (1988), 'Expatriate reduction and strategic control in American multinational corporations', *Human Resources Management*, 27, 63–75.

Lay, R. (1995), 'Einem Stern folgen', *Das Sonntagsblatt*, 17 February, 18.

Löher, A. and Steinmann, H. (1998), 'The ethical dimension of cross-cultural business activities', in H. Lange, A. Löher and H. Steinmann (eds), *Working across Cultures: Ethical Perspectives for Intercultural Management* (Dordrecht: Kluwer Academic).

Los Angeles Times (2000), 'Business etiquette being recognized as a strategic advantage', 14 February, C2.

Los Angeles Times (2000), 'Pope apologizes for Catholic sins past and present', 13 March, A1 and A5.

Lovitt, C. R. (1999), 'Rethinking the role of culture in international professional communication', in C. R. Lovitt and D. Goswami (eds), *Exploring the Rhetoric of International Professional Communication* (New York: Baywood), 1–16.

Mendenhall, M. and Oddou, G. (1986), 'Acculturation profiles of expatriate managers: Implications for cross-cultural training programs', *Columbia Journal of World Business*, 21, 73–9.

Ministry of Finance, Japan (2001), 'Shiokawa zaimudaijin kakugigo no kishakaiken', *www.mof.go.jp/kaiken/kaiken.htm*, 28 August.

Oberg, K. (1960), 'Culture shock: Adjustments to new cultural environments', *Practical Anthropology*, (July–August), 177–82.

Renteln, A. (1988), Relativism and the search for human rights', *American Anthropologist*, 90, 56–72.

Rogers, E. M. and Kincaid, D. L. (1981), *Communication Networks: Toward a New Paradigm for Research* (New York: Free Press).

Sowell, T. (1981), *Ethnic America: A History* (New York: Basic Press).

Taka, I. (1994), 'Business ethics: A Japanese view', *Business Ethics Quarterly*, 4 (1), 53–78.

Triandis, H. C., Brislin, R. and Hui, C. H. (1988), 'Cross-cultural training across the individualism-collectivism divide', *International Journal of Intercultural Relations*, 12, 269–89.

Varner, I. I. (2000), 'The theoretical foundation for intercultural business communication: A conceptual model', *Journal of Business Communication*, 37 (1), 39–57.

Wood, D. J. (1991), 'Corporate social performance revisited', *Academy of Management Review*, 16 (4), 691–718.

15
Networking Bricks and Clicks: Convenience Stores and the Organization of E-Commerce in Japan

Hendrik Meyer-Ohle

Japanese convenience stores are set to assume a crucial role in the advancement of e-commerce in Japan. Located near consumer homes and work places, they enjoy a high reputation with manufacturers and consumers alike for introducing new technologies and products, and seem to be the ideal vehicle to overcome the many hurdles standing in the way of greater acceptance of this new mode of buying and selling in Japan. This chapter categorizes and analyses business models developed by different convenience store operators. It also identifies the alliances formed between corporate actors in the process. While traditional networks in many other areas of Japanese business seem to be crumbling, new networks and alliances are actively being formed in the area of e-commerce.

1 Introduction

Until very recently, e-commerce was seen as a major threat to the established distribution system. This was especially true for Japan, where e-commerce seemed to provide the opportunity of reaching consumers directly without having to go through the complex channels normally associated with Japanese distribution.

This chapter, however, suggests that the reality is different. While minor players in Japan were the first to recognize the opportunities of the Internet as a marketplace, large established companies assumed strong positions relatively quickly in this area, too. The latter seem to be at an advantage in overcoming some of the hurdles blocking e-commerce acceptance in Japan, such as handling payments or delivering merchandise to consumers. The hitherto successful business model of convenience stores evolving into e-commerce outposts, in particular, offers compelling potential for the future development of e-commerce in Japan.

The chapter concentrates on this last aspect with reference to the theoretical debate on consumer-oriented electronic commerce, which is lagging behind developments in practice. Until recently, reports on this area have often been mere descriptions of retail strategies, with specific front runners such as Amazon, Ebay and etoys drawing most of the attention and, therefore, being utilized as benchmarks for the assessment of other retail strategies. With the long-term success of some of these companies looking increasingly uncertain and traditional bricks-and-mortar retailers stepping up their efforts in the e-commerce area, the variety of business models has widened. This demands more comprehensive categorizations and approaches, and the question of how to organize and integrate existing retail networks with e-commerce strategies is gradually taking centre stage in the discussion on e-commerce (e.g., Jones and Biasiotto 1999; Enders and Jelassi 2000).

By analysing the role convenience stores aim to play in the developing e-commerce scene in Japan, this chapter intends to contribute to the discussion and presents the following argument:

1 The utilization of convenience stores seems to present obvious solutions to many of the problems still facing the development of e-commerce in Japan.
2 Convenience store companies have come up with various strategies for participating in e-commerce development. Building on their current strong points, companies not only seek opportunities in consumer markets but also function as service providers by creating e-commerce platforms for other companies.
3 The transformation of convenience stores to e-commerce outposts, however, is not unproblematic since this development requires substantial changes to the Japanese convenience store business model that has been successful up to now. Some of these changes affect elements that strongly contributed to the successful establishment of convenience stores in Japan in the first place.
4 The integration of convenience stores into e-commerce was pushed forward by strong alliances of leading manufacturers, retailers, financial institutions, network providers and the large general trading companies. With some of the established pillars of Japanese industrial organization now crumbling, these new alliances have

the potential to assume prominent positions in the industrial organization of Japan.

The chapter is structured as follows: the first part outlines the development of e-commerce in Japan and the problems which consumer-oriented e-commerce is facing. The main section introduces and discusses current e-commerce strategies utilizing convenience stores. The chapter concludes with some general observations on the future development of Japanese retailing.

Concerned with ongoing developments in Japanese retailing, the chapter is of an exploratory nature. For factual information it had to rely heavily on articles from newspapers, magazines and trade journals, as well as company press releases. In addition, the content of convenience store web pages was examined. Still, it should be pointed out that e-commerce develops fast, and is often experimental in nature. The chapter is therefore more concerned with identifying larger models of e-business engagement and general trends, and should mainly be understood under this objective.

2   E-commerce models by convenience store companies

Since their introduction in the early 1970s, convenience stores have been among the fastest-growing store formats in Japanese retailing. When the last commerce census was conducted in 1999, the almost 40,000 stores in existence accounted for 4.3 per cent of total retail sales (Ministry of Economy, Trade and Industry, or METI 2000). Their success is not only related to favourable acceptance by consumers, but – in contrast to many other Japanese retailers – also firmly based on sophisticated overall systems for product procurement, logistics, market research and merchandising (e.g., Yahagi 1994, Table 2). The Japanese convenience store industry is dominated by a small number of large chains. The industry has seen major reorganization recently with two of the leading companies, Lawson and FamilyMart, coming under the control of general trading companies, and two medium-sized chains, Sunkus and Circle K, in the process of integrating activities under a holding company (see Table 15.1).

2.1   E-commerce development in Japan

METI, the Electronic Commerce Promotion Council of Japan (ECOM) and the consultancy company Accenture have taken on the joint task of assessing the size of Japanese e-commerce markets on a regular basis.

Table 15.1   Leading convenience store companies

Company (affiliation)	Sales in billion yen	Change over last year	Number of stores	Internet venture
Seven-Eleven Japan (Ito-Yokado)	1,963	6.3%	8,153	www.7dream.com
Lawson (Daiei – Mitsubishi)	1,221	5.5%	7,378	www.at-lawson.com
FamilyMart (Seiyu – Itochu)	783	3.3%	5,546	www.famima.com
Sunkus & Associates	342	10.3%	2,593	http://www.toki-meki.com/
Circle K (managed jointly under C&S Holding from 1 July 2001)(Uny)	447	14.1%	2,588	
Daily Yamazaki (Yamazaki Baking)	361	−5.3%	2,571	www.daily365.net
MiniStop (Jusco)	192	11.2%	1,375	https://www.e-ministop.com/
am/pm Japan (Japan Energy)	167	n.a.	1,182	http://www.ampm.co.jp

n.a. = not available.

Sources: Nikkei Ryûtsû Shinbun (2000), 192, 350; (NRS) Ryûtsû Keizai no Tebiki.

They estimate that the business-to-consumer e-commerce market accounted for 824 billion yen in the year 2000, roughly 0.3 per cent of overall consumer spending. The market is expected to expand to 13 trillion yen by the year 2005, which represents 4.1 per cent of overall consumer spending. E-commerce spending can be differentiated into static e-commerce done from home and mobile e-commerce conducted from devices such as mobile phones, car navigation systems, or palm pads. The share of mobile e-commerce is expected to increase from its current level of 7.2 per cent of overall e-commerce to 18.4 per cent in 2005 (Accenture/ECOM/METI 2001, 13). In the survey, the product group with the greatest significance for e-commerce to date was computers and related products with a share of 6.07 per cent of overall sales, followed by automobiles with 2.12 per cent and books and music with 0.75 per cent of their relative markets. The last two product groups are expected to advance most by the year 2005, reaching a share of 19.8 per cent for cars and 17.7 per cent for books and music, which is considerably higher than the 4.1 per cent share estimated for the overall market (Accenture/ECOM/METI 2001, 14–15). While the number of e-commerce sites has been growing rapidly, consumer acceptance in

Japan has for a long time been described as poor. The following points have been raised in this respect (e.g., Webb 1999; Pitchford 2000):

- comparatively high charges for net access and telephone usage
- lack of competition due to excessive regulations by the Japanese government
- comparatively late introduction of information technology to work places
- problems with the Japanese language in designing web pages
- insufficient usage of credit cards in Japan, high transaction charges by banks and a general preference for cash transactions
- long working and commuting hours that leave little time for leisure activities and narrow time slots for home delivery
- importance of shopping as a leisure activity
- closeness of existing stores to consumers
- importance of personal contact in the sales process

Asked about their attitude towards online shopping, consumers voiced concerns about privacy, product quality, and problems in delivery and order processes (Table 15.2). Payment for products ordered online has especially proved to be a major obstacle to the expansion of e-commerce in Japan. Many consumers do not own credit cards and processing credit card payments is often complicated, expensive and time consuming for the retailer.

Table 15.2 Concerns of Japanese consumers about e-commerce

Concerns voiced	Percentage (multiple answers)
Possibility of private data being offered to third parties	73.4
Product delivered differs from product advertised (taste, colour, quality)	72.7
Product is not delivered	52.8
Insufficient trust in Internet store	47.8
Difficulties in correcting mistakes after ordering	44.0
Non-ordered merchandise delivered and charged	43.8
Different product delivered	37.4
Possibility of higher prices	28.0
Time gap until receipt of product too long	27.4
Difficulty in finding product on the Net	18.8

Source: Internet User Survey (conducted 11 December 1999), results in Yûseishô (2000).

Two recent developments, however, have led to a more optimistic outlook in e-commerce. The first breakthrough was the rapid acceptance of mobile access to the Internet by Japanese consumers. In February 1999, NTT Docomo began to offer mobile phones with a permanent connection to online services and the development since then has been truly stunning. As of July 2001, 25 million people were subscribing to this service, with figures showing a continuous monthly growth of more than one million customers (www.nttdocomo.com/i/inumber.html; Noguchi 2000). The second step up the ladder was the advancement of convenience store chains to e-commerce, the topic of this study.

2.2   Attractiveness of convenience stores for e-commerce

The utilization of convenience store networks and their supporting infrastructure of logistics and information technology as outposts and backbones of e-commerce seemed to present compelling solutions to most of the above-mentioned problems that were hindering the development of e-commerce:

1   Convenience store operators control nationwide store networks directly in consumer neighbourhoods and work places.
2   Convenience stores already offer customers the possibility of making payments for a wide range of utility charges. Consumers who are reluctant to use credit cards or who are unwilling to pay comparatively high bank fees for money transfers could make payments at convenience store counters for merchandise ordered online.
3   Convenience stores could act as distribution points near homes and offices for the pick-up of merchandise by customers or delivery to them. In collaboration with major transport companies they already accept parcels for delivery.
4   Convenience store chains have successfully created an image of convenience, speed, reliability and efficiency. This image could inspire confidence in consumers to try out the services of relatively new e-commerce ventures.
5   Convenience stores have a young but relatively affluent customer base, consisting of a large proportion of singles, as well as students and schoolchildren. These groups are responsive to new ways of shopping and also have access to new technologies. Convenience stores have established themselves as a testing ground for new products.
6   Convenience stores have established an advanced business-to-business infrastructure over the years, combining logistics and information technology.

The potentially strong role of convenience stores in shaping the structure of Japanese e-commerce has not only been realized by the convenience store chains themselves but also by investors and potential partners. Convenience store stocks soared with the general enthusiasm for e-commerce and, consequently, plummeted with the on-going disillusionment. The huge potential of e-commerce was also an important reason for general trading companies to acquire controlling stakes in retail businesses. In addition, convenience store companies became popular partners for various manufacturers and companies from the service sector.

2.3   Online operations by convenience stores: examples

As pointed out above, all major convenience store companies currently operate web pages. Company web ventures have advanced to different degrees, with some companies setting the pace. The three largest chains, Seven Eleven, Lawson and FamilyMart, currently run the most sophisticated sites. Their features will be introduced in more detail.[1] Being advanced means here that a site not only offers products but also content, including membership schemes and newsletters: some of the smaller chains have different approaches: some have sites that merely support their store network, while others also offer limited options for online shopping.

2.3.1   7dream.com (Seven Eleven)

Seven Eleven Japan has set up a number of subsidiaries and affiliates in collaboration with other major companies to organize and run e-commerce activities. The main company is 7dream.com, a joint venture with NEC, NRI, Sony, Mitsui, JTB and Kinotrope as minority shareholders. The aim of this company is to establish an e-commerce infrastructure centring on convenience stores, the provision of key services and products, and the development of payment services for other companies. Seven Eleven is also involved in ventures with Softbank, Japan's leading Internet-related company, as well as operating an online bookstore and an online distributor of automobile-related products and services. It is also one of the many partners on Sony's digital game-playing platform, playstation.com. In addition to e-commerce, Seven Eleven explores other ways of utilizing the proximity of convenience stores to consumers. In collaboration with Japan's leading provider of products and services for the elderly, Nichii Gakkan, and with additional support from Mitsui and NEC, it has set up Seven Meal Service. The venture will deliver meals to customers' homes on a regular basis or have them ready for collection at stores. Seven Eleven not only offers access to its online consumer services at home; it has also equipped its stores with multi-media terminals. These terminals provide online access to services, printing of stickers and pictures, or the ability to download digital content on to minidiscs and other storage devices. The company has also launched a membership club which distributes a weekly newsletter that includes special offers for members and introduces new features on the site. In probably its most innovative initiative, the company utilizes its site to interact with users in order to develop new products. Users are asked to suggest new products for development. If the site's operators deem suggestions viable, they create an online forum to discuss realization. Seven Eleven has already succeeded in developing two new products based on suggestions by site users.

It is clearly not the main objective of the 7dream.com website to increase the sales of the Seven Eleven store network. It is an independent site offering services and products. Some of these services and products are provided by companies in which Seven Eleven is itself involved, such as the car and book ventures. Other services are offered by partners in the 7dream.com venture and others yet again by unrelated companies. The involvement of Seven Eleven is mainly symbolized by titles such as 7dream Rent-A-Car or Seven Dream Insurance Shop. Still, the main producers of services and products are clearly named. Seven Eleven contributes the option to pay for products and services in its networked stores. The affiliation to the Seven Eleven mother company, Ito Yokado, can only be seen in a mail order business for larger items and a site for promoting computer games. Most of the offers available on the website are not exclusive to Seven Eleven and can be accessed from other sites, too. This is even true for some of the services offered by companies in which Seven Eleven owns an equity stake. Concerning products handled, so far most of the products and services offered by 7dream.com fall in the category of easy-to-handle and easy-to-explain products. Some of the services on offer give the customer the opportunity to order promotional materials.

2.3.2   at-lawson.com (Lawson)

Mitsubishi and Lawson have set up a number of joint companies with the aim of transforming Lawson stores into bases for e-commerce. Areas of cooperation are the creation of e-commerce portals accessible by mobile phones, the organization of payment and delivery services through the store network, and the installation of automated teller machines and networked order terminals in convenience stores. The companies collaborate with NTT Docomo and Matsushita Electric. They offer tour packages, tickets, books and gifts on their website (http://www.at-lawson.com). Customers can pick up the merchandise and pay for it at a Lawson outlet of their choice. The companies hope the new venture will generate about 10 per cent of Lawson's current sales volume. Lawson does not aim to develop a general shopping mall. The web page is, in fact, very focused and clearly shows targeted customers to be single women and men in their twenties and early thirties, the main customer segment of its existing stores. On a relatively simple web page, which is also designed to be accessed from mobile phones, the company presents a complementary assortment of goods. Several payment and delivery options are on offer, ranging from payment and next day delivery at the store to credit card payment and home delivery. In a separate venture, e-context Lawson is participating in the development of a prepaid card to be accepted for online payments. The aim of the company, however, goes beyond this purpose, extending to providing online sellers with a comprehensive infrastructure. Business clients will be able to choose from a number of service packages which start with the mere handling of payment transactions and gradually extend to product delivery, home page design, electronic data exchange with the provider, automated system updates and, finally, systems for the handling of all aspects of credit card payment. The company will collect extensive information on customers by asking them to enter age group and gender before entering their prepaid card information. Lawson was also the first company to introduce multimedia terminals into its stores on a large scale. It is continuously expanding its base of partners for the usage of these machines. For example, it uses the terminal to supply information on the enrolment in satellite/cable television or Internet services, the calculation of moving services, the registration for newspaper delivery, the provision of information on educational institutions, for health advice or introduction of hospitals, sale of tickets for travel, events and adventure parks, or the prior reservation of newly-launched products.

2.3.3 *Famima.com (FamilyMart)*

FamilyMart operates its e-commerce platform famima.com in collaboration with Itochu, NTT Data, Toyota, Dai Nippon Printing, JTB and PIA Corporation. The aim of the company is to develop a platform to operate e-commerce and the introduction of multimedia terminals in stores. The most interesting aspect of the collaboration is its approach to linking the new platform closely to individual stores of the FamilyMart

Network. In what is described as a unique e-franchise system, the franchisees of FamilyMart are provided with a virtual presence on the Famima.com platform in addition to their physical store presence. When signing up for first orders or the membership club, customers are asked to designate a certain store in their neighbourhood for delivery of goods. After signing on to the website, a link to the website of the designated store appears where store owners have the possibility of providing customers with individual information. Similar to many of the services on convenience store web pages, this feature seems to be still at the trial stage. Only a small number of stores have participated so far and information on the individual pages of participants is limited to a few words of greeting by the store manager and a recommendation for certain products. The list of product categories is similar to other companies, but the comprehensiveness and focus of the assortment at famima.com is still in the early stages. In July 2001, many of the product categories existed only as headers on the top menu; once clicked, only a very small number of products appeared, or else none at all. While FamilyMart also relies on partnering companies to provide services, the names of these companies are presented less prominently on the FamilyMart website than on the site by Seven Eleven. An interesting feature derived from collaboration with its owner company, Itochu, is the offer of free Internet access for its members through the Excite portal, which is operated in Japan by the general trading company.

3   Discussion

Various aspects of convenience store involvement in e-commerce seem worth discussing. The first aspect to be taken up in the following is an assessment of the motives and strategies that convenience store companies pursue. Additional aspects will be the organization of e-commerce within a franchise environment and the formation of e-commerce-related alliances.

3.1   Categorization of e-commerce strategies

Looking at the strategies pursued by convenience stores, three different strategies can be identified: (1) e-commerce and exposure on the web to support the existing store network; (2) e-commerce as an extension of the current programme; (3) e-commerce as an opportunity to provide services to other businesses in the form of e-commerce infrastructure. While most companies pursue somewhat hybrid strategies, some are still leaning more in one direction, others more in another. It therefore seems appropriate to discuss these strategies separately. Still, the question of whether strategies appear to be compatible or not should be brought up.

The first strategy regards the presence of convenience stores on the web as a mere support for the existing store network. The website is used to increase store traffic, raise store loyalty, create new sources of revenue for franchisees or attract new customer groups. Following this strategy, website operators link their e-commerce strategies closely to existing stores, introduce new products handled in the stores and indicate the possibility of home delivery from their stores for the existing product range, as well as store pick-up and payments for items that are not handled in the stores themselves. The e-franchise concept of FamilyMart, aimed at individualizing customer information with regard to the stores in their neighbourhood, clearly pursues these objectives. The meal delivery system of Seven Eleven also points in this direction, attracting elderly people to the convenience stores to order and pay for meals. It thereby contributes to overcoming the heavy reliance of convenience stores on young customers (*Chain Store Age*, 15 January 2000). Another example is the introduction of multimedia terminals that allow access to online services in stores. Following this strategy, companies build on the proximity of stores to the homes and work places of consumers, as well as on their reliability and convenience image. Eventually, convenience stores could become customized entrance and exit points between local communities and the virtual world.

The second strategy is extending the existing business of convenience store operators to create new sources of revenue, not for store owners but for the core company. The company operates the franchised network on the one hand, and the e-commerce venture on the other hand. It offers a wide range of services and products on its e-commerce platform that are not available in the stores. For these ventures companies build on their experience in marketing and market research, their strong brand name, and their existing customer databases. The ventures founded by Seven Eleven with other companies involving the sale of books or automobile-related services are examples of this approach. The services and products of these ventures can be accessed from Seven Eleven's main website but they also have a separate web presence. Aspects shared by both sides, such as payment and delivery options through the store network, might be upheld in the future, but with home delivery systems already quite advanced in Japan and safe online payment options enjoying rapid development, the e-business side could eventually be operated independently of convenience stores.

The third option does not look at the sale of products and services but mainly at the creation of an open infrastructure for the sale of products online. It enables companies interested in building up an online business to source their entire e-commerce infrastructure from convenience store operators. Sellers can source complete e-commerce solutions including web design, presence in a hyper-mall, storage, logistics, payment, and delivery services or parts thereof from the provider, and could have a sophisticated e-commerce infrastructure at a comparatively low initial cost. Companies providing this infrastructure not only increase revenues by fees charged to sellers but also by creating scale economies for their own services and the infrastructure serving their store networks. In offering these infrastructure services, companies build on their existing logistics, store and information networks and their image of reliability and innovativeness. They also profit from their relatively unbiased position in Japan's current distribution structure, since convenience stores, due to their size, only handle a comparatively small assortment of basic products and services.

As mentioned earlier, many companies currently follow a mixed approach. The importance of the physical store network of convenience stores for the development of e-commerce activities will mainly depend on how payment and delivery systems develop in the future. Here, two aspects should be pointed out: first, while convenience stores might lose their importance as payment and delivery outposts in the long run (Kishida 2000, 32), using them at the present time, with sophisticated payment and delivery systems not yet in place, might give convenience store companies and their partners a substantial front runner advantage in creating firm footholds in the e-commerce market. Second, sophisticated payment and (especially) home delivery systems have yet to prove their cost advantages over the store delivery and collection method. Home delivery of small quantities can be extremely costly, and while many companies in the e-commerce sector are currently shouldering costs and accepting losses on home deliveries to build up their customer base, this policy seems unlikely to be sustainable in the long run. Including the customer in the value chain by letting him pick up merchandise at stores or other distribution centres and sharing the existing infrastructure of convenience stores might therefore prove to be a viable and sustainable alternative under cost considerations. This could particularly be the case if companies manage to come up with more sophisticated and consistent models for the first approach, transforming convenience stores into customized community outposts for e-business-related services.

The third option of creating an e-commerce infrastructure seems highly interesting. Becoming an infrastructure provider for e-commerce resembles in many ways the current franchise systems for bricks-and-mortar stores, and therefore fits in well with some of the competencies already present in convenience store companies.

3.2   Transforming the business model of the convenience store

The ability of franchise companies to maintain strong relationships with franchise holders will, as mentioned above, be a major factor in determining the success of e-commerce ventures. If this does not happen, the future development of their current core business will be at risk. While the decision to base convenience stores on the franchise concept was a major factor underlying the success of this store format in Japan, it also forced convenience store company operators to compete for both customers and new franchisees. Ventures in e-business and other services have only recently been introduced so results are not yet available. However, the general characteristics of convenience stores as such, and their organization as franchise systems in particular, put additional pressure on e-business activities to be extremely cost sensitive and become profitable in a comparatively short period of time:

1 The current convenience store concept leaves no space for storing products ordered by customers or introducing multimedia and banking terminals. Franchisees might be reluctant to make space for these services (*Gekiryû Magazine*, 2000).
2 Customers might be confused with the distribution of responsibilities in the order, payment and delivery process. At the moment, stores function solely as delivery and payment points. Customers are repeatedly reminded on the web pages and in the order process to communicate with central call-centres and not with store operators. Still, customers might return merchandise to stores or demand refunds and meet store owners who are extremely reluctant to deny responsibility in a fiercely competitive situation with other convenience stores in their vicinity.
3 Heavy investments, increased complexity, and additional tasks to be performed by headquarters and store owners have to be accounted for. An increasing complexity of tasks might also limit the possibility of running stores almost exclusively with part-timers and fringe employees. Convenience store companies have developed their human resource management based on part-timers to a sophisticated level, and it has been described as one of the major competitive advantages

of this store format (Ribault 1999). Additional time needed to advise individual customers could result in a slowing down of services to other customers. Convenience store owners might therefore have to increase personnel and invest more resources in their training. These disadvantages could overshadow the argument of an increased customer flow.

4   Sharing of profits and costs between franchisees and network operators will become an issue (Katô 2000; *Nikkei Business*, 28 February 2000). As already pointed out, store operators will have to perform tasks for which they will not be reimbursed. At the same time, some stores may profit more from online activities than others. So far, network operators have gone to great lengths to avoid inequality between franchisees.

The introduction of e-commerce is therefore more than a mere addition to the service and product range of convenience stores. It could lead to a profound redesign of the convenience store business model with changes ranging from store layout to franchisor–franchisee relationships and employee qualification. In handling these changes convenience store operators will have to be very responsive to the sentiments of their franchisees, especially since the economic situation of many stores is currently not as satisfactory as it used to be. In many locations, markets are oversaturated. In addition, competition from other store formats has grown. Following a liberalization of regulations, the number of large stores has not only increased dramatically, but many of them have extended business hours and reduced closure days. On the basis of existing stores, sales in most companies are either stagnant or on the decrease (*Chain Store Age*, 15 January 2000). Franchise operators will therefore have to make sure that their e-business ventures quickly lead to new sources of revenue and increased customer flow for store operators.

3.3 E-commerce alliances

Apart from the different models and aims pursued in e-commerce, the organizational arrangements that are created in this area are a major point of interest. Table 15.3 shows that convenience store companies have managed to bring prominent partners together for the organization of their activities. This is especially true for Seven Eleven, which in the organization of e-commerce sticks to its policy of collaboration with and integration of partners in business ventures with equity stakes (*Chain Store Age*, 15 March 2000). All the companies assembled in Seven Eleven's joint venture are leading companies in their respective areas. They bring together knowledge of hardware development, systems

Table 15.3 Organization of e-commerce

Ventures (projects)	Partners (percentage in ventures)	Business area
Seven Eleven		
Seven Dream Dot Com	Seven Eleven (51), NEC (13), NRI (13), Sony (6.5), Sony Marketing (6.5), Mitusi (6), JTB (2), Kinotrope (2)	E-commerce infrastructure centring around CVS, provision of key services and products, provision of payment services for other companies
E-Shopping Books	Softbank E-Commerce (50), Seven Eleven (30), Tohan (10), Yahoo Japan (10)	Online bookstore
CarPoint	Softbank Commerce (45), Microsoft (37), Seven Eleven (10), Yahoo Japan (8)	Provision of automobile-related products and services
PlayStation.com (Japan)	Sony Computer Entertainment other investors: Bandai, Enix, Culture Convenience Club, NTTDocomo, Capcom, Koei, Konami, Square, DigiCube, Namco, Happinet, Seven Eleven	E-commerce related to Game Station
Seven Meal Service	Seven Eleven (60), Nichii Gakkan (30), Mitsui (5), NEC (5)	Home and store delivery of pre-cooked meals
Lawson		
Lawson E-Planning	Mitsubishi Corp (49), Lawson (51)	Incubator for e-business, collaboration with partners from other industries and collaboration with venture companies
E-Context (www.econ.ne.jp)	Lawson (46), Digital Garage (34), Toyo Information Systems (10), Mitsubishi Corp. (10)	Open platform for provision of payment and delivery services (provider for other CVS-chains, total 20,000 outlets)

Table 15.3   continued

Ventures (projects)	Partners (percentage in ventures)	Business area
I-Convenience, Inc.	Lawson (51), Matsushita (18), NTT Docomo (13), Mitsubishi Corp. (18)	E-kiosk: provision of services for mobile Internet users
FamilyMart		
www.famima.com	FamilyMart (50.5), Itochu (14.5), NTT Data (10), Toyota (10), Dai Nippon Printing (5), JTB (5), Pia Corporation (5)	Operation of e-commerce franchise system, introduction of multimedia terminal in stores
E-Plat	FamilyMart (35), Circle K (25), Sankus (10), 3F (10), MiniStop (10), Toyota (5), NTT Communications (5)	Platform for e-commerce and contents provision

Source: Own compilation based on web pages of companies, press releases, etc.

design, consumer goods and service marketing, project management, and web page design. The cooperation with Softbank in the distribution of books and automobile-related services links Seven Eleven to one of the most active companies in Japan's Internet economy. The company not only operates the Yahoo search engine but also finances many of Japan's Internet-related business ventures.

Lawson and FamilyMart seem to take a different approach. While they have also attracted prominent partners such as Matsushita, Dai Nippon Printing, NTT Docomo or Toyota, they rely to a larger extent on their affiliation with general trading companies. Trading companies have been investing actively in IT and multimedia infrastructure with the aim of developing this area as a major pillar alongside their traditional trading activities. Trading companies could therefore contribute to the broad skills of e-commerce ventures in the areas of infrastructure, financing, information technology and content creation. They are heavily involved in digital data transmission, television channels, satellite operation, international telecommunications, cable television, television shopping and the provision of web-related services. Itochu, for example, operates the 'excite' search engine in Japan and, through its satellite communication business, is involved in Japan's leading multichannel digital television provider, SKY-Perfect TV. It is also engaged in the production and provision of content with companies such as Japan Entertainment Network, Star Channel and Space Shower Network. Other companies provide hardware and software as well as Internet services. The engagement of general trading companies in this area is, however, not without its problems. Operators will have to balance carefully the interest of general trading companies in utilizing and developing their capabilities with the need to source the best skills in order to compete with the network set up by Seven Eleven. If general trading companies manage to exert appropriate control over retailers, however, it should bring them a step closer to their goal of playing a larger role in consumer goods distribution. By building on their affiliated retailer's knowledge of consumer markets and by utilizing the unique position of convenience stores in the distribution structure for the purpose of e-commerce, these companies might also be able to assume a more meaningful role with their traditional clients and in the horizontal *keiretsu* again. As Achrol and Kotler (1999, 156) pointed out 'the *sogo shosha* [general trading company] should have transformed into marketing companies for the network; they, rather than the financial companies, should have emerged as the coordinating hub of the network'.

The Internet has often been hailed as a means for new companies to challenge established companies. In Japan, however, the efforts of convenience stores appear to reinforce the position of incumbent companies. With the exclusion of car parts and books, a field where Seven Eleven collaborates with Softbank and challenges existing retailers, the situation in areas such as travel, services for the elderly, digital content provision or insurance is quite different. Established companies collaborate with convenience stores to establish themselves firmly on the Internet. This is not only true for products, but also for the design of systems and the provision of hardware. As previously, involvement in the process is secured by equity investments. While the internationalization of the Japanese economy and its industries has been much discussed over the last decade, it is interesting to see that foreign companies do not seem to be involved or do not opt to secure their interest with equity stakes.

4   Conclusion

Convenience store companies have ventured into e-business in a confident manner. They are determined not only to build on the short-term advantages that come with control over their store networks but clearly aim to establish themselves as long-term players in e-commerce in a sustainable manner. To do so, they go beyond exploiting the opportunity to offer additional products and services to the final consumer by making their infrastructure available to other businesses with the prospect of creating sophisticated e-commerce solutions and platforms.

To be successful, companies will have to stretch their networking capabilities to the fullest in order quickly to create value for prominent alliance partners from other industries as well as for the owners of their franchised stores. Future research should therefore continue to watch the involvement of Japanese convenience stores in e-commerce. This will further contribute to the knowledge of how existing bricks-and-mortar retail operations can be joined to the new possibilities of e-commerce in general, and within the setting of franchise systems in particular. In addition, with traditional relationships in Japanese industries finally losing ground, new alliances created in the process are set to become a key element of Japanese industrial organization in the future.

Note

1   The following overview of strategies is based on information provided by the homepages of the three companies, by observing web pages as such, and by the newsletters distributed to their members. Additional information was taken from *Shûkan Daiyamondo*, 4 March 2000; *Chain Store Age*, 15 January 2000 and Katô (2000).

References

Accenture/ECOM/METI (2001), *Heisei 12 nendo denshi tori hiki ni kan suru shijô kibo/jittai chôsa (Research on the situation and market size of e-commerce in the year 2000)* (Tokyo: Accenture/ECOM/METI).

Achrol, R. S. and Kotler, P. (1999), 'Marketing in the new economy', *Journal of Marketing*, 63, special issue, 146–63.

Aoki, K. (2000), 'Cultural differences in e-commerce: a comparison between the U.S. and Japan', *First Monday – Peer-Reviewed Journal on the Internet*, 5 (11), http://firstmonday.org/issues/issue5_11/aoki/index.html.

Chain Store Age (2000), 'E no nami ni noru (Riding the e-commerce wave)', 15 January, 24–37.

Chain Store Age (2000), 'Konbiniensu sutoa no EC senryaku (E-commerce strategies of convenience stores)', 15 March, 82–8.

Enders, A. and Jelassi, T. (2000), 'The converging business models of Internet and bricks-and-mortar retailers', *European Management Journal*, 18 (5) (October), 542–50.

Gekiryû Magazine (2000), 'Shôsha "kawashimo senryaku" no abunai sokumen (The dangerous side of the downstream strategy of general trading companies)', June, 36–9.

Gekiryû Magazine (2000), 'E-bijinesu Lawson (E-business Lawson)', October, 48–51.

Jones, K. and Biasiotto, M. (1999), 'Internet retailing: current hype or future reality?', *The International Review of Retail, Distribution and Consumer Research*, 9 (January), 69–79.

Katô, N. (2000), 'Chên e tantôsha, netto kanren benchâ ni kikimakuru: "Shikakeru benchâ, noru shôsha, odoru kouri" no Nihon gata e-sukîmu (Listening intensely to the e-business managers of chain stores and net-related ventures: "starting up ventures, riding general trading companies, dancing retailers")', *Konbini* (June), 16–29.

Kishida, M. (2000), 'Atarashii katchi sôzô koso konbini EC no seikô jôken (Success factors of convenience store e-commerce for the creation of a new value structure)', *Konbini* (June), 30–3.

METI (Ministry of Economy, Trade and Industry) (2000), *Heisei 11 gyôtai betsu tôkeihyô no gaiyô (Outline of the survey on retail formats 1999)* (Tokyo: METI) (available at http://www.meti.go.jp/statistics/).

Nakahara, T. (2000), 'Overview of present and future e-commerce', *Journal of Japanese Trade and Industry*, 19 (6) (available at http://www.jef.or.jp/en/jti/200011.html).

Nikkei Business (2000), 'Konbini no mirai (The future of the convenience store)', 28 February, 26–34.

Nikkei Ryûtysû Shinbun (2000), *Ryûtsû keizai no tebiki 2001 (Handbook on the distribution industry 2001)* (Tokyo: Nihon Keizai Shinbun-sha).

Noguchi, S. (2000), 'Impact of mobile communications on e-commerce', *Journal of Japanese Trade and Industry*, 19 (6) (available at http://www.jef.or.jp/en/jti/200011.html).

Pitchford, J. (2000), 'E-Commerce in Japan', *Journal of Japanese Trade and Industry*, 19 (6) (available at http://www.jef.or.jp/en/jti/200011.html).

Ribault, T. (1999), 'Flexible Employment in Japanese Retailing: Toward a Just-in-time Employment Management', in D. Dirks, J.-F. Huchet and T. Ribault (eds), *Japanese Management in the Low Growth Era* (Berlin, Heidelberg, New York: Springer), 295–312.

Shûkan Daiyamondo (2000), 'Konbini e kakumei (Convenience store E-revolution)', 4 March, 26–38.

Webb, A. (1999), 'E-commerce – Japan at the Ready', *J@pan.Inc*, November http://www.japaninc.net/mag/comp/1999/11/nov99_ecom.html.

Yahagi, T. *Konbiniensu sutoa shistutemu no kakushinsei* (*Revolutionary qualities of convenience store systems*) (Tokyo: Nihon Keizai Shinbun-sha).

Yûseishô (Ministry of Post and Telecommunications) (2000), *Tsûshin hakusho* (*White Paper on telecommunications*) (Tokyo: Ôkurashô Insatsukyoku) (http://www.yusei.go.jp/ policyreports/japanese/papers/h12/index.html).

16
Online Marketing: Displaced Dichotomies

Fred Robins

This chapter reflects on examples of apparently successful online marketing. Not surprisingly, the author finds much that is totally familiar but also finds that some novel elements are emerging. The latter include several important and necessary shifts in emphasis away from conventional marketing categories and these shifts are the focus of this study. They include moves away from concern with differences between products and services, mass marketing versus personal service, and between mass communication and human communication. In their place the author identifies new dichotomies. A new one-to-one marketing mix has also emerged with the focus on individuals rather than market segments. The chapter concludes with some generalized statements about the conceptual categories which are useful in organizing our thinking about marketing online.

1　Introduction

Among the most common elements of contemporary marketing thinking are a number of telling contrasts. These are spelt out in every marketing textbook and are deeply embedded in the mind of every marketing professional.

The best known is that between product and service: whereas a product is physical and tangible, a service is not. Another is the contrast between 'mass marketing' and 'personal service'; the former is associated with standardized products in price-sensitive markets, whereas the latter usually relates to non-standard items with emphasis placed on differentiation. A third contrast is between long distribution channels and short ones; long channels tend to be associated with physical products and with loss of control, whereas short channels are commonly associated

1	PRODUCT (tangible) E.g. table or chair	vs	SERVICE (intangible) E.g. medical consultation
2	MASS MARKETING (usually standardized items) E.g. tin of baked beans	vs	PERSONAL SERVICE (usually non-standard items) E.g. restaurant service
3	LONG CHANNEL (usually products) E.g. distribution to overseas retailers	vs	SHORT CHANNEL (usually services) E.g. advance sale of theatre tickets
4	MASS COMMUNICATION (utilizing mass media) E.g. a television advertisement	vs	PERSONAL SELLING (direct human interaction) E.g. house visit to sell insurance

Figure 16.1   Four dichotomies of classical marketing thinking

with intangible services and greater control. Finally, there is the contrast between 'mass communication' and 'personal selling'; the former embraces advertising and use of mass media whereas the latter is a one-to-one or small group activity involving direct, human interaction between buyer and seller. Conventional examples can readily be given for each of these categories. Those included in Figure 16.1 are selected for simplicity and clarity alone.

2   Classic marketing

The four sets of contrasting categories shown in Figure 16.1 largely align with the reduced form of 'the marketing mix', the well-known 4Ps. Thus 'product' and 'service' correspond to the most fundamentally different categories of market offering, or *product*. The key difference of tangibility between the two categories carries a raft of implications for everyday marketing activity and for each element of the marketing mix. Similarly, the categories 'mass marketing' and 'personal service' align with opposite ends of the spectrum with regard to the marketplace importance of *price*: that is, the more standardized and commodity-like the product or service, the greater the likelihood that it will compete primarily on price and that it will consequently require a mass market and mass marketing to be profitable. At the opposite end of this continuum, where the level of differentiation is great, there is correspondingly more room to get away from price comparison and to woo customers with service. The next marketing mix variable, *place*, is better understood as distribution. In distribution, channel length is roughly aligned with the degree of control which a producer can maintain over a product as it moves from its place of production towards its place of final consumption or use. Business concern with control largely accounts for the strategic importance of channel length in classical marketing. Selection of a short, simple channel offers very considerable channel influence to the producer or marketer, if not indirect control; a long and complex channel does not. The final mix variable is marketplace communication, or *promotion*. This may be either personal or impersonal and the two categories, again, are fundamentally different. Impersonal communication reaches its target audience via the intermediary of the mass media, upon which it is dependent. Accordingly, recipients cannot be individually identified or personally addressed. This is quite different in character and in its uses from direct, person-to-person, 'eyeball' communication.

3 Electronic marketing

These classic contrasts, valuable though they have proved to be, are markedly less illuminating and useful in the electronic marketplace. In this new commercial space different categories and different dichotomies offer greater practical value to those with online marketing responsibility. Different choices are more closely aligned with the commercially relevant capabilities of the Internet and the world wide web. Among the more important business benefits available online are cheap interactive, one-to-one communication, high speed, global reach and digital downloadability.

The best known examples of online marketing success are probably Amazon.com and Dell Computers. Each of these companies is the subject of books (Dell and Fredman 1999; Specter 2000). Cursory scrutiny of their businesses reveals that for both of these companies the electronic marketplace offers advantages to both buyer and seller which cannot be obtained in any other way. In the case of Amazon, the buyer obtains maximum product choice combined with maximum convenience of purchase, while the company gains the advantage of maximum channel reach. In the case of Dell.com, the buyer is able to configure the product to an individually preferred specification at no added cost, while the company enjoys savings from side-stepping the cost of supporting conventional channel intermediaries. In such cases, the classic marketing categories do not greatly facilitate our understanding of the choices companies have to make.

At the same time the electronic marketplace is making business look more closely than ever at its customers. This is because online customers are more than ever beyond direct business influence. It is very simple, quick and easy for them to move on when a business fails to hold their attention and interest. The Internet moves control of the *process* of buying and selling away from business closer to the buyer. This is vitally important to understand. It is often said that 'termination of communication by the buyer and/or a move to your competitor is just one quick click away'. So in this online marketplace, the practical utility of classic 4P thinking has become inadequate (Postma 1999, 4). In its place we can focus our thinking instead on the most obviously different and commercially important features of the online marketplace.

3.1   Product categories online

It is not conventional tangibility which distinguishes a product or service online: what matters much more is whether a product or service can be digitized. Software products and information services are among the more obvious digital products. Digitized, or 'virtual', products cut right across the traditional product–service dichotomy. The virtual category embraces both physical products, such as newspapers and compact disks, and services such as the various classes of informed advice. The marketplace significance of digitization lies in the fact that any digitized product or service can be directly downloaded by the buyer. This offers great convenience without the assistance or intervention of any other party. If the product or service cannot be downloaded by the buyer independently, one unique and decisive competitive advantage of the online marketplace is not available. Thus, in the electronic marketplace, the dichotomy between digital and non-digital, or, between downloadable and non-downloadable offerings, is of prime importance. Downloadability can offer a most persuasive benefit to the buyer, combining a maximum of convenience in terms of time and place with great ease of payment. The Internet can thereby offer an unequalled competitive advantage over other channels of distribution. Indeed, for virtual products (but only for virtual products), the defining product feature of downloadability effectively subsumes another classic marketing mix variable, distribution. Of course, other less direct distribution channel options remain available in addition, but in the electronic marketplace digital product and place decisions are made conjointly. The key 'product' question online is: are you digital, or not?

One widely marketed product category online is the compact disk, which remains closely associated with the first online mover in the category, 'cdnow.com' (Lindstrom 2001, 28). The buyer benefit from purchasing this product online is a combination of convenience, choice and immediacy, which illustrates gains from the remote storage of digital data as well as from digital downloadability. The competitive advantage of the online option is decisive in this case since it completely cuts out the offline requirement to manufacture and retail a physical disk. Sooner or later the Internet is likely to dominate the distribution and sale of such products. The short-term problem, however, is identifying a piracy-free and profitable business model. The well-known free music exchange site, Napster, successfully exploited the great ease and high quality of digital downloading to amass some 70 million users before it was effectively suppressed (Grover and Lowry 2001, 54). Even so, by 2000, CDNow had surpassed Amazon in online buyer numbers, servicing over one million customers each day (Hoffman and Novak 2000).

3.2 Price categories online

Examination of the classical categories of 'mass marketed', standardized, fast-moving consumer goods and 'personally served' non-standard items strongly suggests this mass–personal dichotomy is also of limited value online. The electronic marketplace offers no particular advantage in the mass marketing of a highly standardized product, except for the Internet's unrivalled, global reach. At the same time the electronic marketplace offers something much more widely desirable, and that is a wide, accessible path away from product standardization to less price-sensitive, more customized offerings. For example, Mazda in Japan have started offering buyers of their 'Familia S-Wagon' and 'Roadster' models the opportunity to select their preferred car specification from literally thousands of combinations. At the same time the company saves money on distribution and sales transaction costs. Indeed, in this case, online customers gain the further benefit of a slightly lower retail price (TNW 2001, 8). Such an example shows that mass customization need be neither difficult nor costly. One American website, 'nextcard.com', even enables us to customize our credit cards. As time passes, more and more online buyers will be offered the benefit of mass customization in more and more product categories, at no extra cost. The combination of data storage, interactivity and personalization makes customization a fully viable alternative to mass marketing in many markets (Davis 2000, 45). In a situation where individually specified orders can be fed directly into flexible, numerically-controlled manufacturing processes, the classical association between the total output volume of standard items and unit cost is largely lost. Online, the more useful distinction is between automated 'mass customization', for which prices may anyway be varied across hundreds or even thousands of permutations, on the one hand, and unique, one-off, 'bespoke customization' on the other hand. Only the latter, not the former, may need to be a relatively high-cost, high-price activity.

Both mass customization and bespoke customization result in a near unique product or service. Neither category need be associated with emphasis on price competition. In this customized world, price promotion and non-price promotion alike can be totally buried in offers to meet the buyer's own preferences and selections. In this situation, the customization of product and of its price altogether subsumes that other classic marketing mix variable, promotion. So the key online 'price' question is: are you capable of mass customization, or not?

3.3 Place categories online

Online access can dramatically shorten, even short-circuit, classic placement channels. Where *virtual* products are concerned, the online marketplace constitutes a new and superior distribution channel in its own right; could 'patches' to combat computer viruses be distributed as effectively by any other means? More generally, online access offers an additional and often superior channel of communication. A telling example of the Internet's value as a *supplementary* distribution channel is offered by Bridgewater Pottery, a small British firm (www.bridgewater-pottery.co.uk). Bridgewater sells premium pottery through exclusive retail outlets but finds it costly and difficult to identify new retail outlets. Having established its website in 1997, a significant volume of the firm's business is now conducted in countries in which the firm is not even represented. There are thousands of similar examples.

Irrespective of whether online relationships supplement, modify or replace older channel relationships, the character of the electronic marketplace devalues the practical importance of the formerly strategic choice between long distribution channels and short channels. This is because the online channel offers direct, minimal-cost, 24-hour communication between seller, intermediaries and buyer, across the length and breadth of any and every physical distribution channel. Online communication overarches and supplements all other communication at minimal cost and with maximum convenience. This deeply erodes the association which exists offline between the length of a distribution channel and the exactitude of control which a supplier can maintain over a product as it moves towards the final buyer. Online communication keeps everybody who is interested fully informed all the time.

Additionally and importantly, information which in the past would have resided in only one channel of distribution, or customer 'touch point', can now be instantly married with all other bits of related information which have been collected elsewhere. The commercial importance of this development is fundamental. Whereas offline, the customer relationships of a business are both fashioned and often controlled by channel intermediaries and are channel-specific, online this is not the case. Indeed, it is often the opposite. Internet-enabled businesses can share in all customer communication with channel intermediaries, across all the distribution chains utilized and, over time, make use of the much more complete customer information accumulating in a central databank. It follows that in the online marketplace, channel length is of small importance. Of much greater importance is the fact that the online buyer is likely to be fully aware of all the available channel choices. In fact it may well be the buyer, not the business, who drives channel selection as, for example, when the retail buyer of a home computer opts to pick it up from a dealer rather than have it delivered by courier. Most significant in the electronic marketplace may be whether the business can prosper using just a single channel of distribution or whether its target customers want to utilize multiple channels. While it is the business which determines the number and selection of channels made available to customers, it is the online customer who drives actual channel utilization. The central need for the online business, therefore, is to achieve total consistency of information and service level across all channels, or customer 'touch points'. Full channel integration is the order of the electronic day.

It is scarcely possible for the online business to charge widely different prices in different channels for identical products, even should it wish to. Channel integration imposes a degree of cross-channel consistency in pricing if customers are not to be alarmed. Put starkly, full channel integration removes much of the pricing flexibility which used to be available in the offline environment. This gives yet further incentive for business to exploit the capability of the Internet to deliver mass customization. In 'distribution', therefore, the key question for marketing online is: can your channels easily be aligned, or not?

At the same time there is a dilemma with respect to online distribution and pricing. It has been pointed out (Baker, Marn and Zawada 2001) that the Internet channel can offer superior flexibility in pricing. From a technological perspective this is most certainly true. Electronic prices can be set and announced with great speed and precision and different prices can be tested and buyer responses noted instantly. Companies can also adjust prices in response to changes in market conditions and competitor behaviour and use clickstream data to identify individual buyer responses to particular price changes. The unresolved problem is that buyers may not like it.

The limited evidence available tells us such action engenders buyer distrust. In September 2000 Amazon sold popular digital video disk (DVD) movies at varying prices to regular customers in the first major test of 'dynamic pricing' online. Offline retailers cannot often target individuals so Amazon decided to find out how much of a price premium their 'loyal' customers would pay. One DVD was priced variously from $22.74 to $24.49, while others varied by 3–5 per cent. But customers found out about being charged different prices and quickly complained on a chat line. Amazon learnt that word of mouth spreads more quickly online than offline. Once complaints began, the trial was stopped (Melillo 2000). So despite the potential of online distribution for dynamic pricing, widespread adoption of sophisticated yield-optimizing algorithms does not at present seem very likely. Sophisticated yield pricing is nevertheless applied in the online travel industry by airlines. In this case it is possible because the same price fluidity and yield calculations are applied in the offline channels as well.

3.4   Promotion categories online

In classic marketing, the contrast between mass communication, which is impersonal and inefficient, and personal selling, which is precisely targeted and enjoys a relatively high conversion rate, makes a lot of practical sense; not so in the electronic marketplace. This is because there is neither need nor place for impersonal, mass communication. Online, every individual or company has a known electronic address so communications are always targeted and the recipients always identifiable. Online communication is also instantaneous, very cheap, offers global reach and may be encrypted for security if necessary. Instead of the mass–personal dichotomy, technology has made a completely different dichotomy important in the electronic marketplace. This is between automated 'customer relationship management' protocol communication (CRM), on the one hand, and live human communication, on the other hand. The commercial importance of the former derives from the capacity of software to respond in real time to a customer's website tracking patterns and, within one second, to apply the results of systematic mining of pre-existing customer data. This capability permits the business to make automated but highly relevant and informed comment and responses to buyers on a uniquely individualized, one-to-one basis. On the other hand, online responses may be truly personal, as when a business offers private medical, legal or similar services. There is an element of overlap between these two categories. In all cases the website can offer customers a combination of automated response together with a direct link option to a live salesperson or other member of the business. It is noteworthy that while automated, protocol communication offers a more interactive and individualized alternative to personal selling than has hitherto been available, live, human communication retains its classic importance. This continuing importance of live communication is well illustrated by the case of 'cameraworld.com'. When this American retail camera business added a service to its website for those who wished to talk directly with a salesperson via the Internet, the proportion of site visitors who bought cameras jumped from under 10 per cent to 25 per cent (Mullaney 1999). Yet for a host of simple, routine service requirements in the electronic marketplace, including information updates of myriad kinds, human agency is not required for service delivery. So the key 'promotion' question online is: can protocol communication adequately meet your marketplace communication needs yet, or not?

It is not difficult to find examples of automated, protocol communication. These systems operate most usefully when they encompass all relevant customer 'touch points', online and offline together. In Australia, all four of the country's major banks employ CRM systems. These enable the banks to capture information on the behaviour of their account holders, less online and more offline, and use it to create more integrated and effective marketing programmes. The banks know the loyalty of their customers cannot be taken for granted and they believe that their new customer acquisition costs exceed customer retention costs. They also know that a relatively small proportion of their customers, in each category, deliver the bulk of their revenue, so they want automatic CRM systems to help pinpoint individual customer value. Offline, Australia's dominant telecommunications company, Telstra, claims to have doubled its call centre revenue in four months of 2000 after installing CRM software from Siebel (McIntyre 2000). Online, Fosters Brewing operates an Internet-enabled distribution and promotion platform from Oracle, which the company's vice-president for e-business describes as an holistic, end-to-end business strategy (Caruana 2001). In the Internet economy such systems enable a business to personalize what each individual sees. Thus the individual becomes the central focus of attention and the utilization by the business of comprehensive customer data analysis in real time drives professional one-to-one marketing. One little example of how such CRM application works is given by the experience of the Safeway supermarket chain in the UK. Among its many thousands of products, this company retails 200 types of cheese and at one stage considered dropping the slow-moving types of cheese from its product range. Then, it used CRM software to analyse the purchases of its most valuable customers.

This revealed that the slow-moving types of cheese were largely purchased by its very top spenders (Baune 2000), so the planned delisting of the slow-moving cheeses was dropped.

It is also worth noting instances where the Internet is proving well suited to more conventional communication. One interesting case is Blackmores, an Australian supplier of natural diet and medicinal products. The unusual feature of Blackmores' site, (www.blackmores.com) is that it offers no facility to purchase online; instead, it focuses on health information and encourages site visitors to ask online for health advice. For those who do seek advice, there is a promise of an email response from a qualified naturopath within three days. The site does offer to identify the visitor's nearest supplier of company products if the visitor specifies their suburb or postcode. Although the site is transaction free, the company is totally confident it boosts retail sales. In addition, the site has yielded the most focused and valuable mailing list of product category users available in Australia.

4 Dichotomy displacement online

All four of the foregoing pairs of categories focus on the presence or absence of a characteristic which is important to marketing online. Each is more relevant on the Internet than any of the classic dichotomies mentioned at the start of this chapter. For reasons of familiarity, the few examples given are all drawn from the household product domain. In principle, though, each of these categories is as relevant in the business-to-business (B2B) marketplace as it is in the business-to-consumer (B2C) marketplace. Further examples are given in Figure 16.2.

1	DIGITAL ('virtual' products) E.g. online newspapers (FT.com)	vs	NON-DIGITAL (physical products) E.g. garden plants (green.net)
2	MASS CUSTOMIZATION (automated specification) E.g. personal cosmetics (reflect.com)	vs	BESPOKE CUSTOMIZATION (human specification) E.g. hospitals/ car accident repairs
3	INTEGRATED CHANNELS (multiple channels) E.g. supermarkets (tesco.com)	vs	SEPARATE CHANNELS (e-business kept separate) E.g. auction houses (sothebys.com)
4	PROTOCOL COMMUNICATIONS (automated CRM protocol) E.g. banks (anz.com)	vs	HUMAN COMMUNICATIONS (person-to-person) E.g. various (cameraworld.com)

Figure 16.2   Four dichotomies of electronic marketing practice

Each of the categories shown in Figure 16.2 has a practical importance online. The more features an item possesses among those on the left-hand side of the above list, the better suited it is to Internet marketing. If it is characterized by all four of the features on the left-hand side of the list, it is an ideal item for the electronic marketplace: that is, if it can be digitized, mass customized, made available with consistency through multiple channels, and can be adequately supported by automated communication. In the contrary case, when an item is characterized by most or all of the features on the right-hand side of the above list, it is not well suited to online marketing and business should be appropriately cautious. In cases in between, attention should focus on the Internet's two unique capabilities: namely, digital downloadability and interactive customization. It follows that for any item which can be digitized, the electronic marketplace offers unique advantages of ease, speed and quality of purchase and delivery. Similarly, from customization there are the powerful buyer benefits of one-to-one online specification and communication over a very wide range of products and services. Despite the fact that this was recognized at the very start of the internet era by Peppers and Rogers (1993, 5), who wrote of a future characterized by 'customised production, individually addressable media and 1 : 1 marketing', its significance remains underexploited.

5 Task implications

The implications for marketing which derive from these digital dichotomies are still not widely recognized, yet they are very clear and may easily be summarized.

With respect to product or service, a capacity to digitize means that online marketing offers potentially decisive competitive advantages of lower cost production and speedier delivery to the buyer. These benefits cannot be matched by any offline competitor. In the opposite category, that of non-digitization and non-downloadability, online marketing will require the continuing support of a competitive 'fulfilment' capability: that is, competitive delivery and service remains a requirement online, as it does offline. It is the digital product category which is better suited to being marketed online.

With respect to pricing, the online marketing advantage lies with those products which can be mass customized. These can be offered with the valuable buyer benefit of individualized, buyer-selected features, without adding to unit cost, so the seller can be price competitive in the marketplace while at the same time escaping from any exact price comparison with offline competitors. In the contrary case, that of bespoke customization, high-cost human labour is required online just as it is offline. It follows that when bespoke items are marketed online, price should not feature strongly in the pitch to customers. Indeed, the online appeal is likely to combine some of the unique advantages of the channel, such as its convenience and its privacy, with those of the product, rather than focus on product features alone. While both categories of customization enable the marketer to move away from price competition, only mass customization offers a unique advantage online. However, mass customization is an option of potential value to many millions of businesses, whereas bespoke customization is largely the preserve of a minority of smaller, more specialized businesses. Internet-enabled, mass customization is potentially the more significant category commercially.

With respect to distribution, it is the practical desirability of integrating customer information from all distribution channels, or points of customer contact with the business, which differentiates marketing online from offline. One major benefit to business of operating online is enhanced capacity to collate and instantly analyse all available customer information. Electronic marketing can embrace real time tracking of potential customers and instantly drill down into their accumulated purchase history; this cannot be achieved offline. The customer, in turn, expects a business to act with consistency across the different distribution channels they choose to use. For example, the customer does not expect price or delivery time of a non-digital product to differ markedly in a catalogue from that given on a website. Although the Internet provides a perfect mechanism for dynamic pricing experiments, the fraught experience of Amazon indicates that customers are most wary of price manipulations and will respond angrily to those of which they are aware. In the past there were times when it made good commercial sense to price similar products differently in different channels, but this is less the case online. Given the high level of information always available on the Internet, a business has to assume it is unable to hide its offline activities from its online buyers. Online customers are likely to be much better informed than their offline counterparts, so use of multiple distribution channels demands a high level of channel integration to ensure that online customers receive consistent information. Only when this is achieved is online marketing likely to work well. If, for some overriding reason, distribution channels are used differently, online marketing will risk confusing or alienating those customers who receive inconsistent information from the various channels they choose to access. In such a situation online marketing will be handicapped. On the other hand, where different channels can be seamlessly integrated, synergies may well emerge to the benefit of online and offline channels alike. According to Forrester Research, 83 per cent of American retailers find that by offering multiple purchasing channels they increase overall sales. Specifically, online retail customers are estimated to spend 22 per cent more in the retail stores associated with their online purchases (Lindstrom 2001, xiv).

With respect to marketplace communication, or promotion, the two different categories are automated, protocol communication, on one side, and straightforward, direct, human communication on the other. These categories distinguish electronic promotion from live promotion. While protocol communication offers *automated* one-to-one communication, human communication is no different online from offline, except that it has to be requested. Obviously enough, those products for which automated customer relationship management protocols are a suitable communication tool are better suited to online marketing than those which are not. Given that CRM has the capacity to cope with high traffic volume and to personalize at the same time, the Internet's ability to deliver protocol communication can be a major marketing strength. While protocol communication is often criticized as clumsy and risky, this is probably because it is still a relatively new development, the sophistication and quality of which still needs to be improved. Over time there will inevitably be qualitative improvements and effectiveness levels will grow in tandem. It follows that CRM use in electronic marketing will steadily increase. In the contrary case, when direct human communication is preferable, the advantages of marketing online are unlikely to be great.

6   The e-marketing mix

Considering the online marketing mix overall, two general statements may be made. The first is that the online marketplace opens up exciting new marketing possibilities for some product categories, notably the digital and the mass customized, but that the Internet offers much less to other categories. For those categories which can creatively use downloadability and interactivity to their advantage, the electronic marketplace offers plenty of scope for innovation in both marketing practice and in its supporting technologies. The second general statement is that for the other categories, notably items which are mass produced, standardized and mass marketed, the main gain from the electronic marketplace lies in the simple availability of a new and different channel of promotion. However the potential value of *this* additional channel is not to be underestimated. The character of the Internet is such that, for some buyers but not all, it will always offer a uniquely appealing and commercially decisive *convenience*. The corollary for business is that marketing online offers unparalleled reach into the global marketplace.

There is another, less immediately obvious, feature of online marketing, which is that marketing online, even when it relates to a commodity or fully standardised product, always focuses on an identifiable individual at a specified address. Therefore the Internet *always* communicates personally on a one-to-one basis. Classic mass marketing is *never* involved. It follows that the online marketing mix as a whole, unlike the classic 4Ps, needs to be directed at *individuals* rather than large groups. This is always so. It is a feature of online marketing which has been explored elsewhere (Robins 2000, 265), but the key factor to note is that marketing management has succeeded in exploiting the technical capabilities of the Internet in ways which enable it to provide *individualized* customer benefits. These 'new' online benefits include, for example, as much information, or as much involvement, or as much intimacy, as a particular customer wants. Like the classic marketing mix, these features are controllable within the business but, at the same time, engage the interest and interaction of potential buyers. Taken together such online benefits constitute a new, individualized, *online* marketing mix.

7 Market orientation

Internet marketing practice has begun to shift our thinking from standardized products to customized products, from static pricing to dynamic pricing, from single channels to multiple channels, and from mass communication to one-to-one communication. Our whole perspective is shifting from generalities inside the business to the detail of individual buyers in the marketplace outside. We are still taking business control of the marketing mix entirely for granted but becoming more preoccupied with the practicalities of customizing that mix on a one-to-one basis. This individual focus, managed through electronic mix categories and online buyer benefits, is concentrating our attention more than ever on customers. Put simply, the enhanced importance and market power of the individual online buyer is forcing us to be more customer focused than ever before. This shift might end up moving marketing management further away from the inward-looking, inflexible, authority-focused, 'managerial' frames of reference still found today, and further towards the truly outward-looking, flexible and 'market-oriented' mind-set to which most marketing managers have long aspired; time will tell.

8 Conclusions

This chapter has reflected on contemporary electronic marketing and identified a *new* set of marketing mix categories more relevant to the online marketplace than those of classic marketing. The new categories distinguish those products with characteristics which are well suited to being marketed online from those which are not. It is found that products and services characterized by digital downloadability and automated customization are particularly well suited to being marketed online, yet products falling outside these categories still gain from marketing online if interactivity can be utilized to their advantage. Even where there is no apparent online marketing advantage, the Internet offers unparalleled global reach.

The categories identified here can aid modern marketing decision-making. However, they do not by themselves provide a full guide to the art of marketing online. For this reason brief reference is made the fact that marketers have also identified new ways of gaining and maintaining the attention of buyers online. These new ways focus on individuals rather than market segments.

References

Baker, W., Marn, M. and Zawada, C. (2001), 'Price Smarter on the Net', *Harvard Business Review*, Boston (February), 122–8.

Baune, C. (2000), 'CRM: Know your customer – plan your future', *Retail Asia*, Singapore (January), 26–7.

Caruana, L. (2001), 'E-commerce frames group's global network plans', *The Australian*, Sydney, 26 February.

Davis, J. (2000), *A Guide to Web Marketing*, in association with *Marketing* Magazine (London: Kogan Page).

Dell, M. and Fredman, C. (1999), *Direct from Dell* (New York: Harper Business).

Grover, R. and Lowry, T. (2001), 'Can't Get No Satisfaction', *Business Week*, New York, 3 September.

Hoffman, D. and Novak, T. (2000), 'How to acquire customers on the web', *Harvard Business Review*, Boston, 78 (3) (May/June), 179–86.

Lindstrom, M. (2001), *Clicks, Bricks and Brands* (Victoria: Hardie Grant, South Yarra) xiv.

McIntrye, P. (2000), 'Loyalty not enough', *Business Review Weekly*, Sydney, 15 December, 104–7.

Melillo, W. (2000), 'Amazon price test nets privacy outcry', *Adweek.com*, 41 (40) (2 October), downloaded 31 August 2001.

Mullaney, T. (1999), 'E-Biz needs the human touch', *Business Week*, New York, 13 December, 39–40.

Peppers, D. and Rogers, M. (1993), *The One to One Future* (New York: Currency-Doubleday).

Postma, P. (1999), *The New Marketing Era* (New York: McGraw-Hill).

Robins, F. (2000), 'The E-Marketing Mix', *The Marketing Review*, Glasgow, 1, www.themarketingreview.com, 249–74.

Specter, R. (2000), 'amazon.com – Get Big Fast', *Harper Business*, New York.

TNW (2001), 'Mazda site offers customized cars', *The Nikkei Weekly*, Tokyo, 5 February, 8 (anonymous).

Index